Northbound

Northbound

*Travels, Encounters,
and Constructions 1700-1830*

Edited by Karen Klitgaard Povlsen

Aarhus University Press 2007 |

For Mette 1956-2006

Northbound
© Aarhus University Press and the Authors 2007

Cover: *The Nordic House in the Garden at Louisenlund*. Watercolour by J.M. Wagner.
Cover design: Jørgen Sparre
Layout & Typesetting: Anne Marie Kaad
Type face: Minion & Clearface
Paper: Lessebo Design Smooth Ivory
Printed by: Narayana Press, Denmark

ISBN: 978 87 7934 264 4

Aarhus University Press
Langelandsgade 177
DK-8200 Aarhus N
Denmark
www.unipress.dk

Gazelle Book Services Ltd.
White Cross Mills,
Hightown
Lancaster,
LA1 4XS
www.gazellebooks.co.

The David Brown Book Company (DBBC)
P.O. Box 511
Oakville CT 06779
USA
www.oxbowbooks.com

Published with the financial support of
NOS-H
The Aarhus University Research Foundation
The Research Council for Culture and Communication
The Danish Centre for Excellency in the Humanities (DHFC)

Preface

It is a pleasure finally to have the opportunity to thank the numerous people and institutions who have helped me during the protracted gestation of this anthology. It began as a research project from 2001 to 2005 with the involvement of researchers in Nordic literature and culture and it is their analyses that are presented here.

I wish to express sincere gratitude to NOS-H who funded the project for four years. Without this generous help it would not have been possible to undertake the task. Thanks also to Aarhus University Research Foundation and to the Research Council for Culture and Communication for their financial support. And a one-year fellowship from the Danish Centre for Excellency in the Humanities, DHFC in Copenhagen made it possible to finish the first version of this manuscript.

Sincere thanks to the authors for their contributions to this volume and for their patience, having waited for years for editing, funding, editing, and – again – editing. Thanks also to Aarhus University Press for the final English editing, which was not an easy task!

I wish to dedicate this book to my late sister, Mette, who died of cancer in September 2006. I miss her.

Karen Klitgaard Povlsen
Aarhus, 2007

Contents

II: TRAVELS — ENCOUNTERING AND EXPERIENCING THE NORTH

KAREN KLITGAARD POVLSEN

Eighteenth-Century Stereotypes of the North

An Introduction

Today's mediascapes of a globalised world are constantly introducing readers of travel and tourism magazines, viewers of television documentaries and serials as well as participants in games, quizzes and web logs to distant places. We in the West have all become armchair travellers in the evenings or at weekends and most of us have become tourists and business or conference travellers too. Many of us have seen many parts of the world and like to think that we know something about several cultures and that we are reflective travellers and consumers not only of places, but also of trips, hotels, food and various events and luxuries. Tourism as a real and a mediated phenomenon has become a key aspect of modern life and a substantial industry.

Drawing an analogy using Foucault's concept of the gaze, John Urry created the term 'the tourist gaze' (1990, 2002) and wrote about 'consuming places' (1995, 2000). Virtual and imaginative travel is not replacing corporeal travel but is intersecting it in complex ways. If we want to travel somewhere we often 'travel' on the Internet and in various catalogues, guides, magazines and even books before actually boarding a plane:

This omnivorousness presupposes the growth of 'tourism reflexivity', the set of disciplines, procedures and criteria that enable each (and every?) place to monitor, evaluate and develop its 'tourism potential' within the emerging patterns of global tourism. This reflexivity is concerned with identifying a particular place's location within the contours of geography, history and culture that swirl the globe, and in particular identifying the place's actual and potential material and semiotic resources. (Urry 2001: 2)

This contemporary condition of 'fluid modernity' and reflexivity nevertheless has a history. Modernity and industrialism were closely connected to the railway and the transport of goods and tourists (Schivelbusch 1981), but also before mass tourism, travelling and travelogues existed.

For many centuries and even today pilgrims have walked, sailed or been transported by horse and wagon in order to visit the holy places of Christianity or of other religions. They have also written about their experiences – the corporeal (roads, monasteries, passing through the Alps) and the spiritual revelations they received on their tours. For instance, the Swedish Holy Bridget travelled and wrote during the fourteenth century. During the same centuries, Roman soldiers and conquerors travelled and of course tradesmen of all sorts have always travelled – but not necessarily written about their experiences. From antiquity onwards, historians and geographers have tried to make maps of the world they knew or had heard about (Stagl 1995: 1-49) – a tendency that grew fast during and after the Renaissance, when the discovery expeditions of early colonialism and an empirically oriented scientific travelling evolved. Nevertheless, up until the eighteenth century, it can be difficult to distinguish between 'literary' travelogues and scientific ones – the works of Carl von Linné, for instance, were widely read and received also outside botanical circles and his writing created a more general interest in Lapland.

The roads and lodgings of the beaten tracks of the pilgrimages in the sixteenth and seventeenth centuries were also used by young aristocrats travelling southwards on their educational journeys to European universities and fencing, horse riding and dance schools. Since for centuries the earliest and most famous universities and schools were in the south of Europe, most often these young men and their teachers also travelled southwards. They also wrote about their travels in apodemics, often rather short notations of their whereabouts when and with whom. For the young men of the courts and aristocracy, the proof of their travels was inscribed in their body and courtly manners and, of course, in the international connections they had been able to establish.

However, it was not until the eighteenth century that the art of travelling became popular among the educated middle class. The young men – and some women – of the upper middle classes travelled on their 'Grand Tours'. The proof of their travels was most often a travelogue written by themselves or by the tutors travelling with them. During the eighteenth century to travel meant to write. Travelling also meant reading before, during and after the journey. There was a growing desire for empirical knowledge, histories of art, science, geology and so on. Constructions of the world and every part of it – experienced or imagined – were published in Europe and America. The readership for the books and periodicals was also growing and many studies show the importance of travelogues of every kind in the eighteenth-century private or public library. Among the travelogues, more were published concerning the northern part of the world, which during the eighteenth century was still perceived as the near-circumpolar area stretching from Ireland to Siberia. This anthology aims to investigate the when, how and why of this interest in the North, with emphasis on the eighteenth century, since it was a central period of a changing interest in the North.

Constructing the North 1700-1830: Dystopia and Utopia

This was the original title of a research project that was supported by the NOS-H, a joint Nordic research fund, from 2001 to 2005. The hypothesis of the project was that a change had occurred in the perception of the North during the eighteenth century. Up until the first half of the eighteenth century a general perception prevailed of the North as the dark and barbaric margins of Europe (Löfgren in Bergreen/Hastrup I, 1992). In *L'Esprit de Lois* from 1748, C. S. De Montesquieu referred to Cornelius Tacitus and his *Germania* from the first century and his positive picture of the free and strong Nordic people. Montesquieu understood this within the framework of a general theory of climate. He saw the South as agreeable and beautiful but also as softening the morals and ethics of its people, while the North with its cold climate might be frightening and sublime but had strengthened the people living there; they had well-built bodies and a strong tendency towards freedom and democracy. At that point, another image of the North emerged. And while the utopian image did not immediately replace the dystopian one, the European intellectuals and travellers were however becoming increasingly interested in the North. In the second half of the eighteenth century, a number of examples thus depicted the North of Europe and its mythology as a parallel to southern antiquity. The works by the Swiss historian Jean-Paul Mallet helped in particular to popularise the history and mythology of the North. In the same period, a growing self-consciousness in the northern countries along with a general interest in reconstructing the past, the art, and languages culminated in the national romantic period in most of the northern countries in the nineteenth century. The nation-building process began to supersede the patriotism of the first half of the eighteenth century.

Around 1800 some thus saw the North – especially Norway, Lapland, Greenland and Iceland – as the biggest nature reserve and archaeological 'museum' in Europe. The Swiss populariser of philosophy Karl Viktor von Bonstetten stayed in Denmark from 1799 to 1803. Having lived with the English poet Thomas Gray in England during his youth, Bonstetten already had positive feelings about the North when he arrived in Copenhagen. In 1802 he wrote about the Nordic Alps in a book later published in French and German (1826, 1827: Scandinavia and the Alps). Here he tried to use the theories of the Swiss geologist Horace Benedict de Saussure published in four volumes from 1779 to 1796. According to Bonstetten, the Norwegian 'Alps' were older and more original and natural than the Swiss Alps. This he proved with Saussure's geological theories of how the mountains had been born out of the sea. To support his argument Bonstetten referred among other things to the Old Icelandic language, which also seemed older and more original than the German or French languages (Klitgaard Povlsen 1998). Bonstetten connected nature and language through his descriptions of the Norwegian runic inscriptions on stones, speaking of times past and lost greatness, while the peasants living and surviving in this cold climate had long since forgotten the freedom of earlier periods and had lost their eye – and ear – for the natural signs in the harsh climate. Bonstetten was an important link between the early romanticism of Nordic nature and languages and its reception in France by Mme de Staël, for whom every place north of the Alps belonged to the North. She admired the art and literature reflecting the northern climate here.

To Mme de Staël England was thus a Nordic country. A few years before Bonstetten came to Denmark, however, the English traveller Mary Wollstonecraft had visited Scandinavia and had published her *Letters Written During a Short Residence in Sweden, Norway and Denmark* (1796)[1] about her stay. Mary Wollstonecraft was a connoisseur of travel literature. She had written reviews of a number of travelogues for Samuel Johnson's *Analytical Review* (Ryall and Sandbach-Dahlström 2003: 9) during the years 1788-92. Generally she criticised the travelogues for being too empirical, such as William Coxe's *Travels into Poland, Russia, Sweden, and Denmark* (1784, 1790). She was nevertheless positive towards the books of William Gilpin, who emphasized 'the picturesque' in his descriptions of the Scottish Lake District. Her own ambition was to write for 'the armchair traveller' (Ibid.: 10):

I perceived that I could not give a just description of what I saw, but by relating the effect different objects had produced on my mind and feelings, whilst the impression was still fresh. (Wollstonecraft 6, 1989: 241)

Wollstonecraft wanted to give an impression not only of what she had seen but also of her reflections on what she had perceived in her imagination. Her travelogue depicts the three Scandinavian countries as well as her mind and feelings, and since they were melancholic, she also shows the reader a dark and cold landscape, reflecting her own spleen in an era of lost hopes for a successful revolution in France and not knowing what she was going to find upon returning to England.

France and England are the constant references in comparison with Scandinavia, and the two countries appear as the most civilised in the world, while

1   For a number of readings of this book, see Ryall and Sandbach-Dahlström (eds.) 2003

KAREN KLITGAARD POVLSEN

the harsh and cold climate of the North reflects the uncivilised cultures there. In contrast to Bonstetten, Wollstonecraft thus offers a negative image of Scandinavia, and counter to Mme de Staël, she did not depict England as a Nordic country. Wollstonecraft's line of division was more in line with our contemporary one. Wollstonecraft also had a specific interest in her cultural 'anthropology'. Bonstetten looked for and at nature and language, Mme de Staël looked for the sentimental and romanticist literature, whereas Wollstonecraft was interested in the conditions of women and children (Sørensen 2003: 103).

Sweden seemed especially negative in this respect. The Swedish nature with its rocks and cliffs was beautifully gray and melancholic; the people were kind and hospital towards strangers, but their manners and customs were disgusting: The food tasted bad (too much salt or too much sugar), people drank snaps all the time, and the air in the heated rooms was horribly stale because all the men smoked. The children were hardly able to move or exercise because they wore many layers of clothing. When she went to Norway everything seemed better; the people she met in southern Norway reminded her of the old North: "The description I received of them carried me back to the fables of the golden age: independence and virtue; affluence without vice…" (ibid.: 308). She imagined that she might find this utopia further towards the North, but she had to go westward and here, at the limits of Scandinavia towards the sea separating it from England she experienced how international trade had corrupted the imagined original spirit. After Wollstonecraft left Norway in disappointment, she experienced Denmark as another disaster, appealing only to her satirical skills: "There was little to allure the imagination into soothing melancholy reveries" (ibid.: 342). In Denmark the men were tyrants, restricting their women to live as housewives. The women, for their part, spoiled their children, making them too dependent.

Bonstetten imagined the old North of the runes and sagas through the Nordic natural surroundings and thus gave a very positive but astonishingly non-picturesque picture of, Norway, in particular. Wollstonecraft's imagination was more melancholic and rather negative – but surprisingly picturesque (Sørensen 2003: 94-98). The two travelogues used Nordic nature differently, but most important in both of them is the imagination of the writer. Thus Wollstonecraft depicts her own beautiful soul in her melancholic dystopian view, while Bonstetten depicts his political visions in the nostalgic utopia of Nordic nature. Dystopia and Utopia mix in complex ways around 1800 and more subjective reflections find their way into published writing of constructions of as well as experiences from the North.

Today the early stereotypes and heterologies of the different places, languages and cultures in Europe seem interesting because globalisation has intensified our interest in the local and regional specifics in culture. The cosmopolitism of the eighteenth century had somewhat similar effects, focusing as it did on the heterogeneities of the different parts of Europe, especially the differences between northern and southern Europe. At the same time, the educated intellectuals in Europe often shared the same cultures. They were able to speak and read several languages and many still read Latin and Greek. The literary and philosophical canons were mostly shared and books became cheaper and more easily available throughout the century. It was possible to read not only the same classics but also many of the same contemporary works – even in translation (Klitgaard Povlsen 1996).

For a long time the thinking in similarities and unities cultivated by the romanticists of the nineteenth century made the constructions of the eighteenth century seem odd and old-fashioned. Today it is possible to focus upon the tendencies in the eighteenth century without measuring them against the nineteenth century and therefore labelling them as 'pre-'. Also in this respect the relation between the North and Europe might shed new light on the Europe from before the nation-states came to dominate it all.

During the 1970s and onwards, much interest has been given to the constructions of the 'others', the wild ones, the primitives, the cannibals and so forth. Edward Said's *Orientalism* (1978), Anthony Pagden's *European Encounters with a New World* (1993), and Mary Louise Pratt's *Imperial Eyes* (1992) and many others have analysed how Europeans travelled in and wrote about the rest of the world with themselves as the frame of reference, thus constructing 'the rest' as 'others' and as possible objects of colonialism whether it was cultural or political. Post-colonial theories like these offered fine analyses but the theories also often tended to produce new dichotomies of 'us' and 'them'. In this anthology, the attempt is to avoid dichotomies and to focus on detailed analysis in order to develop the complexities of texts and theories. The contributors are not 'resistent to theory', but most of the articles combine theory and analysis to make both more valid. This project should therefore suggest how to map the constructions and reflexions of the North made by contemporary Europeans: the North in the eyes of Europe.

The lapses and blind spots of the project may seem more important than our results. Nevertheless we have tried to investigate as many European cultures and languages as possible and to give examples of their various perceptions of the North. As a result, the general map in this volume is blurred and appears perforated with empty spaces between the single examples. Much is left to the imagination of the readers and to those who we hope will continue and develop our work with new cases, new theories and new readings.

Reflexions and Experiences

Most work on constructions of countries and regions in the northern part of Europe has been oriented towards the factual: How did the countries, cities and landscapes look at the time? This was the point of departure for many of the contributors to this anthology and our original example of this 'tradition' was H. Arnold Barton's *Northern Arcadia. Foreign Travellers in Scandinavia, 1765-1815* (1998). Barton's period differs a little from ours, but mostly we differ from Barton in the sense that our interest is as much in the 'how' as in the 'what' of the material. Thus, we often focus on a single work, several works or a single person, avoiding attempts at creating an overall picture since the range of examples in the book is too vast and varied to be unified in one narrative. We have nonetheless attempted to create not an anthology of single articles but a volume with ongoing common discussions. Unavoidably, this also produces some redundancy.

The eighteen articles of this collection have been divided into two sections: Constructions and Travels. The first section, called "Constructions – Naming and Defining the North", is opened by Jesper Hede and Peter Stadius. Jesper Hede introduces us to the paradigms of knowledge of Nordic literature and the North that were accessible in the southern parts of Europe (Italy and Spain). The question is how much one could know about the North without having travelled there. Jesper Hede focuses on a universal literary history written in the seventeenth century by the Spaniard Juan Andres. Through this focal point Hede develops a rather complex context for the possible constructions and imaginations available at the beginning of the eighteenth century. He develops some of them following for instance the Italian traveller Acerbi through his travelogue. Central to the understanding of the possible negotiations are the cultural quarrels between normative classicism and the rule-bending moderns in France, a discussion also drawn upon by other contributors. Likewise, Jesper Hede comments on the ideas of Jean-Jacques Rousseau in the second half of the eighteenth century, which were crucial to many of the following readings and cases.

Peter Stadius presents a case study of the seventeenth-century Spanish conception of the Swedish king Gustav Adolph and his men during the Thirty Year War as it occurs in two Spanish works on the King by the writers Fadrique Moles (1637) and Fabricio Pons del Castevi (1648). Thus the anthology is not only framed by this introduction, but also by an image of the broad mental schemata as well as a concrete example of this – both seen from the South.

From the North, Hendriette Kliemann-Geisinger outlines not only the mental schemata but also the actual geographical mapping of the North in the eighteenth century. Her concern is the spatial dimension and the varying geographical concepts of Northern Europe. The material she investigates is primarily comprised of German and Scandinavian attempts to localise and define the North. The resulting political consequences are stressed as well as the cartographic flexibility and the shifting geographic extensions. Hendriette Kliemann-Geisinger's definitions of the 'wide' North are important to the understanding of the North in play in the rest of the volume and as such are part of the framing of the book. How this cartographic flexibility was used and the political implications this could have, are discussed and exemplified by Bernd Henningsen in his reading of the German philosopher Johann Gottfried Herder. Following Greenway (1977), Henningsen sees Herder as the key to the romantic view of mythology. He stresses Herder's idea that what we are becomes evident in 'the other'. Henningsen points to the fact that Herder's significance in Scandinavian history of ideas has not been studied as much as other parts of the reception of Herder. Henningsen is convinced of a strong connection between Herder and the Dane N. F. S. Grundtvig, who had a strong influence on the Danish 'folk high school' (folkehøjskole) and on a new interest in Old Norse Mythology among Danish peasants and ordinary people. However, Grundtvig did not have a following like that of Herder, which culminated during the time of German fascism. In Karin Sander's and Karen Klitgaard Povlsen's contributions, they implicitly comment on the discussion raised by Bernd Henningsen, as does Kirsten Gomard from a language historian's point of view.

As a specialist on travelogues written about Iceland, Sumarlidi Isleifsson offers a clear example of how the eighteenth century was a turning point in the European 'Imagology' of the island of Iceland. Isleifsson gives clear evidence of a shift from a dystopian to a more utopian construction of Iceland. This also implies the question whether Iceland should be considered part of Scandinavia or might belong to the 'high' North. Another implied question is the role of Iceland as an island. In the tradition from Thomas More and others we see a number of constructions of islands as utopias – Iceland might be one of them during the eighteenth century, explaining why the turning point is so clear here while it seems more blurred elsewhere where constructions of northern places occur.

Closely connected to the medieval literature of Iceland is the Old Norse mythology of the *Edda* and Snorri Sturleson. In Karen Klitgaard Povlsen's contribution to the constructions, she traces the popular reception of Norse mythology in Northern Europe. As hinted above, she also touches upon Herder and the influence of his works and their fascination with the language, nature and people of the North. A learned interest in Norse myths had existed for a long time; writ-

KAREN KLITGAARD POVLSEN

ten in Latin, they were known in a European context. It was only when the Swiss Paul-Henri Mallet produced a more popular version of Danish history and Norse mythology during the 1750s and 1760s that the impact on European literature was created. This can only be understood within the context of an interest for the primitive, nature (Rousseau), and the notion of original genius (Macpherson) and the cold climate (Montesquieu) that already had been established in Europe. Travelling from Denmark via England to Germany, Mallet's versions came back to Denmark, reinterpreted by the poet Gerstenberg, a mediator between Germany and Denmark. Gerstenberg had a vision of a cosmopolitical third way between patriotism and nationalism and even if he had followers into the nineteenth century, it was Klopstock's, Herder's and Oehlenschläger's nationalistic versions that were written into the canons of German and Danish literary history.

Similarly, Karin Sanders maps mental constructions in her work on the ways in which material remains such as archaeological finds were used in Danish literature and in the Danish tradition of archaeology as a science. She shows how the archaeology of the North competed with established paradigms of classic Greek and Roman antiquity. The point of the article is to follow the long-established perceptions of the North as being closer to its peoples' origin yet further from the Southern regions' depth of culture as factors in the role archaeology plays in the connection between regional (national) claims and aesthetic production, such as for instance literature written by the Danish poets Oehlenschläger and Schack Staffeldt.

Literature is also the topic of Marianne Raakilde Jespersen's article on Anne Louise Germaine de Staël-Holstein. Like several of the other contributors Jespersen exceeds the eighteenth century and follows the trends into the nineteenth century. Again, we go south of the Alps to follow two journeys and the resulting books. Mme de Staël's novel *Corinne ou l'Italy* from 1807 could be read as a guidebook to Italy, but it also contains a description of a journey to England and the northern landscape and culture there. South opposed to North frames a love-story, inevitably ending unhappily because no middle region or third way exists between the two poles that in this context are gendered: the man represents the North, the woman the soft and creative South. Secondly the article discusses Mme de Staël's book from 1812, on the influence of literature on society and how it promoted romantic German and English literature as 'Nordic'. Mme de Staël continued to uphold the stereotypical images of North and South constructed by Montesquieu and Mallet, and with long-lasting effects.

The essay written by Kirsten Gomard closes the first section. It too discusses the mapping of the North, but this time in relation to languages. How was the history of the German and the Nordic languages constructed at the beginning of the nineteenth century? At this point language history tried to establish a connection between language, ethnicity and nation – following the concepts of Herder and others. Comparative linguistics was yet to come (as was archaeology) and the question is which arguments and which lines of tradition between the languages that were construed in the emerging theories of language history. The opponents in the resulting quarrel on the origin of the German and Danish languages built upon the theories of language history elaborated by the German J. C. Adelung, a typical cultural patriot of the eighteenth century. He divided the German languages in a Germanic line and a Scandinavian line, thus laying the basis for a battle between his followers, the Dane Rasmus Rask and the German Grimm brothers, who constructed two versions of language history and termed them differently. The debate was heated, with the brothers Grimm wanting to include the Scandinavian languages in the German line and Rask to exclude them, and hot passions were fuelled by obvious nationalistic interests in the strongest nation-building era in Europe. The quarrel was never settled.

Travels

The second section of this book deals with actual travel and the literature that resulted from these travels. The first chapter understands literature very literally as books in a library. The literary scholar Antje Wischmann describes the topography and history of Lövstabruk, a Swedish ironworks settlement. She analyses the plant according to a spatial concept of a colony in order to discuss whether the plant can be seen as a realized utopia of town planning. Important for the plant and its owner Charles De Geer was the private library and its excellent collection of French, German and English Enlightenment books – placed far north in the Scandinavian periphery. The library is seen as a heterotopia, a connected space, referring to the cosmopolitan utopia of the Enlightenment. Examples from the collection of books are presented and the whole setting is seen in connection with the twentieth-century social-democratic rhetorical exploitation of the eighteenth-century pre-industrial culture (brukskultur) in the concept of the Swedish 'people's home' (folkhemmet).

Actual travelling should also be understood quite literally in the next chapter by the Norwegian ethnologist Bjarne Rogan. He studies the material conditions of travel in Norway during the eighteenth and nineteenth centuries. Of course, these fundamentals of travel have implications for the travelogues written afterwards. Norway is a vast country with relatively few inhabitants, and to help travellers going to and through Norway, the special institution of the 'skyss' – lodging and conveyance – was established by the Danish government. This meant that Norwegian peasants had to provide travellers with horses and/or food and lodging. As a result, foreign travellers came in very close contact with peasants, priests and civil servants in Norway. This became an – if not the – important attraction of travelling in Norway. The rural people and their primitive lodgings and food provided an experience along the same lines as the natural surroundings, the mountains and the waterfalls.

Anka Ryall takes a closer look at two representations of Swedish Lapland: the Italian Guiseppe Acerbi's *Travels through Sweden, Finland and Lapland, to the North Cape* (1802) and the Englishman Edward Daniel Clarke's volumes on Scandinavia in *Travels in Various Countries of Europe, Asia and Africa* (1824). Both journeys were undertaken in 1799. Based on contextualized close readings, the article argues that the North as a particular place comes alive most vividly in these narratives' accounts of both humbling and invigorating interpersonal entanglements and personal and bodily experiences. Marianne Raakilde Jespersen discusses the relevance of (feminine) gender in her close reading of Mme de Staël's books, and Anka Ryall points to the fact that very different versions of masculinity are constructed in her two travelogues. While Acerbi is humbled as a man, Clarke constructs his own masculinity by surviving the cold climate and the simple food, rescued as he was by the local cloudberries.

Implicitly, Stephanie Buus's contribution also revolves around issues of masculinity in her examination of the statistical and topographical account of travel in Norway written by the Dano-Norwegian Christen Pram before the separation of Denmark and Norway in 1814. Pram's account attempts to navigate a growing cosmopolitical void between the two nations in the years around 1814. He nevertheless does not succeed and the account represents an apocalyptic tale of Pram's own disappearance into that void. An important factor in Pram's failure as a civil servant and as a man with a career is a letter written by Pram to the Norwegian king. The letter was never answered, and the article argues why this might be and why Pram was a go-between who had to fail. His project corresponded with the cosmopolitical thinking of the eighteenth century but not with the nation building that became so important in Norway after 1814. In spite of the magnitude of his authorship, Pram, like so many other cosmopolitical go-betweens of the eighteenth century, was not written into the literary annals of Norway – or Denmark – where he is best known as the unhappy husband in the love triangle involving him, his wife and her lover, the poet Jens Baggesen.

Karen Langgård makes an argument for another turning point in the descriptions of the far or 'high' North in her chapter on Greenland. At least in the representations the contours seem to become clearer when we move northward. The first turning point was when Christianity was brought to Greenland by the Danish minister Hans Egede, whose work was later continued by his sons. Egede wrote of his experiences and was rather empathetic towards the Inuit even though he was a missionary whose aim was to Christianise the pagans. Egede and Crantz had an impact on later writers of travel accounts, but they differ through time. How the mixture of the 'primitive' Inuit and their civilised faith could be perceived is argued through a discursive analysis of two such travel reports. Sir John Ross's account from 1818 and 1835, *Narrative of a second Voyage...,* and Frederick Blackley's *The Greenland Minstrel* from 1839 differ from each other not only in relation to genre (Blackley's version is a poem) but also as regards their understanding and depiction of the Inuit.

The question of genre is further developed in Karen Klitgaard Povlsen's chapter on travel accounts. Following a short overview of the genre, she argues for the existence of three predominant models of the genre of travel accounts during the eighteenth century. Joseph Addison (1705) established a new pattern for seeking and describing what had not earlier been described, something 'new' through a represented place seen through classical literature. Laurence Sterne (1762) broke with the established pattern and gave voice to the sentimental account of a journey. His character Yorick represented the traveller who felt deeply, especially for beautiful women, although he had difficulty making contacting with them. The genre developed an ironic and humoristic perspective through this focus on trivial and personal matters that had not previously been seen in this way. Such irony is not evident in Goethe's *Italian Journey,* based on a stay in Italy in 1785-86. Goethe wrote a subjective rather than learned account of how his journey to Italy became a journey to understanding his goals in life. This perception of the genre is still predominant, but Addison's pattern persisted in European travel accounts well into the nineteenth century – partly also for the northbound journeys like Friederike Brun's description of Kullen in Sweden and Karl Viktor von Bonstetten's representations of Denmark.

The Enlightenment was an era obsessed with order – taxonomies were developed and encyclopaedias written. Pär Eliasson discusses how the 'state' of a nation's intellectual and artistic life was reflected by German travellers going to Sweden in the years 1795-1820. The German travellers were all men of literature, and their accounts reflect their interests as well as the stereotypes of the genre. Like Karen Klitgaard Povlsen, Pär Eliasson argues that the genre developed by Addison was used throughout and even after the eighteenth century, maybe especially in the German tradition of encyclopaedic travel. The focus in his article is on the representations of Stockholm and Uppsala, and the many disparate descriptions reveal an author who believed in a rational order more than they reveal the order of Stockholm.

The aim of Sylwia Schab's contribution is to present the elements of Nordic cultures and societies that evoked the interest of Polish travellers in the seventeenth and eighteenth centuries. Very little is known of the Polish travelogues, so Schab's work breaks new ground. She argues that the interpretations of the North in Poland are rooted in this era and can be recognised in the modern stereotypes of the Nordic countries. Among the few travel accounts left by Polish travellers of the seventeenth and eighteenth centuries three are given a closer look. The memoirs of the nobleman J. Ch. Pasek, the letters written by the scholar J. Ch. Albertrandy, and the memoirs of the historian and soldier J. U. Niemcewics. Her key point is that the Scandinavian countries were represented according to the current political situation in the homeland of the travellers. A turning point appears in the representation of Sweden, in which utopia was reversed into at utopia that still exists as a stereotype in modern Polish literature.

Last by not least, Peter Fjågesund brings the reader and the tradition of travelogues into our own time. Rjukan in Norway became a unique tourist destination starting in around 1810. The waterfall at Rjukan was picturesque and appealed to travellers interested in the land of Nordic nature per se. However, around 1910 industrialization changed the scenery. The waterfall was tamed and made into electricity, but being a big power plant it was still an interesting destination to see. The allied heavy water commando raids during the Second World War added new dimensions to this picture. This chapter, an epilogue to the book, discusses how the first myths surrounding Rjukan have been both retained and transformed by twentieth-century events.

The structure of the book is obviously not only determined by the question of constructions versus experiences. A chronology is represented in the ordering of the single chapters. Throughout the book we move from the seventeenth into the nineteenth century and even the twentieth century in the last chapter by Peter Fjågesund. Another underlying structure is an interest in gender and bodily representations, which is explicit in a few chapters but implicitly touched upon in many more. A third recurrent discussion is that of the cosmopolitics of the eighteenth century and its relevance for today's globalization. We just hope that the readers discover other undercurrents and not too many mistakes, knowing that every book has its share.

Note for the Reader

Original titles are in *italics* with an English translation in brackets. If the work was actually published in English the English title is in *italics* – often, but not always – with the English year of publication added. Once mentioned, all titles thereafter are referred to in English.

Quotes are in English, if translated by the author of the contribution, with the original quotes referred at the end of each article.

References

Barton, H. Arnold 1998: *Northern Arcadia. Foreign Travellers in Scandinavia, 1765-1815*. Carbondale and Edwardsville: Southern Illinois University Press.

Berggreen, Britt and Kirsten Hastrup 1992: *Den nordiske verden* 1-2. Copenhagen: Gyldendal.

Bonstetten, Karl Viktor von 1827 (1826): *Skandinavien und die Alpen*. Kiel: Universitätsbuchhandlung.

Klitgaard Povlsen, Karen 1996: Skrifter til tiden. Ed.: Klaus Bruhn Jensen: *Dansk mediehistorie* 1. Copenhagen: Samleren: 49-69.

Klitgaard Povlsen, Karen 1998: Naturmani: Friederike Bruns og Karl Viktor von Bonstettens rejsebreve. Anne Scott Sørensen, ed.: *Nordisk Salonkultur*. Odense: Odense University Press: 425-442

Ryall, Anka and Catherine Sandbach-Dahlström, eds. 2003: *Mary Wollstonecraft's Journey in Scandinavia: Essays*. Stockholm: Almquist & Wiksell International

Schivelbusch, Wolfgang 1981: Geschichte der Eisenbahnreise: zur Industrialisierung von Raum und Zeit im 19. Jahrhundert. Frankfurt am Main: Ullstein.

Stagl, Justin 1995: *A History of Curiosity. The Theory of Travel 1550-1800*. Chur: Harwood Academic Publishers.

Sørensen, Anne Scott 2003: Mary Wollstonecraft's Politics of the Picturesque. Eds.: Ryall and Sandach-Dahlström: *Mary Wollstonecraft's Journey in Scandinavia: Essays*. Stockholm: Aemquist & Wiksell International: 93-113.

Urry, John 2001: *Globalising the Tourist Gaze*. Lancaster University, Department of Sociology. http://comp.lancs.ac.uk/sociology/papers/Urry – Globalising-the-Tourist-Gaze.pdf

Urry, John 2000 (1995): *Consuming Places*. London: Routledge.

Urry, John 2002 (1990): *The Tourist Gaze*. London: Routledge.

Wollstonecraft, Mary 1989: *The Works of Mary Wollstonecraft* 1-7, Eds. Janet Todd and Marylin Butler with Emma Rees-Mogg. London: Pickering.

I: Constructions
– Naming and Defining the North

JESPER HEDE

Northern Time Travel in the Eighteenth Century: European Invention of Nordic Literature

How could an eighteenth century European from Central or Southern Europe attain knowledge of the North of Europe without actually travelling to the region, and what was the content of this knowledge if he or she had access to it? These two questions are explored in this study. The major problem in dealing with them is to find an *Ansatzpunkt*, as Erich Auerbach calls it (Auerbach 1969: 13-14), or a point of departure that can lead to a comprehensive answer. Especially from the second half of the eighteenth century onwards, there are many individual accounts of experiences from the North as well as different kinds of books that contain references to manners, customs and life conditions in the area. However, to survey all these accounts and books is an unmanageable task which, furthermore, runs the risk of simply summarizing individual views and not providing answers. Such a summary can encapsulate all that was known, but it does not necessarily provide an understanding of the paradigms of knowledge that formed the eighteenth century reader's conception of the North of Europe.

By paradigms of knowledge I intend views that determined how the object of inquiry was perceived and what content the object was given due to the perspective. The views involved both ideas and sensibilities. By ideas I mean specific models for organizing the elements of knowledge into systems of meaning, and by sensibilities I mean different forms of intuitions underlining the models of organisation. In considering how ideas and sensibilities determined the conception of the North in the eighteenth century, I will focus on the subject of Nordic literature. The subject is a fruitful point of departure because, during the eighteenth century, literature – besides being considered a reservoir of wisdom and human characteristics, as well as a source of education and knowledge – increasingly became a source of understanding cultural entities, in that the study of literature could lead to the reservoirs that contained the characteristics of these entities. But this kind of cultural or anthropological approach had serious consequences. In the case of the North, it was especially the medieval literature of Old Norse and Old Gaelic that constituted the basis for cultural identification. This meant that certain literary characteristics were given transhistorical value in determining the culture of a geographic region that was not homogeneous in any respect and whose borders were never clearly defined. In addition, many of the early European inventors of Nordic literature had never visited the North and had only studied the literature in translation, relying often on secondary sources in making their judgments.

Transhistorical valorisation and cultural homogenisation are two paradigms of knowledge highly operative in the European invention of Nordic literature in the eighteenth century. It is the significance of such paradigms that I will examine in the following. I will exemplify their application both as systems of meaning and as intuitions of meaning. In considering the difference between ideas and sensibilities, I will emphasise why intuitions of meaning should not be defined merely as prejudicial assumptions because such a definition is misleading when we try to come to terms with the premises and principles that governed the invention of Nordic literature. On that ground, I will turn to the historiographic invention of Nordic literature giving special attention to the first account of world literature by the Spanish born Jesuit Juan Andrés (1740-1817), or Giovanni Andres, as he came to be known, published in seven volumes between 1782 and 1799 under the Italian title of *Dell'origine, progressi e stato attuale d'ogni letteratura* (On the Origin, Progress and Present State of Every Literature). Andrés' work is of particular interest, because he creates a picture of Nordic literature that is taken to reflect the essential features of the Northern culture. Moreover, he contextualises the Nordic literature on a global scale applying a number of mental paradigms characteristic of the period. Hence Andrés' work elucidates not only how the North was conceived seen from Southern Europe. Due to its encyclopaedic ambition and scholarly foundation, the work provides also a picture of what kind of knowledge could be attained from reading about the North.

Experience and Myth

Near the end of the eighteenth century, Friedrich Schlegel wrote of a new kind of cultural hero. This hero was the modern traveller. The exemplum Schlegel had in mind was George Forster, who, at the age of seventeen, had accompanied his father as a naturalist on Captain Cook's second voyage around the world (1772-75). For Schlegel, Forster exemplified, in Harry Liebersohn's words, "a fresh conception of education, his worldly experience a reproach to German bookishness and provinciality" (Liebersohn 1996: 617). Hence, in Schlegel's view, travelling was a new way of education that could bring hope to the future, and experience was at the basis of human understanding, not scholarly learning.

As far as travellers to the North are concerned, the Italian advocate and explorer Giuseppe Acerbi can be seen as an example of Schlegel's new cultural hero (see Anka Ryall in this volume). Twenty five years of age, he travelled through Sweden, Finland and Lapland to the North Cape and in 1802 published his account which earned him a lasting recognition. In the preface Acerbi explains the reason for making the journey, since he imagines that the reader might find it curious that "a native of Italy, a country abounding in all the beauties of nature, and the finest productions of art, would voluntarily undergo the danger and fatigue of visiting regions of the Artic Circle." In fact, he advised that journeys in the North should be undertaken only by those "who have a just and masculine taste for nature, under every respect." But he also claimed that "there is no people so advanced in civilisation, or so highly cultivated, who may not be able to derive some advantage from being acquainted with the arts and sciences of other nations, even of such as are the most barbarous" (Acerbi 1802, I: viii and x., Barton 1996: 1-2). Here, again, the educational purpose is emphasized. But more important is Acerbi's implicit civilisation discourse. The North represents in essential ways the barbarous stage on the ladder of civilisation. This ladder constituted a hierarchical order, but it contained also a temporal dimension. Travelling to the North was not only an arduous and dangerous business; it also meant travelling back in time. To be sure, like many other travellers Acerbi was well aware of the climatic conditions and the natural environment that determined the life conditions in the North, but he was not able to free himself of the mental paradigm of the civilisation discourse.

In many respects, Acerbi reproduced a common idea about the North, perhaps most systematically displayed in Jean-Jacques Rousseau's *Essai sur l'origine des languages* (*Essay on the Origin of Languages*) originally published in 1750. Rousseau combines different sets of binary oppositions in order to bring forth a transcultural and transhistorical conception that can explain differences between cultures and people (Rousseau 1966). For example, Rousseau distinguishes between primitive and cultured people. The former is emotional, whereas the latter is rational. The one is concerned with persuasion and uses figures and tropes as its type of expression through poetry and singing, whereas the other is concrete and establishes proof through the medium of prose. This distinction has a strong teleological dimension in terms of the development of civilisation, and it prepares the way for the distinction between Northern and Southern cultures that indicate two ends on the ladder of civilisation and display two essential elements of human nature. The Southern people worship love, whereas the Northern people strive to survive. The one is tender; the other is aggressive. The language of the South is sonar, harmonic and rhythmical; the language of the North is raw and strong. The former is saying "love me"; the latter is saying "save me". In the *Essay* Rousseau also elaborates on the well-known distinction between speech and script criticized by Jacques Derrida. According to Rousseau, speech reflects feelings, whereas script articulates ideas. The one is expressive, dynamic and vital, while the other is precise, rational and static. For many intellectuals of the period, this matrix of binary oppositions – simplifying, as it may seem to us today, was rationally as well as empirically – and thus scientifically – grounded. It was not Rousseau's invention, but he gave it a systematic quality that appealed to the Enlightenment quest for order. This conception of order emphasised the teleological dimension in the historical development of European civilisation. This meant that a travel to the North was not only a physical experience; it was also a mental time travel.

Although Acerbi mainly reproduced the conventional view of the North, his travel account is interesting because, in recounting a true encounter with the North, it represents in some respects a counter-view to the stereotypical sentiments associated with the North during the second half of the eighteenth century. These sentiments were largely due to James Macpherson's publication of the Ossian poems in the 1760s. The bard Ossian came to represent a Northern Dante or a Northern counterpart to the sensibility of Homeric poetry. This is, for example, manifest in Goethe's novel *Die Leiden des jungen Werthers* (*The Sorrows of Young Werther*) published in 1774, where the opposition between Homeric and Ossianic poetry is an essential theme that demarcates two sides of Werther's nature and two stages in his sentimental development. In *De la littérature considérée dans ses rapports avec les institutions socials* (*On the Influence of Literature upon Society*) published in 1800, Madame de Staël made extensive use of Ossianic poetry in emphasising the significance of Nordic literature for the development and constitution of the European civilization (see Marianne Raakilde Jespersen in this volume). The poetry of the North, she claims, reflects the spirit of a free people much more than the poetry of the South. The Ossian poems possess a power that generates spiritual movements in all people, and this power is due to the profound inspiration from nature imprinted in the poems. Hence, on the one hand, the North was a rough place of strange, sometimes repulsive, customs and manners representing a low rung on the civilisation ladder, whilst on the other, it had a mythological status that appealed to sentimental tendencies in the period and was upheld by the idea of the noble savage. In many cases, however, the two views were mixed and led to uncertainties about what characterized the nature and people of the North. This mixture and the uncertainties it generated are other essential features to keep in mind, when trying to determine the basic elements of the view of the North in the eighteenth century.

In *Travellers and Travel Liars* (1962), Percy G. Adams remarks that there were three kinds of travel accounts in the eighteenth century: true travel accounts, imaginary or extraordinary travel accounts, and travel lies. For the eighteenth century reader, it was not easy to distinguish between these three kinds. According to Adams, this was due to a sort of paradox:

Because the eighteenth century was so avid in its search for data about man and his physical surroundings, it was inclined to be gullible and fall victim to facts that were not facts and to travel books that were partly, even completely, false. (Adams 1962: viii)

To this we may add that just because a travel account was true, it does not follow that it was free of imaginary elements or even lies. Likewise, imaginary travel accounts and travel lies could contain elements of truth.

For example, William Dampier's *A New Voyage round the World* (1691), which Adams counts among "the most admired of true travel accounts," was "written in a fitting style, recording accurate, even scientific, observations, and recounting exciting adventures" (Adams 1962: 163). But as Geraldine Barnes and Adrian Mitchell point out,

It is a fitting irony that under the aegis of the Royal Society, [Dampier] made his greatest continuing impact not on the study of nature but on the writing of books. From Swift and Defoe to Coleridge and, most recently, the Australian writer Roger McDonald, Dampier's scientific exoticism has left its mark more surely on the literary map than on the scientific chart. (Barnes 2002: 56)

This does not mean, however, that Dampier's *New Voyage* should be read as an imaginary travel account or even as a travel lie. It means that if we now attempt to read it as an eighteenth century reader might have read it, we have to remind ourselves that for such a reader it was difficult to distinguish between truth, imagination and lie. It can also be argued that in many cases, the reader would not even pay attention to the necessity of such a distinction. Nevertheless, it is true that in much of eighteenth century writing, accurate observations and scientific facts were presented with commitment to rhetorical and narrative forms that often meant the dramatization of events and the accentuation of the subjective viewpoint in order to attain authority and credibility.

A classical example of the tendency to fall victim of deceit is Daniel Defoe's *Robinson Crusoe* (1719), which some readers took as a true travel account on its publication. But the problem of distinguishing between truth, imagination and lie was not restricted to travel accounts only, but pervaded most areas of communication in the eighteenth century. The way in which Defoe in his *Journal of the Plaque Year* (1722) blends facts and fiction is another example of how difficult it was to identify deceit, since the *Journal* was read as authentic long after its publication. Seen from a twenty-first century perspective, deceit may seem to have been – to use a modern computer term – a virus or spyware in the system of communication in the eighteenth century. But in contrast to our age of information technology, the virus or spyware was far from always created deliberately with the purpose of breaking down a system of communication or playing with its fragile and vulnerable parts. It can be argued that Defoe's blending of facts and fiction in the *Journal*, which has made it hard to define the book as a work of fiction or of history (Mayer 1990: 529), served the purpose of underlining the tendency among the readers of his time to have too much faith in the exactitude and objectivity of books, thus implicitly appealing to a general sharpening of the rational and critical capacity in the public domain. But it can also be argued that Defoe's work shows how much and how often an author of the eighteenth century relied on and appealed to an analytic dimension, which in later periods eventually fell into discredit as a result of different historical developments such as the diffusion of the rationalistic ideals of the Enlightenment and the positivistic standards of modern science. With a modern term, this analytic or reflective dimension can be defined as 'intuition' (Seung 1993: xi-xiv and 1-8).

What intuition means in this context can be exemplified by turning to Macpherson's Ossian poems, which were crucial to the evolution of European Romanticism. Nowadays, it is commonly held that what Macpherson published was a forgery (Bassnett 1993: 15). But, as Aidan Day more cautiously remarks, the poems were rather "highly individual 'translations' of poetry by the ancient Gaelic bard, Ossian" (Day 1996: 50). The view that the poems were a forgery is not new. Already at their publication, different critical voices were heard. The most notable one was that of Samuel Johnson who accused Macpherson of forgery. But as Fiona Stafford more accurately argues,

Fingal may not be a direct translation of Gaelic poems that had survived intact since the third century, but neither is it a "fake" or "forgery", because of Macpherson's peculiar situation at the confluence of very different cultures. As a Highlander, he was at liberty to draw on the common pool of stories and characters, whose chronologies had become mixed in the oral tradition centuries before he began to listen to them and to recreate his own versions of the old tales. (Stafford 1996: xv)

In other words, Macpherson can be said to have used his intuition as a mental tool in ordering the fragments and attempting to create coherent narratives out of oral traditions. The case of Ossian emphasises that it is misleading to maintain that the blend of facts and fictions involved deliberate deceit. What can be argued is that readers and writers were often driven by certain paradigms and intuitions. For example, what inspired Macpherson was the idea that the early poetry of Scotland resembled that of Homeric Greece. This idea was due to a mixture of experience, reading and imagination that enabled him to travel back in time. This mixture was not unique. On the contrary, it is characteristic of other kinds of discovery in the period.

Construction and Invention

In eighteenth century Europe, knowledge of foreign or unfamiliar parts of the world could be attained through three different media: travel, books, and the imagination. An eighteenth century European could travel to foreign parts if he had financial resources; he could read about them if he has access to books; or he could imagine them if he was free of laborious distractions. In all three cases, the eighteenth century European would combine three basic elements of human existence in different ways and to varying degrees: experience, reason and intuition. The traveller to foreign parts of the world would recount the travel experience with rational exactitude coupled with intuitive judgments formed by life experiences and educational background. The reader would judge the content of a travel account and determine its merit by way of reason and intuition; personal experiences, intuitive conceptions of the world and the reading of other books on the subject would be taken into account in determining the authenticity and merit of the travel account. But in many cases, experiences, intuitions and readings would also be combined in a different way which produced imaginary or extraordinary travel accounts, that is, the travel accounts of the imagination in which intuitions and experiences were transferred to a foreign part of the world and recounted with rational exactitude.

Due to our well-developed terminology for narrative strategies, rhetorical devices and generic characteristics, the travel accounts of the imagination are now most commonly treated as a sub-genre or a precursor to the novel. This is all very reasonable seen in a historical perspective and from a modern viewpoint. But the problem is that this genre definition easily distorts the nature and significance of imaginary intuitions in eighteenth century explorations of foreign parts of the world. Imaginary intuitions largely served the purpose of filling in gaps in the comprehension and bringing order to inconsistencies and uncertainties. Sometimes they were clearly prejudicial, but often they were the results of attempts at rational reflection or due to careful studies of books in which other forms of intuitions, imaginations and prejudices were pervasive. But due to the complex nature of these mental paradigms, we do not arrive at any comprehensive understanding of the eighteenth century exploration of the North of Europe, if we reduce them to forms of fiction or define them simply as pure constructions or inventions.

In many studies of historical, cultural and political identifications, the terms 'construction' and 'invention' are used interchangeably. To speak of the construction or the invention of Nordic literature seems to denote the same thing. As the terms are commonly used, they are meant to identify political and ideological projects, most often of social elites, with the ambition of expanding or consolidating their resources. But the two terms contain connotations that complicate their application in any unequivocal sense. Invention can be understood as equivalent to discovery, and construction can be taken to mean understanding. The equivalence of invention to discovery originates in classical rhetoric, whereas the equivalence of construction to understanding has been conveyed especially in the German hermeneutic tradition from Schleiermacher to Gadamer. As far as construction is concerned, the hermeneutic teaching is simple: understanding involves simply the construction of meaning from intuitions or available facts.

In the case of invention, the terminological connotations are more complex seen in a historical perspective. In classical rhetoric, *inventio* was the term for the finding and elaboration of arguments. According to Cicero and Quintilian, the invention of arguments involved the investigation of the facts of the case. On the basis of these facts, the central issue of the case was then determined. Subsequently, the available means of persuasion were explored before arranging the presentation of the argument (*dispositio*), to which style was added (*elocutio*), before the speech was memorized (*memoria*) and finally delivered in a specific context (*actio*). Since invention was an integrated part of the whole rhetorical practice, the presentation of facts was unthinkable without rhetorical ornamentation. As a result, invention implies not only discovery, but also the delivery of the discovery by means of persuasion. These different meanings of invention are significant because many of those we now identify as inventors of traditions and conventions or primary agents of historical, cultural and political constructions were either trained in classical rhetoric or influenced by its common diffusion. Moreover, especially in the eighteenth century, as pointed out by Thomas M. Conley, rhetoric was transformed into a technique for managing appearances; it was less a way of coming to decisions on complex matters (Conley 1990: 224). Hence *elucutio* or eloquence was given high priority.

Due to the rhetorical training and influence, many eighteenth century authors produced texts in which the combination of careful research, logic reasoning, strategic choices and imaginary effects created a fluid mixture of facts and fiction styled with persuasive ornamentation. The elaborate or rhetorical language helped the author to create meaning out of fragments of observations and experiences. Other than providing facts, this kind of language gave the reader the impression that the authenticity of the original experience was imprinted on the text. For those trained in classical rhetoric, the elaborate, artistic language was not artificial or unnatural in comparison to the language of everyday life. On the contrary, it was mimetic of nature and human experiences. This meant, for example, that dramatic events required dramatic language and trivial experiences plain language. These rhetorical strategies were not restricted only to linguistic registers; they were also practiced in the choice of particular words. Hence, to speak of the eighteenth century construction of the North in general, and the invention of Nordic literature in particular, requires different attentions.

As conveyed by the different connotations of the two terms, constructions and inventions of the eighteenth century could be due to thorough investigations and attentive interpretations of facts. Apparently arbitrary statements or historical, cultural and political phenomena could have rational grounding. But in order to bring forth that grounding it is necessary to contextualise the statements and phenomena. The different rhetorical strategies applied are one layer that requires uncovering in order to attain an understanding. The ordering paradigms of intuitions are another layer. Acerbi's emphasis on the necessity of a just and masculine character for travelling in the North reflects his own experience, but it is also a device of eloquence in managing his appearance. In addition, he draws on common ideas about the North in substantiating his appearance of eloquence. This is characteristic of much travel literature in the eighteenth century. But when we turn to literary historiography, another priority becomes manifest. The mental paradigms are still prominent, but the eloquence of appearance is replaced by the eloquence of Enlightenment rationalism.

As often emphasized, the theories of knowledge developed by Francis Bacon and René Descartes profoundly shaped the Enlightenment view of the world (Shoaf 1985: 121). But the result was neither pure description of world experiences nor analytic practice based on principles of formal logic. In the first part of his *Essai sur les Moeurs et l'Esprit des Nations* (*Essay on the Manner and Spirit of Nations*) published in 1756, which contains his philosophy of history, Voltaire could claim,

God has endowed us with a principle of universal reason, just as he has supplied birds with feathers. This principle is so constant that it asserts itself despite all the passions which threaten it, despite the tyrants trying to drown it in blood, despite the impostors endeavouring to destroy it by superstitions (Voltaire 1785: 35).

Moreover, Voltaire declared that his age was the age of reason and as such a model for the future and a stopping point of history. But as Jerome Rosenthal points out,

Rationalism was for Voltaire a platform and an educational program rather than a dispassionate theory. His great aim was to help humanity to become humane, reasonable, clearheaded, free-minded, tolerant and peace-loving. (Rosenthal 1955: 166)

Hence, Enlightenment rationalism was profoundly political. The appeal to reason was a standard of reference by which to judge the present as well as the past in order to bring about changes and found a new conception of order. In addition, the judgment was believed to posses the power of transcending cultural and historical differences.

Literary Historiography

The second half of the eighteenth century witnessed the development of three distinct approaches to literature in Europe. These approaches can be defined as the local, the regional and the global perspective involving discourses on specific national cultures, on the European culture in general, and on the civilisation of the West, respectively. In each case we are confronted with historical and cultural inventions and constructions that are due to acts of discovery and understanding according to the standards and knowledge of the time. In each case the aim was to make a comprehensive account of the object of study combining all facts and sources available, whether it was a national literature, the sum of national literatures in Europe, or the literatures of the European or Western civilisation in comparison with the literatures of other civilisations.

The local perspective is associated with the invention of the genre of the history of national literature in Europe. Although there are many accounts of national histories before the eighteenth century that highlight the literary achievements of European nations, the first major achievement of the genre is Girolamo Tiraboschi's *Storia della letteratura italiana* (History of Italian Literature) published in twelve volumes between 1771 and 1782. Instead of listing works and authors or preparing critical editions of texts in the manner of the French Maurists, who were pioneers in medieval history due to their critical editions of medieval texts, Tiraboschi's objective was to write the history of Italian literature, not of Italian authors (Tiraboschi 1771-82, vol. 1: ix-x). In short, Tiraboschi's approach is cultural, not biographical. He does not use the Italian language as the only demarcating factor in defining Italian culture. He uses it along with historical, political and geographical matters in order to encapsulate the essential qualities of an abstract entity defined as the nation. Hence his objective is to constitute a set of normative standards for identifying Italian culture as manifest in Italian literature. This objective became the standard in many later historiographies of national literatures during the nineteenth century. In a Danish context, it is manifest in Knud Lyne Rahbek's and Rasmus Nyerup's *Bidrag til den danske digtekunsts historie* (Contribution to the History of Danish Poetry) published in four volumes between 1800 and 1808.

As far as the regional and the global perspectives are concerned, they represent two levels of the invention of comparative literature, the former representing it on the European level and the latter on the global level. Although the term 'comparative literature' did not come into use until 1816, the practice predates the term (Bassnett 1993: 12). The same is the case with the term 'world literature,' which is normally associated with Wolfgang Goethe, who in a letter of 1827 to Johann Peter Eckermann stated: "Nowadays, national literature doesn't mean much: the age of world literature is beginning, and everybody should contribute to hasten its advent" (Moretti 2004: 148). But Juan Andrés' work *On the Origin, Progress and Present State of Every Literature*, which Goethe and Johann Gottfried Herder were familiar with, is pioneering in the field of comparative literature on the global scale. Since its focus is primarily set on the European literatures due to the scarcity of sources on non-European literatures at the time, Andrés' work, however, represents at the same time an early example of comparative literature on the European level. When it comes to the strictly regional level, Friedrich Bouterwek's twelve volumes on *Geschichte der Schönen Wissenschaft* (History of Fine Arts), published between 1801 and 1819 and profoundly indebted to Andrés' work, is an early example of comparative literature on the European level, since Bouterwek examines the literatures of England, France, Italy, Germany and Spain, which at the time were considered to constitute the essence of European literature as a whole.

As far as the reception of Nordic Literature in eighteenth century Europe is concerned, Paul-Henri Mallet's *Introduction à l'Histoire du Danemarch* (Introduction to the History of Denmark), published in 1756, is perhaps the earliest work, in which the local or national perspective is elaborated. But as the title says, it is not a study of Danish literature and does not present a comprehensive account of its different elements. Mallet's work had a major impact on the distribution of Old Norse poetry and myth in Europe, where it enjoyed considerable popularity, having been written in French and translated into both German and English at an early stage. As Margaret Clunies Ross and Lars Lönnroth point out, Mallet's promotion of Old Norse poetry and myth represents a new and important turn in the reception history [of Old Norse literature], since his way of looking at Old Norse verse was one of the inspirational forces of the romantic movement in several countries of Western Europe. But Clunies Ross and Lönnroth also emphasise that the sources of Mallet's conceptions "can be traced back to Icelandic and Scandinavian intellectuals like Magnús Ólafsson, Ole Worm, Peder Resen, and Thomas Bartholin – or even Snorri Sturluson himself" (Clunies Ross 1999: 6-7). Although Mallet's contribution to the distribution of Nordic literature was significant for the increasing interests in medieval chivalry and poetry, primitive ways of life and natural environments, and the revival of old forms of poetry – interests supported by Rousseau's notion of the noble savage and the concept of the sublime – his conceptions were not new but were built on a Nordic tradition. Hence, if we are to trace the elaboration of the local perspective in the Nordic context, it is in the Scandinavian tradition we mainly find it explored in the eighteenth century. But the results were only sporadically distributed to the rest of Europe.

For this reason, as far as Nordic literature is concerned, the strictly regional or European perspective had little priority in the writing of literary historiography in the eighteenth century. Madame de Staël's *On the Influence of Literature upon Society* is an exception to this rule, but only to a certain degree, since it is primarily Ossianic poetry she refers to in defining the Northern spirit, not Old Norse poetry. Hence there is no comparative study of European literature that includes Nordic literature. The regional perspective is mainly traceable in Andrés' history of universal literature, which includes the global perspective on the issue and thus disseminates a civilisation discourse. But before we look into Andrés' approach to the Nordic literature and to try to establish the principles by which he uses the global perspective and develops the civilisation discourse, which has consequences for his view of Nordic literature, it is necessary to come to terms with the novelty of Andrés' work.

The Ancients and the Moderns

When we try to determine the ideas that governed the approaches to literature in Europe before the dissemination of conceptions and sentiments that eventually led to European Romanticism, the quarrel of who was superior, the ancients or the moderns, represents a significant event (Aldridge 1974). The quarrel broke out in the later seventeenth century but it soon died out in the first decades of the eighteenth century. No settlement was reached, but on the whole, the ancients were given a certain advantage. The advantage helped to consolidate the system of neoclassical criticism throughout the eighteenth century, inspired by Aristotle and Horace in the field of poetry and by Aristotle, Cicero and Quintilian in the field of rhetoric, and in certain areas of literary criticism it was still highly esteemed well into the nineteenth century and even further, as far as rhetoric is concerned. The quarrel marks out some of the essential premises for discussing poetic and historiographic issues before the diffusion of Nordic Literature into the European context began.

As Jonathan Swift lays out the scenario in his short satire *The Battle of the Books* (1704), the army of the moderns, to name the most prominent ones, consisted of Tasso, Milton, Dryden, Descartes, Gassendi, Hobbes, Guicciardini, Scotus and Aquinas, whereas the army of the ancients, fewer in number, as Swift says, included Homer, Pindar, Euclid, Plato, Aristotle, Herodotus, Livy and Hippocrates and their allies, especially Vossius and William Temple who was Swift's employer. Although Swift's gallery of ancient authors in St. James Library was Greek, authors like Cicero, Quintilian, Virgil, Ovid and Seneca were also included among the ancients. But at the time, no Gaelic or Old Norse bard or Oriental poet had yet seriously arrived on the scene suggesting an alternative to the opposition between the classical and the modern position. As indicated by Swift's gallery of modern authors, the modern position was geographically situated in specific centers of culture in Europe. England, France, Italy and Germany (and later also Spain) were the main lands of Europe and thus the homeland of the modern. This idea was maintained well into the nineteenth century. For example, it is the ordering principle in Bouterwek's *History of Fine Arts* despite the fact that the Old Norse poetry had now entered into the European context, thus suggesting a Nordic dimension of the modern European position.

Although the quarrel only covered a short period of fierce dispute, it has now become equivalent to the question of whether or not the appropriation of the classical heritage is indispensable for the understanding of the modern historical experience. But in considering the controversy in its own context, it should be noticed that historicity or historical awareness was not the essential point of the matter. No doubt, it was a significant aspect of the controversy since the one side stressed the superiority of the ancients and argued for continuity in the distribution of the classical heritage, while the other argued for the superiority of the moderns and stressed discontinuity between ancient and modern times. But when we consider how the two positions looked at the literary or aesthetic elements of the issue, it stands clear that both sides were characterized by the same basic attitude. This attitude can be identified, to paraphrase René Wellek, as "the search for poetics, for laws, or at least for rules or constants in literature, for a universal matrix" (Wellek 1982: 33). That is, the reading of a literary text was a matter of evaluating its content and form according to the authority of certain objective standards based on rationalism and universalism forming a theory of literature that was considered to be scientific.

When Charles Perrault and Bernard Le Bovier de Fontenelle, around 1688, argued in favour of the moderns, they based their argument on what they considered to be an empirical and scientific pattern of thought. They regarded the moderns as more learned than the ancients because humanity was only in its childhood in ancient times but had now reached adulthood in modern times. Thus they symbolically stressed continuity in the history of humanity that echoes the saying about dwarfs on the shoulders of giants ascribed to the twelfth century theologian Bernard of Chartres in John of Salisbury's *Metalogicon*. But at the same time, they emphasized discontinuity in the development of human beings. The principle of discontinuity was the principle of varying degrees of rationality. According to Perrault and Fontenelle, the moderns could now benefit from the imagination of the ancients due to the fact that their reasoning capacity was superior. That adults were more rational in thought and behaviour than children was an empirical fact and a law of nature. Since the development of a human being and the history of humanity were events that took place in the order of nature and both were sooner or later destined to vanish, either by death or universal judgement, it was natural to take it as an objective rule and empirical fact that the course of history was equivalent to the growth of the human mind. To be sure, the growth of the human mind was individual for every human being, but its goal – rational thinking and behaviour – was constant. When Jean Terrasson in 1715 rejected the idea, originally suggested by Nicolas Boileau-Despréaux, that since Homer had always been admired and imitated throughout the ages, he should continue to be so by the moderns, his argument was that a literary work should be judged, not according to its reputation, but according to standards of reason and nature, i.e., constant and objective standards.

The quarrel between the ancients and the moderns was to a large extent a quarrel between two diverse conceptions or intuitions of the idea of a universal matrix, the ancient or the modern. Of course, there were those who completely rejected ancient thinking. For example, in 1649, Descartes argued that the teachings of the ancients were so scanty and so lacking in credibility that any search for truth should start by rejecting it all. But Descartes' position was not the prevalent one. A large number of participants in the controversy took the stand that modern thinking was a more advanced form of thinking than the ancient. As far as literature is concerned, many defenders of the modern position argued that the ancients could be an inspirational source for the imagination and creative process, but the moderns had obtained a rational state of mind that could give imaginative innovations their proper artistic or aesthetic form, i.e., the form of order and beauty. Thus they opposed the system of neoclassical criticism, which at the time was dominant especially in the educational system, diffusing the idea that modern thinking was a degenerated version of ancient thinking.

Although the quarrel was never settled, the attack on the neoclassical system had its effects. During the second half of the eighteenth century, the neoclassical doctrines began to disintegrate. Moreover, as the knowledge of especially Old Norse and Old Gaelic poetry was extended throughout Europe in the second half of the eighteenth century, it was no longer possible to maintain the discussion of ancient versus modern. In fact, it can be argued that the reason why the quarrel did not last longer is that the acquaintance with literatures that could not be determined as either ancient or modern and thus fell outside the existing discourse on universal poetics simply undermined the premises of the quarrel on both sides. As a result, it became necessary to develop a new type of discourse that could handle the new discoveries of differences among European languages, literatures and cultures. A significant result was the increased emphasis on the divisional line between North and South, which became paradigmatic for the determination of differences across cultures and nations. Again we see that the objective was the constitution of a universal matrix. This time, however, it was not a dispute between two different intuitions of the universal matrix. The matrix was now the impact of nature on human beings, especially with regard to climatic differences, as displayed, as we have seen, in Rousseau's *Essay*.

The principles of Rousseau's distinction between Northern and Southern Europe are operative in Andrés' treatment of Nordic literature. But Andrés' treatment of the issue is not simplistic. In accordance with the Enlightenment standard, he elaborates explicitly on the notion of progress. He combines this notion with the idea of progressive rationality. However, he also shows signs of the kind of cultural relativism Herder develops in his criticism of Voltaire in his *Auch eine Philosophie der Geschichte zur Bildung der Menchheit* (Also a Philosophy of History for the Formation of Humanity) published in 1774, arguing, inspired especially by Gottfried Leibniz's *Monadologia* (1714), that each culture, nation or historical period has its own unique set of values that cannot be submitted to the principle of universal reason and placed within a hierarchy of progress or progressive rationality. At the same time, Andrés' work is symptomatic of what Ernst Cassirer (Cassirer 1932) identifies as the fundamental paradox of the Enlightenment. The paradox consists in the fact that while philosophers, scholars and intellectuals of the Enlightenment were fixed on the idea of progress and stressed the necessity of breaking with the past and creating new perspectives on life and even new ways of life, they were equally obsessed with finding and explicating the origin of man, nations, cultures and civilizations. The seeming contradictions and paradoxes detectable in Andrés' work might give the impression of an inconsistent and incoherent position. But it rather underlines the complexity of the Enlightenment. If we define Voltaire's position as reflecting in principle the rationalistic tendency of the Enlightenment, although he never develops it systematically in the manner of Descartes, wherefore it mainly remains an ideal, and at the same time define Herder's position as reflecting the critical stream of the Enlightenment with its emphasis on cultural relativism, we can say that Andrés' work reflects the ideal of combining both positions.

Nordic and Universal Literature

As far as the inspiration of the Enlightenment is concerned Andrés work displays a teleological conception of human history in that it focuses on progress. Moreover, the ideal of historical description is critical objectivity, the method of inquiry is rationalistic, and the objective is encyclopaedic. Thus, in the beginning of the first volume, Andrés writes that his work is "a philosophical work that takes account of all literature and critically describes its developments and present state, now and then making proposals for how it can advance" (Andrés 1782 Vol. I: 1). His inspirational model was the work of Francis Bacon, the French *Encyclopédie* (1751-72), Voltaire's *Essay on the Manner and Spirit of Nations*, and especially John Campbell's *Universal History* (1747) to which he often refers esteeming it highly (Arato 2000). The reason why the work has a representational quality of the attainable knowledge of Nordic literature outside the North in the eighteenth century is due to its encyclopaedic ambition. The scholarly foundation of Andrés' ambitious enterprise is manifest in the fact that he travelled through Europe at least three times to collect material. In Italy alone he visited 23 cities and 121 libraries and centres of study (Mazzeo 1965: 47).

Nowadays, Andrés' work is hardly known. The scarcity of references in modern criticism has several reasons. As far as the function and meaning of literature is concerned, Andrés does not set forth new ideas or argue for a new set of normative standards in evaluating literary works; nor was his ambitious enterprise part of an aesthetic program as in the case of the Schlegel brothers. On the contrary, his method of inquiry can rather be defined as descriptive. To be sure, in describing the diversity of world literature, he uses different historical and cultural paradigms that now stand out as prejudicial or ideologically motivated. But these paradigms were largely scientific at the time. In many respects, Andrés' work can be said to sum up the knowledge of world literature near the end of the eighteenth century. Moreover, it was highly recognised at the time of the publication. Within the first decades, fourteen complete and five summarized Italian editions appeared. A German translation was prepared, and the first volume was published in French at an early stage of the reception history. A Spanish translation was made two years after the first Italian edition, and when it appeared, the Spanish king was so impressed by the quality of the work that he instructed the authorities at the Royal College of San Isidor and the University of Valencia to use Andrés' world literature as the official textbook for their courses on the history of literature, thus making them the first European centres of learning to offer courses on the history of world literature (Mazzeo 1965: 45).

Andrés' work had a significant influence on subsequent generations of literary critics and historians in Europe. With its focus on the history of civilisations, it anticipates historiographic conceptions found in Madame de Staël's *On the Influence of Literature upon Society*, August Wilhelm Schlegel's *Vorlesungen über der drammatischen Kunst und Literatur* (Lectures on Dramatic Art and Literature) published in 1808, Pierre-Louis Ginguené's *Histoire littéraire d'Italie* (History of Italian Literature), published in 1811, and Simonde di Sismondi's *De literature du midi del'Europe* (On the Literature of Southern Europe), published in 1813. In the latter, there are even passages directly translated from Andrés' Italian text. The influence is also traceable in Friedrich Schlegel's *Geschichte der alten und neuen Literatur* (History of Ancient and Modern Literature), published in 1815. In Jean-Jacques Ampère's early works on literature from 1830s, Andrés' work is still a source of knowledge (Arato 2000). Half a century after the publication, the historian Henry Hallam wrote, in his *Introduction to the Literature of Europe during the Fifteenth, Sixteenth and Seventeenth Centuries* (1837-39), that Andrés' work was "an extraordinary performance, embracing both ancient and modern literature in its full extent" (Hallam 1837, Vol. 1: 8). The Italian poet Giosuè Carducci's adverse opinion, stated in a letter of 1860 to Carlo Gargiolli, is rather an exception to the rule. According to Carducci, Andrés was a presumptuous friar who, while attempting to embrace the whole of human culture, was very often inexact and made an enormous number of errors, despising what was truly great and praising mediocrity. However, at that time, much had changed in literature and literary historiography. Although Andrés' work had deficiencies and was inconsistent in different respects, Carducci's judgment mainly reflects the still limited hermeneutic concern, in the nineteenth century, for historicity in criticising historical documents.

Although Andrés' work has now fallen out of the canon of literary historiography, there are important novelties in the work that furthermore were conceived as such by his contemporaries. As Guido Ettore Mazzeo writes about Andrés:

There was no doubt in the minds of [Andrés'] contemporaries that [he] had succeeded in extending the intellectual horizons of his time, if for no other reason than the fact that he had embraced, in his vast design, the little known cultures of the Far East, of Northern Europe, and of Russia. (Mazzeo 1965: 77)

Strictly speaking, we do not learn much about Nordic literature in Andrés' history of universal literature. What he says is coupled with an interest in Macpherson's Ossian poems and is associated with Russian literature which he considers to be a Northern phenomenon that lacks completely the originality of Old Norse and Old Gaelic poetry. But the scarce or superficial treatment of the literatures of Northern Europe is in itself a clear indication of how advanced the European reception of Nordic literature was at the time. For example, in dealing with the discovery of the Old Norse poetry and myth, Paul van Tieghem writes, in *Le Préromanticisme* (*Pre-Romanticism*), that Andrés was the first to introduce the Edda in the history of European literature (Van Tieghem 1924: 188). Thus, in volume two of his history, Andrés describes the Edda as a very famous work that deserves to be widely known. Less than two decades later a number of books on Old Norse poetry and translations had been published, among them the first translation of the Edda into English verse made by A. S. Cottle under the title *Icelandic Poetry*, or the *Edda of Saemund* (1797).

Andrés admits that he is only capable of making a superficial survey of Nordic literature, which he dates back to the fifth century. But he hopes that the survey will stimulate the curiosity of his readers. He presents a brief analysis of some of the critical positions expressed about the authorship, the time of publication, the versification and the themes of the Edda. To this he remarks: "The Icelanders are particularly careful in making their poems enigmatic and unintelligible, not only to the common man but also to minor poets" (Andrés 1782-99, III: 172). And in speaking of poetical and rhetorical devices, he writes: "Antonomasias, metaphors, hyperboles and strange and obscure expressions and sentences constitute the most appreciable ornaments of this poetry" (Andrés 1782-99, III: 172-73). In short, in Andrés' eyes, the Old Norse poetry was mysterious. But the mystery had its reasons. Here the notion of progress and the notion of climatic differences that are operative in Andrés' literary criticism help to elucidate the general perspective on Nordic literature. To paraphrase Rousseau's distinctions, the poetry of the Icelanders is a scriptural reproduction of speech and therefore not a rational articulation of ideas. The poetry contains some of the basic characteristics of primitive cultures as they were developed in Northern Europe. It expresses emotional impulses and is dynamic and vital, and it has strong persuasive qualities and displays aggressive forces that resonate the hard existential conditions of the people of the North and their struggle for survival.

Contrary to what one would expect, Andrés' notion of progress has also its significant traits of pre-modern conceptions. As noted, Andrés defines his work as a philosophical work that takes account of all literature, describes its progress and present state, and suggests how it might advance. He is convinced that cultures and nations of various periods and epochs should be portrayed by its positive rather than its negative sides. Thus, in applying this method, he emphasizes those cultural aspects that best reveal a continuously progressive and upward movement during all centuries. He regards the eighteenth century as the prolongation of the seventeenth century, which he considers to be the foundation of his own century (Andrés 1782-99, I: 1). He emphasizes the fundamentally erudite aspects of his age, thus interpreting it as a historical climax.

In essential ways, the hierarchical order Andrés constructs displays a pre-modern conception of order that is manifest in his emphasis on origin, progress and present state of every literature. Andrés' focus on the past is justified in at least three ways. First, the study of the past provides knowledge of why history has developed as it has. Second, it prepares the way for explaining what might have been lost in the course of history and how the loss might be regained. Third, the study of the past provides insight into why the contemporary state of literature and sciences, which is furthermore associated with the main lands of Europe, surpasses every period and culture of the past. Although this type of perspective has its idealistic foundation, it also displays an ideological conception of history due to its teleology. As the teleological view is manifest in Andrés' work, it has two main features, a diachronic and a synchronic. As far as the former is concerned, the teleology serves the purpose of emphasizing the continual progress in history towards greater understanding and bigger achievements. As far as the latter is concerned, it serves the purpose of establishing hierarchies of advancement within periods and epochs.

These two features elucidate further Andrés' attitude towards Nordic literature. On the one hand, when Nordic literature is compared with other literatures in the course of history, the diachronic perspective provides the basis for underlining how it can advance, taking account of the achievements of other literatures. On the other hand, when Nordic literature is compared with literatures of other areas within the same period, the synchronic perspective makes it possible to place Nordic literature on a less advanced level, as far as its achievements are concerned, since they are not on the level of other European literatures at the particular time in question. Especially the last point helps to explain why Andrés would classify, for example, Indian and Chinese literatures on the level of primitivism. In Andrés' view, none of these two major regional areas ever reached the level of literary inventiveness detectable among the poets of ancient Europe, nor did they undergo a development whose result was modern literature. Hence, Andrés did not regard the difference between the ancients and the moderns as a dispute of great importance. Along with the growth of academic Orientalism in the eighteenth century, the ancients and the moderns were now seen as two significant sides of the same culture – the European culture.

References

Acerbi, Giuseppe 1802: *Travels through Sweden, Finland, and Lapland to the North Cape in the Years 1798 and 1799.* 2 vols. London: J. Mawman.

Adams, Percy G. Adams 1962: *Travellers and Travel Liars, 1660-1800.* Berkeley: University of California Press.

Aldridge, A. Owen 1974: Ancients and Moderns in the Eighteenth Century. *Dictionary of the History of Ideas: Studies of Selected Pivotal Ideas.* 5 vols. Chief editor: Philip P. Wiener. New York: Scribner.

Andrés, Juan 1782-99: *Dell'origine, progressi e stato attuale.* 7 vols. Parma: Stamperia Reale Bodoni.

Arato, Franco 2000: Un comparatista: Juan Andrés. *Cromohs* 5, 1-14.

Auerbach, Erich 1969: Philology and Weltliteratur. *The Centennial Review* 13, 1-17.

Barnes, Geraldine & Mitchell, Adrian 2002: Measuring the Marvellous: Science and the Exotic in William Dampier. *Eighteenth-Century Life*, 26: 3, 45-57.

Barton, H. Arnold 1996: Iter Scandinavium: Foreign Travelers' Views of the Late Eighteenth-Century North. *Scandiavian Studies*, 68: 1, 1-18.

Bassnett, Susan 1993: *Comparative Literature: A Critical Study.* Oxford: Blackwell.

Byron, Lord 1957: *The Poetical Work of Lord Byron.* London: Oxford University Press.

Cassirer, Ernst 1932: *Die Philosophie der Aufklärung.* Tübinen: Morh.

Clunies Ross, Margaret & Lönnroth, Lars 1999: The Norse Muse: Report from an International Project. *Alvíssmál* 3, 3-28.

Conley, Thomas M. 1990: *Rhetoric in the European Tradition.* Chicago: The University of Chicago Press.

Day, Aiden 1996: *Romanticism.* London: Routledge.

Hallam, Henry 1837-9: *Introduction to the Literature of Europe during the Fifteenth, Sixteenth and Seventeenth Centuries.* 4 vols. London: J. Murray.

Liebersohn, Harry 1994: Discovering Indigenous Nobility: Tocqueville, Chamisso, and Romantic Travel Writing. *The American Historical Review* 99: 3, 746-66.

Liebersohn, Harry 1996: Recent Works on Travel Writing. *The Journal of Modern History* 68: 3, 617-628.

Robert 1990: The Reception of A Journal of the Plague Year and the Nexus of Fiction and History in the Novel. *ELH (A journal of English literary history)* 57: 3, 529-555.

Mazzeo, Guido Ettore 1965: *The Abate Juan Andres: Literary Historian of the XVIII Century.* New York: Hispanic Institute in the United States.

Moretti, Franco 2004: Conjectures on World Literature. *Debating World Literature.* Edited by Christopher Prendergast. London: Verso, 148-162.

Rousseau, Jean-Jacques 1966: Essay on the Origin of Languages. *On the Origin of Language: Jean-Jacques Rousseau and Johann Gottfried Herder.* Translated by J. H. Moran and A. Gode. Chicago: The University of Chicago Press.

Rosenthal, Jerome 1955: Voltaire's Philosophy of History. *Journal of the History of Ideas* 16: 2, 151-178.

Schlegel, Friedrich 1967: Georg Forster: Fragment einer Charakteristik der deutschen Klassiker (1797). *Kritische Friedrich Schlegel Ausgabe. Charakteristiken und Kritiken*, 1. Edited by Hans Eichner. Munich: Schöningh.

Seung. T. K. 1993: *Intuition and Construction: The Foundation of Normative Theory.* New Haven: Yale University Press.

Shoaf, Richard 1985: Science, Sect, and Certainty in Voltaire's *Dictionaire Philosophique. Journal of the History of Ideas*, 46: 1, 121-126.

Stafford, Fiona 1996: Introduction: The Ossianic Poems of James Macpherson. *The Poems of Ossian*. Edited by Howard Gaskill. Edinburgh: Edinburgh University Press.

Tiraboschi, Girolama 1771-82: *Storia della letteratura italiana*. 13 vols. Modena: Società Tipografica.

Van Tieghem, Paul 1924: *Le Préromantisme: Etudes d'histoire littéraire européenne* 1. Paris: F. Rieder & Cie.

Voltaire 1785: *Essai sur les Moeurs et l'Esprit des Nations*. *Oeuvres completes*, XVI. Paris: Société Littéraire-Typographique.

Wellek, René 1982: Poetics, Interpretation, and Criticism. *The Attack on Literature and Other Essays*. Chapel Hill: The University of North Carolina Press, 33-47.

The Gothic Tradition and the North: The Image of Gustavus Adolphus and His Men in Seventeenth Century Spain

Few Scandinavians, if any, have enjoyed more widespread fame on the European continent than the Swedish king Gustavus Adolphus (1594-1632). During the Thirty Years War (1618-1648) he, with his army of enrolled Swedish-Finnish peasant soldiers, Baltic officers and hired legionaries, was considered the champion of the Protestant cause both by his own side and by his enemies. The image of the king's person, with its virtues and faults, was vital for the continental image of the Scandinavian kingdoms and the Nordic peoples in a broader sense during the entire Baroque epoch at least up until the mid-eighteenth century. In this article the focus is set on how the king and his men were portrayed in Mediterranean Europe, and especially in Spain. The main analysis will be centred on two Spanish seventeenth century works on Gustavus Adolphus published in Spain. They are Fadrique Moles' *Guerra entre Ferdinando Segundo, Emperador Romano, y Gustavo Adolfo, Rey de Suecia* (The war between Ferdinand the Second, Roman emperor and Gustavus Adolphus, King of Sweden) published in 1637, and Fabricio Pons del Casteví's *Gustavo, Rey de Suecia, vencedor y vencido en Alemania* (Gustavus, King of Sweden, victor and defeated in Germany) from the year of the Westphalen peace treaty of 1648.

When sketching the mental map of Europe during the Baroque epoch, a dichotomy between north and south appears as a central element. The Thirty Years War was, with the notable exception of France, a confrontation between a southern Catholic side and a northern Protestant side. When Sweden entered the main war scene on German soil, the opponents did not lack invectives with which to fight a propaganda war. The general image of the Protestant north and its northernmost warrior king was drawn from a centuries-long tradition of depicting Europe's northern periphery. To picture the northern states, its princes and people as rustic, barbarian, unrefined and uncivilized had played a central role in a self-affirming civilisation discourse in the Renaissance heartland of the south. This negative discourse bore a generational rejection of medieval tradition, describing that epoch as an inter-period in history between a classical time of antiquity and a new era of a reborn European culture. The fall of the Roman Empire became a tragedy that had been inflicted on civilization by northern and eastern barbarian people. The Sack of Rome – *il sacco di Roma* – in 1527 was seen as yet another proof of what barbarians were ready to do. Even though Emperor Charles V (1500-1558) was the head of Catholic Spain, the invasion and plundering were seen as the work of German knights. It is no wonder that the exiled Swedish bishop Johannes Magnus (1488-1544), despite his Catholic faith, would feel a hostile atmosphere towards his person at the Italian universities just about the same time, noting that here the "Goths were cursed as adder bastards and as a people more cruel than the Tatars and the Huns." (Johannesson 1982: 116) This negative image of the Goths would prevail in Italy, while the Gothic issue in early modern Spain, as we will see, was much more complex and ambiguous.

A Gothic Monster or a Gothic Hero?

When the news of the death of the Swedish king at the battle of Lützen on the 6th of November 1632 eventually reached Madrid, the reaction was described as exalted and joyful. The reaction was normal as Gustavus Adolphus was the champion of the enemy side propagating for a Swedish correction of the Christian Church, fulfilling an eschatological role as a northern gothic hero sent to the war by divine providence. As José María Jover and Luis Rosales have shown, Gustavus had been the object of several comments by contemporary Spanish authors, and the attributes were not flattering. Francisco de Quevedo (1580-1645) called him "the monster of Stockholm" (*monstruo de Stocolmia*), while others would use terms such as "Swedish tyrant" (*tirano de Suecia*), "The beast of the North" (*fiera del norte*), "the new Attila" or "proof of Anti-Christ" (Rosales 1943: IX-XI; Jover 1949: 273-275, 290; Clavería 1954: 106-107). These appelations given to the Swedish king are understandable in the general atmosphere of an image propaganda war fought by both sides. The self-image of Gustavus Adolphus was consciously created around Gothic mythology and harsh biblical allusions drawn from the Old Testament. At the crowning ceremony in Uppsala in 1611, the seventeen year old king had proceeded as the Scandic-Gothic king Berig, who in earlier times had bursted out of the clouds of the north to invade the Continent. This image was taken from the Roman-Gothic historian Jordanes' work *Getica* from the sixth century, where the Gothic 'womb of nations' had, conveniently for later Swedish national pride, been situated on an island called 'Skandza'.

Among early modern Swedish scholars there was a firm belief, or at least an opportunistic consensus, that Jordanes' Skandza was nothing but Sweden. In the war propaganda of the Protestant side, Gustavus would be depicted as an apocalyptic proof of a new order. His allies would refer to him as the Old Testament Gideon in The Message of Judges, chosen by God to free the people of Israel. Another biblical allusion was that of Joshua, who would lead the people of Israel from Egypt to their lands in Canaan, fighting violent but victorious battles in the Holy Land. In a letter of defence written to the Emperor in 1632, the city council members of Nuremberg would refer to "the evangelical Joshua, the king of Sweden" (Ahnlund 1932: 354). In the first place, however, the Swedish king was to be referred to as the 'Lion from the North'. After the Swedish victory in Breitenfeld 1631, that would be their greatest victory in the war, a new text to a popular psalm spread around the Protestant German areas. The king addresses himself to the fleeing captain Tilly of the Catholic side (Nordström 1934: 9):

Ich bin der Löw von Mitternacht,
Mit dir will Ich frisch fechten,
Ich streite ja durch Gottes Krafft,
Gott helfe dem Gerechten.

According to the evangelical prophecies a saviour from the north would arrive to carry out God's punishment of Roman Babylon. The Swedish king undoubtedly had a great advantage from these expectations, managing to tie military victories to biblical prophecies in an intricate combination of fact and fiction. Thus his opponents both had to fight a war of arms and a war of images. The negative counter image of the Protestants was forged in leaflets and news pamphlets. From a Spanish perspective the main issue of the religious conflicts was originally tied to the events in the Spanish Netherlands. 'The Dutch rebels' had betrayed the Holy Roman Empire and the Austrian royal family of Spain, and were systematically portrayed as "enemies of our Holy Catholic Faith." (Anonymous 1626a; Anonymous 1626b).

Among news pamphlets available for us today in the Spanish National Library, the true fear and concern also for the Swedish power is made evident. The victory in Nördlingen in 1634 was seen as a much desired turn of the Swedish fortune, when the Imperials would return to victory, and show the world that its hardships were over (Anonymous 1634). The battle of Nördlingen together with other victories for the Imperial side, such as Halberstadt in 1641, inspired pamphlet makers in Spain to signal the end of the Swedish influence. No longer were there "any Imperials that would be afraid of the Swedes" (Anonymous 1641). This sentence found in one pamphlet printed in Sevilla suggests that earlier many on the Iberian Peninsula had been afraid of the Swedes. Gustavus Adophus and his troops had been constant news on the Continent, and consequently their action and their character were of the utmost interest.

In the works of Moles and Pons del Castelvi we can find a more detailed description of the deeds and final destiny of the Swedes and their king. Both works present a chronological narration of the contemporaneous events of the Thirty Years War, starting from when the Swedish king entered the war scene landing his troops at the island of Rügen off the Pomeranian coast at the Baltic in June 1630, until the battle of Nördlingen in 1634, where the Swedish troops, already without their deceased king, suffered a defeat to the Spanish-led imperial troops. This is the period normally referred to as the Swedish phase of the war. The strong Swedish presence on the war scene was from a southern perspective a broader continental issue that also affected Spain. For the reader Moles and Pons del Castelvi initially fix an image of a Nordic and Gothic warrior troop preparing for an invasion of the European continent. The king arrives "with twenty thousand robust Goths, hardened in war" (Moles 1637: 4), according to Moles, while Pons del Castelvi lets Gustavus himself talk to his men preparing them for a "strenuous endeavour, in which you will have to more than over-win your courage." Finally in this fictive speech the king addresses his men with the words, "my Goths" – "Godos mios", when telling his soldiers not to fear entering into the most risky and dangerous of battles and skirmishes (Pons del Castelvi 1648: 17-18).

The tone is thus clear, as the Swedes are depicted as heretic and fearless warriors and a genuine threat not only to the Catholic influence in the northern parts of the continent, but as a serious threat to Rome and all of western Christianity. A comparison to Attila and the invasion of the Huns as well as the Gothic invasion in the fifth and sixth centuries constitutes a central element in these narrations. As both texts were written after the death of Gustavus, it is obvious that both authors have composed their stories according to the final destiny of the Swedish involvement. We cannot know exactly what the feelings still were in 1630 when the Swedish king was busy organizing his military and political platform up in Pomerania on the Baltic shores. Since the advancement of the Swedish troops as well as the extension of the king's influence in central parts of Germany were to be so rapid and spectacular up until 1632, Gustavus is a continental threat in these Spanish narrations right from the moment he sets his foot on German soil. After the Swedish victory at the battle of Breitenfeld in September 1631, the king advanced toward Bavaria, and Munich was occupied early the next year. This had apparently been a shocking warning for the entire Catholic world, which Pons del Castelvi doubtlessly verbalized when narrating the next step of the Swedish king:

Thus Gustavus left Bavaria, and now he was not only a threat to all of Germany, but also to all of Italy, an endeavour I would not consider impossible considering the great spirit and momentum of the king. (Pons del Castelvi 1648: 99)

Vienna, with the imperial throne connected to Spain and the Catholic-Occidental heartland of the Italian peninsula, was now under a substantial threat from a northern Protestant king. Suddenly a peripheral and more or less unknown kingdom of the north constituted a serious threat to everything Spaniards and Italians would consider civilisation. It is in this situation the king, his men and their kingdom become interesting. There is a need to know the enemy, or at least to contemporary society explain who the enemy is. Along with the two Spanish books mentioned, a similar work in Italian by Galeazzo Gualdo Priorato ought to be mentioned. In this work published in Venice in 1640, *Historia delle guerre di Ferdinando II. e Ferdinando III. imperatori. e del re' Filippo IV. di Spagna. Contro Gostavo Adolfo re' di Svetia, e Luigi XIII. Re'di Francia* (The History of the War of the Emperors Ferdinand II and Ferdinand III and the king Philip IV of Spain against Gustavus Adolphus, King of Sweden and Louis XIII, King of France), a not surprisingly similar discourse on the Swedish king is developed. Castelvi mentions this work together with Moles' book among his contemporary sources, so there is an evident intertextual connection between these three.

Curriculum Vitae of the King

Both Moles and Pons del Castevi relate the Swedish participation in the war to the personal life of Gustavus Adolphus. In a typical seventeenth century fashion of princes' handbooks, the narration of contemporary events is interwoven with a biographical meditation on the king's habitus. Bigger events are seen through Gustavus Adolphus' person, and thus his entire lifespan from early childhood to his death on the fields of Lützen contains a moral lesson that is offered to the readers.[1] The king's ancestry is given as an explanation of how he, like his father, King Charles IX (1550-1611), always would be ready to use the sword against his enemies. The Spartan upbringing in the cold north had, "since childhood made his royal body more robust with the continuous military exercise" (Pons del Castelvi 1648: 3). However, the image given of the king is not totally savage, but rather the image of a modern and practical prince who was competent in martial sciences, in various vernacular languages as well as in practical politics. The great Gothic king was a hero of action in the eyes of his contemporaries, and the Spanish author initially finds only one great defect among his virtues.

---

[1] It was common in the Baroque epoch to read so called *Curriculum Vitae*, or grave speeches, where the deeds and morals of the deceased were evaluated.

GVERRA ENTRE
FERDINANDO SEGVNDO
EMPERADOR ROMANO,
Y
GVSTAVO ADOLFO
REY DE SVECIA,

POR DON FADRIQVE MOLES
Cauallero del Orden Militar de San Iuan.

SVPER
ASPIDEM
ET BASI-
LISCVM.
Pſal. 90.

Con Priuilegio. EN MADRID.
Enla Imprenta de Francifco Martinez. Año 1637.

FIG. 1:
The Habsburg Double Eagle is portrayed on the title page of Fadrique Mole's book. The eagle detains the heretic "riper and basilisk" under its feet.

He was sagacious, modest, vigilant, grandeurous, liberal, affable, pious and just; if this last could be included in the deliriums of Luther, that he of unfortunate heredity professed. He was so religious in his superstition, that if he would have been similar in the true Catholic faith, he would have been a unique model for future kings. (Pons del Castelvi 1648: 3)

The moral lesson of a great man fallen into the superstitious heresies of Luther's thesis was thus developed alongside with the narration of the factual events from the war scene. The rise and fall of Gustavus and the Swedish influence on the Continent is developed as a most serious example aimed at provoking both self-affirming and self-critical reflection among Catholic readers. On the one hand, countless examples and small rhetorical reminders are regularly repeated in the texts to point out the danger of Protestant belief. This was of course a central element in a seventeenth century Spanish self-reflection, as well as an obligatory approach in the eyes of the censors. Castelvi's book, printed in Madrid, has no less than four official permits and approbations attached at the beginning. Among these an approbation of the Inquisition's representative, the Jesuit father Augustin de Castro, can be noted. Likewise, a similar set of approbations and permissions is to be found in Moles' book. On the other hand, the story of the Swedish phase of the war is to a certain extent used as a tool to scrutinize the division and in-efficiency on the imperial Catholic side.

The critique directed against France and Louis XIII (1601-1643) is more direct and hateful than the negative otherness discourse developed towards the Swedish side. It was far more normal that a distant Nordic kingdom would act against the Catholic order, but the alliance politics of France were considered scandalous, or as Moles put it: "there is hardly any enemy of God in Europe that has not allied itself or established a friendly relationship with the French." (Moles 1637: 3) So, when the countless bestialities of the Swedish troops are narrated, they are to remind the readers of what kind of ally was fighting with the French. The verbalization of the pure evil embodied by Gustavus' troops do not lack spectacular details. On the battlefields body members are flying in the air, blood is flooding and dead corpses are being profaned and looted. Many are the stories about how Gustavus had seized fortified cities without fight only to break his promise to the burghers and let his troops loot "with insane rage, violate human and Divine rights, and without sentiment satisfy their gaze on miserable corpses." (Moles 1637: 22) The Protestant side was outside the realm of law, order, civilisation and true Christian faith. In the most negative assessments, Gustavus was depicted as half human and half devil:

This atrocious King, or better inhuman beast, could well answer like Timur Lenk did to a friend who wondered if he was human and mortal: You think I am a Man! No, I am a lightning from the Sky, and a plague for mankind. (Moles 1637: 22)

There is only one faith in a well-ending story for such a warrior king, and the king's contemporaneous meridional biographers do make use of the moral lesson offered by his death. Whilst Gustavus' virtues seem to be correctly affirmed, and he is depicted as a just and fearless warrior who does not shun action and danger,[2] Moles, like Castelvi, also states that he would have been a good warrior-king had he been a Catholic, because only the right faith would have corrected some of his most primitive qualities. However, in the end there was no glory for this warrior king, whose ambitions and dreams led to an early death. Castelvi's finishing chapter contains a long evaluation of the life and death of Gustavus Adolphus:

This is the end of this great Goth Gustavus [...] this Gustavus, who from early childhood was brought up among arms, ambitious of glory and fame, prudent in all action, elegant in all speech, friendly in treatment with others, courageous in enterprises, constant in work, sagacious in the most difficult matters, brilliant in fights, fearless in danger, attentive on all occasions, generous in repaying services and a punisher of offences. After all these deeds, after having defended the Kingdom he possessed, after having won entire provinces in Germany in two years, after having subdued two hundred and ninety three fortified cities, after so many victorious combats and so many open field battles, after having made Germany swim in blood, as we have seen, he finally stains that soil with his own, dying in the midst of pistol fire, to die eternally barely reaching the age of thirty eight years. He could have lived to a deserved old age had he been satisfied with his Kingdom, not rebelling in outside lands with the ambition to rule them. (Pons del Castelvi 1648: 12-113)

This extensive passage of Castelvi's text, which is almost a direct citation from the Italian Gualdo Priorato's work of 1640, perhaps raises more questions than it gives clear answers (Priorato 1640: 156-157). Even if the king's death is explained as an unavoidable consequence of heretic hybris, there is an admirable tone amidst the compulsory anti-Protestantism. A certain part of this is perhaps due to a convention to honor great military leaders only for the sake of their martial virtues, and especially in the case of Gustavus an admiration for the vitality and force of a barbarian 'man of nature' (Jover 1949: 290; Clavería 1954: 107).

2   By the mid-seventeenth century it was no longer the rule that a king should lead his troops in battle, as can be seen in the case of Spain's Philip IV (1621-1665), who was mostly informed about a war at the courts in Madrid and El Escorial.

This ambiguous attitude towards the king is a reflection of the following: Firstly Sweden was in the seventeenth century already part of a European political system of states, which meant that a Swedish king could not just be categorized alongside Mongol chiefs of the past, at least not when it was the main ally of France. Secondly, a foreign state and prince was through its otherness a base for reflecting the self. The fact that so many German princes would join cause with the Swedish king was inevitably a fact that awoke self-critical reflection. While the Protestant princes and warlords were re-investing the wealth and riches usurped from Church institutions into the war efforts, the emperor had to balance his politics between conceding the proper rights and riches to the Church and trying to answer the challenge on the battlefields. Both Moles and Castelvi direct critique towards the German princes, whom they see as irresponsible and disloyal to the emperor. In this comparison Gustavus seems much more steadfast and honourable than his Continental allies. Both authors hint that it might be impossible to just lean on faith when defending the only true Church. In order to fight back and destroy the 'heretic hydra', the Catholic side was to be united and prepared with earthly means to fight a violent but just war. The Emperor Ferdinand is actually accused of being too soft when acting according to good faith and benevolence towards his subjects (Castelvi 1648: 22-23). There is a certain militaristic attitude on the part of the Spanish when evaluating what the proper actions would be to fight the Protestant side. It seems like the Spanish authors would have wished to see warlords on their own side that matched the Swedish king. Despite an overwhelming and repetitive demonisation of the Protestants and their main chief Gustavus, an ambiguous discourse is thus developed alongside the narrations of a barbarian Scandinavian invasion of the European continent. This was, as we have seen, a result of a self-critical scrutiny of the politics on the Catholic side. But it also had in the Spanish case, as we will see, certain historical traditions to fall back on.

The Gothic paradox: "Et nos de gente Gothorum sumus"

The terms *Goth* and *Gothic* were frequently employed when referring to both Gustavus Adolphus and his men. During the sixteenth and seventeenth centuries the Gothic historical tradition was revived in many ascending northern powers in Europe. In states like Sweden, Denmark, Holland and even Poland, the Gothic past became a source for building up national self-confidence. Actually the Gothic theme seems to have been almost as popular and debated as was Protestantism. The Gothic tradition was a tool to give these northern nations a longer historical importance. In Sweden the early modern Gothic romanticism was canonized in Johannes Magnus' work *Historia de omnibus gothorum sveonumque regibus* from 1554, where mostly previously unknown references to Gothic history from antiquity and medieval times were brought to general knowledge in sixteenth and seventeenth century Sweden. As we have seen, the Gothic mythology constituted a vital part when forging the image of Gustavus Adolphus, and more importantly the works of both Johannes and Olaus Magnus (1490-1557) were well known to scholars in all parts of the Continent. In Spain this had its special connotations, since the Visigothic tradition was central to the self-image of baroque Spain. Even though the Swedish king represented Protestant heresy, he also descended from the same Gothic line as the Visigothic kings of Spain. This was of considerable importance since the Gothic tradition was a central element in the state-building legend of Christian Spain (Clavería 1954; Söhrman 2000).

The Visigoths had brought Christianity to the Iberian Peninsula, and King Recared converted to Catholicism in 587. The Visigoth and Catholic kingdom around Toledo flourished until 711, when it perished due to the Islamic expansion. Consequently the Visigoth era would soon become a classical epoch, and the idea of re-establishing this kingdom became a leading idea in Christian medieval Spain. Already in two ninth century chronicles the legend of Don Pelayo is presented as the start of a Christian re-conquest, or *reconquista*. Both in the anonymous *Chronicon Albeldense* and in the chronicle of the Asturian king Alfonso III (c. 848-910), the idea of an unbroken chain of Visigoth and Catholic kings is established. According to the legend a small group of Gothic noblemen had fled up north after the fall of Toledo. In the mountains of Asturias their leader Don Pelayo (d. 737) had inflicted the first defeat on the advancing Moorish troops. Driven by the appearance of the Virgin Mary in the cave of Covadonga, Don Pelayo initiated the *reconquista* and was elected king in the new kingdom of Asturias and Leon. This Gothic reign, *regnum gothorum*, was thus considered as a continuum of the kingdom of Toledo. This Christian Spanish kingdom had been described by Isidorus of Seville (c. 560-636) in his Gothic History (*Historia Gothorum*) as the most perfect place on earth, and the Gothic element was contrasted in a positive manner to the Roman influence. Later medieval chronics, like *Acta translationis corporis S. Isidori* (c. 1063), *Historia Silense* (c. 1115), withheld this Gothic history, and for the Castilian historians Lucas de Tuy (*Chronicon Mundi* 1236) and Rodrigo Jiménez de Rada (*Historia Gothica* 1243) the term Goth was equivalent to a Spanish Christian Catholic.

When the *reconquista* was completed in 1492, the Spanish monarchy was thus just as embedded in medieval Gothic-Christian mythology as it was on the verge of establishing a new world empire with overseas realms. The Spanish interest for the Gothic past had been considerably more vivid than the interest for the Roman heritage during medieval times. The Renaissance did not alter this so much as one might expect. As for the knowledge and interest of the most ancient Gothic history and its possible ties to Scandinavia, there had been little notice among the medieval chroniclers. Even though Jiménez de Rada had mentioned Jordanes, he had not connected Scandza with Scandinavia, but with a larger northern area including semi-mythological Scythia as well as Denmark, Norway, Sweden, Flanders, England and German regions. It was at this moment the works of Olaus and Johannes Magnus were to play a considerable role in Spanish historiography. As Johan Nordström has shown, early modern Spanish authors would show great interest in Scandinavian Gothic history that reached the Iberian Peninsula through Italy (Nordström 1945). Even though Spanish history writing of the sixteenth century shows a clear relationship with the formal conventions of the Italian humanist tradition, it differs from that in its attitude towards the Nordic peoples. The Spanish historians did not share the Italian's negative and hateful view of the barbarian invaders. Faithful to medieval historiography, the Gothic tradition still constituted a vital element of Spanish patriotism.

We know that Olaus Magnus sent both his own *Historia de gentibus septentrionalibus* (1555) and his then late brother's work *Historia de omnibus gothorum svonumque regibus* (1554) to the Emperor Charles V, who considered that there was kinship between the Spanish and the Goths of Sweden (Nordström 1945: 41). Once when commenting upon the internal fights in Gustavus Wasa's Sweden (1496-1560), he is said to have uttered the words: Et nos de gente Gothorum sumus – we are also of the Gothic tribe. This supreme approbation of the Gothic-Scandinavian kinship in history on the part of the king, was inevitably to further spark a Gothicist view among Spanish historians. This view came to draw substantial content from the rich descriptions found in the works of the Magnuses. The Gothic historical discourse was cemented by Ambrosio de Morales (1513-1591), chronicler of Philip II (1556-1598), in his work *Crónica general de España* (1574-1586). Unlike many other of his predecessors and contemporaries, Morales did not waste much ink questioning the true origin of the Goths. For him the island Skandza described by Jordanes was nothing other than the Scandinavian peninsula, and the Swedish region of *Gotia* described by Magnus was the original home of all Gothic tribes. For Morales, Gotia is the ancient home of his own people, and with opportunistic selectivity he narrates the most positive descriptions of this land and its inhabitants. Embracing the spirit of the Aristotelean climate theory, Morales emphasizes the ability of the cold and harsh northern climate to generate a numerous, strong and belligerent population.

This still classical idea of the northern Goths is, however, diversified by Morales who adds considerable virtues to their character. He describes the moral and intellectual prowess of the Goths, thus nurturing a positive Spanish self-image in comparison to neighbouring states, and among them first and foremost France. Exactly the same phenomenon can be observed in the Augustinian monk Hieronymo Roman's description of what he calls the 'Northern republic', *Republica Septentrional*. In a vast historical-geographical description of different countries, *Repúblicas del mundo* (1575), he draws his information mainly from Olaus Magnus' history, depicting to his compatriots an image of a golden age with an original state of a pure and true worship of God. The Scandinavian Goths are described with numerous examples of their virtues: they would leave their weapons outside the temples and the doctors would not be allowed compensation for their work before the patient was healed. Extensive descriptions of customs, law and social order are composed to form a truly romantic image of a glorious non-Roman heritage. As was general practice among authors of this time, they would copy directly from the Swedish authors, considering their praise of their home country as uncontested facts. Actually the historical interpretations presented by Johannes and Olaus Magnus could find Spanish defenders when facing contest. In the Franciscan Juan de Pineda's universal history, *La monarchía ecclesiastica* (1588), Johannes Magnus, is held to be correct in comparison with the Dutch Johannes Goropius Becanus (1519-1572), who placed the original Goths on the American continent. 'Our Johannes Magnus the Goth' – 'nuestro Iuan Magno Godo' – as Pineda calls him, is cited extensively in this work, and the author holds a firm belief in the biblical legend of Japhet's son Magog populating "Finlandia, which is the oriental part of Scandinavia." (Pineda 1588: 323). Also for Pineda there is no doubt about the fact that the founders of Christian Spain were descendants of Magog and the Goths that had left Sweden in biblical time. For him the Goths had served the early Christian church persecuted by the Roman Empire. By crushing the empire they had given birth to the Christian monarchy on earth.

"To be of the Goths"

The Scandinavian-Spanish connection was not only considered as part of history but was also a contemporary sixteenth century reality, since Gustavus Wasa and his sons were seen as descendants of Magog in a straight lineage. The royal chronicler Ambrosio Morales actually established a historical relation of a common Gothic blood between Protestant Sweden and Catholic Spain. It is worth noting that in his work he draws very little attention to the Reformation and the religious divide of his own time. Rather he seems eager to strengthen the Gothic elements in his nation's collective historical memory. He undoubtedly experienced considerable success in these ambitions, since his work was still reprinted in the early eighteenth century. Furthermore, he was not solely responsible for spreading the content of these Swedish works in the Spain of the Baroque era, as the perhaps most classical of all general histories, Juan de Mariana's Spanish history *Historiæ de rebus Hispaniæ* from 1592 (1602 in the vernacular), would follow Morales' path idealizing the Gothic heritage of the Spanish crown and Christian Spain at large. This Jesuit father, who exemplifies the scholastic tradition of the university of Salamanca, used Magnus as a main source leaning on the established national tradition of historical writing. Even if Morales' work was reprinted many times, it cannot be compared to the impact Mariana was to have, since his work was to dominate Spanish historical perception for almost two hundred years after its first appearance. So, when Juan Francisco de Masdeu described the deeds of the Visigoths in his emblematic *Historia crítica de España y de la cultura española*,[3] published at the eve of the French revolution (1783-1805), he would still refer to Olaus and Johannes Magnus.

These general histories did not direct specific interest towards Scandinavia. They rather show the longevity of the Visigoth tradition. They are also the most central historical works read by its contemporaries, which suggests a wide acceptance of the Gothic idea. In seventeenth century Spain the Gothic identity was first and foremost connected with the royal family and the nobility, suggesting their straight descent from the original Christian kingdom of Toledo. In popular language the expression "to be of the Goths" became to signify an aristocratic Catholic descent among the nobility (Corominas 1954: 734-737; Clavería 1960). Therefore 'Gothic' features, such as blond hair, a light complexion, corporal magnitude and a robust habitus became admired among those who defended the idea of Spain as a great monarchy and restorer of the Christian order. Inversely the term Gothic, due to this northern otherness, became a pejorative notion for many in the American overseas realms. In this context everything Gothic alluded to the centralised peninsular bureaucracy and the Spanish crown. Thus the Gothic image was tied to the highest caste in the Spanish empire, and it was not just contrasted to what was seen as inferior ethnic elements in the American vice-kingdoms, but also to the Roman heritage. It was important to point out the superiority of the Spanish monarchy and world power in comparison to the ancient Roman Empire.

One of the most emblematic baroque scholars and politicians, Diego de Saavedra Fajardo, gives a clear statement of this in his historical handbook for princes *Corona Gotica* (1645) written for King Philip IV. Saavedra instructs his majesty to read about the Gothic kings, "what they accomplished during many centuries, and learn from their experiences and actions." (Saavedra 1646: 2) Like most of his

---

3   Masdeu was born in Naples, at that time a Spanish-Bourbon kingdom, and his emblematic work in 20 volumes was first published in Italian, *Storia critica di Spagna e della cultura spagnuola in ogni genere*, in 1781-84.

compatriots he would refer to Johannes Magnus, but now in an extended fashion. Not only did he share Magnus' views of the ancient history of the Scandinavian Goths, but he also shared his view of the Visigothic history of Spain. In his introductory letter to the reader he thus justifies his preference for the Gothic tradition over the Roman, asking rhetorically that it "might seem to some that I should not start with the Goths, a nation considered barbarian among the Greeks." For him the true art of state was not to be found in the Greco-Roman heritage, which was too wordy and speculative, but in the simple and just warrior ethos of the Goths. "We have learned more about how to live our lives from the animals than from Man, more from the rustic than from the erudite" (Saavedra 1646: 2), Saavedra states as he continues to point out that the art of statesmanship that invented speculation, the Greeks and Romans in his view, gave birth to tyrants. The Greco-Roman imperial tradition had in his mind been doomed to fail and perish due to its immorality, its corrupted use of intelligence, and arrogance towards others. He compares the softness and delicacy of the highly civilised Greeks with the healthy rudeness of the barbarian tribes. Among these tribes he finds the Goths to be the most educated and thus constituting an ideal historical heritage for the Spanish power of his own time.

Saavedra wrote *Corona Gotica* while staying in Germany as one of the king's ambassadors negotiating the peace treaty of the Thirty Years War. His main interest seems to be the legitimacy of the Spanish crown as the true and just defender of Christianity. He chooses to emphasise the uncorrupted, pure and original faith of God in the religious practices of the Goths. Unlike other lands invaded by barbarians, and later lost by the same, he concludes that the Goths were sent to Spain by God to erect a Catholic kingdom with the total consent of the local peoples (Saavedra 1646: 2). This was the base of the Spanish crown and its ambitions in European politics, and proved Spanish superiority perhaps even before the Papal throne. This Spanish patriotism, or proto-nationalism, had its own level of meaning that surpassed the unity of Catholic Europe. The self-affirming image of Spain and the Spaniards as superior both to contemporary and historical kingdoms and empires, was guided by the idea of purity and divine providence. God was on the side of Spain, the purest and most genuine representative of Christianity. As Peter Burke has noted, purity was a central notion in all except public hygiene during the Baroque epoch (Burke 2004). This obsession with purity was especially visible in Spain, and first of all in the idea of blood purity. This early form of nationalism was centred on the idea of a pure Spanish nation of pure Spanish blood. This blood was neither Moorish nor Jewish, but Gothic. This made Spain different, and superior, to the rest of the old Roman Empire. The "divine blood of the Goths", as Alfonso de Villadiego expressed it in his historical study of Visigoth law published in 1600,[4] was a national identity-shaping factor that complemented a wider Catholic mental geography.

This places the narrations of Castelvi and Moles in a slightly new light. The image of King Gustavus was not simply conditioned by a strictly black and white picture of the war. The Gothic blood that flooded in the veins of the Swedish ruler was a specific concern for both authors. While the general image of the Goths in Italy would remain negative *à la renaissance*, the Spanish national context was somewhat different. Gustavus Adolphus was for Castevi and Moles a contemporaneous monarch that reminded them of Spain's most ancient Christian kings. The king's habitus would awake spontaneous admiration. Gustavus had "wonderful looks, Royal presence, light skin, blond hair (a hereditary beauty of those regions), a stately measured body proportioned with robust arms and legs." (Pons del Castelvi 1648: 3) The incorporation of Gustavus' image in a Spanish-Gothic context was not only limited to a comparison with the traditional description of the Spanish Visigothic nobility and their rulers. The narration of the Swedish entrance into the war was composed according to the generally accepted image of the original Goths. Gustavus and his men would pour out of their northern kingdom that had become too small for their potential. This image was in total conformation with the Gothic myth, adapted mainly from Jordanes, of how the descendants of Magog repeatedly "burst forth like a swarm of bees from the midst of this island and came into the land of Europe." (Jordanes/Mierow 1960: 53) Moles observes this natural need for invading Europe on behalf of the Swedish king, stating that "he is not king, who is king over the sand deserts of Libya or the Arctic Ocean". Consequently he finds Gustavus "taking the example of the Goths, who submerged almost all of Europe" (Moles 1637: 2).

In Saavedra de Fajardo the same kind of intertextual allusion to Jordanes' Gothic mythology is much more explicit. Already before publishing *Corona Gotica* in 1646, he had referred to Gustavus Adolphus and his men as "bears from the north", breaking the ice of Sweden in order to cross the Baltic Sea and inflict harm upon the Holy Roman Empire (Saavedra Fajardo 1949: 557). The same idea is then repeated in his Gothic chronicle:

Not being able to contain themselves in the vapours of the North, they broke through them like puffs pressed out between clouds, and like rays they came forth various times to embrace the world. (Saavedra 1646: 3)

---

4   *Forus antiqvus Gothorum Regum Hispaniæ, olim Liber Iudicum: hodie Fuero Iuzgo nuncupatus* (The Ancient Laws of the Gothic Spanish Kings, then called Book of Jews: today named Fuero Juzgo)

This straight paraphrase of Jordanes is illustrative of the ambiguous Spanish view of Gustavus Adolphus, Sweden, and Protestant Scandinavia at large during the baroque epoch. The Spanish Gothicism was a national peculiarity in the general north and south dichotomy that conditioned mental mapping in most old European civilisations. This Gothicism had a parallel existence with the negative image of the north that built on Renaissance ideals.

Mapping Europe's north 1500-1700

When examining the elements central to the perception of the north in European mental mapping during early modern times, a duality of concepts appears. The traditional image of the north as a periphery of European civilisation fostered an objectifying and poetical *imaganiatio borealis* discourse. However, at the same time an incorporating political process would put the northern kingdoms more firmly on the European map. The French Renaissance specialist Frank Lestringant refers to a *political Europe*, when designating the common family of states that would be considered part of the European balance of power system (Lestringant 1993). At a time when the cosmographical space was revolutionised with the great discoveries, Europe's traditional peripheries would become closer. Olaus Magnus' Nordic history would appear at a time when Turkish expansion was depriving the Christian world of its European Levantine areas. The discovery of the northern peoples, and thus incorporation of the northern kingdoms into political Europe, was a sort of mental re-compensation for the amputated areas on the Balkans.

When Sweden entered on the German scene in the Thirty Years' War and concluded their alliance with France, it was a final consolidation of their status as a European power. This new political situation had its implications on a mental level; the political north and the poetical far north would constitute two sets of northern images often blended in practical image production. On the one hand the Swedish king and his men would be held as equals among continental allies and enemies on a core-European civilisational scale. On the other hand, the Swedes would be depicted through their northerness. This northerness had its peculiar substance tied to that direction, but it also had general features tied to periphery. The values derived from the northern direction, was mostly a practice inspired by climate theory, while an otherness discourse that built on exoticism and remoteness was rather a part of general core-periphery thinking.

The climate theories, first developed in ancient Greece within philosophy and medicine, became vital in the new political science of sixteenth century Occidental humanism. National psychology, temperament, morals and characters were organised in extensive reference systems. In the scheme of reasoning, the north was mostly associated with coldness, brutality and barbarism. In one of the most emblematic Spanish baroque works, Baltasar Gracián's universal novel *El Criticón*, a picaresque story is developed of how all the vices of Man were accidentally freed from where God had locked them up. Out came the vices in the shapes of goddesses, that each would head for one country. While *Pride* would head for Spain, *Gluttony* with her sister *Drunkenness* landed in Germany, *Simplicity* in Poland and *Atrocity* in Sweden (Gracián 1996, 264-266). This was the general idea of early modern national stereotypes. Like in Tacitus' *Germania* (98 AD) – rediscovered by Renaissance humanists – the northern peoples would be defined through a counter-image of civilisation, lacking control over their primitive instincts. This barbarian (Gracián had put the goddess *Barbaria* in Turkey) and brutal force was the force of periphery, well exemplified in Moles' and Castelvi's evaluation of the martial qualities of different nationalities. The Swedish king would several times be saved in his most courageous operations by the seemingly unbeatable 'caualleria Filandesa' (Moles 1637: 5; Pons del Castelvi: 64-65). On the Imperial side the same role was given to the Croats, whose presence on the battlefield would indicate equally violent conditions.

With the climate theory a generally accepted set of graduations evolved, and like in the case of Gothic historiography, also climate theories would soon prove to be part of precise national political ambitions. In France, Jean Bodin (1530-1596) developed a detailed chart of latitude progression from the Equator to the North Pole in his works *La Méthode de l'Histoire* (*Methodus ad facilem historiarum cognitionem* 1566) and *La République* (1577). Among other things he proved that it was climatologically determined that tempered nations like France would be the only capable mediators and defenders of peace in Europe, "with strength to control the ruse of the South and with sagaciousness to end the brutality of the Scyths" (Lestringant 1993: 215). Actually, Bodin presents much of the arguments that Montesquieu would build his climate theory upon in the eighteenth century. Bodin already suggests the inferiority of the European south, which more precisely meant Italy and Spain.

In this context the intense repetition of the Gothic history in Spain gets even more understandable. The biased claim on the part of the French to conquer European hegemony and define the civilisation core included a marginalisation of everything Spanish already in the seventeenth century. The Swedish king had been bought by the French, so it was important to show that the northern king Gustavus had more in common with the Spanish. By claiming the Gothic descent and rejecting the Roman heritage, the Spanish historians and authors of political and philosophical literature would try to avoid their country being downgraded on a civilisational scale, together with Italy, from a French perspective. This was probably a much more important factor than a supposedly genuine Spanish interest for Scandinavia. This would also explain the seemingly unproblematic way in which both positive and negative images of Gustavus Adolphus and his men are portrayed parallel to each other in most narrations. There was a political agenda connected with the massive promotion of the Gothic history, but at the same time a regular European, early modern discourse on the North would prosper to satisfy the needs to demonise the Protestant enemy.

The Gothic theme would lose its importance in Spain as the Habsburg dynasty, with the death of Charles II in 1700, lost the throne to the Bourbons. The romantic revival of the Gothic past in Northern Europe around 1800 was not to be felt on the Iberian Peninsula, where the Moorish heritage rather awoke the passions of romantic souls. The traditional Spanish Gothicism was seen as part of the aristocratic nationalism of the Habsburg Baroque era, and was not found appealing as such. Gradually it was left resting in oblivion, only as a latent historical self-understanding, waiting perhaps to be reused some day.

References

Anonymous 1626a: *Copia sumaria de la consulta de los Reueldes de Olanda.* Handwritten copy, Biblioteca Nacional de España (VE/217/15).

Anonymous 1626b: *Relacion verdadera de la gran vitoria que ha tenido el conde Telli General del exercito de la liga Catholica del Emperador de Alemania, contra los hereges rebeldes enemigos de nuestra Santa Fé Catholica.* Valladolid.

Anonymous 1634: *Sangrienta batalla de Nörlingen.* Madrid.

Anonymous 1641: *Relacion verdadera de la celebre vitoria que han tenido las Armas Imperiales contra las del Coronel Dorstendon General de Suecia.* Sevilla.

Ahnlund, Nils 1932: *Gustav Adolf den store.* Uppsala: Almqvist & Wiksells.

Burke, Peter 2004: *Languages and Identities in Early Modern Europe.* Cambridge: Cambridge University Press.

Clavería, Carlos 1954: Gustavo Adolfo y Cristina de Suecia, vistos por los españoles de su tiempo, *Estudios hispano-suecos.* Granada:

Colleción filológica de la Universidad de Granada: 101-156.

Clavería, Carlos 1960: Reflejos del 'goticismo' español en la fraseología del siglo de oro, *Separata del homenaje a Dámaso Alonso.* Madrid: Gredos: 357-372.

Corominas, José 1954: *Diccionario Crítico Etimológico de la Lengua Castellana.* Madrid: Gredos.

Gracián, Baltasar 1651/1996: *El criticón.* Madrid: Catedra.

Gualdo Priorato, Galeazzo 1640: *Historia delle guerre di Ferdinando II. e Ferdinando III. imperatori. e del re' Filippo IV. di Spagna. Contro Gostavo Adolfo re' di Svetia, e Luigi XIII. Re' di Francia.* Venetia: Bertani.

Johannesson, Kurt 1982: *Gotisk renässans.* Uppsala: Almqvist & Wiksells.

Jordanes 1960 (550, ed. C. C. Mierow): *The Gothic History of Jordanes.* Cambridge: Speculum Historiale.

Jover, José María 1949: *1635. Historia de una polémica y semblanza de una generación.* Madrid: Instituto Jerónimo Zurita.

Lestringant, Frank 1993: *Ecrire le monde à la renaissance*. Caen: Paradigme.

Magnus Johannes 1554: *Historia de omnibus gothorum sveonumque regibus.*

Moles, Fadrique Moles 1637: *Guerra entre Ferdinando Segundo, Emperador Romano, y Gustavo Adolfo, Rey de Suecia*. Madrid: Francisco Martinez.

Morales, Ambrosio 1574-1586: *Crónica general de España*. Alcalá de Henares.

Nordström, Johan 1934: *De yverbornes ö*, Stockholm: Bonniers.

Nordström, Johan 1945: Goter och spanjorer. Till den spanska goticismens historia, *Lychnos 1944*, Stockholm: Lärdomshistorisk Samfundet: 257-280.

Nordström, Johan 1975: *Johannes Magnus och den götiska romantiken: akademiska föreläsningar 1929.*
Uppsala: Almqvist & Wiksells.

Pineda, Juan de 1588: *Segunda parte de la Monarchia ecclesiastica*. Salamanca: Iuan Fernandez.

Pons del Castevi, Fabricio 1648: *Gustavo, Rey de Suecia, vencedor y vencido en Alemania*. Madrid: Domingo Garcia y Morràs.

Roman, Hieronimo 1575: *Republicas del mundo*. Salamanca: Iuan Fernandez.

Rosales, Luis 1943: Prologo, *Poesias heróicas del Imperio*, ed. Rosales &Vivanco. Madrid: Jerarquía: I-XIV.

Saavedra Fajardo, Diego de 1645/1646: *Corona gotica, castellana, y austriaca*. Münster: Juan Jansonio.

Söhrman, Ingmar 2000: The Gothic tradition: its presence in the Baroque period, *Spain & Sweden in the Baroque Era (1600-1660)*, eds Enrique Martínez Ruiz & Magdalena de Pazzis Pi Corrales, Madrid: Fundación Bernd Wistedt: 937-948.

Villadiego, Alfonso 1600: *Forus antiqvus Gothorum Regum Hispaniæ, olim Liber Iudicum: hodie Fuero Iuzgo nuncupatus*. Madrid.

Original Quotes

[…] där goterna förbannades som huggormars avföda och som ett folk grymmare än tatarerna och hunnerna. (Johannesson 1982: 116)

Den evangeliske Josua, konungen av Sverige. (Ahnlund 1932: 354)

Relacion verdadera de la gran vitoria que ha tenido el conde Telli General del exercito de la liga Catholica del Emperador de Alemania, contra los hereges rebeldes enemigos de nuestra Santa Fé Catholica. (Anonymous 1626b)

[…] ya no hay Imperial que tema a los Suecos y rebeldes del Imperio. (Anonymous 1641)

[…] con veinte mil robustos Godos, curtidos en la guerra […]. (Moles 1637: 4)

Este es el principio de una ardua empresa, para que tenga mas que vencer vuestro valor […]. (Pons Castelvi 1648: 17-18)

Salió pues Gustauo de la Babiera, no solo ya con temor de toda Alemania, sino tambien de Italia toda (como se dixo) empresa que no tuuiera yo por imposible, viendo con tan grandes alientos al Rey. (Pons del Castevi 1648: 99)

Hizo desde su niñez mas robusto su Real cuerpo con el continuo exercicio militar, […]. (Pons del Castelvi 1648: 3)

Era sagaz, modesto, vigilante, magnanimo, liberal, afable, piadoso, y justo; si pudiera caber esto ultimo en los delirios de Lutero, que por infeliz herencia professaua, y tan religioso en su supersticion, que à serlo de la verdadera fe Catolica Romana […] diera unico exemplo de Reyes à la posteridad. (Pons del Castelvi 1648: 3)

[…] que apenas ai enemigo de dios en Europa, que no sea confederado, ò amigo del Frances. (Moles 1637: 3)

[...] con colera insana, violando los derechos humanos y Diuinos, los passaron à cuchillo, saciando la vista en los miserables cuerpos. (Moles 1637: 22)

Pudiera este Rey atroz, ò mejor dezir, bestia inhumana, con propiedad responder lo que el Tamorlan à un amigo que le aduirtio era humano y mortal: Piensas que yo soy hombre! no soy sino rayo del Cielo, y peste del genero humano. (Moles 1637: 22)

Este es el fin de aquel grande Godo Gustauo [...] Este Gustauo, que desde su mocedad se alimentò entre las armas, ambicioso de gloriosa fama, este tan prudente en toda accion, elegante en todo discurso, afable en el trato, valeroso en las empresas, constante en los trabajos, sabio en las resolucions mas dificultosas, brioso en las peleas, intrepido en los peligros, desvelado en toda ocasion, remunerados de seruicios, y castigador de delitos, despues de tantas hazañas, despues de auer defendido el Reyno que possèa, despues de auer ganado en Alemania en dos años Prouincias enteras, despues de auer rendido ducientas y nouenta y tres Ciudades, entre fortalezas, y tierras muradas, despues de tan vitoriosos combates, despues de tantas batallas cāpales, despues de auer hecho nadar en sangre a Alemania, como auemos visto, la riega finalmente con la suya, muriendo a pistoletazos, para morir eternamête, a los treinta y ocho años a penas cumplidos desu edad, pudiendo por ventura, auer llegado a la deseada vejez si se contentara con su Reyno, sin auiuar rebeldias en los agenos, por la ambicion de Reynar en ellos. (Pons del Castelvi 1648: 112-113)

No parezca à algunos que yo no debièra empezar de los Godos, nacion tenida por Barvara entre los Griegos [...]. (Saavedra 1646: 2)

No parezca à algunos que yo no debièra empezar de los Godos, nacion tenida por Barvara entre los Griegos [...]; mas emos aprendido à bivir de los animales, que de los Hombres, mas de los Rusticos, que de los Doctos. (Saavedra 1646: 2)

Tenia amable exterior, y Real presencia, rostro blanco, y cabello rubio (hereditaria hermosura de aquellas Regiones) alto de cuerpo, y proporcionado con robustos miembros. (Pons del Castelvi 1648: 3)

[...] no pudiendo contenerse dentro de los Vapores del Norte rompieron por ellos semejantes à las exalaciones constreñidas entre las, y como rayos salieron diversas vezes à abrazar el Mundo. (Saavedra 1646: 3)

HENDRIETTE KLIEMANN-GEISINGER

Mapping the North – Spatial Dimensions and Geographical Concepts of Northern Europe

How to locate the North? One might think it would be an easy task to define the borders of that region. As one of the four cardinal points the North obviously marks the opposite direction of the South. Viewed more closely, things are not that simple any more: throughout time the North has symbolized different regions with shifting extensions, the particular definition depending on the context and the viewpoint, the intention and interests of the observer. Due to this lack of a universally valid concept it is important to remember the fact that eighteenth and nineteenth century scholars and travellers had different spatial concepts in mind when they were writing about the North, whether they were defining them explicitly or not. Therefore, this essay[1] is about the spatial dimension (Osterhammel 1998b, Schlögel 2003: 7-37) of the North. The leading question is where the North has been located – in contrast to the question of how it has been culturally defined (Lewis, Wigen 1997: 48, 84-75).

The focus of this essay lies on the academic attempts made by German and Scandinavian scholars during the eighteenth and early ninteeth centuries to define and locate the region. They started to do systematic research on the North and therefore had to define their object. Spatial concepts of the North and descriptions of its extension can mostly be found in eighteenth and nineteenth century geographical, statistical and historical studies as well as in studies in the political sciences. Explicit definitions of the North's geographical range are usually the subject of large volumes, not of short essays. On the other hand, periodicals dealing with Nordic themes can give information about their geographical concepts of the North. Here the geographical dimension is usually discussed in the introduction describing the spatial concepts that lie behind a study.

During the eighteenth and early nineteenth centuries the North was mainly a political and less a purely geographical concept. The focus of this analysis there-

---

1   The article is based on parts of the author's dissertation: *Koordinaten des Nordens. Wissenschaftliche Konstruktionen einer europäischen Region 1770-1850.*

fore lies on the political appearance of the North and its role among the European states as well as on its cartographic flexibility, with its varying borderlines and steadily changing geographical extensions. Concretely, the following sections deal with three different aspects of academic attempts to locate the North. The first is about the wide concept of the North and the Nordic image of Russia, which dominated the European perception of that region during the eighteenth century. The second presents attempts to create a geographical concept of Europe based on natural criteria and different approaches to define nature-given regions in Northern Europe, especially at the beginning of the nineteenth century. It also discusses why the North is not described as a coherent region during that time. Finally, the third and last points out different regions of the North, presenting alternatives to the wide concept of the North.

The wide concept of the North

The image of the North has its roots in the ancient worldview with its general division into the known and civilized world, the Mediterranean South, and the unknown, barbarian North. This dichotomy was not always present on the mental map of the Europeans. During the Middle Ages an east-west division characterized the image of Europe, but in the Renaissance the ancient north-south dichotomy once again returned and dominated the image of the North for the following centuries. According to this concept the North included Iceland, Scandinavia, Russia, and today's Eastern Europe, and could even cover parts of Asia. The structures of the ancient north-south dichotomy and the continuing usage of the terms North and South arose from the tradition of dividing Europe into the civilized Mediterranean South and the barbarian North. Stratification from east to west or vice versa were not yet common. The term North was still used in contexts that from an academic point of view could, geographically, have been recognized as eastern long ago. The wide concept of the North was dominating the European perception of this region until the late eighteenth century. It did not change before the turn of the nineteenth century, when the idea of a Scandinavian/Germanic North and the concept of Eastern Europe emerged (Lemberg 1980, Kliemann-Geisinger 2002a: 47-50).

During the eighteenth century, Russia was generally regarded as Nordic – from the inside as well as from the outside. The decisive reason for this goes back to the politics of Peter the Great (1672-1725). By opening Russia to Europe Peter the Great made it a European and at the same time a Nordic power (Lindsey 2001). Russia's involvement during the Nordic Wars 1700-21 made it impossible for the Europeans to see it as an isolated state. Instead it was integrated into the

HENDRIETTE KLIEMANN-GEISINGER

European system of powers. At the same time Russia's advance to the Baltic affected Western European trade interests because the eastern parts of the Baltic, especially the Baltic provinces, were some of the most important suppliers of shipbuilding materials for the Europeans. Russian access to the Baltic Sea was therefore decisive for its belonging to the North and drew attention to Russia (Mediger 1968). The foundation of St. Petersburg on former Swedish territory in 1712 symbolized the emergence of the new Nordic power in the eastern parts of the Baltic Sea and further contributed to Russia's Nordic image.

International politics took Russia's new position into account by creating a system of political balance, the so-called Balance of the North, similar to the one already existing in the south of Europe (Brandt 1929, Rahbek Schmidt 1957). From then on, the shaping of a northern and a southern state system characterized the discussion about the political structure of Europe. The so-called Balance of the North became an object of research in statistics and the political sciences (Rassem 1980). The aim was to achieve a balance of power for the whole of Europe, in which the northern and the southern nations could be seen as two independent groups of states. To eighteenth century opinion, the two systems had nothing in common and did not influence each other.

Johann Jacob Schmauß (1690-1757), Professor of law at the University of Göttingen, adopted this dichotomy in his *Einleitung zu der Staatswissenschaft* (Introduction to Political Sciences), published between 1741 and 1761. He differentiated the history of Europe, by which he meant the South (Schmauß 1741), and the history of the northern states, by which he meant Denmark, Sweden, Russia, Poland and Prussia (Schmauß 1760). He argued for this dichotomy by referring to the isolation of the North, which in his opinion made the Nordic powers "participate more seldom in the European conflicts because of their remoteness, but [...] quarrelled instead with each other about their special equilibrium." Therefore the system of the North did not have "any precise connection with the first ones [the South]", for which reason both "necessarily must be distinguished from each other, to prevent any confusion" (Schmauß 1741: introduction).

The Nordic image of Russia is reflected in eighteenth century linguistic usage and can be found in numerous expressions. The Northern Palmyra and the Amsterdam of the North were for example used for the capital St. Petersburg. Peter the Great was called the Northern Star, Ludwig of the North, or even the Turk of the North, while Catherine the Great (1729-96) was admired as the Northern Minerva and the Semiramis of the North. The German scholar Johann Gottfried Herder (1744-1803) regarded Sweden, Russia and Prussia as Nordic states and called Charles XII (1682-1718) of Sweden and Peter the Great the Nordic heroes (Herder 1802: 415).

The so-called Northern Tours of young wealthy men led them to Copenhagen and Stockholm as well as to St. Petersburg or Poland. Periodicals published in Russia as well as periodicals about Russia were called Nordic. The *Nordische Miscellaneen* (Nordic Miscellanea) published in Riga 1781-91 concentrated for example on the Baltic parts of Russia, Poland and Prussia, and the *Neue Nordische Beyträge zur physikalischen und geographischen Erd- und Völkerbeschreibung* (New Nordic Contributions on the Physical and Geographical Description of the Earth and the Races) published in St. Petersburg 1781-96 referred to Russia and Asia as well as to Scandinavia, Iceland and Greenland. The journal *Der Orient und der Norden* (The Orient and the North) published in St. Petersburg 1805-06 was even bound up with two of the old regions: the North and the Orient.

In the East and North of Europe shine, like suns in the sky, dazzling the eye by the splendour of their brightness [...] two amazing cities, both residences of powerful gods on earth, both metropolises of kingdoms, of empires, immeasurable in their extent, rich in an unlimited number of products [...] Who would – even if he had not read the headline – doubt for a single moment, that there can only be talk about *Constantinople* and *St. Petersburg*? They can be seen as the great representatives of the Orient and the North, and what could this journal dedicated to these regions better start with than a short parallel between them? (Anonymous 1805: 1-2)

The author took it for granted that St. Petersburg symbolized the North whereas he regarded Constantinople as the capital of the East, the Orient. Here the traditional north-south dichotomy still exists. There is no talk about Russia lying in the East.

Nevertheless the wide concept of the North had already started to pale. Early indications of its decline can be found already during the second half of the eighteenth century. They appear on the one hand as uncertainties concerning the real geographical position and the designation of Nordic, on the other hand as an increased usage of the term Nordic in the meaning of Scandinavian.[2]

A striking example of the Nordic image of Russia and its approaching decline during the second half of the eighteenth century is the voluminous *Allgemeine Nordische Geschichte* (Universal Nordic History), published by the German historian August Ludwig Schlözer (1735-1809) in 1771. It deals more with Russia and

---

2   In his article about the invention of the term *Osteuropa* Hans Lemberg describes this process in detail and makes clear that Eastern Europe is a construction of the early nineteenth century. Cf. Lemberg 1980. In contrast, Larry Wolff postulates the invention of Eastern Europe in the eighteenth century, although the contemporary linguistic usage still referred to the North and knew the East only in the meaning of the Orient. Cf. Wolff 1994.

FIG. 2:
August Ludwig Schlözer 1771: Allgemeine Nordische Geschichte, front page.

Asia than with Scandinavia. Although Schlözer was aware of the geographical in-accuracy of his definition of the North, which he placed rather in the east than in the north, he was not able to break with the common north-south dichotomy and could not yet introduce the term Eastern Europe. Instead he argued for his concept of Nordic history:

I could not define the concept of Nordic history in another way than very arbitrarily; like all terms based on the climate and the geographical position, it is totally relative: but it had yet to be defined at last. [...] I have taken the liberty of defining the Elbe and the Danube as borderlines, and in this way I have divided the whole of European history into two grand parts, of which the one on this side of the rivers is covering Southern European history, and the other, on the other side, Nordic. (Schlözer 1771: 2-3)

Schlözer was aware of the blurring of his definition, which he himself called "partially even geographically incorrect" because "not all the people who belong to the so-called Nordic history live in the North" (Schlözer 1771: 212). Therefore he fixed on his geographical concept but was not able to solve the contradiction:

By this I assume Germany as the border of the North, I exclude Britain, Hungary etc. I count Greenland to America; indeed the Greenlanders are Eskimos, too. (Schlözer 1771: 291)

Schlözer was the first scholar who systematically tried to define his own object of research, i.e. Nordic history. Thereby, he was the first to concentrate on mapping the North (Kliemann-Geisinger 2002b).

Half a century later the German historian Arnold Herrmann Ludwig Heeren (1770-1842), still used the common north-south dichotomy when describing the history of the European states. His *Handbuch der Geschichte des europäischen Staatensystems* (Guide to the History of the European State System) marks a climax in statistical research. From Heeren's point of view, it was "the nature of things" that made it "necessary to distinguish the history of the northern Europeans state system from the southern one" (Heeren 1822: I: 17). He included Russia, Sweden, Poland and Denmark into his concept of the North, and described Prussia as the link between the North and the South. But even if Heeren still used the common north-south division of Europe for the history of the eighteenth century, he was uncertain concerning the validity of this concept for his own century, because "the position of the major powers of the Continent" and not at least the Russian position, "had fundamentally changed". Because of that, Heeren argues, "the hitherto existing division of the northern and southern group of states" does not make sense any longer: "From now on, Europe is forming only one system of states" (Heeren 1822: II: 247-248).

The decline of the old wide North and the emergence of both a new Scandinavian North and of Eastern Europe were long and slow processes. For some

HENDRIETTE KLIEMANN-GEISINGER

centuries both constructions existed side by side. It took until the middle of the nineteenth century before the term Eastern Europe was generally adopted in contemporary linguistic usage (Lemberg 1985: 60-62). At the same time the North was transformed into a Scandinavian-Germanic concept. Russia was identifying itself with its Nordic image until the mid nineteenth century. The official journal for European readers published by the Russian government in Brussels was called *Le Nord* (The North). The archive of the Foreign Office in London kept both Russia and Poland together with Scandinavia in the section North until its reorganization after World War II.

The transformation of the North around 1800 cannot be explained and described without the European context. There is a strong interdependence between the development of the concept of the North and structures and processes in the history of science and universities. The Humboldt reforms and the demand for research led to a fragmentation of knowledge (Schwinges 2001). As a consequence of this differentiation, a general specialization took place and led to independent branches of study. This applied also to Slavic, Scandinavian and Germanic studies. Because each of the disciplines had to define its own topic of research, the fragmentation of the old wide North was only a question of time.[3]

The changes in the perception of the North took place against the background of a far-reaching transformation process leading to fundamental changes in Europe on the threshold of modernity. In the context of nation building and the search for a national identity, criteria of language and nationality became more important and advanced the cultural construction of the North (Sørensen, Stråth 1997, Henningsen et al. 1997). With a stronger focus on Europe, the Europeans and the European nations in general, there was no longer room for a broad and overlapping regional concept like the wide North.

The political development at the beginning of the nineteenth century contributed to the fragmentation of the North. As a consequence of the Napoleonic Wars, Russia retained the formerly Swedish Finland in 1809. Norway was transferred from the Danish to the Swedish crown and got its own constitution at Eidsvoll in 1814. Western Pomerania, which Sweden had ceded to Denmark in the Treaty of Kiel in 1814, was given to Prussia, which compensated Denmark with the duchy of Lauenburg. Thus, Scandinavia was lying at the edge of Europe after 1815. In contrast, Russia's political influence in Europe was growing. As one of the major powers it became part of the Concert of Europe after the Congress of Vienna in 1814-15.

---

3   Jürgen Osterhammel argues the same way explaining the construction of Asia by European scholars during the eighteenth century. Cf. Osterhammel 1998.

This development contributed to general changes in the (mental) mapping of Europe (Gollwitzer 1964). The North is not unique as a region and cannot be seen as an isolated case. There are similar examples in Europe (Schenk 2002), such as the Balkans (Todorova 1999), the Orient (Said 1995) or the East (Lemberg 1985, Wolff 1994) at the same time. These regions stand for parallel developments, which indeed were characterized by the particular regional conditions, but like the North they were as a whole also dependent on the European development and the contemporary image of Europe and were thus influencing each other. At the beginning of the nineteenth century a new East emerged in the form of Eastern Europe. It was more comprehensive than the traditional, oriental East and included also today's Eastern Europe and Russia. The barbarian image of the North was henceforth transferred to the new East, whereas the new, Germanic-Scandinavian North was supplied with a positive, pure and natural image (Thom 1995). Thereby, changes in the perception of Europe and a shifting of its centres led to a change in the perspective of the European regions, too.

Geographical concepts of Northern Europe

The extensive political changes of the Napoleonic Wars made it almost impossible to publish geographical up-to-date material based on political structures, borderlines and states. Teachers and parents were constantly complaining about out-dated schoolbooks and maps (Beck 1980: 280-281). In this situation one solution seemed to be to concentrate on the more quiet and stable regions. For those reasons the German geographer Carl Ritter (1779-1859) chose the North to open his geographical, historical and statistical description of Europe. In *Europa ein geographisch-historisch-statistisches Gemälde* (Europe a Geographical-Historical-Statistical Portrait), published between 1804 and 1809, he argued:

I have chosen the so far quiet *North* for the first part; it is not possible yet to decide *when Germany* is going to calm down and when a description of it will be possible, and therefore it is not included in these three parts. (Ritter 1804: I: XIV)

To Ritter, the North included Russia, Sweden, Denmark and Prussia. This region appeared as a sufficient and solid object of research at the beginning of the nineteenth century. The scientific focus on the North of Europe corresponded with the fact that travels and journeys to Northern Europe increased around 1800, too (Bring 1954). Not only scholars but also travellers preferred the quiet and stable regions in an age of change.

HENDRIETTE KLIEMANN-GEISINGER

To focus on the more quiet parts of Europe was a short-term solution and an immediate reaction to the extensive political changes that were caused by the Napoleonic wars. Another and more lasting solution was to focus on natural structures. This was the starting-point for physical geography, which developed into an independent discipline during that time. Physical geography was concentrating on the natural appearance of the earth and was trying to arrange countries into groups on the basis of common geographical criteria instead of describing them one by one as in statistical literature (Schultz 2000). Therefore it seemed to be an alternative way out of the dependency on political structures (Beck 1980: 280-281).

To find new ways of describing the geographical appearance of Europe, scholars of the early nineteenth century proposed multifarious concepts. One example is August Ludwig Bucher's *Versuch das Europäische Continent in natürliche Länder abzutheilen* (Attempt to divide the European Continent into Natural Countries), published in 1812. Here the North consists of a number of different regions, the names of which Bucher derived from mountains, rivers and seas, for example the 'Baltische Länder' from the Baltic and 'Kölen-Land' from the Latin notation of the Scandinavian mountains, i.e. 'kiöl montes' (Bucher 1812: fig. 3).

The German historian and geographer Johann Christoph Gatterer (1727-99) was one of the first to spread the idea of natural borders. His geographical approach was no longer based on political and statistical criteria but instead on the natural structures of the earth's surface, which he called "natural-division" (Gatterer 1789: 83). Gatterer gave a striking example of the variability and casual arbitrariness of such concepts. Still influenced by the chronological trichotomy of geography, which was divided into an ancient, a middle and a modern period, Gatterer distinguished between two chronological levels: "Alt-Europa" and "Neu-Europa" (Gatterer 1775: 165), old and modern Europe.

Old Europe was, according to Gatterer, divided into the North and the South along a borderline marked by the Rhine and the Danube. He based this distinction on the dichotomy of the Roman South and the non-Roman North, and divided the northern parts of Europe into the regions that were known and the ones that were unknown to the Romans. Gatterer drew the borderline of this "*terra incognita*" (Gatterer 1775: 166) north of the line Thule, Shetland, Stockholm, Reval and Moscow.

In contrast to the historically determined north-south dichotomy, Gatterer invented an east-west division of modern Europe (Gatterer 1775: 141). For further divisions he used the concept of natural lands based on the European rivers. Within the western part, which he also called Germanic Europe, he distinguished between the British Isles and the Baltic Lands in the North. The latter were divided into the Northern and Western Baltic Lands, respectively Scandinavia, i.e.

Denmark, Norway, Iceland and Sweden, and the South-eastern Baltic Lands, i.e. Prussia (Gatterer 1775: 141-142).

It was common to divide Northern Europe into a western, northern and eastern part, but also into the North Sea Lands and Baltic Islands or Baltic Lands. There was an even more detailed breakdown of these entities into the western and eastern North Sea Lands and the northern, southern and eastern Baltic Lands. The classification of the single states varied within these regions. The final classification depended on the particular interests of the observer and his perception of Europe as a whole, but also on the context and purpose of these geographical constructions. Generally the attempts to compose useful and meaningful geographical concepts of Europe based on natural criteria showed the same variables that were appearing in statistical approaches.

First of all, Russia's position was unclear. It was ranging between the North and the East depending on the general division of Europe (Cannabich 1821: 21-22). But Denmark, Sweden and Great Britain were causing confusion, too. Denmark's position between Germany and the Continent, on one hand, and Scandinavia, on the other, made it impossible to define its affiliation (Bucher 1812: 84-85). Actually it was more a political than a geographical question, because from a geographical point of view at least Jutland was a continuation of Northern Germany (Frandsen 1994).

In his *Haandbog i Geographien* (Guide to Geography), published in 1819-20, the Danish geographer Ludvig Stoud Platou (1787-1833) based his concept of Northern Europe on the two northern seas: the North Sea and the Baltic. Like many of his German colleagues he distinguished between the North Sea Lands and the Baltic Lands, "Nordsøiske Lande" and "Østersøiske Lande", the first of which included Norway, Denmark, the Netherlands and the British Isles, the second of which included Sweden, Russia, Prussia and Germany. But there is one decisive difference: in Platou's concept not only Denmark but also Germany were counted among the Nordic states (Platou 1819: I: 47).

Sweden was regarded as part of Scandinavia, forming the Scandinavian Peninsula together with Norway, but it was also counted among the countries around the Baltic Sea. In this context it was usually placed together with Prussia and Russia. Finally Great Britain's position was unclear, too. It was sometimes counted among the Nordic countries, sometimes it was seen as part of Middle or Western Europe (Anonymous 1828: 33, Hassel 1821: IX-X).

These various concepts and geographical inventions, most of which were forgotten shortly after, bear witness to early nineteenth century scholars' imagination and creativity (Schultz 2000). Nevertheless, a unanimous concept did not exist. The so-called natural classification of Europe was as dependent on (political)

HENDRIETTE KLIEMANN-GEISINGER

interests and viewpoints and was often a result of the particular context, such as the statistical and political approaches of defining the North.

The North itself is not placed among the naturally given geographical entities. Sometimes Scandinavia is mentioned, mostly as the Scandinavian Peninsula or in the context of the Scandinavian mountains. But usually the North is divided into smaller entities, based on the structure of rivers or mountains, as are the remaining parts of Europe. Instead the scholars attempted constructions like the North Sea Lands or the Baltic Lands while at the same time they invented terms like the Pyrenean Peninsula, the Apennine or the Balkans, which are still in use today. This suggests that the North was first and foremost a cultural and political, not a spatial construction. From a geographical viewpoint the North is not a coherent region, nor was it seen as such around 1800. It is and was a temporarily and spatially flexible construction with variable borderlines. This becomes evident not least by the fact that a geographical region of that name was not mentioned in any geographical study of the time.

Regions of the North

The definition of the North is and was always dependent on the contemporary perception of Europe. The North is characterized by variable borderlines that are neither constant in time nor in space. Despite this shifting appearance some core regions or centre zones have served as projection screens for spatial constructions of the North time and time again.

The Alps were the borderline between North and South especially in classical times but were still seen as a demarcation of the North around 1800. They were one of the oldest and most common borderlines to define the North and were still used in the eighteenth century when the fascination with ancient geographical knowledge was still unbroken. Because of this interest in Greek and Roman geography it is hardly surprising that the Alps kept their role as a frontier of the North for centuries. The Hyperboreans, who according to Greek mythology were dwelling in a state of perfect bliss in the Far North, fascinated many eighteenth century scholars (Käppel 2001: 20-25). But to them Hyperborean meant not only this people but also the unknown regions of the North in general (Buhle 1810: 142-143).

According to Johann Gottfried Herder, the Alps were not only a geographical and climatic frontier. They also divided ethnic characteristics.

Northwards, under a different sky, on such a different soil, the people necessarily had to adopt an appearance and a manner unfamiliar to the southern peoples: because nature has not created more lasting differences on earth than those created by the mountains. There she is sitting on her eternal throne, sending out streams and weather, and is distributing the climate as well as the tendencies, often even the fortune of nations. (Herder 1909: 257-258)

The German poet and historian Ernst Moritz Arndt (1769-1860) described the Alps as "the holy frontier-guards of fortunate peoples" and highlighted their function as a meteorological divide. Switzerland and Tyrol were according to Arndt the southern frontier of Northern Europe. But the Alps were "at the same time a remarkable division of life, because all minds, manners and ambitions are so different from these on the other side of the mountains" (Arndt 1810: 98-99). People were even-tempered and considerate in the North and hot-tempered and mettlesome in the South (Arndt 1810: 103-108).

There are numerous maps from the eighteenth and early nineteenth centuries showing the ancient image of the North, whilst almost none dealt with the contemporary image of the region. Though detailed maps on specific countries increased around 1800 due to more detailed information and fast-growing needs of up-to-date geographical material, especially after the French Revolution and during the Napoleonic Wars, it is hard to find maps explicitly dealing with the contemporary appearance of the North as a whole (Black 1997: 25-27). The reason is the same as above: the contemporary North was not regarded as a regional entity. Instead scholars focused on the ancient worldview. August Ludwig Schlözer for example even added two historical maps to his *Allgemeine Nordische Geschichte* and spent a large chapter of his voluminous Nordic history on the geographical knowledge of ancient times. As already mentioned in the title, the whole work was written "as a geographical and historical introduction [...] especially in ancient times and the Middle-Ages" and did not claim to offer solutions for the eighteenth century North (Schlözer 1771. The front page clearly shows the ancient influence on the perception of the North and the presentation of Nordic topics. Six angels, each of them holding a parchment with one of the headlines of the different chapters of the Nordic history, including Russian, Slavic and Scandinavian history are presented. In the background one can see an ancient map of the northern parts of Europe showing the land of the Hyperboreans, Thule, the Baltic and Scandinavia. Also an obelisk referring to Greek and Roman geographers, historians and philosophers is to be seen (fig. 3).

Among the regions in the North the Scandinavian Peninsula is one of the few geographically coherent areas. Here Sweden and Norway are linked together by the Scandinavian mountains and this gave reason to regard Scandinavia as a geographical entity. eighteenth and nineteenth century encyclopaedias distinguished a geographical and a political definition of Scandinavia. In a geographical context it meant only Sweden and Norway but politically it also included Denmark (Kliemann-Geisinger 2002a: 39-42).

HENDRIETTE KLIEMANN-GEISINGER

FIG. 3:

August Ludwig Bucher 1812: Versuch das Europäische Continent in natürliche Länder abzutheilen. This map is one of the few examples of a cartographic illustration of the geographic attempts to structure the Continent into so-called 'natural' lands.

Supporters of Scandinavianism, the cultural and political movement for a unified Scandinavia during the first half of the nineteenth century, stressed the nature-given entity of the three kingdoms Denmark, Sweden and Norway. In most cases, however, nature did not mean geography but culture: a common language, religion and history (Grundtvig 1810: 4, Schimmelmann 1810: 6). The Swedish historian Erik Gustav Geijer (1783-1847) therefore could announce the natural as well as the historical entity of Scandinavia (Geijer 1826: 34). In the context of Scandinavianism the term Scandinavia was gradually used synonymously with the North.

The territorial changes in Northern Europe between 1809 and 1815, the loss of Finland and the personal union between Norway and Sweden, led to a concentration on the Scandinavian Peninsula. Strategically it became a near-island surrounded by waters on three sides and subarctic wilderness on the fourth, which made it easier for contemporary scholars to see it as an entity and to argue for the coherence of the region. The Baltic Sea was constructed likewise as a Germanic Mediterranean by German authors and politicians, especially in the 1840s. They emphasized the pretended relation between the Germanic and Scandinavian peoples around the Baltic/Germanic Sea, intending to form a Germanic alliance against the Slaves. Both constructions lie close to politics and show the close connection between science, politics and national interests.

The Danish and the German landscapes were often compared, and so were the ethnic characteristics of the Danes and the Germans. According to this general idea Denmark was attached to Germany both in natural and in political respects. After 1814 the Danish monarchy was not a coherent state. Denmark consisted of landscapes that were traditionally close to the Danish crown but at the same time they were, as in the case of Holstein and Lauenburg, members of the German Confederation. The city of Hamburg became one of the most important trade partners of the Danish provincial towns and displaced Copenhagen as a financial centre after 1814. This complexity and Denmark's close cultural connection to Germany made it difficult to decide whether it should be counted as Scandinavian or German. Therefore Denmark bridges the gap between the North and the South. It is either counted as a part of Scandinavia or of the Continent, which means Germany, depending on the particular political interests (Detering 1996, Frandsen 1994, 1996).

By the middle of the nineteenth century the province of Jutland was still a *terra incognita*. Its infrastructure was not yet developed and could not draw the attention of Danish islanders or foreign travellers. Jutland remained a kind of minor Siberia without attractions. Like the North, Jutland was regarded as underdeveloped. The unspectacular heather-clad landscape seemed to underline this image. Nevertheless it was precisely the heather that was seen as the constituting element of the North by the Swiss philosopher and politician Victor von Bonstetten (1745-1832). Travelling northwards to Scandinavia the heathland near Lüneburg appeared to him as the boundary of the North, typifying the Nordic landscape. In *Der Mensch im Süden und im Norden* (Man in the South and in the North)[4] he wrote:

Near Lüneburg the look of the country starts changing; in these heathlands I saw for the first time those lakes that are spread plentifully over the ground of northern countries. These bodies of standing water on moorland enhance the sad impression of the landscape; the similarly lifeless ground narrows the horizon; a depressing feeling of loneliness takes possession of the soul; it seems as if the earth is nothing more than a dark spot, with which fogs might shortly mingle. (Bonstetten 1825: 6)

4   French orig. L'homme du Midi et l'homme du Nord, ou l'influence du climat.

Here, not only Denmark but also the northern regions of Germany marked the passage between the North and the South. Their belonging to either the North or the Continent depended on the viewpoint of the observer, his interests and intentions and on the context.

The exploration and discovery of the North was a precondition for academic research in that region. Expeditions brought necessary knowledge and supported the research and exploration of the North. Those journeys and the travelogues on them became themselves objects of research. In the *Geschichte der Entdeckungen und Schiffahrten im Norden* (History of the Explorations and Sea Passages in the North), published in 1784, the geographer Johann Reinhold Forster (1729-89) described for example the gradual discovery of the North since ancient times based on travelogues. In this context the North referred to the respectively unknown and unexplored parts of the northern hemisphere. More important than the actual direction seemed the fact that the North represented the unknown and that it was characterized by wilderness and distance. Forster distinguished between the well-known European North, which he called "our North" and the still unknown areas of the whole northern hemisphere, the Far North (Forster 1784: 7, 10-12).

Siberia and Lapland represented the boundaries of the map for a long time and formed the Far North of Russia and Scandinavia. Because of their unknown areas and waters the Scandinavian North and the North and East of Russia (Zorin, Zorina 1992) epitomised wilderness and distance and provided space for the image of fabulous and mythical places and people. At the same time these regions represented the exotic. At the beginning of the eighteenth century, the Scandinavian North was still widely unexplored and inspired scientists as well as adventurous travellers. National borders were not drawn before 1751 and in the Swedish-Russian case not until 1826. Lapland (Sörlin 1988) as well as Siberia (Bassin 1991a, 1991b) seemed to symbolize a promising future for their nations because of their immense natural resources. Thus, they became projection screens for the future of their particular nation.

At the beginning of the nineteenth century the image of Siberia was changing. It lost its economic impact, and became instead a place of banishment (Bassin 1991a, 1991b). The reversal of the Siberian image, the Russian North, from the positive to the negative came along with the general transformation of the European North, its replacement and relocation and restriction to Scandinavia. The barbarian image, which so far had been connected with the North, was now primarily referring to the East and to the Orient (Schenk 2002: 500-501). At the same time the purpose of travelling to the northern parts of Europe was no longer to explore that region but to experience the romantically transfigured wilderness, while scientific Nordic expeditions turned to the Polar Regions, which henceforth became the unknown Far North in science.

Final remarks

The North is a spatially flexible construction, the definition of which is dependent on the location, the objective and the interest of the beholder. These facts and not real existing geographical common conditions or differences determine the contents of the definition. This becomes evident especially in the context of alliances and in the interaction between science and politics. The alternative classification of Denmark as belonging either to the Continent or to Scandinavia is a political and not a geographical question. There is no doubt, however, that from a geographical point of view Jutland is a continuation of Northern Germany. These regional and national interests that focus on particular areas of Northern Europe are the reason why the North is neither seen as a political nor a geographical entity. Due to this lack of geographical homogeneity, asking for the spatial dimension of the North always means asking for the (political) unit too. If it is possible to define the latter, as in the case of the Nordic powers during the eighteenth century, it is also possible to mark the borders of the North. But the sharply defined concepts of the Nordic powers and the Balance of the North are limited to a certain period and lose their meaning after the Napoleonic Wars when new political constellations and shifts of power make the concept of a northern and a southern system of states and of the balance of power between the Nordic countries obsolete. If the (political) situation is diffuse and unclear, as in the case of the classification of Denmark during the nineteenth century, it also influences the definition of the Northern coordinates: mapping the North becomes impossible.

References

Anonymous 1805: Konstantinopel und St. Petersburg. Eine Parallele. *Konstantinopel und St. Petersburg. Der Orient und der Norden* 1,1: 1-10.

Anonymous 1828: *Kleine Schulgeographie oder erster Unterricht in der Erdbeschreibung.* Königsberg: Friedrich Thewing.

Arndt, Ernst Moritz 1810: *Einleitung zu historischen Charakterschilderungen.* Berlin: Realschulbuchhandlung.

Bassin, Mark 1991a: Russia between Europe and Asia: The Ideological Construction of Geographical Space. *Slavic Review* 50: 1-17.

Bassin, Mark 1991b: Inventing Siberia. Visions of the Russian East in the Early Nineteenth Century. *American Historical Review* 96: 763-794.

Beck, Hanno 1980: Geographie und Statistik. Die Lösung einer Polarität. Eds.: Mohammed Rassem, Justin Stagl: *Statistik und Staatenbeschreibung in der Neuzeit vornehmlich*

HENDRIETTE KLIEMANN-GEISINGER

im 16.-18. Jahrhundert. Bericht über ein interdisziplinäres Symposion in Wolfenbüttel 1978. Paderborn, München: Ferdinand Schöningh: 269-281.

Black, Jeremy 1997: *Maps and History*. New Haven: Yale University Press.

Bonstetten, [Carl] Victor von 1825: *Der Mensch im Süden und im Norden oder über den Einfluß des Climas*. Leipzig: Wilhelm Zirges.

Brandt, Otto 1929: Das Problem der 'Ruhe des Nordens' im 18. Jahrhundert. *Historische Zeitschrift* 140 : 550-564.

Bring, Samuel E[ ] 1954: *Itineraria Svecana. Bibliografisk förteckning över resor i Sverige fram till 1950*. Stockholm: Almkvist & Wiksell.

Bucher, August Leopold 1812: *Betrachtungen über die Geographie und über ihr Verhältnis zur Geschichte und Statistik*. Leipzig: Gerhard Fleischer d. J.

Buhle, Johann Gottlieb 1810: *Versuch einer kritischen Literatur der Russischen Geschichte. Erster Theil. Enthaltend die Literatur der aelteren allgemeinen Nordischen Geschichte*. Moskau: Buchdruckerey N. S. Wsewolojsky.

Cannabich, J[ohann] G[ünther] F[riedrich] 1821: *Lehrbuch der Geographie nach den neuesten Friedensbestimmungen*. 8. Auflage. Sondershausen: Bernhard Friedrich Voigt.

Detering, Heinrich, ed. 1996: *Grenzgänge. Skandinavisch-deutsche Nachbarschaften*. Göttingen: Wallstein.

Forster, Johann Reinhold 1784: *Geschichte der Entdeckungen und Schiffahrten im Norden*. Frankfurt Oder: Carl Gottlieb Strauß.

Frandsen, Steen Bo 1994: *Dänemark – der kleine Nachbar im Norden. Aspekte der deutsch-dänischen Beziehungen im 19. und 20. Jahrhundert*. Darmstadt: Wissenschaftliche Buchgesellschaft.

Frandsen, Steen Bo 1996: *Opdagelsen af Jylland. Den regionale dimension i Danmarkshistorien 1814-64*. Aarhus: Universitetsforlag.

Gatterer, Johann Christoph 1775: *Abriß der Geographie*. Göttingen: Joh. Christian Dieterich.

Gatterer, Johann Christoph 1789: *Kurzer Begriff der Geographie*. 1. Göttingen: Johann Christian Dieterich.

Geijer, Erik Gustaf 1826: *Schwedens Urgeschichte*. Sulzbach: J. E. v. Seidel.

Gollwitzer, Heinz 1964 (1951): *Europabild und Europagedanke. Beiträge zur deutschen Geistesgeschichte des 18. und 19. Jahrhunderts*. München: C. H. Beck.

Grundtvig, Nicolai Severin Frederik 1810: *Er Nordens Forening ønskelig? Et Ord til det svenske Folk*. Kopenhagen: Andreas Seidelin.

Hassel, [Johann] G[eorg] [Heinrich] 1821: *Vollständiges Handbuch der neuesten Erdbeschreibung von Ad. Chr. Gaspari, G. Hassel, J. G. Fr. Cannabich und J. C. F. Gutsmuths. Dritte Abtheilung. Zweiter Band, des ganzen Werkes eilfter Band, welcher das Europäische Rußland und Polen, mit einer statistischen Einleitung in das ganze Russische Reich enthält*. Weimar: Geographisches Institut.

Heeren, Arnold Herrmann Ludwig 1822: *Handbuch der Geschichte des Europäischen Staatensystems und seiner Colonien, von seiner Bildung seit der Entdeckung beider Indien bis zu seiner Wiederherstellung nach dem Fall des Französischen Kaiserthrons, und der Freiwerdung von Amerika*. 1-2. 4. Edition. Göttingen: Johann Friedrich Römer.

Henningsen, Bernd 1993: *Der Norden: Eine Erfindung. Das europäische Projekt einer regionalen Identität*. Berlin: Humboldt-Universität.

Henningsen, Bernd, Janine Klein, Helmut Müssener, Solfrid Söderlind, eds. 1997: *Wahlverwandtschaft. Skandinavien und Deutschland. 1800-1914*. Berlin: Jobis.

Herder, Johann Gottfried 1885 (1802): Ereignisse und Charaktere des vergangenen Jahrhunderts. *Herders Sämtliche Werke* 23. Ed.: Bernhard Suphan. Berlin: Weidmann: 415-505.

Herder, Johann Gottfried 1909 (1791): Ideen zur Philosophie der Geschichte der Menschheit. *Herders Sämtliche Werke* 4. Ed.: Bernhard Suphan. 14. Berlin: Weidmann.

Hughes, Lindsey, ed. 2001: *Peter the Great and the West. New Perspectives*. Basingstoke: Palgrave.

Jessen, Ralph, Jakob Vogel, eds. 2002: *Wissenschaft und Nation in der europäischen Geschichte*. Frankfurt am Main: Campus.

Käppel, Lutz 2001: Bilder des Nordens im frühen antiken Griechenland. Eds.: Annelore Engel-Braunschmidt, Gerhard Fouquet, Wiebke von Hinden, Inken Schmidt: *Ultima Thule. Bilder des Nordens von der Antike bis zur Gegenwart*. Frankfurt am Main: Peter Lang: 11-27.

Kliemann, Hendriette 2002a: Aspekte des Nordenbegriffes in Deutschland um 1800. Ed.: Bernd Henningsen. *Das Projekt Norden. Essays zur Konstruktion einer europäischen Region*. Berlin: Berliner Wissenschafts Verlag: 37-57.

Kliemann, Hendriette 2002b: Ett mångfaldigt begrepp. August Ludwig Schlözers konstruktion av Norden. *Norden som tanke och resemål*. Historisk Tidskrift för Finland 87: 315-336.

Kliemann, Hendriette 2005: *Koordinaten des Nordens. Wissenschaftliche Konstruktionen einer euorpäischen Region 1770-1850*. Berlin: Berliner Wissenschafts Verlag.

Konstantinopel und St. Petersburg. Der Orient und der Norden 1805-06. St. Petersburg.

Lemberg, Hans 1985: Zur Entstehung des Osteuropabegriffes im 19. Jahrhundert. Vom 'Norden' zum 'Osten' Europas. *Jahrbücher für die Geschichte Osteuropas* 33: 48-91.

Lewis, Martin W., Kären E. Wigen 1997: *The Myth of Continents. A Critique of Metageography*. Berkeley: University of California Press.

Mediger, Walther 1968: Russland und die Ostsee im 18. Jahrhundert. *Jahrbücher für die Geschichte Osteuropas*. Neue Folge 16: 85-103.

Neue Nordische Beyträge zur physikalischen und geographischen Erd- und Völkerbeschreibung, Naturgeschichte und Oekonomie 1781-83, 1793-96. St. Petersburg.

Nordische Miscellaneen 1781-91. Riga.

Osterhammel, Jürgen 1998a: *Die Entzauberung Asiens. Europa und die asiatischen Reiche im 18. Jahrhundert*. München: C. H. Beck.

Osterhammel, Jürgen 1998b: Die Wiederkehr des Raumes: Geopolitik, Geohistorie und historische Geographie. *Neue Politische Literatur* 43: 374-397.

Platou, L[udvig] Stoud 1819-20: *Haandbog i Geographien*.1-2. Christiania: Jacob Lehmann.

Rahbek Schmidt, K. 1957: Wie ist Panins Plan zu einem nordischen Mächtesystem entstanden? *Zeitschrift für Slawistik* 2: 406-422.

Rassem, Mohammed, Justin Stagl, eds. 1980: *Statistik und Staatenbeschreibung in der Neuzeit vornehmlich im 16.-18. Jahrhundert. Bericht über ein interdisziplinäres Symposion in Wolfenbüttel 1978*. Paderborn: Ferdinand Schöningh.

Ritter, C[arl] 1804 (1807): *Europa ein geographisch-historisch-statistisches Gemälde, für Freunde und Lehrer der Geographie, für Jünglinge, die ihren Cursus vollendeten, bey jedem Lehrbuche zu gebrauchen*. 1-2. Frankfurt am Main: Joh. Christ. Hermann'sche Buchhandlung.

Said, Edward W. 1995 (1978): *Orientalism. Western Conceptions of the Orient*. London: Penguin.

Schenk, Frithjof Benjamin 2002: Literaturbericht Mental Maps. Die Konstruktion von geographischen Räumen in Europa seit der Aufklärung. Ed. Christoph Conrad: *Mental Maps*. Geschichte und Gesellschaft 28: 493-514.

Schimmelmann, Ernst Heinrich 1810: *Til Skandinaverne*. København: Bonnier.

Schlögel, Karl 2003: *Im Raume lesen wir die Zeit. Über Zivilisationsgeschichte und Geopolitik*. München: Carl Hanser.

Schlözer, August Ludwig 1771: *Allgemeine Nordische Geschichte. Aus den neuesten und besten Nordischen Schriftstellern und nach eigenen Untersuchungen beschrieben, und als eine geographische und historische Einleitung zur richtigen Kenntnis aller Skandinavischen, Finnischen, Slavischen, Lettischen*

HENDRIETTE KLIEMANN-GEISINGER

und Sibirischen Völker, besonders in alten und mittleren Zeiten. Halle: Johann Justinus Gebauer.

Schmauß, Johann Jacob 1741: *Einleitung zu der Staats-Wissenschaft, und Erleuterung des von ihm herausgegebenen Corporis Juris Gentium Academici und aller andern seit mehr als zweyen Seculis her geschlossenen Bündnisse, Friedens- und Commercien-Tractaten. Erster Theil. Die Historie der Balance von Europa, der Barriere der Niederlande, der Oesterreichischen Sanctionis pragmaticae, und anderer dahin gehörigen Sachen und Tractaten in sich haltend.* Leipzig: Johann Friedrich Gleditsch.

Schmauß, Johann Jacob 1760: *Einleitung zu der Staatswissenschaft, und Erleuterung des von ihm herausgegebenen Corporis Juris Gentium Academici und aller anderen seit mehr als zwey Seculis her geschlossenen Bündnisse, Friedens- und Commercien-Tractaten. Zweyter Theil. Die Historie aller zwischen den Nordischen Potenzen, Dännemarck, Schweden, Rußland, Polen und Preussen geschlossenen Tractaten in sich haltend.* Leibzig: Johann Friedrich Gleditsch.

Schultz, Hans-Dietrich 2000: Land – Volk – Staat. Der geografische Anteil an der 'Erfindung' der Nation. *Geschichte in Wissenschaft und Unterricht* 51: 4-16.

Schwinges, Rainer C., ed. 2001: *Humboldt International. Der Export des deutschen Universitätsmodells im 19. und 20. Jahrhundert.* Basel: Schwabe & Co.

Sørensen, Øystein, Bo Stråth, eds. 1997: *The Cultural Construction of Norden.* Oslo: Universitetsforlag.

Sörlin, Sverker 1988: *Framtidslandet. Debatten om Norrland och naturresurserna under det industriella genombrottet.* Stockholm: Carlssons.

Thom, Martin 1995: *Republics, Nations and Tribes.* London, New York: Verso.

Todorova, Maria 1999: *Die Erfindung des Balkans. Europas bequemes Vorurteil.* Darmstadt: Wissenschaftliche Buchgesellschaft.

Wolff, Larry 1994: *Inventing Eastern Europe. The Map of Civilization on the Mind of the Enlightenment.* Stanford California: Stanford University Press.

Zorin, Andrei, Irina Zorina 1992: Russia's two Nordic landscapes. *The Source of Liberty. The Nordic contribution to Europe. An anthology.* Ed.: Svenolof Karlsson. Stockholm: The Nordic Council: 105-113.

Original Quotes

… "die Abgeschiedenheit des Nordens", die dazu geführt habe, dass die nordischen Mächte an den Konflikten in Europa "als am weitesten davon entlegen, gar selten Antheil genommen, sondern […] unter sich selbst um ihr besonderes Aequilibrium gestritten" hätten. Das nördliche System habe demnach "mit den erstern keine genaue Connexion, weshalb beide "um alle Verwirrung zu verhüten, notwendig voneinander unterschieden werden müssen."

Im Osten und Norden Europa's strahlen gleich Sonnen am Firmament, das Auge blendend durch des Glanzes Pracht, […] zwei Wunderstädte, beide Residenzen mächtiger Erdengötter, beide Metropolen von Reichen, von Kaiserreichen, unermeßlich an Umfang, reich an der Produkte unendlicher Zahl, […] Wer würde – hätte er auch die Ueberschrift nicht gelesen – einen Augenblick daran zweifeln, daß hier nur von *Konstantinopel* und *St. Petersburg* die Rede seyn könne? Sie können als die großen Repräsentanten des Orients und des Nordens angesehen werden und womit könnte darum diesen Himmelsgegenden geweihete Zeitschrift besser begonnen werden, als mit einer kurzen Parallele zwischen ihnen?

Den Begriff der Nordischen Geschichte konnte ich nicht anders als sehr willkürlich bestimmen; er ist völlig relativisch wie alle Namen, die von Klima und geographischer Lage hergenommen sind: allein bestimmt mußte er doch einmal werden. […] Ich habe mir die Freiheit genommen, die Elbe und die Donau zu Gränzlinien anzunehmen, und solchergestalt die ganze Europäische Geschichte in zwey große Hälften zu zerlegen, wovon die eine, diesseits dieser Ströme, die Südliche, und die andre, jenseits derselben, die Nordische Europäische Geschichte begreift.

Er selbst bezeichnete sie als "zum Theil selbst geographisch unrichtig," denn "nicht alle Völker liegen Nördlich, die in die sogenannte Nordische Geschichte gehören.

So nehme ich zur Gränze des Nordens Deutschland an, Britannien, Ungern etc. schließe ich aus. Grönland rechne ich zu Amerika, wirklich sind auch die Grönländer die Eskimaur.

"Die Natur der Dinge" mache es "erforderlich, die Geschichte des *nördlichen* Europäischen Staatensystems von der des *südlichen* zu trennen". "… hatte sich die Lage der Hauptmächte des Continents […] wesentlich verändert. […] So verschwindet von jetzt an von selbst die bisherige Trennung des Nördlichen und Südlichen Staatenvereins; bei der engen Verschlingung von beiden bildet Europa von jetzt an nur Ein Staatensystem.

Ich habe den bisher ruhigen *Norden* zum ersten Theile gewählt, *wann Deutschland* zur Ruhe kommen und eine Schilderung nach diesem gange zulassen wird, läßt sich noch nicht bestimmen, und ist daher nicht mit in den 3 Theilen begriffen.

Natur-Eintheilung

Germanisches Europa, Baltische Länder, Nord- und Westbaltische Länder, Südostbaltische Länder.

Nordwärts derselben, unter einem so andern Himmel, auf einem so andern Boden, mußten die Bewohner desselben nothwendig auch eine Gestalt und Lebensweise annehmen, die jenen südlichen Völkern fremd war: denn auf der ganzen Erde hat die Natur durch nichts so dauernde Unterschiede gemacht, als durch die Gebürge. Hier sitzt sie auf ihrem ewigen Thron, sendet Ströme und Witterung aus, und vertheilet so wie das Klima, so auch die Neigungen, oft auch das Schicksal der Nationen.

die heiligen Gränzhhüter glücklicher Völker

zugleich eine merkwürdige Scheide des Lebens, da an Gemüth, Sitten und Streben alles sogleich ganz anders ist, als jenseits der Berge.

als eine geographische und historische Einleitung […] besonders in alten und mittleren Zeiten.

Bei Lüneburg beginnt der Anblick des Landes sich zu verändern; in diesen Haiden sah ich zum ersten Male jene so reichlich über den Boden nördlicher Länder hingebreiteten Seen. Diese stehenden Gewässer auf morigen Ebenen vermehren den traurigen Anblick der Landschaft; der gleichsam leblose Boden verengt den Horizont; ein niederdrückendes Gefühl von Einsamkeit bemächtigt sich der Seele; es scheint als sey die Erde nichts wie ein dunkler Punct, den Nebel bald vermischen würden.

HENDRIETTE KLIEMANN-GEISINGER

BERND HENNINGSEN

Johann Gottfried Herder and the North: Elements of a Process of Construction

Nord oder Süd!

Wenn nur im warmen Busen

Ein Heiligtum der Schönheit und der Musen,

Ein götterreicher Himmel blüht.

Nur Geistesarmut kann der Winter morden;

Kraft fügt zu Kraft und Glanz zu Glanz der Norden!

Nord oder Süd!

Wenn nur die Seele glüht! …

> Karl Lappe, set to music by Robert Schumann, 1848

Johann Gottfried Herder (1744-1803) was an author who was well read and discussed in Scandinavia in the nineteenth century. However, his significance for the Scandinavian history of ideas has by no means been investigated to the same extent as for other spheres. This is the starting point for the following considerations.[1] That there is a strong connection between John Gottfried Herder and Nikolai Frederik Severin Grundtvig (1783-1872), the father of the Danish political and cultural self-definition, is conceded among Scandinavian researchers and also quite obvious. However, has anybody ever done any work on this subject, perhaps even exhausted it? How far-reaching was the Scandinavian Romanticists' reception of Herder in fact? What immediate, identifiable influence did he have on the process of nation-building in northern Europe?

In what follows I shall be addressing these questions; however, it is not possible to provide any definitive answers. The first is the question as to Herder's 'presence' and thought in the North; I shall then draw attention to some of the characteristics of Herder's mode of construction in the Scandinavian political process (Hettne, Sörlin, Østergård 1998) and discuss these before and together with the

---

1   Kliemann-Geisinger 2005 discusses Herder's influence in detail. Korsgaard, 2004 also repeatedly cites Herder and describes him as a "folklorist".

respective German contexts. After all, *German* literature, *German* philosophy and *German* education were invented at this time – but no German *political order* was established (cf. Gebhardt 1968: 7-16).

Works and influence

Basically, all has already been said about Herder, the eighteenth century Classicist from East Prussia. No serious work on national identity or self-interpretation, political self-definition or the process of nation building of the nineteenth and twentieth centuries, and no serious work on the development of the cultural sciences, can afford not to cite Herder (cf. Kittler 2000, Slotderdijk 2004: 127). Since Herder culture has been referred to in the plural. Yes, the analysis of the aberrations of National Socialism and the ideological mass movements of the twentieth century, racism and mass murder – and not only during the *European* civil war – points towards Herder. It has long been promulgated and firmly established that he was the father of the idea of national construction based on identity and of the functionalisation of political symbolism and the instrumentalisation of language. While this was not only so in Germany, it was there that it had the most fatal political consequences. What was thought of him in Kant's era of the Enlightenment was spread further by his successors, as we can infer from the above verse by Lappe and Schumann. Herder has become a "see also" author.

Herder is seen as being the opposite pole to Immanuel Kant (1724-1804), whose lectures he heard in Königsberg, and is counted as one of the great Four of the Weimar Classical Period – alongside Johann Wolfgang von Goethe (1749-1832), Friedrich Schiller (1759-1805) and Christoph Martin Wieland (1733-1813). He was the "Copernicus of history", as Cassirer has dubbed him (Cassirer 2000 (1957): 254). Madame de Staël (1766-1817) spoke of the "magic" that emanated from his writings (de Staël 1985 (1814): 466). Michael Zaremba's "poetic encyclopaedist" (Zaremba 2002) sounds somewhat more profane. Ernst Cassirer names a different triumvirate in his evaluation, namely Johann Joachim Winckelmann (1717-68), Kant and Herder and expresses the view that all three had a "common characteristic" in which the general intellectual and material state of Prussia at that time is reflected: it is that of an embittered struggle to escape the "deficits" and "narrowness" of a "political and intellectual milieu" (Cassirer 2001 (1918): 32). Herder was respected and admired and his work was received with acclaim; his thought had an intellectual and political echo. He faded into the collective memory, so to speak – and was soon no longer read. This is due to the fact that, according to his grateful disciple, the poet Jean Paul, "he [had] the fault that he was not a star of

BERND HENNINGSEN

the first water or other degree of greatness, but a cluster of stars, from which each engenders its own constellation (cited in Wölfel: 15).[2]

Herder's continuing presence in relative insignificance arises from our memory of associated work; as Kurt Wölfel comments, Herder became a chapter in the biography of Goethe (Wölfel: 16). He was on everyone's lips, but there was never "a cult that formed" around him. And thus in the same way as it has become customary since Montesquieu and Herder, as Cassirer notes with a certain justified annoyance (Cassirer 2004, 226f.), to use the term 'Geist' (spirit) to refer to the *a priori*, the essence and the ground of 'Geist', Herder is the nameless wizard of national identity.

All his life Herder was dissatisfied, even surly, hot-tempered, gloomy, sentimental, a misanthropist and a hypochondriac. He was a theologian by profession, full of plans for a literary career, a great pedagogue (also on the theoretical side), but not a good speaker, although he was a gifted conversationalist, as Wilhelm von Humboldt (1767-1835) comments (Humboldt 1986 (1830): 362). He was a critic, but no academic. He was born the son of a verger in a tiny Masurian hamlet, Mohrungen. When he died he was the General Superintendent of the intellectual hub of Weimar, a town of 6,000 inhabitants, a post which he had obtained through the efforts of Goethe, who was younger than he (Bollebeck 2001: 207-224). Even the different places where he lived – Mohrungen, Königsberg, Riga, Nantes, Paris, Strasbourg, Bückeburg and, finally, Weimar – would on their own provide sufficient material for an evocative biographic novel (for further details of his life history see Kantzenach 2002 (1970); Zaremba 2002).

To quote Jean Paul again:

One could say that, with regard to his life, Herder was composed in Greek [...]. Few were as comprehensively learned as he [...]. Thus he demonstrated Greek humanity, to which he gave back its name, in the most tender respect for all purely human relations and with a Lutheran anger against all its poisons that were blessed by religions or the state. Thus he was a fortress full of flowers, a Nordic oak whose branches were plants of meaning. (cited in Zaremba 2002: 7f.)

The North between Enlightenment and Romanticism

The nation-building process in the Scandinavian countries in the late eighteenth and early nineteenth centuries[3] took place between and on the basis of the ideas of

---

2   Transl. note: apart from the quote from Gellner, all quotations in English are *ad hoc* translations by the translator of the present text.

3   The political process took longer, of course. The Swedish-Norwegian Union was dissolved in 1905 and Finland did not become independent until 1917.

FIG. 4:
Johann Gottfried Herder (1744-1803). Sally von Kügelgen, 1909

the Enlightenment and Romanticism.[4] The only problem with this not so unusual statement is that the way in which the Enlightenment and Romanticism were manifested in Scandinavia differed from how it was evidenced in, for example, Germany or even France. There are several reasons why this was so, however we cannot go into them in any detail here. They have to do with national, political, social and economic crises, from which Scandinavia, like the rest of Old Europe, was not spared (for a detailed account see Trägårdh 1990).

4   For more on the definitions of both epochs cf. Berlin's criticism, 2004.

Thus, while a civil nation-building effort rooted in the Enlightenment, taking as its model the American and French revolutions, relied on the self-regulating and self-determining individual, this was opposed by a conceptualisation of the nation based on special qualities – race, blood, culture, language and history. Herder and Fichte, who represented this German paradigm, i.e. an ethnic one, had a great influence in the Scandinavian (and Baltic) countries. While on his voyage from Riga to Nantes, which he undertook in an attempt to escape from a petit-bourgeois existence at the European periphery and the narrowness of his office ("Liefland, du Provinz der Barbarei"; Herder 1997 (1769): 128), contrary to his original plans Herder by-passed Denmark and Copenhagen and thus Friedrich Gottlieb Klopstock (1724-1803), who lived there, whereas Johann Gottlieb Fichte (1762-1814), a "wild German patriot and nationalist" (Berlin 2004, 162), did in fact visit his Romantic friends in Copenhagen when he was fleeing from Napoleon's troops. Fichte had a lasting influence, while Herder resounds like a *basso continuo*, but is seldom cited.

However, there can be no doubt that this notoriously narrow intellectual (and political) influence on Scandinavian thought by the great thinkers of the country to the south that was later to be called Germany did exist. Herder's ethnocentric 'Geist' was to flow into the Danish political self-image via Grundtvig. However, a number of Danish scholars with whom Herder had already been in personal contact had already been influenced prior to Grundtvig (Korsgaard, 2004, 199ff.).

As far as the Norwegians are concerned, as Øystein Sørensen (2001: 17-21) points out, the usual glorification of the peasants, borrowed from the Romantics, was filtered by a deeply entrenched Enlightenment tradition. The idealisation of the past, the dream of the old Golden Age became intermingled with Enlightenment thought in Norwegian academic and political life in the nineteenth century:

A romantically modified, pragmatic and rustic Enlightenment tradition – during the long Norwegian nineteenth century this is the main line of the national development of ideas. (Sørensen 2001: 21)

The Norwegianisation of the Danish written language, which was tantamount to an admission that there was no original Norwegian language, and the fact that it is still sometimes difficult to find a Norwegian 'Volksgeist', a specific Norwegian individuality, do not fit into Herder's identity construct. What happened was rather a pragmatic modification of the Romantic claim to originality on one of the main battlefields of both the ideological and the practical nation-building process. Jacob Aall (1773-1844), a pragmatic representative of the Enlightenment, a purged

Romantic, should be mentioned in this context. The solutions arrived at in the controversy over the Norwegian language, the ideological roots of which can doubtlessly be sought in the work of Herder, turned it from its German (Romantic) head on to its Norwegian (pragmatic) feet.

On the other hand, it was precisely the philosophers of the Norwegian university in Christiania, which was founded in 1811, who were strongly influenced by Herder (and Fichte) and developed into sceptics, if not opponents of German idealism and Hegelianism. Among them was the Wolffian Niels Treschow (1751-1833) (cf. also Koch 2003: 156ff. and also Aall 1919: 101), prior to whom it can be demonstrated that Tyge Rothe (1731-95) was influenced by Herder. Rothe in turn made an impression on Henrik Steffens (1773-1845) (Koch 2004: 259ff, 269ff). The Danish Norwegian Steffens was a pioneering figure who initiated Romanticism in Denmark and later became a professor, also at Berlin University. In his memoirs he describes in warm tones his encounters with Herder and the influence that the older man had on him (Steffens 1995-96 (1840-46) 4:421).

The reference to the Romantic concept of the organism, which was introduced into Danish philosophy by Steffens and then presented in unusually explicit terms, is striking. Whereas it remains implicit in the work of many continental Romanticists, in the North it is addressed directly. This would appear to be the most marked indication of Herder's legacy in northern Europe, despite the fact that Goethe is frequently cited as the originator of organismic theory (Koch 2004: 23ff.; Henriksen 1973). The unity or holistic philosophy of the Romanticists, the idea that nature and history proceed from a single fundamental principle and that there is teleological process that develops to perfection became the determining line of thought in the epoch around the turn of the century; key words such as nature, development, personality, identity, history, the unconscious, inspiration and genius took on the meanings that are still conventional today (Henriksen 1973: 7). The theory that plants are determined by their seeds that Goethe presented in his *Die Metamorphose der Pflanzen*[5] has its precursors, for example, in the mysticism of Jakob Boehme (1575-1624). The Romantic paradigm change for which Herder stands is based on the transposition of the organismic concept to history and politics, the sphere of peoples and nations. The cultural development of mankind develops in a similar manner to the growth of plants and individuals: through childhood, youth, adulthood and old age.

In regular periods the air, fire, water and the earth developed out of spiritual and physical stamina. Many different compounds of water, air and light had to have existed before the

---

5   Metamorphosis of Plants.

BERND HENNINGSEN

seed of the first plant organisation, for instance moss, could be produced. Many plants had to have developed and died before an animal organisation came into existence; and the higher animals of the earth and the day were also preceded by insects, birds, water and nocturnal animals, until finally the crowning glory of the organisation of our earth, the human being, appeared; microcosm. He, the son of all elements and beings, their most exquisite essence and the blossom of earthly creation, so to speak, could not be anything else than the last spoilt child of nature, whose creation and reception had to be preceded by many developments and revolutions. (Herder 1989 (1784): 31)

The German 'Sonderweg'[6] and the Scandinavian systems of thought

The nationalistic blood and earth camarilla of the 1920s and 30s in Germany had a much more simple reception in Scandinavia. For the Scandinavians Herder was the main motor in the Romantic struggle against the Enlightenment; he had influenced Thomas Thorild (1759-1808), the Swedish intellectual outposted in Greifswald who was to make a lasting impression on the Uppsala philosopher Benjamin Karl Henrik Höijer (1767-1812); Herder's genealogy was finally followed back as far as Erik Gustaf Geijer (1783-1847), who was a conservative and later became a liberal professor of history in Uppsala. From Geijer, Esaias Tegnér (1782-1846) and also Selma Lagerlöf (1858-1940) the German nationalists adopted the idea of the tribal community in the 'Geist' (spirit) and in the 'Volk' (the people) that Herder had introduced: "Their dependency on the German spirit is a weapon in the struggle against the thinking of the Enlightenment" (Petersen 1937: 456). Herder's postulate of the "Germanic-Nordic community" was still being defended in the 1970s (Gerhardt/Hubatsch 1977: 327).

This was an attempt to include the Scandinavian countries in the 'German Sonderweg'.

The second half of the eighteenth century creates the profound philosophical and social turn in the Western world, in which German and Western thinking finally part company. The French movement, from Voltaire's entrance on the scene to the finishing of the Encyclopaedia, completes the construction of thought based on natural law and individualism, [...], while at the same time the great German countermovement, from Lessing through Herder and Winckelmann to the classic Goethe is concerned with the construction of a new image of man, the ideal of human totality. (Gerhardt/Hubatsch 1977: 429)

6   Unique course.

The notion of the organism – conceptualized as a "totality", was interpreted by Carl Petersen, a university professor in Kiel, as a philosophical and social (!) event. We are all too familiar with the consequences. What Carl Petersen, a nationalist, was evidently not familiar with, are the traditions of the Scandinavian history of ideas, which in fact continued to link these to the humanity of the western world and immunised it against the totalitarian philosophical and political tendencies of the Left and Right (cf. Henningsen, B. 1977). Herder became the godfather of the German 'Sonderweg' and was labelled as the "great initiator of German species-specific thinking and feeling" (Petersen 1937: 431).

At the same time, it is possible to show with and on the basis of Herder and his reception in the Scandinavian countries that both the civil society *and* nationalism can exist side by side as allies and not as enemies of the modern conceptualisation of society and the state and remain so.

At the start, they tended to be allies. For one thing, early nationalism was modest and timid, the Herderian defence of the charms of folk cultures against imperialism of the French court or of British commercialism or the bloodless universalism of abstract man of the Enlightenment. (Gellner 1995: 46)

The Scandinavian coalition of liberal nationalism and national identity, which was thus effortlessly able to adapt the non-aggressive Herder, had its humus in an interpretation of the Enlightenment that had already been justified by Ludvig Holberg (1684-1754). In opposition to Montesquieu (1689-1755) he had rejected circumstances, the climate and similar basic constructs used to explain the characteristics of peoples, preferring the respective peculiar developments of their political regimes (Hettne, Sörlin, Østergård 1998: 79-94).[7] *National* culture is *political* culture because it is rooted in politics. Politics and political culture are the bases of the Scandinavian nations, not, as in Herder, language and poetry. Thus, Herder, who hated politics and viewed it as a cold monstrosity (Craig 1982: 36), laid the foundation stone for the German antagonism between the state (= bad) and community (= good), an antagonism that remained foreign to Scandinavian politics and language until far into the twentieth century. 'Samfund' (Community) is the Scandinavian synonym for 'state' *and* 'society' (Henningsen, B. 1977). In his *Allgemeines Staatsrecht*,[8] which was published in 1793, the influential historian August Ludwig Schlözer (1735-1809) from Göttingen, a contemporary of Herder's, restricted the social existence of human beings to the role of subjects. This is an accurate

7   See also Hovde, 1943, on Herder's influence in Scandinavia.
8   General Constitutional Law.

description of the German political and societal disaster of the post-revolutionary era: "Politics is [...] identified with dominion over the subject" (Gebhardt 1968: 10). State and society are separate and in Germany the crisis of Old Europe led to a loss of 'common sense'.

The search for the 'symbolic universe' of a people and its objectification in the 'Volksgeist' (spirit of the people), as described by Herder while on his journey from Riga to Nantes and Paris (cf. Henningsen, M. 1989: 31-52) did not, in the case of the Scandinavian countries in the twentieth century, lead to an exclusive nationalism as in other regions of the world,[9] but rather promoted the civil society traditions of thinking and acting. The question as to why nationalism and the civil society remained allied in the Scandinavian countries, despite the strong influence of Herder *and* the infiltrations from the South, must and can only be explained on the basis of the bodies of thought mentioned above, which retained their immunising effect (Henningsen, B. 1977). To what extent their peripheral location and early political withdrawal from the European political theatre played a role must remain an open question.

Eric Voegelin pointed out in his study *Rasse und Staat*,[10] which was published by Mohr as late as 1933, that the "Nordic idea" of German origin is unpolitical because it is an idea of the middle classes which in Germany – at least until 1933 – never had a political idea:

Its position as a political power factor should not be characterised as ruling, but as a desperate rebellion against total proletarisation, against the demise into a mass without status. (Voegelin 1933: 221)[11]

In a brief discussion of Hans F. K. Günther's *Rassenkunde des Dritten Reiches*[12] Voegelin came to the conclusion that the "Nordic idea" was not able to find the support of any relevant social group in Germany and thus had no "political grounding in reality":

---

9   This is not to claim that there was or is no racial hatred in Scandinavia.

10   Race and State.

11   As far as I know this early study by Voegelin has never been cited in analyses of the history of Nordic studies. I find this all the more surprising in view of the fact that Voegelin, who was forced into exile by the National Socialists in 1938, was known to be not only well versed in the writings of the racist and nationalist authors, but also in those of Otto Höfler, a central figure of the SS Ahnenerbe (ancestral heritage foundation of the SS) and academic Scandinavian studies before and after the Second World War, who was also teaching in Vienna at the same time as himself.

12   Racial Theory of the Third Reich.

Thus the object of the Nordic idea must not be to maintain an existing view of humanity, but simply to shape the people according to its image. (Voegelin 1933: 221)

Voegelin did not employ the concept of construction, however. What is meant here is precisely: the construction of political reality in accordance with any idea, whatever it may be. This is the meaning of the notion of the 'Revolution des Geistes' (revolution of the spirit), following Fichte and Schlegel (Gebhardt 1968). That the Scandinavian countries remained immune to this revolution of the spirit was due to their traditionally western-oriented history of ideas, political thinking that was rooted in existential experience and to an apologia for the political middle road which must be termed Aristotelian. These differences can be considered to be responsible for the fact that the Herderian concept of the 'Volksgeist' did not result in a nationalist refusal of apperception and the Scandinavian countries remained open and liberal societies – at least up until the 1980s. At the same time it must be said that during the two centuries since Herder there has also been a national discourse, i.e. one dominated by a nationalistic ideology, in the Scandinavian countries. However, up to the end of the twentieth century it met with little or no resonance in the parliaments or state chancelleries and, above all, no determining influence on behaviour at the polls after the introduction of parliamentarianism. Constitutions, human rights, the sovereignty of the people, justice and institutions were the points of reference in public political discourse – not language, history, culture or blood. This has changed in the new millennium. Now nationalism has stepped out of literature and the newspaper supplements and is determining thought and behaviour in politics and society.

Language

From Johann Georg Hamann (1730-88), his teacher and friend, Herder adopted the conviction that language, people and nation constitute a single unit, and he developed it further. The idea that language and the people have spirit originates from Hamann. Speculation about language became an important core element of Herder's thought. In the course of the nineteenth century it was to become effective politically and, in Germany, at least, have fatal results. Starting from the conviction represented by Hamann that there is a single human nature and that language is a constituent part of this nature, Herder arrived at the conviction that language is not only the expression of the 'Volksseele' (people's soul), but that it has a soul itself – "everything has its genius, its spirit" (Herder 1985 (1772): 738; cf. Vondung 1988: 169ff.).

From the analogy between body and spirit, spirit is reified, language and poetry become the "reified manifestation of the Holy Spirit", the word becomes a divine, creative *logos* (Vondung 1988: 171). Poetry, which is older than prose, becomes the "dictionary of the psyche" (Herder 1985 (1772): 740). Thus, anyone who wishes to create a 'Volkskörper' (people's body) must not only master language, but also employ language to build the nation.

If language is the organ of our soul forces, the means of our innermost education, we cannot do other than be well educated in the language of our people and country (Herder 1991 (1792): 597)

Only in its language does a nation become a nation, only through language is a national feeling of community engendered and – constructible. Herder therefore also employed the term "national language" and of course also that of the "mother tongue" (Herder 1985 (1772): 794 and idem 1997: 54ff).

By means of language a nation is raised and educated, by means of language it becomes order and honour-loving, obedient, civilized, pleasant-natured, famous, hard-working and powerful. He who despises the language of his nation dishonours its most noble audience; he becomes the most dangerous murderer of its spirit, its inner and outer fame, its inventions, its finer morality and activity. He who elevates the language of a people and elaborates it to be the strongest expression of every sensation, every clear and noble thought, helps to spread or unify and more stably establish the widest and finest audience. (Herder 1991 (1792): 305)

No element of Herderian speculation had such a profound and sustained effect in Scandinavia as that of the central significance of language for national identity and political and cultural self-definition. The after-effects of Herder, which since Grundtvig have been fostered, are always appreciable when attention is drawn to the beauty and uniqueness of the respective "mother tongues". Herder believed that the complexity of feelings and thoughts could only be expressed in the mother tongue. The significance of the 'Sprachgeist' (spirit of language) is raised to the level of the 'Volksgeist' (spirit of the people), the 'Volksgeist' is manifested in the 'Sprachgeist' and the soul of a 'Volk' or people is evidenced in its language. The Others are those who do not understand the soul of one's own language and cannot fathom its emotional depth. Language becomes the *corpus mysticum* of the nation. In Herder's works this reification is not yet pronounced. We find it in the work of Fichte (and that of his keen student Ernst Moritz Arndt) (Vondung 1988:

173), in Grundtvig's writings it is clearly evident – and it becomes politically tangible in the Norwegian language controversy.

It was already evident in Herder's time that neither does language have a soul. Nor is there a genetic link between the development of language and the development of nations. There were no homogenous languages that made communication possible even on a regional or national level, let alone across the barriers of social rank or class, either in France, Italy or Germany, quite apart from in multicultural areas such as the Baltic region (cf. Hobsbawm 1991: 59-96; Schulze 1999: 172-177).

The spirit of the people that was conjured up to justify the nation was entirely the spirit of a small class of educated enthusiasts. (Schulze 1999: 177)

An admiration for the old poets and of Shakespeare in particular is common to all the identity constructors of Romanticism. They sought the 'Volksseele' (people's soul) in traditional mythology, history, the oral narratives of the peoples and in literature. Nowhere is the constructive impulse as evident as in the epidemic enthralment of this epoch with Ossian. All actors, Herder included, were deceived by the forgery of this supposedly ancient Celtic poetry by James MacPherson. *The Poems of Ossian* (1760-65) fulfilled the need for construction in the European crisis period. However, they were not *discovered*, but *invented* (Jansson 1996; 192-208). At this point the spirit of the age proved to be exactly what its contemporaries hoped – a stroke of genius. This was indeed pure genius, devoid of all connection with reality.

Without the notion of the creation of a nation on the basis of language there would be no disputes about language. Ideologically and in concrete terms the conflict over the Norwegian national language was fuelled by the value that Herder attributed to language in the national consciousness. Language was considered to be sacred and anyone who desecrated it thus became a "murderer". It therefore also reflects the extent to which politics have been "sacralised" (cf. Vondung 2004). This refers not to the turn in the philosophy of language initiated by Herder and Wilhelm von Humboldt, which was in fact a new direction of thought, as Ernst Cassirer repeatedly stresses (cf. for example Cassirer 2001 (1918): 84ff.), but to a political functionalisation of language that culminated in linguistic purism. This began to spread, particularly in Germany, and became a political issue that had genocidal consequences (cf. Henningsen, M. 1989). Since Herder, the only route of access to the truth has been language.

BERND HENNINGSEN

Mythology, the education of the people and stolen identity

When the modern nation states developed at the end of the eighteenth and beginning of the nineteenth centuries they did so on the basis of their respective histories, literatures and mythologies. That is, the discovery of what is one's *own* results to a great extent from the discovery of the *Other*. Herder's postulate that what is one's own becomes manifest in the Other has since been a recurring theme in the history of his reception and of the construction of collective identity, and not least in its political branches. While the tiresome certainty that *we* are different from our neighbours is not new, since the Romantic era it has become highly political, for since this time *we* have been 'better' than the *Others*.

The continuity of political history is preceded by the continuity of the notion of the *construction* of continuity: before we can say what we *are* and *will be*, we need to know what we *were*. After the French revolution the Idealists and Romanticists therefore embarked on a search for the political roots, the national literature, the mythology, the roots of their own countries. Out of this historical material, which had not previously been put into any kind of order, they invented a continuity that stretched from the past through the present and into the future. They make us forget that there is a rupture in the construction of identity marked by the French revolution. Before the French revolution national identity had been a question of loyalty to a dynasty, after its ideas and putative foundation myths ruled the day. This is the basis of national identity: a cultural construction out of different materials that were *declared* essential at the respective points in time. Following Herder, Ernst Cassirer identifies the myth as the "magic key" that "opens the world of history" (Cassirer 1995: 86).

The construction of continuity works if the individual can be convinced of the plausibility of the construction, the material is original and autochtonous and if – and this describes the interaction between continuity and construction – it can be integrated into the citizens' current experience without interruptions. This was the case in the Nordic countries and also in France and England. Norse mythology and literature were originally Nordic, the languages also, but the history was the main source of national identity construction. This is an exact description of what Ernest Renan gave as a definition of the nation in his Sorbonne lecture in 1882: an agreement on affiliation that is established every day (Renan 1995: 57). Because citizens found themselves reflected in society's self-interpretation they identified with their nations and were less liable to be influenced by substitute identities or ideologies. Renan was able to make such a clear definition because he knew 'his' Herder so well – he called him his "master thinker" (cf. Euchner 1996: 47) and thus Renan can be seen as a ghost of Herder who was able to be clear about the constructivist nature of nationalism owing to the French experience with the German interpretations of nationalism after 1871. His sentence "a nation is a soul, a spiritual principle" (Renan 1995: 56) is more easily understandable seen against the backdrop of this familiarity with Herder's philosophy.

Here again the German case provides the comparative explanation. I present an example: in the process of national identity-finding at the end of the eighteenth century and beginning of the nineteenth century in German-speaking countries there was also a search for the specifically Germanic prehistoric era and for original German mythology and literature (cf. for example von See 1994). Since these do not exist, the problem was solved by falling back on the construction trick of declaring Norse mythology and literature, which had by then been re-discovered, to be German mythology. Walhall became a *German* hall of fame, the gods of Norse mythology became *Germanic* - meaning German.[13]

Some German Classicists believed that Greek mythology had lost its attraction for the education of the people and thus in 1797 Herder made a proposal that was to have serious consequences and in fact 'point the way ahead' for the construction of the north (Kliemann-Geisinger 2005: 231), namely that related material should be adopted from the immediate vicinity of Germany in order to construct a national, *German* identity: the development of a Germanic-German national identity out of Norse mythology (cf. also Rühling 1996: 67ff.). Through the medium of the brief Socratic debate between Frey and Alfred published under the title "Iduna" in the *Horen,* and in disagreement with and differentiation from Friedrich Schiller, he suggested that Greek mythology should be replaced by Norse mythology and literature as the basis of education.

[We are, however] what we are, *human beings.* Our reason develops only *through fictions.* We are forever searching and creating a *one in many* and developing it into a *'Gestalt';* from this *concepts, ideas and ideals* are created. If we use them wrongly or even become accustomed *to configuring incorrectly,* we marvel at shadows and, like beasts of burden, become weary of bearing false *idols* as holy relics: thus the blame is on us, not on the matter. We cannot exist without poetry, a child is never happier than when it is *fantasising* and even *imagines* itself in foreign situations and persons. All our lives we remain such children, only in *composing our souls in poetry,* supported by *intellect,* ordered by *reason,* do we find the happiness of our existence. Permit us them, *Frey,* these innocent joys, let us keep them. *The fictions of jurisprudence and politics* are seldom as pleasant as they. (Herder 1998 (1792-1800): 156-157)

Since the importance of Greek mythology for the education of the people had dissolved it was now a question of adapting related material from the close vicinity.

---

13   See also Karen Klitgaard Povlsen in this volume.

Norse mythology [… has] retained a genuine, purely German 'Stammsprache' and we therefore wish to adopt some of it. Peoples of Teutonic origin have spread wide and far, even as far as Africa; we shall take what serves us as we find it. (Herder 1988. (1792-1800): 164)

Herder was referring to the materials of modern identity construction. He provided the 'national' symbols and also at the same time – at the inception of European nationalism, which was based on people, language, literature and history – the strategy with which these symbols can be generated and national identity derived. It had become evident that the old symbolic order was irrelevant and the political order required a new symbolism after the French revolution and the destruction of classical Europe. Old Europe was engaged in its most serious political, economic, social and legitimation crisis between 1770 and 1830 and its own national heritage had no symbolic material to offer. Herder thus fell back on a plausible adaptation strategy which subsequently was willingly taken up by German contemporaries and brought into the political discussion (von See 1994; Weber 1996). As already noted by the Danish German scholar Carl Ross in the 1930s, the North subsequently became the "lost German tradition" (Roos 1938: 82; Jansson 1996). Ernst Bloch describes this in more poetical terms in his "Konstruktion"[14] and "Grundriss einer besseren Welt"[15] which he called "The Principle of Hope":

Ultima Thule attunes one in a very special way to the last frontier, the end of the world. Thus Thule's past simultaneously discloses itself in its very meaning of boundary: it is, as Herder says, 'an exit of the world in relief'. […] Northwards a magic of doom geographically forms a utopia which contains the complete destruction of a world, but also wants to overcome it, with a paradoxical homeland. Thule is the geographic-dialectical utopia of a world that is coming to an end and perishing, but with the contrasting image of a stormy night and fortress permanently contained within it. Thule in the Arctic Ocean is the mysticism of bad weather with an open hearth right in the middle. (Bloch 1982: 914)

The North in Herder's Works

Following the (pre-)classical climate theory, and then Montesquieu's Enlightened climate theory in geography, the doctrine of the harmony of space with the peoples inhabiting it became established. Herder is the German propagandist of this "prestabilised harmony" (Schultz 2000). While Goethe had already replied to

14   Construction.
15   Basic Outline of a Better World.

Eckermann in 1828 that the tribes usually took possession of the land that was in harmony with the congenital character of the people, in 1833 an anonymous text on "natural diplomatics" was published in which a kind of "elective affinity" between the tribes and the land was postulated (Schultz 2000: 10). According to this theory, which was conclusive in the truest sense of the word, the peoples wander around in the world in search of a harmonious place until they find the spot that fits their mission in world history, true to Napoleon's maxim "The history of the peoples is written by their geography" (Schultz 2000: 16).

While we need go into no further detail as regards the disastrous consequences of this mode of thought, Napoleon's name marked an initial climax. At the end of the twentieth century it was evident that the postulated agreement between land, state and people encouraged genocide also – and precisely in Europe – and continues to do so today. However, if we go into detail we must also remember that in the genealogy of the constructions of the climate theory the idea of spatial boundaries of culture originated in particular in the age of the Enlightenment. When Ernest Renan summarised the nature of the nation in his metaphor of the daily plebiscite in his Sorbonne lecture (Renan 1995) over a hundred years later, he discovered the constructivist thought of the "will to nature" – frontiers are not natural, but constructed by the senses.

The preference for theories that did *not* result from 'natural' opposites and cultural boundaries but from commonalities and elective affinities (cf. Henningsen, B. et al. 1997) was kindled at the end of the eighteenth century and was to pour forth like an ideological cataract throughout the nineteenth and early twentieth centuries. Herder and Winkelmann introduced a new cultural theory according to which the identity-linked, national origins were sought and found in the respective 'Volksgeister'. This philosophy marked the end of the supreme reign of Cartesian and Enlightenment thinking and welcomed the entrance of the free, embodied individual onto the scene as the new hero. The focus shifted from humanity as a whole and the individual nation became the reference point and actor. Whereas the seventeenth century still had the entire history of civilisation in its purview, particularly in Scandinavia – take, for example, Olaf Rudbeck (1630-1702) and Carl von Linné (1707-1778), who were still able to cast their glance as far as Egypt and Asia (cf. Henningsen, B. 1997) – in the Romantic era (roughly) European cultural memory was reduced to the period of and after the Greeks (cf. Assmann, 2000: 221). Herder was probably the most important representative of this anthropological turn.

While in his brief *Auch eine Philosophie der Geschichte zur Bildung der Menschheit,*[16] published in 1774, the cultural and educational development of humanity

16   Also a Philosophy of the History of the Development of Humanity.

BERND HENNINGSEN

ends in the North, in his monumental treatise entitled *Ideen zur Philosophie der Geschichte der Menschheit*,[17] published in 1784, the description of the development of mankind and nature based on space and climate begins in the North; all life begins in the North:

Thus one can still see the northern sea with its large number of inhabitants as the womb of life and its shores as the margin on which the organisation of earthly beings begins in mosses, insects and worms. (Herder 1989 (1784): 210)

The construction of the North, an ideological process that began with the Greeks and the Romans, partly out of curiosity and partly for autostereotyped, didactic reasons, took on an anthropological dimension with and after Herder, the after-effects of which became political in the course of the nineteenth century and today still determine the 'image of the North'.

17   Outlines of a Philosophy of the History of Man.

References

Aall, Anathon 1919: *Filosofien i Norden. Til oplysning om den nyere tænknings og videnskaps historie i Sverige og Finland, i Danmark og Norge*. Kristiania: Dybwad.

Assmann, Jan 2000: *Religion und kulturelles Gedächtnis*. München: Beck.

Berlin, Isaiah 2004: *Die Wurzeln der Romantik*. Berlin: Berlin.

Bloch, Ernst 1982: *Das Prinzip Hoffnung*. 1-3. 8. Edition. Frankfurt am Main: Suhrkamp.

Bollenbeck, Georg 2001: Weimar. Ed.: Etienne François, Hagen Schulze: *Deutsche Erinnerungsorte*. 1. München Beck: 207-224.

Cassirer, Ernst 1995: *Nachgelassene Manuskripte und Texte*. Hamburg: Meiner.

Cassirer, Ernst 2000 (1957): Das Erkenntnisproblem in der Philosophie und Wissenschaft der neueren Zeit. *Gesammelte Werke Hamburger Ausgabe*. 2-4. Hamburg: Meiner.

Cassirer, Ernst 2001 (1918): Kants Leben und Lehre. *Gesammelte Werke Hamburger Ausgabe*. 8. Darmstadt, Hamburg: Meiner.

Cassirer, Ernst 2004: *Nachgelassene Manuskripte und Texte*. 5. Hamburg: Meiner.

Cassirer, Ernst: 2001: Philosophie der symbolischen Formen. Erster Teil: Die Sprache. *Gesammelte Werke Hamburger Ausgabe*. 11. Hamburg: Meiner.

Craig, Gordon A. 1982: *Über die Deutschen*. München: Beck.

Euchner, Walter 1996: Nation und Nationalismus. Eine Erinnerung an Ernest Renans Rede 'Was ist eine Nation?' Ed.: Ernest Renan: *Was ist eine Nation?* Hamburg: EVA: 41-68.

Gebhardt, Jürgen 1968: Zur Physiognomie einer Epoche. Ed.: Jürgen Gebhardt: *Die Revolution des Geistes. Politisches Denken in Deutschland 1770-1830*. München: List.

Gellner, Ernest 1995: The Importance of Being Modular. Ed.: John A. Hall: *Civil Society. Theory, History, Comparison*. Cambridge/Mass.: Polity Press: 32-55.

Gerhardt, Martin, Walther Hubatsch 1977: *Deutschland und Skandinavien im Wandel der Jahrhunderte*. Darmstadt: Wissenschaftliche Buchgesellschaft.

Henningsen, Bernd 1977: *Die Politik des Einzelnen. Studien zur Genese der skandinavischen Ziviltheologie*. Göttingen Vandenhoeck & Ruprecht.

Henningsen, Bernd 1997: *Die schwedische Konstruktion einer nordischen Identität durch Olof Rudbeck*. Berlin: Humboldt-Universität.

Henningsen, Bernd, Janine Klein, Helmut Müssener, Solfrid Söderlin, eds. 1997: *Wahlverwandtschaft. Skandinavien und Deutschland 1800 bis 1914*. Berlin: Jovis.

Henningsen, Manfred 1989: The Politics of Purity and Exclusion: Literary and Linguistic Movements of Political Empowerment in America, Africa, the South Pacific, and Europe. Ed.: Björn H. Jernudd, Michael J. Shapiro: *The Politics of Language Purism*. Berlin, New York: Mouton de Gruyter: 31-52.

Henriksen, Aage 1973: *Organismetanken – en hovedlinie i det 19. århundredes tænkning og digtning*. Kopenhagen: Gyldendal.

Herder, Johann Gottfried 1797 (1769): Journal meiner Reise im Jahr 1769. *Werke in zehn Bänden*. 9/2. Frankfurt am Main: Deutscher Klassiker Verlag: 9-126.

Herder, Johann Gottfried 1985 (1772): Abhandlung über den Ursprung der Sprache. *Werke in zehn Bänden*. 1. Frankfurt am Main: Deutscher Klassiker Verlag: 695-810.

Herder, Johann Gottfried 1989 (1784): Ideen zur Philosophie der Geschichte der Menschheit. *Werke in zehn Bänden*. 6. Frankfurt am Main: Deutscher Klassiker Verlag.

Herder, Johann Gottfried 1991 (1792): Briefe zur Beförderung der Humanität. *Werke in zehn Bänden*. 7. Frankfurt am Main: Deutscher Klassiker Verlag.

Herder, Johann Gottfried 1997 (1769): Gedanken bei der Lesung Montesquieus. *Werke in zehn Bänden*. 9/2. Frankfurt am Main: Deutscher Klassiker Verlag: 204-208.

Herder, Johann Gottfried 1998 (1792-1800): Schriften zu Literatur und Philosophie. *Werke in zehn Bänden*. 8. Frankfurt am Main: Deutscher Klassiker Verlag.

Hettne, Björn, Sverker Sörlin, Uffe Østergård 1998: *Den globala nationalismen. Nationalstatens historia och framtid*. Stockholm: SNS.

Hobsbawm, Eric J. 1991: *Nationen und Nationalismus. Mythos und Realität seit 1780*. Frankfurt am Main: Campus.

Hovde, B. J. 1943: *The Scandinavian Countries, 1720-1865. The Rise of the Middle Classes*. 1-2. Boston: Chapman & Grimes.

Humboldt, Wilhelm von 1986 (1830): Ueber Schiller und den Gang seiner Geistesentwicklung. *Werke in fünf Bänden*, 2. 4th Edition. Darmstadt: Wissenschaftliche Buchgesellschaft: 357-394.

Jansson, Bo G. 1996: Nordens poetiska reception av Europas reception av det nordiska. Ed.: Else Roesdahl, Preben Meulengracht Sørensen: *The Waking of Angantyr. The Scandinavian past in European culture. Den nordiske fortid i europæisk kultur*. Aarhus: Aarhus University Press: 192-208.

Kantzenbach, Friedrich Wilhelm 2002 (1970): *Johann Gottfried Herder mit Selbstzeugnissen und Bilddokumenten*. Reinbek: Rowohlt.

Kittler, Friedrich 2000: *Eine Kulturgeschichte der Kulturwissenschaft*. München: Wilhelm Fink.

Kliemann, Hendriette 2005: *Koordinaten des Nordens. Wissenschaftliche Konstruktionen einer europäischen Region 1770-1850*. Berlin: Berliner Wissenschafts-Verlag.

Koch, Carl Henrik 2003: *Dansk oplysningsfilosofi 1700-1800*. Copenhagen: Gyldendal.

Koch, Carl Henrik 2004: *Den danske idealisme 1800-1880*. Copenhagen: Gyldendal

Korsgaard, Ove 2004: *Kampen om folket. Et dannelsesperspektiv på dansk historie gennem 500 år*. Copenhagen: Gyldendal.

Petersen, Carl 1937: Die Überwindung des Aufklärungsdenkens im Norden. Ed.: Hans Friedrich Blunck: *Die nordische Welt. Geschichte, Wesen und Bedeutung der nordischen Völker.* Berlin: Propyläen: 423-456.

Pross, Harry 1991: Ritualisierung des Nationalen. Ed.: Jürgen Link, Wulf Wülfing: *Nationale Mythen und Symbole in der zweiten Hälfte des 19. Jahrhunderts. Strukturen und Funktionen von Konzepten nationaler Identität.* Stuttgart: Klett-Cotta: 94-105.

Renan, Ernest 1995: *Was ist eine Nation? Und andere politische Schriften.* Wien, Bozen: EVA.

Roos, Carl 1938: *Germanica.* Copenhagen: Gyldendal.

Rühling, Lutz 1996: Das deutsche Bild Skandinaviens: Von barocker Poeterey bis zum wilden Norden. Ed.: Heinrich Detering: *Grenzgänge. Skandinavisch-deutsche Nachbarschaften.* Göttingen: Wallstein: 60-77.

Schultz, Hans-Dietrich 2000: Land – Volk – Staat. Der geografische Anteil an der 'Erfindung' der Nation. *Geschichte in Wissenschaft und Unterricht* 1: 4-16.

Schulze, Hagen 1999: *Staat und Nation in der europäischen Geschichte.* München: Beck.

See, Klaus von 1994: Bar*bar. Germane. Arier. Die Suche nach der Identität der Deutschen.* Heidelberg: C. Winter.

Sloterdijk, Peter 2004: *Sphären III. Schäume.* Frankfurt am Main: Suhrkamp

Sørensen, Øystein 2001: *Kampen om Norges sjel 1770-1905.* Oslo: Aschehoug.

Staël, Anne Germaine de 1985 (1814): *Über Deutschland.* Franfurt am Main: Insel.

Steffens, Henrik 1995-96 (1840-46): *Was ich erlebte. Aus der Erinnerung niedergeschrieben.* 2. Stuttgart: Fromann-Holzboog.

Trägård, Erik 1990: Varieties of volkish ideologies. Sweden and Germany 1848-1933. Ed.: Bo Stråth: *Language and the construction of class identities.* Göteborg: Gothenburg University: 25-54.

Voegelin, Eric(h) 1933: *Rasse und Staat.* Tübingen: Mohr.

Vondung, Klaus 1988: *Die Apokalypse in Deutschland.* München: dtv.

Vondung, Klaus 2004: Die Tücken des millenarischen Sendungsbewusstseins. *Frankfurter Rundschau* 20.7.

Weber, Gerd Wolfgang 1996: Nordisk fortid som chiliastisk fremtid. Den norrøne arv og den cykliske historieopfattelse i Skandinavien og Tyskland omkring 1800 – og senere. Ed.: Else Roesdahl, Preben Meulengracht Sørensen: *The Waking of Angantyr. The Scandinavian past in European culture. Den nordiske fortid i europæisk kultur.* Aarhus: Aarhus University Press: 72-119.

Wölfel, Kurt 1994: Hundert zerstreute Spiegelscherben zu stellen, daß sie die Strahlen auf *einen* Punkt werfen. Ed.: Stiftung Weimarer Klassik Goethe Nationalmuseum: *Johann Gottfried Herder. Ahndung künftiger Bestimmung.* Stuttgart: Metzler: 13-23.

Zaremba, Michael 2002: *Johann Gottfried Herder. Prediger der Humanität. Eine Biografie.* Köln, Weimar, Berlin: Böhlau.

den Fehler [hatte], dass er kein Stern erster oder sonstiger Größe war, sondern ein Bund von Sternen, aus welchem sich dann jeder ein beliebiges Sternbild buchstabierte. (zit. n. Wölfel :15)

Herder war gleichsam nach dem Leben griechisch gedichtet […] Wenige Geister waren auf die große Weise gelehrt wie Er […] So zeigt' Er die griechische Humanität, der Er den Namen wieder gab, in der zärtlichsten Achtung aller reinmenschlichen Verhältnisse und in einem Lutherischen Zorn gegen alle von Religionen oder vom Staat geheiligten Gifte derselben. So war Er ein Festungswerk voll Blumen, eine nordische Eiche, deren Aeste Sinnpflanzen waren. (zit.n. Zaremba 2002:7f.)

Eine romantisch modifizierte, pragmatische und bäuerliche Aufklärungstradition – das ist die Hauptlinie in der nationalen Ideenentwicklung des langen norwegischen 19. Jahrhunderts. (Sørensen 2001: 21)

In periodischen Zeiträumen entwickelte sich aus geistigen und körperlichen staminibus die Luft, das Feuer, das Wasser, die Erde. Mancherlei Verbindungen des Wassers, der Luft, des Lichts mußten vorhergegangen sein, eher der Same der ersten Pflanzenorganisation, etwa das Moos, hervorgehen konnte. Viele Pflanzen mußten hervorgegangen und gestorben sein, ehe eine Tierorganisation ward; auch bei dieser gingen Insekten, Vögel, Wasser- und Nachttiere den gebildetern Tieren der Erde und des Tages vor; bis endlich nach allen die Krone der Organisation unserer Erde, der Mensch, auftrat; *Mikrokosmos*. Er, der Sohn aller Elemente und Wesen, ihr erlesenster Inbegriff und gleichsam die Blüte der Erdenschöpfung konnte nicht anders, als das letzte Schoßkind der Natur sein, zu dessen Bildung und Empfang viele Entwickelungen und Revolutionen vorhergegangen sein mussten. (Herder 1784/1989: 31)

Die zweite Hälfte des 18. Jahrhunderts bringt den großen geistigen und sozialen Umschwung der abendländischen Welt, in dem sich deutsches und westliches Denken endgültig scheiden. Die französische Bewegung vom Auftreten Voltaires bis zur Beendung der Enzyklopädie vollendet das Gebäude des naturrechtlich-individualistischen Denkens, […] während gleichzeitig sich die große deutsche Gegenbewegung von Lessing über Herder und Winckelmann bis zum klassischen Goethe vollzieht: die Aufrichtung eines neuen Bildes vom Menschen, das Ideal der menschlichen Totalität. (Gerhardt/Hubatsch 1977: 429)

seine Stellung als politischer Machtfaktor ist nicht als Herrschen zu charakterisieren, sondern als ein verzweifeltes Aufbäumen gegen die völlige Proletarisierung, gegen den Untergang in einer Masse ohne Status. (Voegelin 1933: 221)

When Sprache *das Organ unsrer Seelenkräfte, das Mittel unsrer innersten Bildung und Erziehung* ist: so können wir nicht anders als in der Sprache unsres Volks und Landes gut erzogen werden …

Mittelst der Sprache wird eine Nation erzogen und gebildet; mittelst der Sprache wird sie Ordnung- und Ehrliebend, folgsam, gesittet, umgänglich, berühmt, fleissig und mächtig. Wer die Sprache seiner Nation verachtet, entehrt ihr edelstes Publikum; er wird ihres Geistes, ihres inneren und äusseren Ruhms, ihrer Erfindungen, ihrer feineren Sittlichkeit und Betriebsamkeit gefährlichster Mörder. Wer die Sprache einer Volks emporhebt, und sie zum kräftigsten Ausdruck jeder Empfindung, jedes klaren und edlen Gedankens ausarbeitet, der hilft das weiteste und schönste Publikum ausbreiten, oder sich vereinigen und fester gründen.

Der Geist des Volkes, der beschworen wurde, um die Nation zu rechtfertigen, war ganz und gar der Geist einer kleinen Schicht gebildeter Enthusiasten. (Schulze, 1999: 177)

(…wir sind nun aber,) was wir sind, *Menschen*. Unsre Vernunft bildet sich nur *durch Fiktionen*. Immerdar suchen und erschaffen wir uns ein *Eins in Vielem* und bilden es zu einer *Gestalt*; daraus werden *Begriffe, Ideen, Ideale*. Gebrauchen wir sie unrecht, oder werden wir gar gewöhnt, *falsch zu konfigurieren*; staunen wir Schattenbilder an und ermüden uns wie Lasttiere, falsche *Idole* als Heiligtümer zu tragen: so liegt die Schuld an uns, nicht an der Sache. Ohne Dichtung können wir einmal nicht sein; ein Kind ist nie glücklicher, als wenn es *imaginiert* und sich sogar in fremde Situationen und Personen *dichtet*. Lebenslang bleiben wir solche Kinder; nur im *Dichten der Seele*, unterstützt wom *Verstande*, geordnet von der *Vernunft*, besteht das Glück unsres Daseins. Lass uns, *Frey*, diese unschuldigen Freuden; lass sie uns. *Die Fiktionen der Rechtswissenschaft und der Politik* sind selten so erfreulich wie sie.

…die nordische Mythologie…(hat) eine *echte, reine deutsche Stammsprache* aufbewahrt, und deshalb wollen wir uns etwas von ihr zueignen. *Völker von teutonischen Stamm* haben sich weit umher getummelt, sogar nach Afrika verloren; wir nehmen das, was *für uns dient, wie wir's finden*.

…ultima Thule stimmt auf ganz besondere Weise zur letzten Grenze, zum Ende der Welt. Damit erschleisst sich die Verhangenheit Thules zugleich in ihrem Grenzsinn selbst: sie ist, wie Herder sagt, ein Ausgang der Welt in Erhabenheit'…nordwärts utopiert sich ein Todeszauber geographisch, der eine ganze Weltvernichtung in sich einschliesst, aber auch überwinden will, mit paradoxer Heimat. Thule ist die geographisch-dialektische Utopie einer Welt, die ausgeht und untergeht, doch mit dem dauernd ineinander verschränkten Kontrastbild von Sturmnacht und Burg. Thule im Nordmeer ist die Mystik des schlechten Wetters, mit dem Kaminfeuer drin.

…so kann man das nordliche Meer mit der grossen Fülle seiner Bewohner noch jetzt als eine Gebärmutter des Lebens und die Ufer desselben als den Rand betrachten, auf dem sich in Moosen, Insekten und Würmern die Organisation der Erdgeschöpfe anfängt.

SUMARLIDI R. ISLEIFSSON

Barbarians of the North become the Hellenians of the North

Iceland, a faraway island in the North, has long attracted the imaginations of people in Western Europe. One way to obtain an impression of this interest is to examine the holdings of the National Library in Reykjavík where many books on Iceland written by foreigners can be found; for instance, *C.G. Zorgdragers alte und neue Grönländische Fischerei und Wallfischfangst mit einer kurzen historischen Beschreibung von Grönland, Island, Jan Mayen Eiland, der Strasse Davis u.a.* from the year 1723.[1] From the nineteenth century, there is, for example, *An American in Iceland. An Account of its Scenery, People, and History* by Samuel Kneeland, published in 1874. Among the newest accounts, from 2003, is *Waking Up in Iceland. Sights and Sounds from Europe's Coolest Hotspot* by Paul Sullivan. These works represent only a tiny part of the literature on Iceland by non-Icelanders. The bibliography *Writings of Foreigners Relating to the Nature and the People of Iceland* (Sigurðsson 1991), which covers books and articles on Iceland published in other countries, lists more than 3000 titles, most of them travel accounts or books on Icelandic history and nature.

In this article I will examine images and ideas that appear in texts on Iceland, mainly from the eighteenth and nineteenth centuries, in order to identify changes in the image of Iceland which may have occurred during that period. Was there a substantial change in the image of Iceland during that period? Was there perhaps a turning point in the image of the country in the late eighteenth century? If there was a significant change during this period, what were the main reasons for it? The 'classification' of Iceland and of the Icelanders will also be discussed. It is clear that Iceland's location was in the North, more precisely in the far North. However, it is a question whether Iceland, before the nineteenth century, should be considered a part of Scandinavia, or whether it belonged culturally and geographically to another region – and if so, to which region?

---

1   C.G. Zorgdrager's Old and New Greenlandic Fishing and Whaling, with a Short Historical Description of Greenland, Iceland, Jan Mayen, the Davis Strait a.o.

At this point, I would like to introduce some important concepts. First, there is the term *image*. As the Dutch scholar Joep Leerssen has explained, image studies start from "the presupposition that the degree of truth of such commonplaces is not a necessary issue in their scholarly analysis." (Leerssen 2005) The texts that imagologists work with are commonly "conventions … inherited from a pre-existing textual tradition [that] fully overshadow the experience of reality." They are usually based on other sources, not "reality," and obey "built-in rules," which are most often unrelated to the real situation in the relevant country (Leerssen 2005).[2]

Another important term is the *island*. As is well known, in Western intellectual history and the history of ideas, islands have since Antiquity been endowed with special qualities. They were commonly described as places of wonder, either good or bad, as the American historian John Kirtland Wright has stated: "Islands were convenient topographic units to which the medieval mind was wont to attribute fabulous and supernatural qualities" (Wright 1965: 229-230).

The terms *utopia* and *dystopia* are closely related to the term *island*; Thomas More's *Utopia*, for instance, is located on an island. As scholars of ideal societies have pointed out, many different types of utopias have been posited over the course of history. Among them are the land of abundance (Land of Cockaygne); Arcadia, where people live a simple life on what Nature has to offer; and, finally, the Ideal City, referring to the Greek 'golden' heroic past (see e.g. Kumar 1987: 19; Davis 1984).

Distance – center-periphery – is another crucial concept in this context and also closely related to the term *island*. Increased distance from the cultural centers of Europe entailed heightened, and in Iceland's case, mostly negative, exotic and otherness, as the scholar John Gilles has stated: "The link between difference and distance is virtually axiomatic" (Gillies 1994: 31). Another scholar, James S. Romm, investigating the complex relationship between center and periphery, has described how the image constructed by some observers present "the center of the world as the best or most advanced location and therefore demotes distant peoples to the status of unworthy savages. An inversion of this scheme, by contrast, privileges the edges of the earth over the center" (Romm 1992: 46).

Until the eighteenth century and even later, Classical views, following the climatology of Aristotle, still had a significant influence on European ideas of the world. According to the Classical view, the climate in the far South and North was so extreme that these areas were more or less uninhabitable; civilized life was

---

2   It is for this reason that different countries are often described in similar ways. Among the structural constants Leerssen mentions are, for example, the terms *North-South* and *center-periphery*.

impossible and, it seemed, only monsters, giants or dwarfs could survive. In Central and Southern Europe, this negative image of the North generally prevailed throughout the Middle Ages and until the eighteenth century, not forgetting "those swarms of barbarians, who for several ages under the names of Danes and Normans, ravaged the different countries of Europe" (Adam 1797: 584).

What kind of texts?

According to Haraldur Sigurðsson's bibliography, *Writings of Foreigners Relating to Iceland* (1991), travel accounts on Iceland dating from before 1830 are few, only around a dozen, but after that their number rapidly increases in the latter half of the nineteenth century. Some travel accounts will be taken into consideration in this paper but I will also rely on other sources focusing on geographical texts and related materials. The reason is that the geographical texts are well suited for my purpose: to study images.

It is important to keep in mind when discussing texts on geography from before 1800 that they were not concerned primarily with describing the geographical conditions in individual countries. In contrast to contemporary practice, these texts were more historical and ethnographical, though they did also include descriptions of concrete geographical features. In the early nineteenth century, physical geography came to dominate geographical practice, supplanting the previous historic-ethnographic emphasis of such texts (Feldbæk 1991: 285-286).

The dystopia

Most texts dealing with Iceland dating from the Middle Ages until the mid-eighteenth century were short, typically only a few lines, perhaps only mentioning that Iceland was an island at the end of the world. Generally speaking, it can be said that Iceland hardly existed for educated Europe until after the middle of the eighteenth century. "Of Yseland to wryte is lytill need" (here after Wawn 2000: 10, 17) is the characterization of Iceland in an English text from the 1430s. According to such writers, there was hardly anything remarkable about the island but fish, and that topic was not regarded as interesting for the educated classes. If Iceland was mentioned in more than one or two lines, it was described as some kind of faraway island of wonders, extremely cold, where nothing could grow – a place with no trees or grain. There were poisonous fountains and destructive volcanoes, and Hell or Purgatory might even be found on the island, with devils flying about. Living there were superstitious and rude people, far beyond the reach of civilization, in a nearly demon-like state: half animal, half human, not knowing whether they were men or monsters (Ísleifsson 1996).

Andrew Boorde's book *The first Boke of the Introduction of Knowledge* from the middle of the sixteenth century is a good example of this tradition. In his book the author describes the different nations of Europe, among them the Icelanders:

And I was borne in Islond, as brute as a beest
Whan I ete candels ends, I am at a feest.
Talow and raw stockefysh, I do loue to ete
In my countrey it is right good meate
Raw fysh and flesh I eate whan I haue nede;
Upon suche meates I do loue to feed (Boorde 1870: 141)

Dystopian descriptions of Iceland reached a peak with Johann Anderson's book *Nachrichten von Island* (1746) (Accounts from Iceland) [etc.] from the mid-eighteenth century. Anderson, a merchant and mayor in early eighteenth-century Hamburg, never visited Iceland but based his book on other sources. According to him, Iceland was the true dystopia of Europe: a place of ugliness, misery and evil, where barbarism prevailed in a nature that was more like Hell than an environment for living creatures. According to him, the 'Laplanders' were the people to whom the Icelanders could best be compared (Anderson 1748: 136-137).

Another tradition

On the other hand, there is also a very different tradition in describing Iceland, according to which the country is even depicted as a utopia of Arcadian paradisaic abundance, with reference to Christian legends. This tradition can be traced back all the way to antiquity, to the Greek legends of the Hyperboreans in the far North, who lived to old age in abundance and ease (see e.g. *Reallexikon für Antike und Christentum*, 16, 1994). As early as the eleventh century, the German cleric Adam of Bremen connected the Icelanders to this tradition, which can be traced up to the present day (Boas 1948: 52).[3]

3   The American anthropologist George Boas mentions this in his book *Essays on Primitivism and Related Ideas in the Middle Ages*, 1948. Referring to the power of distance, he concludes the following: "Like so many other writers, of antiquity as well as of our time, the more remote the people whom Adam is describing, the more noble. Thus the Icelanders have the palm among his island tribes for virtue" (p. 52).

According to this tradition the Icelanders are healthy, live to advanced ages and there is so much food that it can hardly be stored. Examples of texts of this kind can be found in e.g. Peter Heylin's *Cosmographie* from 1666:

Iseland … yeeldeth neither Corn nor Trees … yet there is grass in such abundance, that the people are of opinion, that if they doe not sometimes keep their cattell from feeding, they are in danger to surfeit and dye with fulness. … The people for the most part, are of a plain and simple nature, living (as in the Golden Age) on that which Nature gives them, without help of Art, more than that making of Cheese and Butter. … They use neither Physick, nor Physitians, yet live so long (and probably the longer for it) that many of them attain to the age of 150 years and more. The women are exceedingly fair, but they know not how to attire themselves. (Heylin 1666: 495-496)

Comparing Heylin's blend of Arcadia and the Land of Cockaygne with Boorde's and Anderson's dystopia it becomes evident that these, and many other authors on Iceland up to the eighteenth century, were describing an island of wonders. Furthermore, the descriptions of this strange place clearly oscillated between two poles, negative and positive, dystopian and utopian, though the negative side dominated at least until the late eighteenth century.

Borders

In his book *Dannemarks og Norges Beskrivelse*, (Description of Denmark and Norway) Ludvig Holberg tells a story from a stay in Italy during his youth:

Here I can't resist telling something that happened once to me when I was young. I was staying in Rome and occasionally met a fellow from Piedmont who had been reading something about Germany and the Nordic countries. He noticed that I had some familiarity with these countries, so he asked me if I had ever seen a Norwegian. When I told him that I was myself from Norway he was quite astonished and said after some reflection that my parents must then be of foreign origin, because he knew well that the Norwegian people were deformed and had faces that were more like pigs' heads. (Holberg 1729: 20)[4]

Holberg has an explanation for this 'misunderstanding'. People in the South writing on the countries in the North were confusing the 'real' Norwegians with the "Finnlapps", who, according to him, seemed as strange to the Norwegians as Greeks and Persians (Holberg 1729: 20). What Holberg is doing here is suggesting a differ-

4   Translation by the author.

ent border between civilization and barbarism than his Italian friend, with at least the southern part of the Scandinavian countries and Denmark within the border of civilization but the northern part, Lapland, beyond the frontier.

Holberg's suggestion was not without precedent. Even though the countries we now know as the Nordic countries or Scandinavia were in the eighteenth century still regarded by some as uncivilized, the trend was clear: to include the southern parts of these countries, or the kingdoms of the North, as they were often called, in the civilized world. The question was in fact not whether they were civilized, "but the degree of civility," as the British scholar Brian Dolan has put it (Dolan 2000: 181).

But where was the border, then, to be drawn between barbarism and civilization? From geographical works and travel accounts dating from the Middle Ages up to the mid-eighteenth century it is possible to trace this line, though it is sometimes obscured; outside the borders were the areas and islands we still regard as the periphery of the Nordic region, namely Iceland, the Faroe Islands and Greenland. Nova Zembla and Svalbard (Spitsbergen) were also commonly included on this list. To these islands, often named the "Northerne Ilands" or the islands in the Hyperborean sea, were frequently added the northernmost areas of Scandinavia and Russia, where only "wild pigmies" were living, as one source names the inhabitants of Lapland (see e.g. Münster 1628; Capel 1678; also Dolan 2000: 183). These areas were outside the civilized world, and the inhabitants had more in common with people in other parts of the world which explorers from the West had been 'discovering' over the previous two or three hundred years.

Image in transition

Iceland was outside the frontier of civilization, at least until the late eighteenth century, as Holberg illustrated quite well in his books on Nordic history, for example, telling the story of an Icelander who ate his shoes like pancakes (Holberg 1729: 31-32).[5] A brief look at geographical literature in the latter half of the eighteenth century, however, makes it clear that the image of Iceland was rapidly changing. The old authority, chiefly sixteenth-century publications mentioning Iceland, lost its hold on the imagination and a new one emerged after the middle of the eighteenth century.[6]

5   Translation by the author.

6   In addition to the sources already mentioned, authors such as Olaus Magnus' *Historia de Gentibus Septentrionalibus, Rome 1555* and Sebastian Münster's *Cosmographia* should be noted. As is well known, Olaus' *Historia* was for a long time one af the most important sources on the Nordic countries; the same can also be said of Münster's *Cosmographia*, published originally in 1544 but later republished in at least 46 editions in several languages.

SUMARLIDI R. ISLEIFSSON

These new canonical works gradually became the authoritative texts about the country. The first publication in this category is a book by the Dane Niels Horrebow, *Tilforladelige efterretninger om Island*, published in Danish in 1752 and later translated into English, French, Dutch and German (*The Natural History of Iceland*) (1758). The author wrote his book after spending a year in Iceland; his aim was to undermine Johann Anderson's *Nachrichten von Island* from 1747, mentioned above. Second, there is the encyclopedic work by the Icelanders Eggert Ólafsson and Bjarni Pálsson, *Reise igiennem Island*, a result of years of research and travel, originally published in Danish (1772) but later also published in the main European languages, two volumes totaling some 1100 pages with more than 50 illustrations (*Travels in Iceland*) (1805). The third work to be discussed here is the encyclopedic travel account *Letters on Iceland* by the Swede Uno von Troil, later bishop, who went to Iceland with the well-known British explorer Joseph Banks in 1772. In his book, Troil describes Icelandic nature, society and culture, drawing on many sources.

The aim of Horrebow's book can be illustrated with a quotation from the English version of it. He says he wanted to rescue Iceland

from the obscurity in which it has so long drooped; for so much the more, as there is scarce a country the world has less knowledge, or has conceived a less genuine idea of, chiefly by reason of the accounts published of it, which are far from being true, or to be depended upon. (Horrebow 1758: iii)

One of the examples he cites from Johann Anderson's book is Anderson's claim that a certain lake in Iceland burns regularly every two weeks. Horrebow's response to this is that "two opposite elements will not unite in this country no more than in any other" (Horrebow 1758: 20).

The books by Horrebow, Eggert Ólafsson and Bjarni Pálsson, and Troil were part of a new trend. All over Europe the authorities, sometimes under the auspices of scientific societies, were financing research and publications on faraway regions within and beyond Europe. As Brian Dolan has pointed out, information on these areas, on "climate, natural history, diet, migration, clothes, language, and physiological appearance was gathered in an attempt to explore the possibilities of some shared cultural ancestry amongst populations at different areas in the European frontier" (Dolan 2000: 70). This was done, as Dolan explains, in an attempt to "distinguish degrees of Europeanness" perceived as equivalent to civilization by the Eurocentric mind (Dolan 2000, 180). – With the works of Eggert Ólafsson and Bjarni Pálsson, Troil and Horrebow the foundation was laid for other authors to reconsider and reconstruct the image of Iceland, to find out whether the Icelanders were dwarfs or giants or more or less normal people.

GEYSER.

FIG. 5:

Geysir, the great Icelandic hot spring, attracted the interest of Joseph Banks and his company, among them Uno von Troil. Geysir was to be a token for the evolution of the image of Iceland in late eighteenth and nineteenth century, from the frightful Icelandic landscape to the sublime. Uno von Troil, 1780

118   SUMARLIDI R. ISLEIFSSON

It is impossible not to mention the changing attitude to the North in the eighteenth and nineteenth centuries. It was as if the traditional North-South polarity had suddenly been inverted. The North became positive and the South negative; the North was stable and the South treacherous; the North loved liberty, while servitude dominated in the South. Cold and difficult conditions were challenges which made people strong, while heat made people inactive and lazy. A changed and more positive image of the North (generally) was important. However, in the case of Iceland and other areas in the periphery this was not sufficient as the country had not been considered part of the (more or less) civilized North, but outside that frontier.

Late eighteenth century

Let us now investigate how writers on Iceland in the late eighteenth century depicted the country. What image, for example, did the explorer Joseph Banks have of Iceland? Banks came to Iceland in 1772 after having resigned from Captain Cook's second voyage to the Pacific. One of the books Banks might have read was a new edition of *A New Geographical and Historical Grammar* by Thomas Salmon (1772). From that book and several others from that period we can discern the image Banks and his company might have had of this "property of a Danish trading company" (Banks 1973: 197). Certainly, the island was no paradise,

....scarce any thing thriving there besides juniper shrubs, birch, and willow; the bread used here is made of dried fish ground to a powder; and the flesh eaten, beside mutton, is of bears, wolves, and foxes; but fish, with their roots and herbs, are their greatest dainties. (Salmon 1772: 255)

This description is in many ways not unlike the description of Iceland by Andrew Boorde from the mid-sixteenth century, mentioned above, and it cannot have seemed very attractive to Banks and his company. However, as we read further in Salmon's *Grammar* it becomes evident that the image of Iceland was changing. According to the author's description of the Icelanders,

they are Christians, and an honest, industrious, and hardy people; amusing themselves in singing, playing at chess, and other innocent amusements; they differ very little from the Danes and Norwegians from whom ... probably they were descended (Salmon 1772: 255).

Reading further in Salmon's book provides additional evidence for the classification of Icelanders; when describing the Norwegians, Salmon states that they are "in general comely; the men strong, robust, brave, and industrious, the women handsome and affable … not much unlike the people in many parts of England." The people of Lapland, however, are totally different. According to the author, these "human species of these cold and sterile climates seem very different from those to the Southward of them: the people … are ill-shaped, with large heads, and short, scarcely exceeding in stature five feet; and their intellect is very inconsiderable" (Salmon 1772: 256-257).

This new image is confirmed in many other publications in the late eighteenth century, e.g. in William Guthrie's, *A New System of Modern Geography*. According to him the Icelanders are

in general middle-sized, and well-made, though not very strong. They are an honest, well intentioned people, moderately industrious, and very faithful and obliging. Theft is seldom heard of among them. They are much inclined to hospitality, and exercise it as far as their poverty will permit. … their chief pastime consists in reading their history. (Guthrie 1782: 59)

It is evident that the frontier of civilization in the far North was on the move in the late eighteenth century; the image of Iceland was changing. Writers and explorers in this age of classification were reconsidering the situation of Iceland. Should the Icelanders be classified as Europeans or outside civilization, together with the Greenlanders and the Laplanders?

Awakening interest in the Sagas

In Joseph Banks' account of his visit to Thingvellir in Iceland, he describes the great rift Almannagjá as "romantick & pretty" but does not mention any connection with Icelandic history. What Banks was interested in was not primarily Icelandic culture or people; it was the volcanoes, hot springs and lava fields he wanted to see. Nonetheless, as can be seen from the above quotation from Guthrie's book, interest in Icelandic culture was awakening in the late eighteenth century. Uno von Troil, who, as mentioned above, was one of the members of Banks' crew, discusses these matters in a chapter in his book *Letters from Iceland*. According to him, Icelandic poetry was interesting but not great:

I will readily acknowledge they have no poem that can be proposed as pattern of wit and elegance; yet it cannot be denied, but that very sublime thoughts and expressions and sometimes very beautiful comparisons, are to be met with in them. (Troil 1780: 202)

SUMARLIDI R. ISLEIFSSON

Generally it can be said that the Icelandic cultural heritage and the *Sagas* became more and more visible from the late eighteenth century onwards. Icelandic cultural history had been discussed in earlier texts, for instance, by Saxo Grammaticus already in the twelfth century (Saxo 2000: 15). Later, the Icelander Arngrímur Jónsson and other writers in the sixteenth, seventeenth and eighteenth centuries – most of them Danes – introduced medieval Icelandic literature to an international reading public. Echoes from these texts often found their way into the geographical literature. Some of the *Sagas* and parts of the *Eddas* were translated into Latin and later into English, French, German and other European languages, though only a few such translations appeared in the seventeenth and eighteenth centuries (see e.g. Wawn 2000: 17-21).

Most important in this connection was the work by the Swiss author Paul Henry Mallet, published in French in 1763. Parts of it were later translated into English and edited by Thomas Percy, and published in 1770 under the title *Northern Antiquities*. A few years earlier, in 1763, Percy had also published translations of Old Icelandic texts, *Five Pieces of Runic Poetry, Translated from the Icelandic Language.* (see further Clunies Ross 1994: 107-117). Both works were well received and *Northern Antiquities* was later republished – and edited – many times, gaining status as an authority on Nordic cultural heritage for more than a century.

Other authors, presumably relying on Mallet, Percy and Uno von Troil, began to describe how poetry had flourished in Iceland in earlier times. The island was "one of the few countries in Europe, and the only one in the North, wherein the sciences were cultivated and held in esteem," as William Guthrie stated (Guthrie 1782: 60). Another author, William Coxe, in his book *Travels into Poland, Russia, Sweden, and Denmark*, stated how astonished he had been to discover that "Iceland, which was considered by the antients as the *Ultima Thule*, or the extremity of the world, and by us scarcely habitable, abounded in learning and science, at a time when Europe was involved in darkness" (Coxe 1784: 377).

The Hellas of the North

After an interval of twenty years because of the Napoleonic wars, travelers were again setting sail to Iceland around 1810 and after that, foreigners other than Danish officials or merchants were not the rare sight they had previously been in the country. Until the 1840s most of these travelers paid more attention to Icelandic nature than to its culture and cultural heritage, but from that time on there was a growing interest in these aspects of Iceland. One focus of attention was the language. In the process of determining how to classify the Icelanders or other nations on the frontiers, the language was estimated quite important, providing

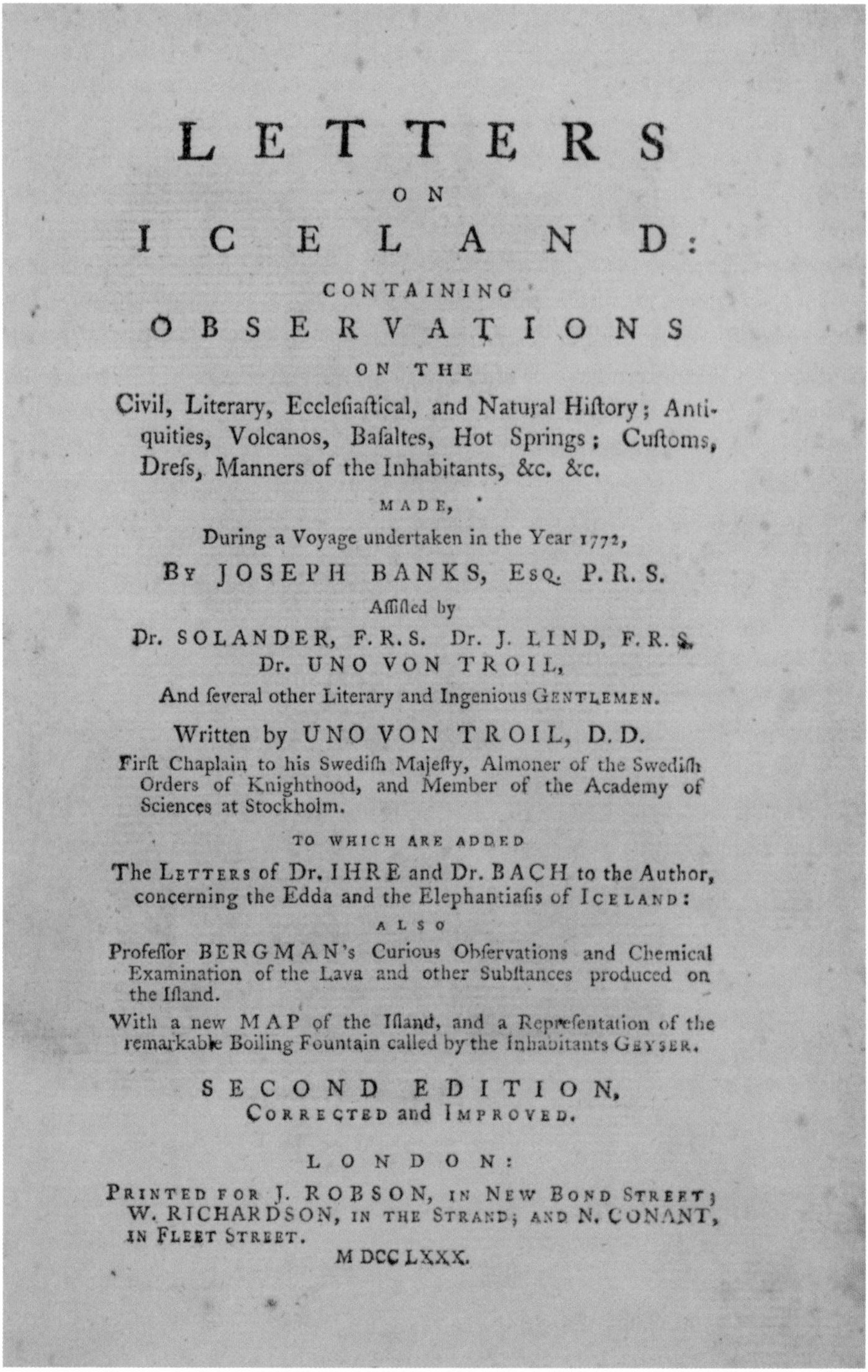

LETTERS

ON

ICELAND:

CONTAINING

OBSERVATIONS

ON THE

Civil, Literary, Ecclefiaftical, and Natural Hiftory; Antiquities, Volcanos, Bafaltes, Hot Springs; Cuftoms,
Drefs, Manners of the Inhabitants, &c. &c.

MADE,

During a Voyage undertaken in the Year 1772,

By JOSEPH BANKS, Esq. P.R.S.

Affifted by

Dr. SOLANDER, F.R.S. Dr. J. LIND, F.R.S.
Dr. UNO VON TROIL,

And feveral other Literary and Ingenious GENTLEMEN.

Written by UNO VON TROIL, D.D.

Firft Chaplain to his Swedifh Majefty, Almoner of the Swedifh
Orders of Knighthood, and Member of the Academy of
Sciences at Stockholm.

TO WHICH ARE ADDED

The LETTERS of Dr. IHRE and Dr. BACH to the Author,
concerning the Edda and the Elephantiafis of ICELAND:

ALSO

Profeffor BERGMAN's Curious Obfervations and Chemical
Examination of the Lava and other Subftances produced on
the Ifland.

With a new MAP of the Ifland, and a Reprefentation of the
remarkable Boiling Fountain called by the Inhabitants GEYSER.

SECOND EDITION,

CORRECTED and IMPROVED.

LONDON:

PRINTED FOR J. ROBSON, IN NEW BOND STREET;
W. RICHARDSON, IN THE STRAND; AND N. CONANT,
IN FLEET STREET.

M DCC LXXX.

FIG. 6:

The title page from the second edition of Uno von Troil's book, Letters from Iceland. The book was
the only publication from the Banks expedition to Iceland in 1772 and was for decades one of the
most important sources on the country. Uno von Troil, 1780.

SUMARLIDI R. ISLEIFSSON

fundamental information about the value of cultures of different nations. It was stated that the Icelandic language was

the most ancient and venerable of any spoken throughout Scandinavia, and being esteemed the most pure dialect of the Gothic, has engaged the attention of many profound scholars, who have considered it as the parent of the Norwegian, the Danish, and the Swedish, and in a great degree of the English. (*The European Delineator* 1815: 137)

As mentioned above, Uno von Troil was of the opinion that the *Sagas* and Old Icelandic poetry were admittedly interesting but could not be compared with the masterpieces of Greek and Roman antiquity. This view was to change in the early nineteenth century. With increasing nationalism and Romanticism, the significance of the *Sagas* and of the society of the *Saga* Age was emphasized in various texts, e.g. in Henry Wheaton's book *History of the Northmen* from 1831. Lyrically, he describes how "the flowers of poetry sprung up and bloomed amidst eternal ice and snows." And how the Icelanders with their "familiarity with the perils of the ocean, and with the diversified manners and customs of foreign lands, stamped their national character with bold and original features, which distinguished them from every other people" (Wheaton 1831: 54-55).

The North was in need of a counterpart to Herodotos and Homer; this was found in the *Sagas* and Snorri Sturluson, "Snorro in particular being styled the Herodotos of the North" (*The European Delineator*: 137). With this 'invention' the demand for translations of the *Sagas* increased rapidly. The first English version of *Heimskringla* was published in 1844 and of *Njáls Saga* in 1861, followed by several other translations of the *Sagas*. (Wawn 92: 156-157). The *Sagas* were also translated into German and other European languages; by the early twentieth century most of the *Sagas* had been published in German (Bjarnason 1999: 53-88).

As mentioned earlier, Joseph Banks found the Almannagjá rift in Thingvellir "romantic and pretty" but did not connect it in any way with Icelandic history. Ninety years later, in 1861, the rift was described as the "famous Almannagiá down which so many a free-born peasant-legislator of Iceland used to journey to the parliament; the kindred of those fine fellows, so unlike the slave-born founders of old Rome" (Metcalfe 1861: 66). When the well-known Viennese traveler Ida Pfeiffer came to Reykholt in Borgarfjörður, where Snorri Sturluson had lived, she "picked all the buttercups … on the grave" in order to "give pleasure to several of my countrywomen by offering them a floweret from the grave of the greatest of Icelandic poets" (Pfeiffer 1853: 130).

In the space of less than a century Iceland had become a place of pilgrimage. Interested members of the educated classes in Central and Northern Europe more and more often wrote of the country as a holy place "where the powerful genius of liberty, and the no less powerful genius of poetry, have given brilliant proofs of the energies of the human mind at the farthest confines of animated nature" (Malte-Brun 1834: 193). The most holy places should be visited, places like Thingvellir, Reykholt and the sites of *Njáls Saga*.

Many travelers in the nineteenth century continued to describe the "filthy dens" of the Icelanders, "infested with vermin to a degree which can certainly not be surpassed, except in the dwellings of the Greenlanders and Laplanders" (Pfeiffer 1853: 24). In other words, the dystopia still had its place in the literature on Iceland – and it still does. But it was not the dominant image in the nineteenth century; the dominant image was that of medieval Iceland, a kind of 'Ideal City', or simply the Hellas of the North.[7] Iceland was described as a society of spiritual and physical superiority where all the best qualities of the German race were united, "a race whom their admirers compare with the Spartan in deliberate valour and mother wit; with the Athenian in daring and genius" (Metcalfe 1861: 393). According to accounts from this period the medieval Icelanders had succeeded in creating a culture and literature that were unrivaled in the entire Teutonic world, the main explanation for this achievement being all the noble people of Norwegian and Celtic origin who had colonized Iceland and formed a society there. The *Sagas* were the key to this unique society: they showed the real image of medieval Iceland, as reflected in all the travel accounts, travel handbooks and newspapers.

The admirers of and visitors to Iceland were aware that much had changed in Iceland since the Golden Age, when the Icelanders "were the bravest warriors, the boldest sailors, and the most obstinate heathens," as Frederick Howell described the medieval Icelanders in his book *Icelandic Pictures* from 1893 (Howell 1893: 20). Fortunately, it was possible to discern in other countries the same spirit as once had been found in medieval Iceland, as the Englishwoman Elisabeth J. Oswald told her countrymen in the late nineteenth century:

…we have inherited, with a strain of their race, their spirit of enterprise and their love of the sea. Everything relating to them has therefore a special interest for us; and when we inquire into their history we find that Iceland holds the key to the knowledge we desire to gain. (Oswald 1882: 280)

---

7   This expression, "Hellas of the North," is not my invention. References to Ancient Greece are common in texts on Iceland in literature of the late nineteenth and early twentieth centuries; see e.g. Poestion, Josef Calasanz 1882, *Aus Hellas, Rom und Thule. Cultur- und Literaturbilder,* Leipzig: Verlag von Wilhelm Friedrich.

Elizabeth J. Oswald is typical for many of the travelers that went to Iceland in the mid- and late nineteenth centuries. They were interested in the past in the same way as travelers to Greece at the same time. According to Brian Dolan, travelers' visits to Greece were "a quest to discover *classical* antiquity, not modern Greece, which was thought to hold value for illuminating Western values. Those born and bred in the East were irrelevant – almost transparent – in travelers' accounts" (Dolan 2000: 126). Although it would be an overstatement to say that this was the case for the travelers to Iceland, there was a tendency in that direction. Writers on Iceland were well aware that much had changed in Iceland since the old days, and, as in the case of Greece, the Icelandic past was used to support "national claims to superiority" (Dolan 2000: 179). At least some of the Iceland travelers were, however, interested in the lives of contemporary Icelanders. Even though they were sure that much had changed, some of the "golden" spirit was still to be found there:

The general diffusion of knowledge which took place in Iceland during the period of its prosperity, is still continued in a degree unknown in any other country. It often happens that travellers may find their guide address them with fluency and elegance in Latin. During the long winter nights the reading of the ancient Sagas and the classical writings of antiquity is a favourite occupation with families. (*Hand-Book for Travellers* 1858: 100)

Many of those who were interested in Iceland in the nineteenth and twentieth centuries, not least writers and politicians, were sure that Iceland and the Icelanders would one day rise again. In the first decades of the twentieth century, not least in Nazi Germany, where Iceland was to play a significant role, it was claimed, stating the superiority of the Icelanders, that with the advent of independence Iceland should and could again become the ideal society it once had been. (Prinz 1935: 82)

Final remarks

For centuries Iceland was the dystopia of Europe. It was far away from the main centers of Europe, which increased the otherness of the country, it was an island in the far North, beyond the frontier of civilization. The change in the image of the country in the eighteenth and nineteenth centuries was nearly unbelievable: this evil island in the North was transferred, politically and culturally, from the periphery to the center of the world. With the rise of Romanticism and nationalism in the nineteenth century, Iceland became a place where "wild and savage grandeur everywhere predominates," as Friedrich Howell wrote in 1893 (Howell 1893: 31). This was combined with the wish to find the "Teutonic cradle," a place which everyone of the Teutonic race could read about or visit, becoming acquainted with their origins and their so-called German or Teutonic qualities. Thus, instead of being at the world's end, Iceland became an insular magnet, a center like Jerusalem, Athens and Rome, an important place of pilgrimage. Hence, a utopia based on the *Sagas* emerged in the nineteenth century, replacing the dystopian view of Iceland that had been dominant for centuries. German, British and other interested scholars, writers and travelers in the nineteenth century discovered and found in Iceland what they were looking for, a counter-Rome, a new Athens or Hellas of the North.

References

Adam, Alexander 1797: *A Summary of Geography and History, both Ancient and Modern; Containing, an Account of the Political State, and Principal Revolutions of the Most Illustrious Nations in Ancient and Modern Times* [etc.]. London: A. Strahan; T. Cadell; W. Davies.

Anderson, Johann 1746: *Nachrichten von Island, Grönland und der Strasse Davis, zum wahren Nutzen der Wissenschaften und der Handlung* [etc.]. Hamburg: Georg Christian Grund Buchdr.

Anderson, Johann 1748: *Johann Andersons, fordum første Borgemester i Hamborg ... Efterretninger om Island, Grønland og Straat Davis* [etc.]. København: Hos Gabriel Christian Rothe.

Banks, Joseph 1973: The Journals of Joseph Banks's Voyage up Great Britain's West Coast to Iceland and to the Orkney Isles July to October, 1772. *Proceedings of the American Philosophical Society* 117. Philadelphia: 186-226.

Bjarnason, Óskar 1999: Þegar Íslendingar urðu forfeður Þjóðverja. Eddur, Íslendingasögur og þjóðmenntastefna Diedrichsforlagsins 1911-1930. *Skírnir* 173, 2. Reykjavík: 53-58.

Boas, George 1948: *Essays on Primitivism and Related Ideas in the Middle Ages.* Baltimore: The John Hopkins Press.

Boorde, Andrew 1870: *The Fyrst Boke of the Introduction of Knowledge.* London: Early English Text Society.

Capel, Rudolff 1678: *Norden Oder Zu Wasser und Lande im Eise und Snee mit Verlust Blutes und Gutes zu Wege gebrachte und fleissig beschriebene Erfahrung und Vorstellung des Norden.* Hamburg: Bey Johann Nanmann.

Clunies Ross, Margaret 1994: Percy and Mallet. The Genesis of Northern Antquites. *Sagnaþing helgað Jónasi Kristjánssyni sjötugum 10. apríl 1994.* Reykjavík: Hið íslenska bókmenntafélag, 107-117.

Coxe, William 1784: *Travels into Poland, Russia, Sweden, and Denmark. Interspersed with Historical Relations and Political Inquiries,* 1-3. vol. Dublin: Printed for S. Price, R. [etc.]

Davis, J.C. 1984: Science and Utopia: The History of a Dilemma. *Nineteen Eighty-Four: Science between Utopia and Dystopia.* Eds. Everett Mendelsohn and Helga Nowotny. Boston: 21-49.

Dolan, Brian 2000: *Exploring European Frontiers. British Travellers in the Age of Enlightenment.* London: Macmillan Press Ltd.

Feldbæk, Ole 1991: Skole og identitet 1789-1848. Lovgivning og lærebøger. *Dansk Identitetshistorie 2. Et yndigt land 1789-1848.* København: C.A. Reitzels Forlag.

Gillies, John 1994: *Shakespeare and the Geography of Difference.* Cambridge: Cambridge University Press.

Guthrie, William 1782: *A New System of Modern Geography: or, a Geographical, Historical, and Commercial Grammar; and Present*

SUMARLIDI R. ISLEIFSSON

State of the Several Kingdoms of the World. London: Printed for C. Dilly and G. Robinson.

Hand-Book for Travellers in Denmark, Norway, Sweden and Iceland. 1858. London: John Murray.

Heylin, Peter 1666: Cosmographie, in Four Books, Containing the Chorograpie and Historie of the World, and all the Principal Kingdoms, Provinces, Seas and Isles thereof. London: Printed for Anne Seile and are to be sold at her Shop.

Holberg, Ludvig 1729: Dannemarks og Norges Beskrivelse ved Ludvig Holberg. København: Trykt hos Johan Jørgen Høpffner.

Horrebow, Niels 1758: The Natural History of Iceland. Containing a Particular and Accurate Account of the Different Soils, Burning Mountains, Minerals, Vegetables, Metals, Stones, Beasts, Birds, and Fishes; together with the Disposition, Customs, and Manners of Living of the Inhabitants. London: Printed for A. Linde [etc.].

Howell, Frederick W.W. 1893: Icelandic Pictures. Drawn with Pen and Pencil. London: John Murray.

Ísleifsson, Sumarliði R. 1996: Ísland, framandi land. Reykjavík: Mál og menning.

Jónsson, Arngrímur 1985: Crymogæa. Þættir úr sögu Íslands. Reykjavík: Sögufélagið.

Kumar, Krishna 1987: Utopia and Anti-Utopia in Modern Times. Oxford: Blackwell Publiacations.

Leerssen, Joep 2005: Images – information – national identity and national stereotype. http://cf.hum.uva.nl/images/

Malte-Brun, M. 1834: A System of Universal Geography, or a Description of All the Parts of the World. Boston: Samuel Walker.

Metcalfe, Frederick 1861: The Oxonian in Iceland; or, Notes of Travel in that Island in the Summer of 1860, with Glances at Icelandic Folk-Lore and Sagas. London: Longman, Green, Longman and Roberts.

Münster, Sebastian 1628: Cosmographia, Das ist: Beschreibung der ganzen Welt. Basel: Bey den Henricpetrinischen.

Oswald, Elizabeth 1882: By Fell and Fjord or Scenes and Studies in Iceland. London: William Blackwood and Sons.

Ólafsson, Eggert; Pálsson, Bjarni 1772: Vice-Lavmand Eggert Olafsens og Land-Physici Biarne Povelsens Reise igiennem Island. Sorøe: Videnskabernes Sælskab i Kiøbenhavn.

Pfeiffer, Ida 1853: Visit to Iceland and the Scandinavian North. London: Ingram, Cooke, and Co.

Poestion, Josef Calasanz 1882: Aus Hellas, Rom und Thule. Cultur- und Literaturbilder. Leipzig: Verlag von Wilhelm Friedrich.

Prinz, Reinhard 1935: Geist und Geschichte des isländischen Volkes. In Heering, Walther, ed. Das unbekannte Island. Ein Fürer in das Land der Edda. Harzburg: 36-84.

Reallexikon für Antike und Christenthum, vol. 16. 1994. Stuttgart: A. Hiersemann.

Romm, James S. 1992: The Edges of the Earth in Ancient Thought: Geography, Exploration, and Fiction. Princeton: Princeton University Press.

Salmon, Thomas 1772: A New Geographical and Historical Grammar; Containing the True Astronomical and Geographical Knowledge of the Terraqueous Globe: And also the Modern State of the Several Kingdoms of the World. London: Printed for W. Johnson [etc.].

Saxo, G. 2000: Saxos Danmarks historie. København: Gads Forlag.

Sigurðsson, Haraldur 1991: Ísland í skrifum erlendra manna um þjóðlíf og náttúru landsins. Ritaskrá (Writings of Foreigners Relating to the Nature and the People of Iceland. A Bibliography). Reykjavík: Landsbókasafn Íslands.

The European Delineator: Containing Brief, but Interesting Descriptions of Russia, Sweden, Denmark, Norway, &c. &c. &c. 1815. Leeds: S. & T. Topham.

Troil, Uno von 1780: *Letters on Iceland: Containing Observations on the Civil, Literary, Ecclesiastical, and Natural History; Antiquities, Volcanos, Basaltes, Hot Springs; Customs, Dress, Manners of the Inhabitants* [etc.]. London: W. Richardson.

Wawn, Andrew 2000: *The Vikings and the Victorians. Inventing the Old North in Nineteenth-Century Britain*. London: D. S. Brewer.

Wheaton, Henry 1831: *History of the Northmen*. London: John Murray.

Wright, John Kirtland 1965: *The Geographical Lore of the Time of the Crusades. A Study in the History of Medieval Science and Tradition in Western Europe*. New York: Dover Publications.

Original Quotes

Jeg kand ikke forbigaa her at fortælle en ting, som mig udi min ungdom er vederfaren. Da jeg opholdt mig til Rom, og af en hendelse kom i selskab med en Piemonteser, der havde læst adskilligt om Tydskland og de nordiske lande, og same Piemonteser fornam, at jeg havde nogen kundskab derom, spurte han mig: Om jeg ikke nogen tid havde seet en Normand, da jeg nu sagde ham, at jeg var selv fra Norge, forundrede han sig ikke lidet derover, og endelig efter nogen betænkning svarede, at jeg maatte da være fød af fremmede foreldre; Thi han vidste vel at norske folk vare vanskabte, og havde ansigter der lignede mere svinehoveder.

Saaledes har en iislandsk kiøbmand engang fortalt mig, at han saae en Iislænder tage sine skoe af føderne, og at æde denne op, som det kunde have været et par pandekager, og da jeg ved rysten med hovedet gav tilkiende min vantroe, besejlede han historien med en eed, saa jeg der udover ikke havde et ord at sige derimod.

SUMARLIÐI R. ISLEIFSSON

KAREN KLITGAARD POVLSEN

Travelling Mythologies of the North around 1760
Molesworth, Mallet, Gerstenberg and several others
in Copenhagen

North of Copenhagen near Hillerød, the Danish royal palace of Fredensborg ('palace of peace') is situated in a baroque park with rococo trimmings. During the years 1984-2002, the park was reconstructed by the Danish state: the great old romantic lime trees were cut down, new formally cut trees were planted, and the old ruined sculptures overgrown with algae and moss were replaced by bright copies.[1] A neoclassical, Roman-inspired column with a golden ball at the top, drawn by the Danish neoclassical sculptor Johannes Wiedewelt, was placed at the centre,[2] with alleys extending from the column in a cross and terraces were placed in half circles around and about the column, three terraces on the right and two on the left. Behind the park are big broadleaf trees and groups of fir, so that 'nature' surrounds the park and farmland is not visible. In this amphitheatre made in a former gravel pit, approximately 60 out of originally 70 sculptures have been placed so that they all face the column in the middle, which represents the Danish absolute monarchy and King Frederik V. The design of the park, but not the sculptures in it, was borrowed from the Bosquet des Domes at Versailles (Lund 2004: 68-69).

The Italian-style palace was built in the years after 1719 by King Frederik V, who reigned from 1746 to 1766. He wanted the castle to be a celebration of peace after the peace treaty on the great Nordic war had been signed in 1720. During the years around 1750 the park was laid out by the French architect Nicolas Henri Jardin. Frederik V stayed here during the summer – a habit continued by his queen, Juliane Marie, after she became a widow until she died in 1796. After her death, the castle and the park were neglected for many years (Scavenius 1997: 145ff.).

---

1   For a more detailed description see Priskorn 2004, and Sanders in this anthology. For a very fine introduction to Nordmandsdalen see Skousbøll 2004.

2   If Wiedewelt himself or Grund cut the column is not testified. For more on Wiedewelts statues at Fredensborg see Scavenius 1997: 117, Bukdahl 1993.

In 1764, King Frederic V placed the first sandstone sculptures in the park. These were made by the German sculptor Johann Gottfried Grund. The Danish sculptor Johannes Wiedewelt already had many neoclassical works represented there. Wiedewelt is regarded as one of the first neoclassical sculptors to base his work on the theories of the German art historian Johann Joachim Winckelmann, whom he had come close to during a stay in Italy in the 1750s. Some of the works at Fredensborg, like the statue *Forblommet Antik* (Equivocal antiquity), however, related not only to Greek and Roman antiquity but also to Nordic mythology (Scavenius 119-112). This theme was highly accented by Grund's statues. They were based on a number of small figures, originally cut in wood, later in walrus tooth by a Norwegian post coach, Jørgen Garnaas (Priskorn 2004: 10-15). He had sent a few of his figures as a present to the Danish-Norwegian king, who liked them and ordered them as large-scale sandstone statues. Over the years Grund made 70 sculptures: 60 Norwegian fishermen and women and 10 fishermen from the Faeroe Islands: plump, ordinary people in their daily clothes with utensils from everyday life and work placed in a refined French baroque park. During the twentieth century, the original sculptures were ruined by the weather and 70 new sculptures of harder sandstone from the former GDR were made for the reconstructed baroque park. Today, the original 'originals'are placed in museums and storerooms and are no longer considered bad taste, which they were for centuries.

It may thus be said that three historical narratives meet in Hillerød: the northern way of life consisting of simple people's hard work (Grund), the southern hedonism in the park, which was developed in the aristocracy and at the royal courts, and Wiedewelt's neoclassical, refined works balancing between antiquity and northern mythology. In this way, the design of castle, park and statues represents a mediation between simple, harsh northern ways of life and southern refinements. The question is whether this kind of third way was possible. Was this idea which was fostered by an absolute king shared by other artists and poets of the time?

I shall attempt to answer this question in the following discussion of the status of Nordic mythology around 1750. But first I shall briefly introduce the context for my questions: the European image of Denmark-Norway around 1700.

Molesworth: *An Account of Denmark 1693*

In 1693, Robert Molesworth (1656-1725), the Anglo-English diplomat at the Danish court, published a critique of Danish society and absolutism in his book *An Account of Denmark as It was in the Year 1692*. Molesworth's book created a sensation in Denmark and abroad because of its pointed criticism of the Danish court. During its first year, it was published in four English editions and was re-issued several times until 1738 (Brasch, 1879: 62ff.). Several translations were made, and the book was even published in French in many editions until 1714 and again in Desroches de Parthenay's *Histoire de Dannemarc* (Amsterdam 1730). Voltaire[3] and Montesquieu (*De l'Esprit des Lois* 1748) referred – explicitly and implicitly – to Molesworth, and in the first part of the eighteenth century it became the standard reference to Denmark-Norway or to absolutism as a specific form of government. Many essays appeared in Danish and German periodicals criticising Molesworth's image of Denmark. However, in Molesworth's preface he stresses a general dichotomy between South and North by mentioning Italy and Greenland and thereby establishing a contrast between freedom and tyranny:

But as an *Italian* that passes a Winter in *Groenland*, will soon be convinc'd through his want of the kind Influences of that glorious Planet, how much Misery he endures, in companion of those who dwell in his Native Country, so he that knows by *Experience* the trouble of languishing Sickness, or the loss of his *Liberty*, will presently begin to have a right esteem of that which formerly he scarce thought worth his notice (preface).

Molesworth presents himself as an observer speaking from experience, but in reality he had never travelled to Greenland. The dichotomy he sketches between North and South repeats the seventeenth-century stereotype of the greatness of the Arcadian South and the barbarism of the cold North that would change during the eighteenth century. We have to consider, however, that Molesworth was an Englishman who had lived in Ireland at his estate, which he had lost because he and his equals did not succeed in importing the English revolution from 1688 to Ireland. Molesworth thus fled Ireland and the position as envoy at the Danish court was given to him by the English King. When he arrived, Molesworth was an inexperienced diplomat with a political vision. His first deed was to protest against the etiquette at the francophile and ceremonial court, and he experienced three difficult years in Denmark. Absolutism as he saw it at the Danish court and around the Swedish king imitated absolutism practised at the French court. It was a southern model in translation, but in Molesworth's book it represented the barbaric North itself.

The preface is rather long and mostly deals with England. England is declared the only democratic and free nation in Europe. Molesworth wanted to export the English revolution and the role of the monarchy to Scandinavia and his book was thus an apology for the English revolution as another version of antique 'democracy' and an attack on the French system of centralised absolutism, which the kings in Sweden and Denmark-Norway had adopted. Molesworth is an early voice

3   See Dillmann 1996: 19: "La lumiere du Nord".

in the choir criticising the French system of government and culture that would dominate the European debate in the eighteenth century, culminating in the discussions of the French revolution in the 1790s (Klitgaard Povlsen 2005: 18-22). He does so in the traditional dichotomy of North and South even if this dichotomy opposes his argument.

Half a century later, the French philosopher Charles Secondat de Montesquieu also criticised absolutism in *De l'Esprit des Lois* (1748), but following the tradition from Cornelius Tacitus's *Germania* (from around year 90), he turned the North-South dichotomy upside-down and saw the North as the smithy of the tools meant to break the southern chains of serfdom. Montesquieu's view was mechanical: the climate had softened the people in the South but strengthened them in the North. Tacitus's work had been rediscovered in the fifteenth century, and in the years after 1700 it spread rapidly in Europe through translations (Greenway 1977: 65ff.). Tacitus wrote about the "baritus" (barditen) songs and about the solid, fair-haired, blue-eyed men with brave and beautiful wives (www.heimkringla.no/dansk/tacitus 2006) and placed them in present-day Germany. In northern Germany, a small tongue of land was inhabited by the Cimbrians, who were the biggest warriors of all the Germans and constantly fighting with the Romans (Tacitus: chapter 37). The people from the North resisting and conquering the Romans from the South became an important theme in the arts.

Already in the 1690s, the German writer Daniel Kasper von Lohenstein wrote 3000 pages on *Arminius* – later called Hermann in Germany – who fought the Romans in Teutoburger Wald in the first century of our time. In 1740, the German J. E. Schlegel published his drama *Hermann* in Copenhagen. And Klopstock's *Hermanns Schlacht* (1769, followed by two more Hermann pieces in 1784 and 1787) attracted great popularity, as did H. v. Kleist's romantic drama *Hermanns-schlacht* from 1808. The English historian Edward Gibbons also described the clash between the brave men from the North and the softened Roman soldiers in his *Decline and Fall of the Roman Empire* (1776-88). It was a theme that prevailed through the second half of the eighteenth century.

In 1753, however, the Norwegian-Danish author Ludvig Holberg (1684-1754) opposed Montesquieu. As a historian Holberg looked for cause and effect more than chronology (Greenway 1977: 87), he saw the king as dependent on alliances with the aristocracy and as a result on a balance of power with the aristocracy (Østergaard 1997: 31). But it was the young Swiss teacher of French at the Royal Academy in Copenhagen Paul-Henri Mallet who at last created a positive picture of Danish absolutism satisfying the European intellectual need for mythic origins in his work of Danish History, commissioned by the Danish government and in particular by the German-speaking Prime Minister J. H. E. Bernstorff (Greenway

1977: 87). Soon after Mallet, two other Swiss writers, André Roger and Elie Salo-mon-Francois Reverdil, contributed to the picture of the ancient people from the North with an original instinct for freedom in *Lettres sur Dannemarc 1-2* (Letters on Denmark, 1757-64). In 1756, Mallet paraphrased some of the Nordic myths in French, and when he was translated into English and edited by Bishop Percy (1770) – who had already published *Five Pieces of Runic Poetry* in 1763, which heavily draws upon Mallet – the bonfire was soon burning brighter than anyone could have imagined twenty years before.

Mallet's northern antiquity

In 1934 – before the Second World War – Thor A. Beck, professor of French liter-ature in New York, summarized the current political and aesthetic developments:

The theory which holds that a reign of Freedom and Equality was planted on the ruins of the Roman Empire by barbarians who issued from the womb of nations in the North is *eo ipso* anti-classic and romantic; and has political bearings which vary according to the views of the nationality of its proponents. It is pro-Scandinavian and nationalistic in Scandina-via. It is pro-German and racial in Germany. It is pro-Germanic and anti-nationalistic in France. (Beck, 1934: 116)

Romanticism subscribed to the free spirited genius from the North and was joined by a new nationalism in northern Europe. For a brief period, the utopias of the North presented the possibility of a third way between cosmopolitanism and na-tionalism, stressing the free peasants in the northern hemisphere like the Nord-mandsdalen [the Norwegian Valley] did at Fredensborg, or combining the Nordic elements with antique mythology as Wiedewelt did. This utopia was nevertheless soon fragmented and domesticated in many small utopias of the pasts of the many new or old nations in the northern parts of Europe.

When Mallet's book was published in the 1750s, some basics on Nordic mythol-ogy were already known, and this contributed to its success (Kliemann-Geisinger 2005: 73, Böldl 2000: 136-138, Ross 1998). Mallet followed Montesquieu's theories of climate and migration and the idea of the North as the origin of European democ-racy. Mallet described how tribes had left Asia or Scythia and headed towards the northwest, where they lived so well that the areas became overpopulated. A new migration towards the South then began: "like a tree full of vigour, extending long branches all over Europe" (Mallet 1847: 56).[4] People became softened by their easy living conditions in the South, while humans in the northern regions were still healthy and brave because of the cold climate there. At last Rome was defeated by conquerors from the North with

…that spirit of independence and equality, that elevation of soul, that taste for rural and military life, which both the one and the other had originally derived from the same common source, but which were then among the Romans breathing their last." (Ibid.: 57)

So the people from the North were seen as the healthy root of the decadent Romans. Mallet did not distinguish between Teutons and Celtics; he assumed that in ancient times only one worldwide mythology existed, which then developed different branches according to the climate and living conditions of the tribes and people. The Norse monotheistic mythology was therefore a result of the climate: simple, strong and healthy! In Mallet's version, Odin arrived in Denmark 70 years before our time (Ibid.: 61); after twenty years he had conquered all of Scandinavia, which he reformed into a kind of 'original' democracy. To Mallet, Odin represented a historical fact *and* an ancient deity. The mythology was widespread:

These are the principal heads of that ancient religion which probably prevailed for many ages through the greatest part of the north of Europe, and doubtless among several nations of Asia. When it began to lose the most beautiful features of its original purities….is difficult to decide. (Ibid.: 90)

Mallet followed Montesquieu closely in his construction of a 'back to nature' or 'back to the original mythology' version of ancient Norse mythology, just as he followed Montesquieu in his conception of history as progressive: the northern mythological origin was not depicted as a golden age, but as the cultural foundations that could still appear in glimpses. Mallet's version was the basis for numerous histories, mythologies, poems, elegies and so on. As Thor J. Beck notes, Mallet himself was split between enjoying this mythology and considering it to be tales for children with traces of enlightened deism. But when he experienced the success of his book and of *Ossian* in the 1760s, he wrote three more volumes of ancient

---

4   The references are to Percy's English translation and edited version of Mallet' *Northern Antiquities* (2. vol. 1770).

Danish history – and it was the second volume on the ancient myths that was most acknowledged in Europe.[5] What Beck concludes in 1934 is true for both editions:

Mallet tries to follow a middle road and be both Pro-Scandinavian and Pro-German, or rather Pro-Gothic. By doing so he appears to be in accord with contemporary, pre-revolutionary Pro-Germanism. (Beck 1934: 116)

Because Mallet did not distinguish between Celtic, German, Dane or Teuton and because he followed the middle ground as a kind of third way, he invited the reader to see Norse mythology and past as an original example of a united northern Europe with a common ancient language. When *Ossian* was published in 1760 the poems of MacPherson were received as another example of this common origin. For the poetry of the 1760s a new world opened up: a fresh and 'natural' mythology that appealed to sublime descriptions of Nordic nature from Ireland to Asia.

Homesickness for a lost past

At the end of May 1769, the young Johann Gottfried Herder (1744-1803), who had studied with Kant in Königsberg, travelled by ship towards Copenhagen from Riga in Latvia. At the time, Riga was an important city with a German cultural and economic elite, but Herder opens his rather peculiar travelogue by describing how boring Riga and his life as a teacher had become. He had to go away but he did not know his goals. The travelogue he writes on the ship is a search for a new beginning in himself, so the travelogue is more a work of introspection than extrospection. When Herder eventually reached Helsingør, he therefore hardly wrote anything in his diary of his experiences of the North; he only made some statements revealing that he had read important works in Latin of the North and of the Edda.

Herder had not only read Pontoppidan and other learned writings of the North, he had also read Mallet's introduction to Nordic history and myths. A review of the German version of the French original by Mallet was printed in the *Königsberger Gelehrten und Politischen Zeitungen auf das Jahr 1765*.[6] The review is very positive; Herder views Mallet as being on a par with Dalin from Sweden, Hume from Britain, Giannoni from Naples and Salignac from Poland – and wishes

---

5   Mallet's oeuvre:
     1755: *Introduction à l'historie de Dannemarc*, 1756
     1756: *Monumens de la mythologie et de la poesésie de Celtes et particulièrement des anciens Scandinaves*
     1758-77: *Historie de Dannemarc* 1-3. I quote from the Danish translation from 1755 and Percy's translation with commentaries, which is also commented by Bohn, the editor of the 1847 edition of *Mallet's Northern Antiquities*.

6   The Königsberg learned and political newspaper. The review was reprinted in Suphan 1877, 1: 73-77.

that Russia and Germany also had such history writers. But the best parts concern northern mythology:

The lovers of antiquities are here led to the solemn field, filled with honourable monuments of the Scandinavians and we feel our German blood, that our old Germans were brethren of the brave Danes, their religion, laws, customs and habits. (Suphan 1: 73-74)

The ocean between the Baltic and Scandinavia was the dystopian version of the North upon which the small vessel with Herder on board balanced: "Here the cold North seems to be the birth place both of the sea monsters and of barbarians, human giants and the destroyers of the world" (Herder 1976 (1769): 15).[7] Amidst this angst and existential crisis the question is "Was North or South, Morning or Evening the *Vagina Hominum*?" (Ibid.). In short, where was the origin of humanity? Following Tacitus and Montesquieu's *De l'Esprit de Lois* from 1748, Herder chose a 'both/and' solution and replaced the dystopian view of the North with a utopian one:

Should this be the case, I see two currents, the first one coming from the Orient gently lowering itself towards southern Europe via Greece and Italy – this one also invented a gentle, southern religion, a poetry of imagination, music, art, modesty, science of the eastern south. The second current goes from Asia by the north into Europe; wherefrom it floods over the first one. Germany belongs to the second current, so it should be only reasonable in its fatherland to study this history of the north.... (Ibid.: 15-16)

Herder regarded Germany as part of the North, thereby creating an excuse for studying the history of the North – i.e. German history.

Herder did not, however, immediately follow up on this. On the contrary, the majority of his travelogue of 1769 deals with the French tradition of art and aesthetics: "France: its literary era has ended: The century of Louis is over; over are the Montesquieus, D'Alemberts, Voltaires: one lives on ruins" (Ibid.: 92). France imported art and literature from Spain and Italy – so it was not originally French but southern and of foreign origin. For Herder, the only original thinker in France was Montesquieu, who pointed towards the North (Ibid.: 95-96); other French philosophers were victims of "galanterie" ("gallantry"; Ibid.: 107-108), they were excellent rhetors, but

---

7   All the quotations from Herder's travelogue are translated by the author of this article. Parts of the text are available in English: F.M. Barnard 1969: *J. G. Herder and Social and Political Culture*. Cambridge: C. U. P.

...where is genius? Truth? Strength? Modesty? The French philosophy lies in the language, its riches in abstractions, is *learned*, thus only dimly decided, thus used over and over: thus no philosophy any more. (Ibid.: 109; Herder's italics)

The French were not able to be "ein Vorbild Europens" ("a model for Europe"; Ibid.: 121). France was 'not', while the North was 'hot'. As soon as Herder left his ship in Painbeuf, he therefore regretted only having visited Helsingør and Kronborg but not Copenhagen. In Copenhagen he would have liked to have visited "Der Geist Klopstocks" (The spirit of Klopstock: 118), Resewitz, Cramer, and last, but not least

Gerstenberg... to sing about the bards and skalds, to embrace him because of his love and funny sketches in the Hypochondrit, to read with him his letters on the Remarkable, to talk about Hamann, Störze, Klotz etc. and to make sparks, to a new spirit of literature, beginning from the Danish end of Germany and refreshing the country. To write then about the skalds and to disappear to Kiel into the Arab language. That was my first period; shall I obtain it in France? (118-19)

The attraction in Denmark, or "the Danish end of Germany", was the Germans, especially Gerstenberg and his Nordic poems and visions, which shall be considered below. As we have seen, the immediate answer to Herder's question was no. But when at last Herder arrived in Nantes he met a young Swede, Koch, who was the incarnation of a northern personality: "This young man had great taste for truth, good and the really beautiful" (Ibid.: 133). They met in a library, but the young man is not a man of reading; he is a man of doing, concerned with reality rather than rhetoric, and this becomes a new kind of the Nordic utopia for Herder. The man from the North in the South is a man of the future because he wants to learn from reality rather than books – like Herder and the Germans in Copenhagen. On the last pages, Herder then describes a book that he plans to write, a book on a pedagogy of the senses aimed at preserving the child in man until old age. He seems to have read J.J. Rousseau's *Education of Emile* (1762). Herder's goal in the travelogue seems to be to re-educate the German-speaking parts of Europe to enable them to imagine and thus preserve their childhood and pasts.

I dwell on Herder because he depicts a general turn in European thinking, but also because in his later works he lays the groundwork for German Nationalism.[8] Herder 'comes home to Germany' when he replaces the South with the North. In between North (Latvia/Denmark) and South (France) lies Germany and Herder's

8   See Bernd Henningsen in this volume.

future. However, his inner destination is to imagine the past and describe it as if he had been there. So for Mallet and Herder the impetus is to look back for nostalgic imaginations as reflections of their contemporary society; they are both occupied with the contents of Old Norse mythology and history.

Aesthetics of place

Theories of a sublime aesthetic were formulated in antiquity by Pseudolonginus in *Peri Hypsous* from around the year 100. This work was found and published in Basel in 1554, but it was the translation into French by Boileau in 1674 that made the theories interesting to contemporary writers. Boileau stressed that Longinus expressed the highest feelings in the simplest language and was therefore able to create an emotional response in the reader whose imagination was roused. The theories of the sublime were popularized by Edmund Burke in *A Philosophical Inquiry into the Origin of our Ideas of the Sublime and the Beautiful* from 1757. Starting in the 1750s, landscapes were described with a new sensibility for the mountains, the sea, stormy weather and lonely moors. The poems of Thomas Gray are an early example of this tendency. He was famous for his *Elegy Written in a Country Churchyard* (1751), a meditation on death and life after death. But Gray also had an interest in Old Norse mythology and its dark, melancholic and sublime 'feeling'. Gray combined this interest with the study of Celtic and early Welsh poetry (Reeves, 1973: 22 and 29). Gray wrote two poems, *The Bard* and *The Descent of Odin*, which were published in 1757 and can be considered the first example of how the 'Nordic' is transformed into a new kind of emotional sensibility that culminated in 1760 when MacPherson published his poems on *Ossian*, a presumed Scottish poet from around 1200. The extreme popularity of these poems all over Europe can only be understood in relation to this new fascination with the North, an absorption which represented a homesickness for the sublime, the melancholy, and dark pasts. With this we see a change from classically and rhetorically oriented poetry to a new kind of sensibility: 'sensibilité' or 'Empfindsamkeit'.

One of the key concepts of this new literature was the aim to write in symbols rather than allegories[9] – it should appeal to the imagination and the senses, as we have seen in the reading of Herder. A new way to create authenticity was by using 'strong' symbols, and old Norse (and Celtic) mythology offered a reservoir

---

9   For a definition of the terms 'allegory' and 'symbol', see for instance Bengt Algot Sørensen 1972: *Allegorie und Symbol*. Frankfurt am Main: Athenäum; Angus Fletcher 1995 (1964): *Allegory*. Ithaca: Cornell University Press; Maureen Quilligan 1992 (1979): *The Language of Allegory*. Ithaca: Cornell University Press. In Paul de Man's work he problematises a simple distinction between allegory and symbol; see for instance *Blindness and Insight*, 1996 (1971), London: Methuen, or *Allegories of Reading*, 1994 (1979) New Haven: Yale University Press.

KAREN KLITGAARD POVLSEN

of possibilities in this respect that still felt new and different, while the mythology of classical antiquity was often regarded as outworn. It had been used as a literary pattern for centuries, with Virgil as an icon of how to write about antique myths – an icon that was slowly replaced by Homer in the second half of the eighteenth century. The new Homer of the North, Ossian, did not replace the old Homer, but the popularity of the poems meant that a critique and modernization of classical allegorical and rhetorical patterns developed rapidly, especially in the North, which at the time was still considered to extend from Ireland in the West to Russia, maybe even Japan, in the East; the East-West dividing line in Europe only slowly began to develop after 1814.[10]

À la française: old and modern

The redefinition of North and South in the years before and after 1800 thus had its roots in a reformulation of classical aesthetic theories. A direct connection from Cicero, Horaz and Longin (Pseudolongin) to French classicism was established by Charles Batteaux (1713-1780), among others. He interpreted the classical idea of mimesis in the sense that the imitation of nature should be an imitation of the ideal way the antique artists had imitated nature. Therefore, he could approve of Boileau's (1636-1711, 1676: *L'Art poetique*) normative system of rules for poetry along the lines of the Horatian school of *Ars poetica*. In contrast to this school, the tradition of Dubos (1670-1742) was formulated. In his *Refléxions critiques sur la poesie et sur la peinture (1719)*, Dubos emphasized the sentiments and the heart – the subjective imagination – as the decisive element in the reception of poetry or visual arts. Dubos based his ideas in part on the philosophers John Locke and the Earl of Shaftsbury, and was deeply influenced by empiricism and sensualists. In his view, the heart and the senses rather than reason alone should determine whether a piece of poetry is excellent or not. No normative rules for poetry could exist even though he thought the sentiments of the heart were trans-historical. In French theory itself, two opponents thus faced each other – for and against French classicism. When Dubos was translated into German by Funk in Copenhagen in 1760/61, Gerstenberg and Klopstock, two German writers and friends of Funk who lived in Copenhagen at the time, soon developed an interest in Nordic mythology and immediately became his followers. To be against French taste – as we have already seen in the case of Herder – was equated with being for Norse mythology and with a new sensibility for symbols and an appeal to the imagination. But the

10   Kliemann-Geisinger, 2004: 93ff., and Kliemann-Geisinger in this volume; see also: Hans Lemberg 1985: Zur Entstehung des Osteuropabegriffs im 19. Jahrhundert. *Jahrbücher für Kultur und Geschichte der Slaven*. Breslau, vol. 33, 1: 48-91.

arguments really came from a discussion among French theorists and represented a general modernization of literature and arts more than anything geographical or nationalistic. At the time, however, the North was considered in line with the modern, and the South in line with the old antique norms – even though the fascination with the North was triggered by old myths.

The groundwork was thus laid when Paul-Henri Mallet published his introductions to Danish history and Old Norse mythology in the 1750s, and the timing of the translation of his works into German and English was perfect.

Go-Betweens of the eighteenth century

Herder regretted not having visited Copenhagen and Heinrich Wilhelm von Gerstenberg (1737-1823). Gerstenberg was the first to write a skaldic poem in 1766, thereby founding the Barden literature that appealed to the nostalgic imagination of Herder, Klopstock and others. Gerstenberg was born into a German family in the Danish town of Tønder and attended university in Jena. Gerstenberg was interested in old Danish and German literature. He spoke and read both languages and also acquired knowledge of the Old Norse language. In the 1760s, he was also occupied with MacPherson's *Ossian* and he enjoyed the style of the poems, even if he was one of the first to seriously doubt their origin.[11] The German translation of Mallet was published in 1764, and that same year the first volume of *Ossian* was also translated – and both were read by Gerstenberg (Gerecke 2002: 121). In 1765, Gerstenberg moved to Copenhagen, where he socialised with the German circle there: J. E. Schlegel, Klopstock, J. A. Cramer and many others. Gerstenberg had already published some works but during his first years in Copenhagen he was acknowledged as a rather famous German poet w ith, for instance, the first skaldic poem, *Gedicht eines Skalde* (Poem by a Skald), from 1766. The same year he began publishing the periodical *Briefe über Merkwürdigkeiten der Literatur* (1890 (1766-67, 1770), Letters on literary remarkables). Both works show that Gerstenberg studied the old literature in Denmark and Iceland in detail; he analyzed the rhymes and rhythms and was fascinated by the new aesthetic possibilities that he found in, for example, the Danish *Kiæmpeviser* (giant songs). His fascination was directed more toward aesthetics than content, but he studied both for years and he criticized Mallet for being superficial in popularising the *Edda* (1890: 238). Like Mallet, Gerstenberg imagined a North from somewhere west of Ireland to somewhere east of Russia; he therefore explains the complicated prosody of the ancient poems as follows:

---

11   See his discussion on MacPherson in his 8th Letter on literary remarkables 1890 (1765): 66-67, where he questions the originality of the poems.

You will already have noticed, how detailed these rules are, what a finely tuned ear they presuppose and how accurately they agree with the prosodie of the first oriental people. However that which was called Asamal, or the language of the Ases (Asian, Gods), makes this correspondence even more striking. (Ibid.: 153)[12]

Gerstenberg maintained that German and Danish literature could profit from using themes and not least the style from the ancient Norse past and mythology:

In my opinion no nation in the world could show a richer treasure of relics of this kind than our Nordic, especially the Danish, if we first begin to become very conscious of our own advantages as most others are of theirs. (1766: 58)

Clearly, Gerstenberg saw Germany and Denmark as "Nordic", and he wrote as if the North was one nation including England, among other countries. Gerstenberg is not sympathetic towards either Germany or Denmark but to both. As a person he was *in between*: he had two languages and two cultures, and his solution was to develop a cosmopolitan patriotism towards both cultures – and his utopian projection was to see this culture as one. He saw Old Norse literature as a common possibility for both languages and their literature, because the old forms could renew the classical rules and norms and a new and original literature could be created. In Gerstenberg's view, the old songs and sagas were old and in opposition to French classicism and Batteaux's norms and rules based on antiquity. He preferred English literature – Shakespeare, Young and MacPherson – and even though he did not believe in the authenticity of the *Ossian* poems (1890: 114-115), his style in *The Poem of a Skald* was clearly influenced by it – and by Percy's *Reliquies of Ancient Poetry* (1890: 58). Gerstenberg was not anti-French, but anti-classical. He agreed with Montesquieu and his climate theories and J. J. Rousseau and his back-to-nature theme (Gerecke 2002: 129). According to Gerstenberg, 'Nature', 'Sentiment' and 'Genius' were one and the same thing: "– where there is genius, there is invention, something new, the original, not the other way around" (1890: 228) – and Old Norse literature could be a vehicle for this new invention. His own poem *Poem of a Skald* was an experiment to prove this point, which he elaborated theoretically in *Literary remarkables*. In five songs – with additional factual information in the 21st letter in *Literary remarkables* – and a glossary of the mythological names at the beginning of the poem, we have five different formal experiments with rhymes, alliterations and rhythms from Old Norse literature. The speaker is the skald Thorlaugur, who

---

12   For further discussion of Gerstenberg and a comparison with the position of Böldl 2000: 142ff.

killed himself when his friend Halvard died. Now, in the eighteenth century, he is awakened after 1000 years and descends from the barrow where he and Halvard were buried. The old gods have disappeared as in a Ragnarok and he is stunned by the new Christian world he sees. We have past and present represented as parallel to each other, and Gerstenberg insists on their staying parallel by ending the poems in the present tense (Greenway 1977: 128-29). It is not denied that the present is more advanced than the past. So, metaphorically, the old pagan world was resurrected in Christianity at a time when the same cult of friendship was flourishing as in pagan Nordic culture – and as in classical antiquity. The point is that through the myth, Gerstenberg created metaphors or images in his text which could or should be understood through the reader's emotional response – instead of through the classical reasonable understanding of allegorical images.[13] He was sentimental or 'Empfindsam', wanting to talk to the heart more than the brain.

The poem and the letters in *Literary Remarkables* had an impact on German – and Danish – literature. Gerstenberg was in search of a transnational identity and poetry. He did not want to take sides in the escalating conflicts between the Danish and German Copenhagen of the 1760s, a conflict that culminated years later in new rules for citizenship (1776) and the literary debate "Tyskerfejden" (1784). He tried to define a third form of cosmopolitan identity and poetry (Gerstenberg 2002: 62-65). He thought that together *Ossian* and old Norse literature could create a new aesthetic beginning for a poetry without homeland (*fædreland/Vaterland*), and in this way combine cosmopolitanism with an anticlassical aesthetics. For most of his followers, however, the question was more of content and nation-building than of anti-classicism as in Gerstenberg's case: and as it later would become to Herder, who did not stop over to visit Gerstenberg in Copenhagen in 1769.

Klopstock and Herder revisited

After publishing the first part of his *Messias* in 1758, Friedrich Gottlieb Klopstock (1724-1803) was invited to Copenhagen and stayed there for almost 20 years. He was inspired by Gerstenberg to write odes and bard poems and to use Norse mythology in his works, such as for instance the already mentioned trilogy on Hermann (or Arminius), who fought the Romans in the forests of Teuton. Klopstock did not have Gerstenberg's vision of a third way. In his youth, Klopstock had written about the antique Greek myths in, for instance, his poem *Der Lehrling der Griechen* (The pupil of the Greeks) from 1747, but around 1765, under the influence of Gerstenberg, Mallet and MacPherson, he shifted his focus to Nordic mythology,

---

13   For further arguments and examples of this, see Gerecke 2002: 157-207.

i.e. Celtic and old Norse versions of myths – for example, in the 1767 poem *Der Hügel und der Hain* (The mound and the grove), which would become one of the favourite poems of the Göttinger Hain circle of poets from the 1770s. Klopstock's vision was not of a cosmopolitan Europe based on common mythological roots or an ancient language. His vision was of a united Germany. The poet here is angry with the author because he listens for something that has disappeared: "Also for my fatherland sang the Bards/And alas! Their song has come to an end!" The poet is convinced that if the Bard reappeared, he would sing much better than the Greek poet because he "Is a Bard of my Fatherland…" And then the Bard appears and sings about the Nordic oak, which should be preferred to the Greek laurel. The poet decides not to go to the Greek mountains, but to stay at the small spring in the Teuton grove, and the poem culminates in a vision of the Fatherland: "…and it sounds by itself: Fatherland". The bard ends the poem by stating that he will return to Valhalla, where "unmourned/also the Noble ones hover, who for the Fatherland/on the bloody flower of the shield sank".[14]

Klopstock gave voice to a German nationalism that denied the ideals of Gerstenberg. Also, Klopstock reacted against French classicism; he was a poet of sentimentalism and he created an interest in English poetry and theory in Copenhagen as he translated for instance Young's *Conjectures on Original Composition* (1760: *Der nordische Aufseher*). According to Klopstock, however, ancient Norse mythology should serve the more limited ideal of anticipating a reborn German nation. Following Klopstock after 1770, Herder began reconstructing another version of German history, and to this end began collecting old songs in *Stimmen der Völker in Liedern* (Voices from the people in songs 1778/79). Herder did not consider the skaldic poems of Gerstenberg or Klopstock the real thing, but even Herder searched for old songs all over Europe, not only in Germany. Klopstock was the first to define Norse mythology as a means to build a German nation. In the nineteenth century, many countries in the north of Europe began to use ancient Norse mythology in the same way as Klopstock – and Herder, in his way – did: as a means of nation-building. Then the question became who had the birth-right to which myths and histories, and another fight began.

Return to Sender

English authors like Shakespeare, Milton, Young and Ossian were thus introduced in Denmark by German authors. In 1769, the young poet Johannes Ewald (1743-81) was introduced to Klopstock and his circle in Copenhagen where Shakespeare and

14   The translations are by the author of this article.

Ossian were discussed. Ewald learned to read English – for example, Shakespeare – and in 1770 wrote his own tragedy in prose, *Rolf Krage,* with a plot from Saxo's chronicle – a dramatic Shakespearean plot. During the 1770s, Ewald wrote several unfinished and one finished tragedy with plots from Saxo in several styles and forms, from the Greek alexandrines to Shakespearean blank verse. With *Balders Død* (The Death of Balder) he introduced his personal version of Italian prosody – very similar to blank verse – while the melancholy setting is still along the lines of Ossian. The scene is a Norwegian mountain fir forest where Balder is in love with the virtuous Nanna, who is also courted by Hother. This unnatural love becomes the end of Balder, who commits suicide, consumed by passion. Ewald did not follow the nationalistic line of Klopstock; *The Death of Balder* was nevertheless a huge success. So great was the impact that the young Friederike Münter (born 1765) fainted and had to be carried out when she saw the play in the spring of 1778 (Brun 1917: 96-99). Ewald might not be as nationalistic as Klopstock, but his success was perceived as a Danish and national success. Gerstenberg's third way seemed to be an anachronism. With *The Death of Balder,* Ewald was seen as the first Danish poet to take back the heritage from the German occupation. The new agenda was one language, one nation, one past and one mythology. The climax was the dawn of a new national literature with Adam Oehlenschläger and Nicolai Severin Grundtvig at the beginning of the nineteenth century.[15]

Norse and Celtic mythology – including Ossian – had been Gerstenberg's utopia of an aesthetics of a new common ground in Northern Europe around 1760. Ten years after, it was reduced to an archive of metaphors and symbols. Oehlenschläger conveys this idea in his prize essay from 1800 (published 1801):

Could it be good for the fiction of the North, if the ancient Norse mythology was introduced and generally accepted, in stead of the Greek one?

Our Nordic countries own many beauties, and even if we lived in Kamchatka, the great National Poet would be able to conjure it into a Paradise, and to awaken love to the Nation (Fædrelandet) in his fellow citizen's hearts.

(1801: 272, 294-95)

Oehlenschläger preferred Norse mythology to Greek mythology because it had not been yet used much by poets and therefore represented new contents and new images: "a whole new poetical world is opened for the poet" (Ibid.: 283) – "it only awaits the hand of the artist to be formed" (Ibid.: 284):

---

15   See Karin Sanders and Bernd Henningsen in this volume.

And which true artist does not find the simple marble-block more suitable for his creative genius, than the already finished statue, where he has not anything more to do for him than to lay hands on the last, nearly invisible polish. (Ibid.)

Oehlenschläger makes references to Klopstock's *Hermann* and Herder's *Fragmente über die neuere deutsche Literatur (*Fragments on modern German literature) and concludes as follows:

But the one, who in particular can be seen as a model for how poems of this sort should be treated, is in my thoughts Ossian! Who would deny, that lovable gentleness, mixed with masculine mind sounded from the strings of this great natures poet harp; …(Ibid.: 293)

His last and best argument is however that Norse mythology "is Nordic" (Ibid.) and therefore suitable for writing the history of the Fatherland; in addition, Oehlenschläger saw the Norse gods as real historical persons.

Other endings

Oehlenschläger did not deny that his inspiration for his national and romantic poetry was based on Norse mythology that came from England via Germany. But in the aftermath, most researchers, such as Gerecke (2002), seem to have forgotten that his version was not the only one. A number of essays in contemporary theory went against Oehlenschläger and some poets continued to write according to Gerstenberg's suggestions. Oehlenschläger himself referred to Sulzer's *Allgemeine Theorie der schönen Künste* (General theory of the arts) from 1792-94, a work of great influence on the German debate on arts and aesthetics. Sulzer prized Greek mythology and wrote about the "poor mythology of the Celts" (Ibid.: 275). The same opposition towards Norse mythology can be found in Fr. Rühls's "Ueber die Bedeutung und den Werth der nordischen Mythologie und Poesie" (On the meaning and worthiness of Nordic mythology and poetry, 1802: 2: 106-119). Rühls did not know what to do with all the words and names from Norse mythology and he saw the trend as merely replacing Greek with Norse (107). He agreed that the tradition of German mythology should be researched, but clearly found the use of Nordic mythology in German literature empty and unnecessary. The debate went on for several decades for aesthetic reasons – as in Rühls's case – and not least political ones. It was a debate between, on the one hand, the romanticists and nationalists and, on the other, a number of 'old-fashioned', learned poets and often go-betweens, authors of what we regard as minor works today because they did not follow the main trend of the time; they remained cosmopolitically oriented and some of them shared Gerstenberg's vision of a third way traversing cultures and nations.

An example of a go-between is the German-Danish author Friederike Brun, born Münter (1765-1835), who grew up in the German circle in Copenhagen and read Klopstock and Gerstenberg when she was very young. They both associated with her parents, and all her life Friederike Brun admired them and visited them in Germany, where she travelled extensively. Friederike Brun wrote in German and was inspired by Norse and Greek mythology: by Ossian and Virgil, by Klopstock and Ewald. She wrote many travelogues from her travelling life and was a beloved poet of the *Empfindsamkeit* movement. Today she is perceived as a sentimental writer, but her poems and ballads with motifs from Norse mythology are simple and easy to read and sing even today. Her ballad *Die sieben Hügel* (The seven groves) from 1791 draws upon Danish mythology and folk poetry, while *Das Mädchen Mona* (The girl Mona) from 1801 blends the tradition of folk poetry about unrequited love and Norse mythology. The love story of Mona ends at the cliffs of Arcona and hence is placed in a historical setting with Danes and German tribes fighting – resulting in women suffering. Friederike Brun thus displayed her own sense of misplacement or role as a go-between in a hostile culture in the way she used the tradition of old Norse literature, and the effect is an accentuation of (Nordic) melancholia.

Return to Nordmandsdalen around 1800

Friederike Brun and others of her kind were exceptions in their cosmopolitan attitude. They included her Swiss friend Carl Victor von Bonstetten, who stayed in Denmark for several years and studied old Icelandic language and literature. He began to write in German instead of French, because the German language was closer to the Nordic languages. Bonstetten liked Nordmandsdalen, describing it in 1799 as a symbol of the many Danish nationalities joining around their king. He would like to create an English garden with cottages from Lapland around the statues (Skougaard 2004: 124), thus completing the 'Nordic' feeling. Bonstetten associated with the Coppet circle and Mme de Staël and thus introduced her to the Nordic spirit in literature and mythology (Klitgaard Povlsen 1998: 225ff.). However, he might have written about Nordmandsdalen to argue against another German traveller in Denmark, F. W. B. von Ramdohr, who found Nordmandsdalen most distasteful (1792: 234), just as he found the Danish margins of Europe backwards, barbaric and lacking in culture. In this way, the debate between Ramdorh and Bonstetten repeated the pattern we have already seen between aristocratic classicism (southern) and modern sensibility (northern).

The go-betweens of the eighteenth and nineteenth centuries, however, were not good examples when the national literary histories were written – such as Rahbek and Nyerup's four volumes in the years 1800-1808. The dominant and national development was seen in the tradition of Oehlenschläger and his admirer N. F. S. Grundtvig (1783-1872),[16] who popularised Norse mythology more than anyone, but who also created a strong bond between Christianity, nation-building and Norse mythology in Denmark in his *Nordens Mytologi* (Mythology of the North, 1808). For Grundtvig, an important reason to work with Nordic mythology was the general crisis of Christianity in the last part of the eighteenth century, when deism and atheism were on the agenda (Auken 2005: 15). Grundtvig might have thought that he could save Christianity with Norse mythology. Grundtvig had many traits in common with Herder: He was a nationalist and he wanted not only to equate Norse mythology with Christianity, but also to understand the Danish landscape through this mythology. Grundtvig admired the work of Oehlenschläger, and parts of his *Mythology* can be read as a very positive review of Oehlenschläger's early works, but he also found Oehlenschläger too southern in his positive understanding of Norse mythology. For Grundtvig, the myth of Ragnarok was also a doomsday myth, which might make the foundations of a new world freed from sin. The interpretations of Grundtvig's role vary. Even today he is used by extreme Danish nationalists as well as by liberal groups – in his work of 1808, his aspirations were artistic: he wanted to become an even better writer than Oehlenschläger. Whether he succeeded is questionable, but he did popularize Norse mythology and make it an important political weapon for nationalism and against go-betweens of German-Danish origin.

16   See also Bernd Henningsen in this volume.

References

Auken, Sune 2005: *Sagas Spejl*. Copenhagen: Gyldendal.

Barton, Arnold, 1998: *The Northern Arcadia*. London: Eurospan.

Beck, Thor J., 1934: *Northern Antiquities in French Learning and Literature 1755-1855, 1-2*. New York: Columbia University.

Bonstetten, Karl Viktor von, 1799: *Neue Schriften* 1. Copenhagen: bei Friedrich Brummer.

Böldl, Klaus, 2000: *Det Mythos der Edda. Nordische Mythologie zwischen europäischer Aufklärung und nationaler Romantik*. Tübingen und Basel: Francke Verlag.

Brasch, Christian A., 1879: *Om Robert Moleswort's Skrift: "An Account of Denmark as it was in the Year 1692*. Copenhagen: E. A. Reitzel.

Brun, Friederike 1917 (1824): *Ungdoms-Erindringer*. Copenhagen: H. Hagerups Forlag.

Bukdahl, Else Marie 1993: *Johannes Wiedewelt*. Hellerup: Edition Bløndal.

Dillmann, Francois-Xavier, 1996: Frankrig og den nordiske fortid. Ed. Else Roesdahl and Preben Meulengrath Sørensen: *The Waking of Angantyr*. Aarhus: Aarhus University Press: 13-26.

Dyserinck, Hugo, 1977: *Komparatistik*. Bonn: Bouvier Verlag.

Fjågesund, Peter, and Ruth Simons, 2003: *The Northern Utopia*, Amsterdam: Rodopoi.

Gerecke, Anne-Bitt, 2002: *Transkulturalität als literarisches programm: Heinrich Wilhelm von Gerstenberg*. Göttingen: Vandenhoeck & Ruprecht.

Gerstenberg, Heinrich Wilhelm von, 1766: *Briefe über Merkwürdigkeiten der Litteratur*. Schleswig und Leipzig.

Greenway, John L., 1977: *The Golden Horns. Mythic Imagination and the Nordic Past*. Athens: University of Georgia Press.

Hartmann, Regina, 2000: *Deutschsprachige Reisende in der Spättaufklärung unterwegs in Skandinavien*. Frankfurt/Main: Peter Lang.

Herder, Johann Gottfried, 1976 (1769): *Journal meiner Reise im Jahr 1769*. Stuttgart: Philipp Reclam Jun.

Herder, Johann Gottfried, 1877 (1765): Rezension von Mallets Geschichte von Dänemark. Ed. Bernhard Suphan: *Herders sämtliche Werke* I. Berlin: Weidmann: 73-77.

Kliemann, Hendriette, 2005: *Koordinaten des Nordens*. Berlin: Berliner Wissenschafts-Verlag Gmbh.

Klitgaard Povlsen, Karen, 2005: Kulturrevolution og Kulturkamp: 1789 og reaktionen i England. Eds. Klitgaard Povlsen and Anne Scott Sørensen: *Kunstkritik og Kulturkamp*. Aarhus: Klim: 16-32.

Lund, Hakon, 2004: Nordmandsdalen. *Nordmandsdalen i Fredensborg Slotshave*. København: Slots-og Ejendomsstyrelsen: 67-77.

Mallet, Paul-Henri, 1756 (1755): *Indledning udi Danmarks Riges Historie*. Copenhagen: Ludolph Henrich Lillie.

Mallet, Paul-Henri, 1847: *Northern Antiquities;* translated from the French by Bishop Percy and ed. I. A. Blackwell, with an abstract of the Eyrbyggja Saga by Sir Walter Scott. London: Henry G. Bohn.

Molesworth, Robert (1693), 1977: *En beskrivelse af Danmark 1692*: Aarhus: Wormanium.

Oehlenschläger, Adam, 1801: Var det gavnligt for Nordens skiønne Litteratur, om den gamle nordiske Mythologi blev indført og almindelig antaget, i stedet for den grædske? *Minerva*, 1801:2: 272-297.

Priskorn, Ole, 2004: Nordmandsdalens tilblivelse. *Nordmandsdalen*. Copenhagen: Slots- og Ejendomsstyrelsen: 10-24.

Ramdohr, Friedrich Wilhelm Basilius von, 1792: *Studien zur Kenntniss der schönen Natur, der schönen Künste, der Sitten und der Staatsverfassung auf einer Reise nach Dännemark*. Hannover: Verlage der Helwigschen Hofbuchhandlung.

Reeves, James, ed., 1973: *The Complete English Poems of Thomas Gray*. London: Heineman.

Roesdahl, Else and Preben Meulengracht Sørensen, 1996: *The Waking of Angantyr*. Aarhus: Aarhus University Press.

Ross, Margaret Clunies, 1998: *The Norse Muse in Britain 1750-1820*. Trieste: Edizioni Parnaso.

Scavenius, Bente, 1997: *Fredensborg Slotshave*. Copenhagen: Gyldendal.

Rühls, Friedrich, 1802: Ueber die Bedetung und den Werth der nordischen Mythologie und Poesie. *Der neue Teutsche Merkur* 2: 106-119.

Skougaard, Mette, 2004: Det norske haveteater. Nordmandsdalen i Fredensborg. Ed. Mette Skougaard: *Norgesbilleder. Dansk-norske forbinderlser 1700-1905*. Copenhagen: Gads Forlag: 104-125.

Strich, Fritz, 1962, (1922): *Deutsche Klassik und Romantik oder Vollendung und Unendlichkeit*. Bern und München: Francke Verlag.

Sulzer, 1792-94: *Allgemeine Theori der schönen Künste* 1-4. Leipzig: Weidmannschen Buchhandlung.

KAREN KLITGAARD POVLSEN

Tacitus, Cornelius, around 90: Germania. www. heimkringla.no/dansk/tacitus.

Wawn, Andrew, ed., 1994: *Northern Antiquity. The Post-medieval Reception of Edda and Saga.* Middlesex: Hisarlik Press.

Østergaard, Uffe, 1997: The Geolitics of Nordic Identity. Ed Øystein Sørensen and Bo Stråth: *The Cultural Construction of Norden.* Oslo: Scandinavian University Press: 25-71.

Original quotes

Der kalte Norden scheint hier der Geburtsort so gut der Seeungeheuer zu seyn, als ers der Barbaren, der Menschenriesen, und Weltverwüster gewesen. (Herder 1976 (1769): 15)

Ist Norden oder Süden, Morgen, oder Abend die *Vagina hominum* gewesen? (Ibid.)

Ist dies so, so sehe ich zwei Ströme, von denen der Eine aus Orient, über Griechenland und Italien sich ins südliche Europa sanft senkt, und auch eine sanfte, südliche Religion, eine Poesie der Einbildungskraft, eine Musik, Kunst, Sittsamkeit, Wissenschaft des östlichen Südens erfunden hat. Der zweite Strom geht über Norden von Asien nach Europa; von da überströmt er jenen. Deutschland gehörte zu ihm, und sollte recht in seinem Vaterlande seyn, diese Geschichte Nordens zu studiren: ... (Ibid.: 15-16)

Frankreich: seine Epoche der Literatur ist gemacht: das Jahrhundert Ludwichs vorbei; auch die Montesquieus, D'Alemberts, Voltaire's, Rousseau sind vorbei: man wohnt auf den Ruinen: ..." (Ibid.: 92)

...wo ist Genie? Wahrheit? Stärke? Tugend? Die Philosophie der Franzosen, die in der Sprache liegt: ihr Reichtum an Abstraktionen, ist *gelernt*; also nur dunkel bestimmt, also über und unter angewandt: also keine Philosophie mehr. (Ibid.: 109)

Gerstenberg.... Mit ihm über die Barden und Skalder zu singen, ihn über seine Liebe und Tändeleien im Hypochondristen und wo es sey, zu umarmen, die Briefe über die Merkwürdigkeiten *etc.*, mit ihm zu lesen, von Hamann, Störze, Klotz u.s.w. zu sprechen, und Funken zu schlagen, zu einem neuen Geist der Literatur, der vom Dänischen Ende Deutschlands anfange und

das Land erquicke. Alsdann über die Skalden zu schreiben, und nach Kiel ins Arabische zu verschwinden. Das was meine erste Periode, werde ich sie in Frankreich erreichen? (Ibid.: 118-19)

Dieser junger Mensch hatte vielen Geschmack am Wahren, Guten, und würklich Schönen! (Ibid.: 133).

Sie werden schon angemerkt haben, wie sehr diese Regeln ins Feine gehen, was für ein richtiges Gehör sie voraussetzen, und wie genau sie mit der Prosodie der ersten orientalischen Völker übereinstimmen. Allein das, was man Asamal, oder die Sprache der Asen (Asiaten, Götter) nannte, macht diese Übereinstimmung noch frappanter. (Ibid.: 153)

Keine Nation in der Welt müsste, meines Erachtens, eine reichern Schatz an Ueberbleibsln dieser Art aufzuweisen haben, als unsre Nordische, vornehmlich die Dänische, wenn wir erst einmal anfingen, so aufmerksam auf unsre eignen Vortheile zu werden, als die meisten andern auf die ihrigen sind. (Gerstenberg 1766: 58)

-wo Genie ist, da ist Erfindung, da ist Neuheit, da ist das Original; aber nicht umgekehrt. (Gerstenberg: 1890: 227f.)

Auch meinem Vaterlande sangen Barden,/Und ach! Ihr Gesang ist nicht mehr! (Klopstock)

Ist ein Barde meines Vaterlands ... (Klopstock)

und sie tönt von sich selbst: Vaterland! (Klopstock)

unbeweinbar/ Auch die Edlen schweben, die für das Vaterland/Auf des Schildes blutige Blume sanken! (Klopstock)

Var det gavnligt for Nordens skiønne Litteratur, om den gamle nordiske Mythologie blev indført og almindelig antaget, istedet for den grædske? (*Minerva 1801:* 272)

Vore nordiske Lande besidde mange Skiønheder, og boede vi end i Kamschatka, saa stod det i den store geniefulde Nationaldigters Magt at trylle det om i et Paradiis, og at opvække Kiærlighed til Fædrelandet i sine Medborgeres Hierter. (Ibid: 295)

… aabner Digteren en heel nye poetisk verden. (Ibid.: 283)

…, som kun venter en Kunstnerhaand for at dannes. (Ibid.: 284)

Og hvilken sand Kunstner finder ikke ogsaa den simple Marmorklods mere passende for sit skabende Genie, end den allerede færdige Billedstøtte, hvor der i det høieste ikke er andet tilbage for ham end at lægge Haand paa den sidste, næsten umærkelige Politur? (Ibid.)

Men den, som især kann tiene til Mønster for, hvorledes Digte af dette Slags skal behandles, er i mine Tanker Ossian! Hvo vil nægte, at elskelig Blidhed, blandet med Mandigheds Aand tonede fra Strengene paa denne store naturdigters Harpe; … (Ibid.: 293)

…schlechte Mythologie der Kelten… (Sulzer 1792-94: 275)

KARIN SANDERS

"Upon the bedrock of material things": The Journey to the Past in Danish Archaeological Imagination

"In the snow-bound North the past does not reveal itself in the friendly way that belongs to temperate lands" writes the French archaeologist Alain Schnapp, but "for those who took the trouble to look at the landscape, the earth revealed its secrets: megaliths, barrows and even runic inscriptions (the first Scandinavian writing) were everywhere" (Schnapp 1997: 156). In fact, early "Scandinavian antiquaries" Schnapp points out, went "further and faster than their European colleagues [...] because they could apply their knowledge to a much closer past, for which they sensed a formal continuity with the present" (Ibid: 150-1) Schnapp's statement is telling in a number of ways in that he reveals how the Northern landscape as frozen and hostile became a conventional trope in early archaeological imagination; how conceptions of landscape factored into the archaeological imagination of regional and national pasts.[1] Defined by its limitations (the apparent unfriendliness and implicit lack of historical depth) the snow-bound North offered access to "a much closer past" and hence to a more immediate sense of the presence of the past (*anamnesis*) than did the warmer (read: deeper) Southern soil.

Such long-established perceptions of the North as both closer to its peoples' origin yet further from the Southern regions' depth of culture implied that the North was too shallow and climatically hostile to yield profound archaeological artifacts in line with the plethora of ancient art excavated from the Grecian-Roman soil. How then can an archaeology of the North compete with established paradigms in European archaeology in which the grandeur and nobility of classic Greek and Roman antiquity is cast against a perceived sense of Nordic crudeness? How can rune stones and barrows compete with the sublime marble figures of Apollo and Venus? Does the perceived lack of temporal depth and the hostility of the landscape factor into the role of archaeology as a nation's discipline? Is there

---

1   Unlike early English antiquarians' interest in the picturesque, for example, early Danish antiquarians were partial to seeing the landscape as a site which provided knowledge about epigraphy rather than one which offered a site for sentimentality.

a way in which we can rethink the connection between regional (national) claims and aesthetic production?

Museum and chronology

Although archaeology itself does not seem to have any fixed origin, convention holds that modern Western archaeological interests developed out of the mid-eighteenth century discoveries of Herculaneum and Pompeii and gelled in the mid-nineteenth century with the birth of archaeology as a professional discipline. In this history of archaeology the North figures prominently and early antiquarians of the North are credited in most archaeological textbooks with considerable contributions to the making of the discipline; most significantly, they would help untie the close bond between art and archaeology which had marked the seventeenth, eighteenth and early nineteenth century. Thus the term archaeology, known since the sixteenth century, was not fixed in the modern sense and understanding until the nineteenth century. In the centuries before, the conflation of *archaeologist* and *aesthete* into *antiquarian* and the interest in finding artifacts which could testify aesthetically and implicitly morally to the progress of civilization was emblematized in the celebration of fine arts, particularly beautiful statuary. Although such refined statuary was not to be found in the Northern part of Europe, the past in this region could be seen as part of the landscape – in form of barrows, rune stones etc. – and it was to be found in the myths.

While "the fabric of history is a fragile thing," as Schnapp points out, "archaeology will always preserve some of the threads. However, for memory to persist mankind must observe, interpret and create the narrative upon the bedrock of material things" (Schnapp 1997: 33). And, one could add, for archaeology to exist there has to be some form of observable process in place. Such a process is outlined already in 1638 by the Antiquary-Royal of Denmark and Norway, Ole Worm (1588-1654). In *Om historieskrivning løsrevet fra den antikke tradition* (On History Writing Unshackled from the Antique Tradition) from 1633, Worm complained that many of his contemporaries were unwilling to see the significance in descriptions of the Nordic countries unless looked at through the prism offered by Greek and Roman historians. Worm's instructions for examining a site therefore paid attention to the details of the material landscape at hand.[2] His methods were essentially the same as those for modern surveys; the information was collected

---

2   Also Sweden's Johan Bure [Bureus] 1568-1652, transformed archaeology and completed the first professional archaeological survey supported by the king, making the kingdom of Sweden "the first state to endow an archaeological service which foreshadowed in many ways the role of our modern agencies." Schnapp 1997, 159; see also Klint-Jensen 1975, 14-31.

KARIN SANDERS

first-hand, measured, analysed and contextualized by gathering local perceptions and judgements.

Worm's famous collection, *Museum Wormium*, inaugurated a museum tradition in Denmark, but it was a heterogeneous collection not earmarked specifically to (although certainly including) prehistoric Danish treasures. Not until the founding in 1807 of *Den Kongelige Commision til Oldsagers Opbevaring* (The Royal Committee for the Preservation and Collection of National Antiquities) which marked an attempt to put a stop to the ongoing destruction of prehistoric artifacts, was a sanctuary provided for the nation's antiquities at the Trinitatus Church loft in Copenhagen. The Danish literary scholar Rasmus Nyerup (1759-1829) initiated the Royal collection in the loft and worked to fulfill a dream of a national museum. In 1806, Nyerup published a request to the public asking for archaeological finds for the collection, calling for objects which would: "allow the viewer to know the transition of our ancestors from wildness and vileness to culture and virtue" (Here cited from Jensen 1992: 20; see also Nielsen, I. 1987: 81).

That the initiator of museum collections of ancient Nordic artifacts was a literary scholar speaks volumes about the way in which material culture was viewed in early museum history. Nyerup's interest in both literary and material culture can be seen in his description of the museum visits as a walk through time, a place where the visitor could amble from room to room and study the successive progress in the nation's culture and concepts, customs and conventions. It was his idea to name the new museum *Nationalmuseet* (The National Museum). Nyerup's interest in the nation's past also led him to write, with Knud Lyhne Rahbek (1760-1830) the first Danish Literary History: *Bidrag til den danske Digtekunsts Historie* (Contributions to the History of Danish Literature) published in 1800-8. Nyerup (as did Rahbek) belonged to the Enlightenment, but his work on the ancient past would inspire the generation of Romanticists who – each in their way – attempted to build a sense of nationhood from the past.

The collection in Trinitatis Loft would become the center for important archaeological activities resulting already in 1809 in the first methodical survey of mounds in Denmark by B.S. Thorlacius (1775-1829), (Kristiansen 1998: 12-13). Material culture, then, gradually found its way into the institutional realm in the beginning of the nineteenth century, and the language and methods with which to approach the artifacts began to resonate with vocabulary specific to its material reality – and not as beforehand primarily as verification of literary, historical or mythological thoughts. The antiquarian, E.C. Werlauff (1781-1871), for example, advocated that fieldwork needed to be carried out systematically and not just through questionnaires to clergymen in the country. In 1812 he wrote:

So, then, into the field! Must be the first and last cry of the antiquarian eager for knowledge, to those who honor and speak on behalf of the past? [....] When all this has come to pass, when all our antiquities have been collected and placed in our museums, then the time will come for the archaeologist to arrange and set in order all this material and, if possible, organize it into a system; only then can he decide what we know, with some degree of certainly, and where gaps exists which cannot be filled. The historian will assist by comparing the data provided by the archaeologist with the insights gleaned from nature and myth, and [...] perhaps shed new light on the early mythical past of the Nordic countries. (Ibid: 21)

In 1819, with the director C.J. Thomsen (1788-1865) as guide, the doors were opened on a regular basis for visitors to the Trinitatis Church loft. He had found the artifacts in chaos but systematized the collection and hereby laid not only the ground for the National Museum as a weighty institution, but also pointed the direction which archaeology was to take over a century. Thomsen continued the work of Nyerup and established prehistoric chronology located as temporal blocks in three Ages – Stone, Bronze, and Iron.[3] He grouped the artifacts through a principle of association and allowed the cultural traces around the finds to determine their places in a prehistoric chronology. While Thomsen labored to give archaeology status as a self-sufficient discipline independent of philology and literature studies, his successor J.J.A.Worsaae (1821-1885) would extend and revise Thomsen's work in a continued effort to replace the traditional literary model of interpretation – which had been the guiding principle of early archaeological discourses – with a model in which artifacts and material culture was allowed to determine interpretations. Thomsen too subscribed to the importance of actually seeing the 'things themselves'; the past was tangible and not to be found in books. Under his leadership the museum became a unique national institution and was the "most interesting and instructive sight in Copenhagen" according to the Swedish poet Erik Gustaf Geijer in 1825 (Kristiansen 1985: 13). Since the events of the Napoleonic wars where Denmark lost its control of Norway and other territories, experienced the defeat of its fleet, endured the massive bombardment of Copenhagen by England, followed by the state bankruptcy in 1813, a wave of national Romanticism swept the county and facilitated interest in the ancient past both in the arts and in literature. In time, the National Museum would come to play a central part in the formation of a renewed sense of national Danish identity.

---

3   In "Ledetraad til Nordisk Oldkyndighed" published by *Oldskriftsselskabet* in 1836, Thomsen defined the prehistoric chronology and designated them as Stone, Bronze and Iron Ages. See also *Dansk Biografisk Leksikon*, XXIII, MCMXLII: 553. Kristian Kristiansen points out that the "Three Age System" has become a metaphor "for any arbitrary cultural and chronological division" and, in spite of the value of such groupings, has partly resulted in "distorted, historical conceptions of the past": 24.

It has been pointed out by many that there is an almost unavoidable relationship between archaeology and nation building, and the ways in which prehistoric artifacts frequently supply tangible aid to constructed narratives of a nation's past has been scrutinized in a number of archaeological studies (Kohl and Fawsett 1995; Lotte Hedeager and Karen Schusboe: 1989).[4] In recent years, however, the past is often referred to as an idea or as a construction, a fabrication, as something imagined. It comes as no surprise, then, that the *Cambridge Illustrated History of Archaeology* introduces its subject with these words:

[...] the development of archaeological theory has made us more aware that we do not simply rediscover the past: we create it. For the raw materials dug up from the earth, do not tell us much directly. They have to be interpreted. And it is we who do the interpreting. The past as we understand it is thus, in a sense, our own creation, although it is built up out of all the great discoveries made by the archaeologist's spade. The history of archaeology is therefore a complex one – a story not only of discovery and of new research techniques, but also of new interpretative frameworks. For if we are shaped by our past, we also, in a very real sense, through the practice of archaeology, create the past for ourselves. The history of archaeology is the history of self-awareness. (Renfrew 1996: vii)

If the history of archaeology is the history of self-awareness, how then does this apply to a Northern self-awareness? More specifically, how does the archaeological knowledge translate into other fields than the one put forward by museums. How, for example, do poetry and visual arts offer imaginative articulations of regional or national claims?

4   As Neil Asher Silberman argues: "archaeological narratives cannot help but be constructed in contemporary idiom, with emphasis on each society's specific hopes and fears." (Silberman 1995: 261) But to see archaeology as a form of narrative does not exclude a plausible reconstruction of the past built on archaeological data or on "scholarly standards of logic and evidence." (Ibid.: 249) Archaeological narratives are not inherently deceptive or in themselves suspect. Still, the association between archaeology and nationalism or national identities and the uses of archaeological discoveries in nation building contexts can easily take on accents of manipulation: the assertion of ownership of the past to support present political claims and so forth. The archaeological stories told (and presumably verified by material remains) are not interchangeable, each equally true, or each equally imagined. As Philip Kohl and Claire Fawsett put it: "one story is not as convincing as another." They continue: "Some archaeological tales are not innocuous, but dangerous in that they fan the passions of ethnic pride and fuel the conflicts that today pit peoples against each other....a fine line separates legitimate from questionable research." Kohl and Fawsett 1995: 6. Neither an extreme positivism nor exaggerated relativism, will help us to steer clear of the many pitfalls in interpreting the past, but an awareness of how and what is at issue in each case, is cardinal. The question is and must be *how* and *when* the line has been crossed between a past which is excessively constructed and manipulated and one which can be carefully ascertained from available empirical data. In the work of leading archaeologists such as Ian Hodder, Michael Schanks, Meg Conkey, Julian Thomas and others, archaeology is no longer a matter of identifying similarities or differences among the cultural products of the human past, it is also a matter of acknowledging interpretation, and discussing how these interpretations come about. Also see Sanders 2002: 259-261.

Daniel Rantzav.

FIG. 7:

After a call for an awakening to a new awareness of national sovereignty, Lund brings his poem Lunden ved Jægerspriis to a close: "Behind the hedge the shielded barrow rests/And nature's beauty embraces it with smiles/And great men from the oldest days of North/In undying marble, live once again." In S.L. Lange's unfinished watercolor (seen here) a tree literally bleeds into one of Mindelunden's marble monuments. Jægerspris. S. L. Lange, 1797.

KARIN SANDERS

To engage the past is nearly always about reconstruction. It is about 'making again' that which *was* but *is* no longer – a shift in tense from present to past – and it is an (often utopian) attempt at constructing a past-present. The past is frequently seen as a foreign realm, a faraway place, a paradise lost and a golden age. The longing for such a past is implicitly a longing for innocence and virtuousness. But the past, when it is engaged in nation building contexts, is also always about the present. A *present* that needs to be defined, constructed, understood as a *presence* which can lay claim to roots and identities; not an imaginary tale, but a 'saga' nevertheless. This 'saga' can be told by looking at the use of landscape as an archaeological-artistic-poetic hybrid.

If digging through the soil is a journey in and through time and a quest for finding hidden objects from the past, then the visible surface in form of accultur-ated landscapes testifies to the ways in which the present articulates *visions* of this past. In fact, such landscape articulations in Denmark in the late 1700s and early 1800s allow us once again to observe the emergence of two trajectories: one point-ing South to the Grecian-Roman soil, the other pointing North; one to classical sculpture (predominantly), the other to burial mounds and to rune stones. At times the two combine into one. And this combination, as we shall see, becomes an attempt at defining a particular kind of *national* landscape which has roots in the local soil but also tentacles which stretch beyond narrowly defined national borders. The sculptor Johannes Wiedewelt (1731-1802), for example, would play a key role in bringing neo-classical form to and merging it with the Danish land-scape – and the Danish past. He had close ties to the German archaeologist and art historian Johann Joachim Winckelmann (1717-1768); they traveled together to the excavations in Herculanum and were room-mates in Rome for a while. Through Winckelmann, Wiedewelt was inspired by neoclassical ideals and adhered to Winckelmann's principle that the 'noble simplicity and calm grandeur' of Greek antiquity should be emulated. But after his return to Denmark, the sculptor was engaged by the Danish Prime Minister Ove Høegh-Guldberg (1731-1808) to place monuments in the park surrounding the ancient burial mound at Jægerspris.[5] As Marjetta Nielsen points out:

The project of 'restoring' the Neolithic mound Julianehøj at Jægerspris had also raised the question of chronology within the Nordic past, and it kept intriguing him. But at that time not even the professional scholars had any idea of the age of the mound, so this Stone Age

---

5   For the most informative introduction to the Memorial Grove at Jægerspris and the burial mound (re)named Julianehøj, see Lund, H. 1976.

monument came to be seen as the memorial of legendary Viking-Age kings. The sense of the recalled past reached only that far, the error margin being some 4000 years. (Nielsen, M. 2003: 202)

Nevertheless, Wiedewelt would bring a sense of time and memory into play with the Danish landscape. His tenure in Rome and experience with the ancient city's funerary memorials and temporally layered – yet clearly visible – past would inspire a new view of the Nordic past as well. At Jægerspris, Wiedewelt would place "monuments whose symbols, liberated from classical antiquity, were created in a Nordic idiom and yet were easy to understand" (Karin Kryger 2003: 238).[6] Wiedewelt himself argued in a letter in 1776:

[I have] endeavored to give posterity a reminder of national things: the first stones are simple and marked solely with inscriptions; afterwards I commence to introduce representations, and I continue with allegories. In the same way as the monuments of the Greeks and the Romans are ornamented with their mythology and historical characteristics, I have tried here to use our own. (Cited from Bukdahl 1993: 45; see also Lund, H. 1976: 21)

The Jægerspris project was three-fold and existed of monuments memorializing 'ordinary' men and women who had served their country; a reconstructed barrow with commemorations of mythical Danish kings; and finally a garden parterre with "four vases representing the elements (earth, water, fire, air) and, in the middle of the parterre, a column with an urn" (Kryger 2003: 241; see also Damsholt 2000: 158-169). This was in tune with the wishes of the heir presumptive, Frederik (later Frederik V), or rather with the objective of Ove Høegh-Guldberg, who was the mastermind behind *Mindelunden*. After an excavation in 1776 of the mound in Jægerspris it was decided, as the historian C.F. Wegener puts it in 1856: to make "The mound and its surroundings into a patriotic memorial able to combine ancient and contemporary times" (Wegener 1856: 178).[7] To combine prehistory with the present, also became a matter of assigning national meaning, or, as Else Marie Bukdahl expresses:

6   Else Marie Bukdahl gives a more full explanation: "Wiedewelts reading of Burke's analyses of 'the sublime' (which released him from his dependence on Antique models), his encounter with English landscape gardens (which shattered his concept of rationality) and his pre-Romantic interpretation of Winckelmann's views on history resulted in fractures and fissures in his Classical artistic idiom while at the same time almost draining it of complicated conceptual allegories and artificial literary content" (Bukdahl 1993: 45). This in turn leads to Wiedewelt's creation of a "vocabulary of form that was abstract […]because he believed that 'Nordic antiquities' – unlike those of Antiquity – were built up of abstract forms. It could have been his encounter with Stonehenge in England or the Danish prehistoric tombs and stones with runic inscriptions that gave rise to this view" (Ibid.: 45-6).

7   Wegener catalogues the numerous monuments and includes drawings of them.

Ove Høegh-Guldberg undoubtedly saw the memorials as a visualization of – or perhaps even as a monument to – his own struggle to promote Danishness, but his politico-cultural programme had no clear connotations of national Romanticism, whereas Wiedewelt's artistic interpretation of it certainly has. He saw quite clearly that the rational philosophy and unhistorical attitude of the Age of Enlightenment had been replaced by a philosophy of culture which regarded history as an organic whole and exposed the characteristics and the history of the development of the individual peoples. (Buhdahl 1993: 44)

While the inspiration behind the monuments might in part have been a written source, most likely inspired by Ove Malling's *Store og Gode Handlinger af Danske, Norske og Holstenere* (Great and Good Deeds by Danes, Norwegians and Holstein-eans) from 1777, the memorial park when finished would not only honor great poets (amongst this pantheon to worthy commoners, one of the monuments carries the names of no less than five poets from 1500-1800: Anders Arrebo, Anders Bording, Thomas Kingo, Christen Bauman Tullin, and finally Johannes Ewald, while Ludvig Holberg for example was honored with his own,) but also find its way as a patriotic *topos* into poetry.

Lunden ved Jægerspriis, for example, written by C.A. Lund in 1783 (published in 1788) as an entry for a competition announced by *De skjønne Videnskabers Selskab* (The Academy of Fine Arts) addressed both the natural trees and the man-made marbles in the memorial park, allowing each to testify about ancient times. While the trees recall "Nordens Genius", the marble monuments evoke historical figures like Juul and Tordenskjold. This twofold path into the landscape is an attempt to fuse prehistory, history, and present, while allowing the visitor to experience a physical and emotional belonging to the nation (See Damsholt 2000: 162-4). To walk into this combined nature-culture realm was designed as a trajectory into a place which had created itself, so to speak, a kind of romantic English garden yet still embodying the features of classical patterns and protocols.

"Receive your poet, dim grove! Your shadow/ against the rays of midday sun calms me" Lund writes and thus places the poem's narrator symbolically in the comfortable dimness of the past, which the park presents: "But trees of fir! You, who majestically/ with dark crowns strut toward heaven/ and invite me; what grand deity builds his sanctuary in your gloomy shadows?" he asks, and then shifts from natural to manufactured memorials: "To whom do you belong, proud marble! – on who's honor/ do you tell tardy eternities?" (Lund 1788: 6-7). The noun, "marmor" (marble), is repeated again and again as a symbolic reference to a material which holds (eternal) stories of ancient heroes:

The opening grove reveals before my eyes,

How nature without artistry and tenfold charms

smiles solemnly, like the place

where Adam woke, amongst the trees of Eden.

Here old beech trees bend down their massive boughs

To kindly shade the splendid scene of joy.

The marble pantheon is here clearly matched with nature's own unformed material: the trees of the nation, which are also the trees of Eden. The marble monuments and the trees each in their way harbor the nation's past and the names of its heroes. The poem progresses as a stroll into and around the memorial park and the narrator imagines various moments in the history of the Danes as it plays out with a multitude of historical actors inscribed in the marble monuments and placed as if by happenstance amongst the trees. Marble stones, trees, and proper names coalesce until the poem's narrator reaches zenith, the ancient burial mound, now renamed Julianehøj.

Material Presence vis-à-vis Poetic Articulation

Wiedewelt's and Høegh-Guldberg's vision of the memorial park as a symbolic manifestation which aimed to educate the wanderer in the garden of his or her Danish roots and ancestry had an abstract quality, which only in part, at least in aesthetic terms, spilled over into the next generation.[8] Yet, knowledge of and interest in archaeology would sharpen noticeably in Danish literature at a time when endangerment of the nation gave rise to interests in origin and national identity. The inauguration of the *Royal Committee for the Preservation and Collection of National Antiquities*, for example, was linked to the Romantic Movement and the nationalism following the Napoleonic wars. Authors of the so-called Golden Age, like Adam Oehlenschläger, B.S.Ingemann, and N.F.S. Grundtvig would play important parts in the dialogue between history, archaeology, and literature.[9] But, different as they were, neither Oehlenschläger nor Grundtvig would

8   See Hakon Lund's description of H.E. Freund's reaction to the monuments and his task of restoring them in 1831. The first restoration of the stones were necessary already in 1810, so the memorial stones, ironically, did not hold well against the ravages of *time*.

9   Kristian Kristensen writes: "The 'fateful years' of 1807, 1848, 1864, 1920 and 1940-45 are reflected in the archaeological activity of the time, and prehistory in these years of crisis was frequently used as symbol of national identity. After all, it was not only through museums and archaeological books that knowledge of archaeology spread. Most of the population got to know of it at second or third hand – primarily though the literary traditions extending from Oehlenschläger, Ingemann and Grundtvig to Johannes V. Jensen and Martin A. Hansen, but also in an attenuated form through school text books, children's books, folk high schools etc." (Kristiansen 1985: 26)

160   KARIN SANDERS

endorse archaeological excavations of the many burial mounds scattered over the Danish landscape. Their interest in the past was colored by romantic ideology, not scientific interest. Grundtvig complained that Werlauff, for example, was an "attacker of graves" (gravstormer). Werlauff had argued that after excavating and mining the mounds for their artifacts they could well be leveled and hence more useful for the peasant. This "grave-attack-song" (gravstormersang) as Grundtvig grumbled, showed no veneration for the soul of the ancient landscape. That "the shadow was revered more than the body" outraged Grundtvig and he argued for the rights of the mounds in anthropomorphic terms: "the unique value of these memorials lies in the fact that they, like embalmed giants, grant us insight to past times." (Here cited from Jørgen Jensen 1992: 37; see also Lundgreen-Nielsen 1980: 293-294). Only if untouched, he maintained, would the mounds remain meaningful.

Oehlenschläger too protested in *Sankt Hans-Aftenspil* (Midsummer Night's Play, 1802) against the destruction made by avaricious peasants. And in his poem "Guldhornene" (The Golden Horns, 1802/3), which according to literary tradition inaugurated the Romantic Movement in Denmark, Oehlenschläger famously spoke of the blindness of the antiquarians. Here, archaeological artifacts in form of the two Golden Horns became a perfect model for imaginative projections of a national past. When they disappeared, stolen and then melted down to coins by the thief, they changed from objects of the Enlightenment to tropes for Romanticism, from archaeological treasures to poetical images.[10] This relationship between poetic language and material artifact is worth a closer look.

At the threshold between Enlightenment and Romanticism, the Nordic past, argues John L. Greenway, "found expression on both an empirical-rational and mythic level." He goes on to say:

Consciously, Nordic subject matter was either derided in formal literature or, when seriously studied, searched for concealed historical or conceptual content and treated as allegory, conforming to neoclassical esthetics. On the mythic (unconscious) plane the Norseman became the central figure in major social myth of Enlightenment origins – the myth of northern freedom – and developed from this into a minor literary myth of the golden age. This myth, however, ran counter to the controlling myth of the Enlightenment – progress. (Greenway 1977: 84)

---

10   See also Bernd Henningen's article in this volume.

But what role do the ancient artifacts play in the literary or poetic imagination – what task do they perform as materiality? Is it the material (its thing-ness if you will) that is of interest? Or is it the emanation, the 'spirit' of the fabric and substance from the past that vibrates in the literature and poetry of this period? As a national literary history became important and as the nation started to house its treasures and prehistoric artifacts in museum spaces, how did the two meet?

Gold, Marble and other Material Imaginations

It is not possible to answer this question in a Danish context without another brief comment on Oehlenschläger's poem on the Golden Horns. The poem still looms large in Danish literary history, not only as the symbolic launch of a new poetic language with which to address the past in romanticist terms but also because of the conciliation (or the "myth of synthesis", see Greenway 1977: 157) the poem performs between historical facts (the horns' actual existence as archaeological artifacts and the empirical events linked to the finding of the horns in 1639 and 1734 respectively, the loss of them in 1802 etc.) and poetical imagination. The fact that the horns existed in reality was not as important to the poet, however, as the metaphysical possibility they offered as vessels from – and for – a mythical past. What Oehlenschläger wanted to extract from the earth and from the symbolic value of 'gold' was not tangible proof of a past but a sense of its spirit. Therefore, he was rather hostile to the efforts of archaeologists, who in his view were akin to dusty and myopic librarians. Their efforts at comprehending the past by way of digging for empirical bits and pieces were consequently described in the poem as blindness.

But what significance can we mine from the *gold* of the Golden Horns? It seems that we can think of it at three different levels ranging from the concrete to the symbolic; first: the materiality, the actual metal of the archaeological artifact; second: the ancient Greek concept of a first (and idealized) Golden Age; and third: the metaphorical meaning that the poet (Oehlenschläger) constructs, which in turn becomes emblematic for the start of the Danish Golden Age in the nineteenth century. To think of the past in terms of materials and metals was not an archaeological invention of the early 1800s; it was a well-known construction by the Greeks (Hesiod, for example, in *Works and Days* writes about four ages (or races) – Golden, Silver, Bronze, and Iron). The concept of the Golden Age resonated in a metaphorical sense both with a Hellenistic inspired concept of a past that never grew old, a world idealized, free of toil – a *first* age; and with what later would be seen as the Golden Age of the Danish nineteenth century. The gold and the symbolic values assigned to it, then, have their own temporality. Not a

KARIN SANDERS

temporality that is necessarily progressive and linear, but one that appears to hold more than one moment in time.[11]

If we look at The Golden Horns as both text and artifacts we are able to ascertain two parallel tracks, one visual and material and another verbal and metaphysical. One leads to the museum, the other to the reading room and the library. In a museum context, at the National Museum in Copenhagen, the significance of the *metal* of the horns continues to be at issue. In September 2004, for example, the public was invited to a display of jewellery supposedly made from the melted gold of the stolen horns. The value of the metal – now reshaped as earrings – has museal significance as the tangible and authentic material from which the national treasures had once been formed. Yet when the only surviving material traces of the original horns takes a radically different form from the original vessels which spoke so forcefully to the romanticists, and when these new forms (earrings) are displayed in the same showcase and next to replicas of the original horns, one has to ask: what is authenticity? Is it lodged in the fabric of the material (gold) or is it to be found in the shape of the artifact it once was (horns)?

Although Oehlenschläger's 'golden' poem expressed a new moment in which the old was rearticulated, poets of the nineteenth century did not entirely lose sight of the metaphorical value of another material which had captured the poetic imagination during much of the eighteenth century: marble. An example of this can be found in the poems of Schack Staffeldt (1769-1826). Ten years older than Oehlenschläger, Staffeldt too articulated a relation to the past, but did not publish his poems until one year later than his rival. Unlike Oehlenschläger, Staffeldt did not favor the North over the Grecian-Roman. Rather his poetic verve was tied intimately to the artistic paradigms formed by the conventional classical ideals. Furthermore, Staffeldt drew heavily on Neo-Platonism and in "Kunstnerlængsel" (Artistic Longing) published in 1804, the past is anthropomorphized as a tangible manifestation of loss and longing: "The silent past turns back/in flight and looks at me/through smiles and tears." We are presented with a corporeal experience, where the past is perceived by the poem's 'I' as a partner in longing for a meeting which cannot fully take place. Resembling platonic love, Staffeldt's artistic longing is about the pain of non-fulfillment; and about the memory of potential pleasures. In fact, the silent past (den stille Fortid) is, as we see in the stanza above, made human and therefore able to return a gaze, full of smiles and tears, to the poem's wounded and yearning

---

11 Ironically, the Golden Horns were given currency as national treasures precisely at a time when endeavors were commenced to fine-tune an understanding of the past through chronologies based on empirical findings of other (less precious!) material: stone, bronze and iron. To group the prehistoric past – that is, the time before written sources – according to metals or material found in geological layers is both a concrete and symbolic act.

'I'. The past is a lover lost, a platonic lover never held. Staffeldt's gesture of making the past both historical and personal is unambiguous:

Oh! There was a time
when innocence, youth, bliss and song
in the valleys of earth, were restored:
Sheer spring and daylight, then,
rapture and embrace
and dawn of life.

But is the soil from which this past is emanating Nordic? Staffeldt is clearly not interested in emblematizing the past in or as a particular regional artifact, and only in the poem's reference in the fourth stanza to "On the rare cut of the saga-stone/ still many saved features are kept/ as if the vanished speaks;" can we locate a possible reference to the culture of the North. This dearth of specific allusions to the North is characteristic of Staffeldt's poetry. The past here is colored by a classical notion of a Golden Age, not one specifically Nordic.

In another poem, "I Canovas Værksted" (In Canova's Workshop), also from 1804, Staffeldt places himself squarely in antiquity as the aesthetic model for romantic poetry. (See Sanders 1996) Here, Staffeldt is inspired by Herder's notion that the world is created from a "boulder" or a "rock" fallen from heaven, which forms the earth's initial substance, and by Herder's idea that the ideal sculptural form lies hidden in the marble, already shaped, waiting to be released from its prison by the artist. It is this emancipation process which is at the core of the poem. It starts with a question: "Did a marble block fall sunder? // is it a relic of a fallen past?" The marble block is to be reshaped and re-articulated to create a tangible point from which to start the process – as the poem progresses – of chiselling out and reshaping the original material into ethereal poetic 'matter'. The relic of the past is not pried from the soil of the Nordic past, such as in Oehlenschläger's poem, but implicitly accredited as an aesthetic debt to (neo) classical ideals.

Competing Disciplines

While the poets wrestled with which past they should turn to (be it Nordic or Grecian-Roman) as the repository for poetic language, the interest in separating material culture and literary culture also started to take form institutionally. This story is best told by looking briefly at two combatants, N.M. Petersen (1791-1862), a philologist and historian and eventually the first Professor of Nordic Languages in 1845 at Copenhagen University, and the younger J.J.A.Worsaae who, as mentioned, would become C.J. Thomsen's successor as Denmark's key archaeologist. The former represented a literary approach to interpreting material artifacts from the past, the latter an archaeological. Each, in their own way was engaged with national identity. Petersen's literary and linguistic explanations of the past in particular were not lacking in patriotic fervor and like many of his contemporaries he shared in the belief that national identity was tied to language. In "Ledetraad til Nordisk Oldkyndighed" (Guidelines to Nordic Antiquarianism, published in 1836 and edited by Thomsen), to which Petersen had written a section on Old Norse literature, his glorification of the Nordic past focused on language, and he located in the Danish tongue the authenticity and honesty that he saw as emblematic of its people. He was an industrious contributor on matters relating to the past, but would show little interest in, and indeed neglected, prehistory (See Conrad 1996: 296; Sanders 2004: 203-6). Worsaae too was engaged in an ideological dispute about language and national identity, particularly with the German linguist and folklorist Jacob Grimm, whom he accused of misusing science in a fanatical nationalistic interest (See Kirsten Gomard in this volume). Grimm's thesis, that Jutland linguistically had been German until the 5th and 6th century was to Worsaae yet another abuse of historical facts. History was to be understood, not misunderstood.

Although Petersen, the literary-scholar, had harbored dreams of becoming a poet and saw his work as influenced by poetry, Worsaae, the archaeologist, was more directly connected to the influential poets and authors of the time. As was the case with most of his contemporaries, the dramatizations of the Danish past, particularly those by Adam Oehlenschläger, the principal Danish Romanticist, would inspire Worsaae. In *En Oldgrandskers Erindringer* (Memoirs of an Antiquarian) he reflects:

My studies were carried forth by the surge of national movements. The awakening public spirit sought rebirth and refreshment from the memorable past, which Oehlenschläger's works had brought to general ferment. I shall never forget the powerful impression I received when I, who had previously only seen poor comedies in Jutland, visited the Royal Theater for the first time and saw "Hakon Jarl" [...] I felt as if I was placed directly in ancient times as an eye witness [...] As an antiquarian I had not had a more moving experience." (Worsaae 1879/1935, 70)

Worsaae also comments on another dramatization of the Danish past at the Royal Theater, Henrik Hertz's *Sven Dyring's House*, in which a specter appears in a house at night. "I found myself close to taking the same position as did H.C. Ørsted's waiter, who, after seeing [it], exclaimed in full honesty: 'in that house he would under no circumstances take employment'" (Worsaae 1935 (1879): 70). Worsaae is clearly ambivalent when it comes to fictionalizing history. Although fascinated by the dramatist's renditions of the past, he too, like Ørsted's valet, was not to take up employment in "that house". With his nationalistic inclination he was a man of his time, and as such the literary world with its celebration of the past would be of influence. But Worsaae kept his distance. His interest in the "the marvelous memories of the old North" (det gamle Nordens herlige Minder: 91) and his belief in a spiritual unity "aandelig Eenhed" between the Scandinavian peoples did not spark an active political involvement in the Scandinavian cause. He remained a national aristocrat not a populist. Archaeology, in Worsaae's universe had to rest on facts not emotion: "In archaeology as well as in other areas, the loosest, most fanciful claims were brought forth. I therefore found it to be an urgent necessity, to lay the ground for a more true system through critique and the certainty of facts, less dependant upon old prejudice" (Ibid: 93). Yet, he was by no means blind to the relation between archaeology and literature. He had access to Adam Oehlen- schläger's home and would exchange information with the poet. In fact, he would bring historical and archaeological works to the bard and in return Oehlenschläger would read to him from his latest poems. Oehlenschläger apparently recognized in Worsaae a fellow enthusiast for the ancient North. Worsaae writes:

I expressed my own and many other antiquarians' admiration for his ability to give, from his readings of poor translations of the Edda-songs, of Saxo and Snorre, a fresher and more truthful image of the Nordic past, than we antiquarians had so far been able to cre- ate from all of our memorial stones and written sources. Rightly, Oehlenschläger pointed out, that the true antiquarian-and historian [...] also had to be a poet or have poetic abil- ities in order to be able to penetrate the spirit of past times and collect the fragments left behind into a perceivable whole for the present. To me it seemed that in this regard the poet's position was more enviable than the antiquarian's was. The poet could more freely follow his instinct and by its creative force give his picture accurate light and shadow. A poor antiquarian on the other hand had to constantly tame his imagination, even if he was convinced that an inner truth lay therein. He had to patiently wait for *impervious facts*. If he transgressed even the slightest bit, a whole army of un-poetical critics would call in arms. (Worsaae 1935 (1879): 119)

Although Worsaae here positions himself as a "poor antiquarian", who had to tame his imagination, he had of course already proven himself to be one of the "un-poetical critics". Oehlenschläger in turn understood the poetical aspects of archaeology, but had no sense for or particular interest in its scientific potential. To him, as we could see, and as was the case with most other poets at the time, ancient artifacts and monuments spoke most forcefully when left untouched by

166

scientific, un-poetical, dissections. Interestingly, Petersen would not share Worsaae's gesture of acceptance toward Oehlenschläger's use of the Danish past. To him, Oehlenschläger corrupted the national heritage and produced "Gibberish" (Ruskomsnusk) (Conrad 1996: 305).

Worsaae's description of Oehlenschläger's ability to provide a "fresher and more truthful image of the Nordic past" than the archaeologists, and Petersen's assessment of the poet's accomplishments as 'Gibberish,' were, each from their perspective points, what can best be described as a vacillating tension and cross-pollination between the disciplines and between material artifacts and written words. In his *Moralske Tanker* (Moral Reflections) from 1744, written several generations before the quarrels described here, Ludvig Holberg famously growled that "studying Nordic antiquities is like scrabbling in dung-hills: it is like an occupation to which certain people might well be sentenced for their crimes, if there were not so many keen amateurs in the field" (Holberg 1992 (1744): 303). The generations of scholars and poets which followed Holberg would both consent to and dispute his biting observation. Undeterred by perceptions of frozen hostility or by Holberg's deprecating comment about "scrabbling in dung-hills," Worsaae and Petersen in the end joined a host of Danish eighteenth and nineteenth century poets, visual artists and archaeologists who – occasionally in sync, oftentimes not – had dug into the earth in order to tease out a sense of nationhood and identity from "the bedrock of material things."

References

Bukdahl, Else Marie 1993: *Johannes Wiedewelt,* Edition Bløndal.

Conrad, Flemming 1996: *Smagen og det nationale. Studier i dansk litteraturhistorieskrivning 1800-1861.* Copenhagen: Museum Tusculanum Forlag.

Damsholt, Tine 2000: *Fædrelandskærlighed og borgerdyd: patriotisk diskurs og militære reformer i Danmark i sidste del af 1700-tallet.* Copenhagen: Museum Tusculanum Press.

Eman, Karin 2001: Landskabshavens tableauer, *Tableau. Det sublime øjeblik.* Eds. Elin Andersen, Karen Klitgaard Povlsen. Aarhus: Klim.

Fejler, Jane 2003: Wiedewelt, Winckelmann and Antiquity, *The Rediscovery of Antiquity: The Role of the Artist.* Eds. Jane Fejfer, Tobias Fisher-Hansen, Annette Rathje. Copenhagen: Museum Tusculanum Press.

Greenway, John L. 1977: *The Golden Horns: Mythic Imagination and the Nordic Past.* Athens, GA: University of Georgia Press.

Hedeager, Lotte, Karen Schusboe (eds.), 1989: *Brugte Historier.* Copenhagen: Akademisk Forlag.

Holberg, Ludvig 1992 (1744): *Moralske Tanker.* Ed. Billeskov-Jansen, F.J. Copenhagen: Det Danske Sprog og Litteraturselskab & Borgen.

Jensen, Jørgen 1992: *Thomsens Museum. Historien om Nationalmuseet.* Copenhagen: Gyldendal.

Klint-Jensen, Ole 1975: *A History of Scandinavian Archaeology.* London: Thames and Hudson.

Kohl, Philip L., Clare Fawsett 1995: Archaeology in the service of the state: theoretical considerations, *Nationalism, Politics, and the Practice of Archaeology.* Eds.: Kohl and Fawsett. Cambridge: Cambridge University Press.

Kristiansen, Kristian 1998: *Europe before History.* Cambridge: Cambridge University Press.

Kryger, Karin 2003: Julianehøj and the Memorial Grove at Jægerspris, *The Rediscovery of Antiquity: The Role of the Artist.* Eds. Jane Fejfer, Tobias Fisher-Hansen, Annette Rathje. Copenhagen: Museum Tusculanum Press.

Lowenthal, David 1985: *The Past is a Foreign Country.* Cambridge; New York: Cambridge University Press.

Lund, C.A. 1788: *Lunden ved Jægerspris.* Copenhagen: Johan Fredrik Schulz.

Lund, Hakon 1976: *Mindelunden ved Jægerspris.* Jægerspris: Kong Frederik den Syvendes Stiftelse.

Lundgreen-Nielsen, Flemming 1980: *Det handlende ord. N.F.S. Grundtvigs digtning, litteraturkritik og poetik, 1798-1819.* Vol. 1, Copenhagen: G.E.C. Gad.

Nielsen, Marjetta 2003: Between Art and Archaeology, *The Rediscovery of Antiquity: The Role of the Artist.* Eds. Jane Fejfer, Tobias Fisher-Hansen, Annette Rathje. Copenhagen: Museum Tusculanum Press.

Nielsen, Ingrid 1987: Den Kongelige Commission for Oldsagernes Opbevaring, *Bevar din arv.* Ed. Ingrid Nielsen. Copenhagen: Gad.

Renfrew, Colin: 1996. Foreword, *Cambridge Illustrated History of Archaeology.* Ed. Paul G. Bahn. Cambridge; New York: Cambridge University Press.

Sanders, Karin 1996: Plastiske objekter – romantiske tekster, *Runer Paa Blad.* Ed. Henrik Blicher, Copenhagen: Copenhagen University & Akademisk Forlag.

Sanders, Karin 2002: The Archaeological Object in Word and Image, *Edda. Nordisk tidsskrift for litteraturforskning.* 3/02. Eds. Unni Langås, Andreas G. Lombnæs, Jahn Thon. Universitetsforlaget.

Sanders, Karin 2004: Fra 'Sølen' og 'Pølen'. Et moseligs fortælling i material- og litteraturhistorien, *Kampen om litteraturhistorien .* Eds. Marianne Alenius, Thomas Bredsdorff, Gert Emborg. Copenhagen: Dansklærerforeningens Forlag.

Schnapp, Alain 1993 (1996): *The Discovery of the Past.* London: The British Museum Press.

Silberman, Neil Asher 1995: Promised lands and chosen peoples: the politics and poetics of archaeological narrative, *Nationalism, Politics, and the Practice of Archaeology.* Eds. Philip Kohl and Claire Fawsett. Cambridge, Great Britain: Cambridge University Press.

Staffeldt, A.W. Schack von 2001 (1804): *Samlede Digte.* Ed. Henrik Blicher. Copenhagen: Det Danske Sprog og Litteraturselskab & C.A. Reitzel.

Stangerup, Haakon 1940: *Schack Staffeldt.* Copenhagen: Gyldendal.

Wegener, C. F. 1856: Historiske Efterretninger om Abrahamstrup Gaard i den Ældre og Nyere Tid, *Annaler for Nordisk Oldkyndighed og Historie.* Copenhagen: Det Kongelige Nordiske Oldskrift-Selskab.

Worsaae, J.J.A. 1935 (1879): *En Oldgrandskers Erindringer.* Copenhagen: Gyldendal.

KARIN SANDERS

sætter Beskueren paa Spor til at kjende vore For-fædres Overgang fra Vildhed og Raahed til Cultur og Sædelighed. (Nyerup)

kunde studere den successive Fremgang i Natio-nens Kultur og Begreber, Sæder og Skikke, (Ny-erup)

Mit Studium blev ligesom baaret og løftet af de mere og mere svulmende nationale Bevægelser. Den nyvakte folkelige Aand søgte Gjenfødelse og Forfriskelse i den minderige Oldtid, for hvilken Oehlenschlägers Digterværker havde fremkaldt en almindelig Begeistring. Indensinde kan jeg glemme det mægtige Indtryk, jeg selv modtog, da jeg, som hidtil kun havde kjendt slette Comedier i Jylland, for første Gang besøgte det Kongelige Theater og netop saa "Hakon Jarl" […] Jeg følte mig umiddelbart hensat i Oldtiden mellem dens store Helteskikkelser som et virkeligt Øienvidne til den stolte Jarls og det grumme Hedenskabs Fald./ En for mig, især som Oldgransker, saa gri-bende og vækkende Forestilling har jeg ingensin-de siden overværet, […]. (Worsaae *Oldgranskers Erindringer*, 70)

Jeg befandt mig noget nær paa det samme naïve og lykkelige Standpunkt som H.C. Ørsteds Tjener, der efterat have seet Hertz's "Sven Dyrings Huus", hvori en Stedmoder sulter Børnene, medens Mo-deren gaaer igjen om Natten, i fuld Alvor bestemt erklærede, at "i det Huus vilde han ikke for nogen Priis tage Tjeneste." (Ibid.)

I Archæologien saavel her som andetsteds op-stilledes fremdeles de løseste, mest phantasifulde Paastande. Jeg fandt det derfor paatrængende fornødent, ved Kritik og ved sikre Kjendsgjer-ninger, at lægge Grunden til et rigtigere, af ældre Fordomme mere uafhængigt System. (Ibid.: 93)

Jeg udtalte min og mange Oldforskeres Beun-dring over, at han alene ved Læsning af slette Oversættelser af Edda-sangene, af Saxo og Snorro var bleven istand til at give et friskere og sandere Billede af den nordiske Oldtid, end vi Oldgranskere med alle vore Mindesmærker og Kildeskrifter hidtil havde formaaet at skabe. Med

rette bemærkede Oehlenschläger, at den virkelige Old-og Historieforsker […] jo ogsaa maatte være Digter eller have en digterisk Begavelse, for ret at kunne trænge ind i de svundne Tiders Aand og samle de talrige efterladte Enkeltheder til et for Nutiden anskueligt Heelt. Mig forekom det dog, at Digterens Stilling i saa Henseende var mere misundelsesværdig, end Oldforskernes. Dig-teren kunde langt friere følge sit Instinkt og ved dets skabende Kraft give sit Billede behørig Lys og Skygge. En stakkels Oldgransker derimod maatte idelig søge at tøjle sin Phantasie, om han end var nok saa fuldt overbeviist om, at der laa en indre Sandhed til Grund derfor. Han maatte taalmod-igt vente paa *bevisende Kjendsgjerninger*. Gik han den ringeste Smule udenfor det Givne, stod der strax en heel Skare upoetiske kritikere, som raabte "Vagt i Gevær."(Ibid.: 119)

Høien og den Omgivelse til et fædrenelandsk Minde, der saa at sige skulde forene Oldtiden med Nutiden. (Wegener)

Modtag din Digter, dunkle Lund! Din Skygge/ mod Middagssolens Straaler mig betrygge

Men Graner! I, som majestætiske/Med mørke Top mod Himlen kneisende/Indbyde mig; hvad mægtig Guddom bygger/Sin Helligdom i eders skumle Skygger? (Lund: 6-7)

Hvis er du, stolte Marmor! – om hvis Hæder/For-taeller du de seene Evigheder?" ((7) Lund, 1788: 6)

Bag tætte Hegn indfredet Høien hviler,/Og al Naturens Skønhed om den smiler,/Og Nordens ældste Dages store mænd/i varigt Marmor leve her igjen. (Ibid.: 28)

Med aabne Lund sig for mit Syn udbreder,/ Hvor uden Kunst med tifold Yndigheder/Na-turen smiler højtidsfuld, som der/Hvor Adam vaagnede blandt Edens Træer./Hist gamle Bøeg nedbøier tætte Grene/Til venlig Lye for Glædens store Scene. (Ibid.)

Hvad er det, som Jorden her/Saa mægtigt drager /Og dybt mit Hjerte saarer?/Den stille Fortid vender sig/I flugten om og seer paa mig/Igjennem Smiil og Taarer. (Staffeldt)

Ak! Vist en Tid der var engang,/Da Uskyld, Ungdom, Fryd og Sang/I Jordens Dale bøde:/Da var der idel Vaar og Dag,/Henrykkelse og Favnetag/ Og Livets Morgenrøde. (Staffeldt)

Sagatavlens sjeldne Skaar/ End mangt et reddet Træk der staar, / Som om det Svundne taler

Styted' en Marmorklippe sammen?/ Er det Vrag af den faldne fortid? (Staffeldt)

Det er højligen at beklage, at der endnu findes mange, som ikke vil give noget magt, som skrives om disse nordiske lande, undtagen det kan bevises med nogle af de græske eller romerske historikere. Ligesom de skulle bedre have vidst, hvad herhjemme skete, end indbyggerne selv: da dog ingen af dem har været i disse lande, intet heller om disse rigers tilstand kunne vide andet, end hvad de ungefær af andre af vores modstandere hørte. (Worm)

Skyggen skal agtes mere end Legemet; hine Mindesmærkers ejendommelige Værd for os bestaar deri, at de som balsamerede Kjæmper skænker os et Blik tilbage i de svundne Tider. (Grundtvig)

KARIN SANDERS

A Map of Words

Mme de Staël's Three-dimensional Cartography and Gendered Geography in *The Influence of Literature upon Society* and *Corinne, or Italy*

On her journey to Italy in 1804-5, Mme Anne-Louise-Germaine de Staël (1766-1817) writes a letter to Jean-Baptiste-Antoine Suard, an old friend of her family and a respected literary critic, telling him about a novel she is working on. It is, she writes, "a kind of novel", which primarily takes place in Italy, and which can work as a guide for travelling there (Staël 1970: 306).[1] The novel, she is referring to is *Corinne, ou l'Italie*, 1807 (*Corinne, or Italy* 1833) – a bestseller in which the young Scottish Lord Nelvil falls in love with the beautiful, multitalented, apparently Italian Corinne. As Mme de Staël's letter to Suard shows, the novel combines prose fiction and travel writing. This double function was, however, not unusual. Chloe Chard points out in her book, *Pleasure and Guilt on the Grand Tour*, that "even works that proclaim themselves as fictional offer both information and practical advice." (Chard 1999: 9). Mme de Staël's novel is an example of this. It worked as a guide for travellers in a much more personal way than today's guide books – at least for British travellers: "Early nineteenth-century British travellers in Italy constantly refer to Germaine de Staël's novel *Corinne, ou l'Italie* (1807), in order to define and reflect on their own experiences of travel."(Chard 1999: 16). As the allegorical title suggests, Corinne is the personification of Italy, while Oswald is England. This cartography reflects an idea of Europe being divided in two cultural, political, and artistic hemispheres, which Mme de Staël previously had unfolded in her work on literature in its relation to society, *De la littérature considérée dans ses rapports avec les institutions sociales*, 1800 (*The Influence of Literature upon Society*, 1812).[2] While *Corinne* could serve as a guide for travellers in Italy, *The*

1   "I will write a kind of novel which serves as a frame for travelling in Italy, and I think that a lot of the thoughts and feelings will take place there." Rome, April 9, 1805. (Staël 1970: 306; my translation).

2   Mme de Staël translated *De la littérature…* to English in 1803, using the title *A Treatise on Ancient and Modern Literature. Illustrated by striking references to the principal events that have distinguished the French Revolution.* In 1812, however, she published a second edition, now entitled *The Influence of Literature upon Society.* I have chosen to use her revised title, due to its exactness and her own choice of changing it. Unfortunately it has not been possible for me to quote directly from neither the 1803- nor the 1812-edition. All translations of passages from *De la littérature…* in this article are mine.

Influence of Literature upon Society – at least metaphorically – was a guide for arm-chair travelling in the world of literature.

In the following I shall present a close reading of these two texts, which are written in different genres but have a narrative dynamic in common, based on an opposition between north and south in Europe. My main focus shall be how Mme de Staël stages and invigorates this dichotomously formed map. Due to her Enlightenment upbringing, her intellect, and her wide reading, she manages to communicate complicated theories on history, politics, social institutions, climate, art, literature, aesthetics, gender etc. in plain language and in handy images. Adjusted to her own time, she popularizes and reformulates theories by, among others, Tacitus, Paul Henri Mallet, Edward Gibbon, Charles de Secondat Montesquieu, Jean-Jacques Rousseau, Edmund Burke and Johann Joachim Winckelmann, and synthesizes these different approaches in a functional and easily understood image of Europe. Her image is, I will argue, a three dimensional cartography: In the intersection point between a specific time and a specific place, space emerges. This space is emphasized by her (modern) making the body the pivotal point, and in her cartography, I propose, it is a gendered space.

The Influence of Literature upon Society

The Influence of Literature upon Society was originally published in 1800 and consists of two parts: "On ancient and modern literature" and "On the current state of the Enlightenment in France and its future progress". I shall, exclusively, concentrate on the first part and on the North-South cartography.

In her preface for the second French edition of *The Influence of Literature upon Society*, Mme de Staël describes her intention with the book as a wish to prove the relationship that had existed between literature and the social institutions in every century and in every country (Staël 1844: 196).[3] Her intention presupposes a mutual relationship between time ("every century"), place ("every country") and society. Thus, in her introduction she writes: "I intend to examine the influence of religion, customs, and laws on literature, and the influence of literature on religion, customs, and laws." (Ibid.: 199). She remarks, that this is a work not yet done in any other book, and that no French treatise on literature has presented sufficient research on the moral and political reasons for changes in the literary spirit.

From today's perspective her project is a combination of literary history, criticism, sociology and comparative literature. Her idea of literature is relativistic and evolutionary and is reflecting her Enlightenment upbringing. The main thought

3   The following quotations referring to Staël 1844 are my translations.

FIG. 8:

Mme de Staël painted as Corinne. The picture reinforces the general identification of Corinne as Mme de Staël's alter ego. Elisabeth Vigée-Lebrun, 1807-1807.

of her treatise is the ongoing intellectual progress of mankind (ibid.: 207), and her description of her project reveals an encyclopaedic research:

I will try to show the character that such or such kind of government gives to the eloquence, the moral ideas that such or such religious belief develops in the human spirit, the effects of imagination which are produced by the credulity of the people, the poetic beauties which belong to the climate, the degree of civilisation which is most favourable for the force or perfection of the literature, the different changes which are introduced in the writings as well as in the customs by the existence of women before and since the establishment of the Christian religion; finally the universal progress of enlightenment as a simple effect of the succession of time […] (Ibid.: 207)

Her investigation of this armchair travel does not surprisingly resemble that of travel writing: She focuses on government, religion, moral, climate, civilization, enlightenment, and women's situation.[4] She relates it to literature, however, and her main interest is the local and epocal manifestation in literature, and conversely, the effect of literature on the social institutions and on mentality. In this sense she regards literature as being seismographic – as registering and reflecting cultural, political, social, religious, and climatic circumstances.[5]

Mme de Staël's definition of literature is rather broad. Literature includes poetry, eloquence, history and philosophy or the study of 'our' intellectual life. She differentiates between the branches of literature which belong to imagination (fiction) and those which belong to thinking (philosophy) (ibid.: 208). She regards fictional literature as mimetic and defines poetry as exactly the art of depicting in words that which catches the eye (ibid.: 209). Poetry as an imitation of physical nature is, she writes, not evolutionary. The sensual impression is limited by the senses, and though the description of various natural phenomenons may vary in detail, the strongest impression must, she argues, be made by the first author who managed to describe them (ibid.). Since the ancient Greeks were the first to trans-form nature and things seen, sensed and experienced into literature, their version is supreme. In contrast to fiction, philosophy has developed from the Greeks and onwards. Its influence on science, method, and analysis is immense, Mme de Staël points out, and furthermore, philosophy's exploration of the human heart has influenced fictional writing.

Two literary hemispheres: North and South

Mme de Staël's cartography is based on an already existing idea of Europe, but her valuation of the two European hemispheres along with her remarks on the present situation in France, upset Napoleon.[6] In her preface for the second French edition,

---

4   H. Arnold Barton mentions similar key topics for travellers in the 1760s and 1770s and detects a shift in interest: "While the literary travelers [sic] of the 1760s and 1770s tended to concentrate upon what I have described as the 'public visage' of the lands they visited – government, public institutions, higher culture, and upper-class social life – those of succeeding decades and their readers showed a growing interest in folk customs and culture." (Barton 1998: 95).

5   Like travel writing, her book reveals, however, as much about her own time and country as about the country in question. As Fjågesund & Symes point out, travel writers' investigation of the other is in general as much about themselves (Fjågesund & Symes 2003).

6   See for instance the preface by the translator, Robert L. Hansen, in the Danish edition of *De la littéra-ture: Litteraturen og samfundet* (Staël 1973: XV).

MARIANNE RAAKILDE JESPERSEN

she notes, that she has been criticized for preferring literature from the North (ibid.: 196). Her view of northern literature is, as this shows, pointing towards a general revaluating of the northern part of Europe as a utopia.

All in all, her map of Europe follows Tacitus, whom she refers to several times: Europe is divided into two parts by the Alps. The ancient Greece and Rome formed the cradle of civilisation, while the people from the North were barbarian tribes. Upon this pre-existing map she applies her literary criticism, roughly following the lines already drawn on paper. She distinguishes between two fundamentally different literatures: One coming from the southern countries, and one from the northern. The source of the first is Homer, the second originates in Ossian.[7] The literature of the South covers the Greeks, the Italians, the Spanish, and the French at the time of Louis XIV. Consequently, the literature of the North covers English writings, German writings, and some books by Danish and Swedish authors, and is seen as originating in the Scottish bards, the Icelandic legends and the Scandinavian poetry (ibid.: 252). Thus, her definition of the northern countries is broader than our present understanding of north Europe.[8] Her references, in her general sketch of the history of Europe, are both explicit and implicit. For instance her avoidance of epochal markers creates a mythological time, which ascribes a kind of universal validity to the two European regions: As the people of the North/South were then, they are now and forever. Her contemporaries have most probably been able to detect the implicit references, but still she creates an illusion of eternal characteristics caused by the geographic belonging. According to this mythology, the people of the North were barbarians who invaded the southern countries and made their literature and art disappear for a while. The northern people, who came with a warlike cruelty and absolute ignorance, gained the advantages of civilisation, enlightenment and knowledge, and obtained a kind of flexibility which would help them to complement their intellectual skills. The weakened people in the southern countries gained, on the other hand, strength from being mixed with the northern people. The merging of the northern spirit with the southern way of living was, however, according to Mme de Staël, only possible due to Christianity (Ibid.: 236-237).[9]

7   For further discussion of the polemic about Ossian, see the articles by Karen Klitgaard Povlsen and Jesper Hede in this volume.

8   For elaboration of the definition of north Europe, see the article by Hendriette Kliemann-Geisinger in this volume.

9   The fact that Mme de Staël stresses the importance of Christianity and Protestantism has to be seen in the context of the religious conditions in her own country, France. However, it exceeds the limits of this article to go further into it.

Her characteristic of the northern people elaborates the idea of the warrior spirit but surprisingly connects this mentality to a certain appreciation of literature:

The people of the North did not attach any value to life. This disposition made them individually courageous, but cruel toward others. They were imaginative, melancholic and had a tendency towards mysticism, but a deep contempt for enlightenment as a weakening of the spirit of the warrior: the women were more educated than the men because they had more spare time than them. The men loved them, they were faithful to them, they worshipped them; they could show a certain sensibility caused by love. (Ibid.: 237)

Warriors of the North, hedonists of the South

In general Mme de Staël describes the ancient Nordic people as disciplined and physically strong. Their virtue, she argues, prescribed them to show wisdom and competence through ways of living which demanded a supernatural control of pain (ibid.: 245). Their devastating fearlessness was, she argues, changed to unyielding firmness due to Christianity. The Christian religion controlled the people in the North by using their predisposition for melancholy, their inclination for sombre images, and their continual and profound occupation with the memory of the dead and their destinies (ibid.: 238). The religion and happiness at home stabilized the otherwise vagrant life of the ancient Nordic people. The women did not create superior literary works, but nevertheless they served the progress of literature by inspiring their husbands thoughts by being emotional and sensitive (Ibid.: 240).

Thus, while the ancient Nordic people were melancholic and obsessed with physical strength due to their living under a misty sky (ibid.: 238), their neighbours in the southern hemisphere had surrendered to pleasure. The Roman character of national pride and civilisation no longer existed, the Italian people were sick and tired of the idea of honour and believed in nothing else but pleasure. The intoxication of vice and ordinary ruin destroyed every kind of virtue, and the moral nature of the southern people was absorbed by the joys of pleasure, until Christianity – the great saviour in Mme de Staël's European history – came along and taught them duty, sacrifice and faith and gave their otherwise enslaved women equal rights in moral and religious issues (Ibid.: 237-239).

Mme de Staël rewrites an already known mythology of the early European history. The basic idea of geographical location determining the character and mentality of the people living there is even more obvious when she moves on to describe the two literary hemispheres. The most striking feature of her charac-

FIG. 9:
Corinne gives a feast for Oswald in order to compensate for delaying her story. She is begged by him and the other guests to improvise. Her improvisation at Miseno, as depicted here, shows that the human subject is regarded as being a part of the surrounding nature, and that body and nature is mutually reflecting. Aubrey-Lecomte, lithograph after the painting Corinne Improvising at Miseno, 1827, which the lithograph reverses.

teristics is the interdependence between climatic circumstances and literature. In this she refers to Montesquieu who formulated the idea of climatic differences as determining in *De l'esprit des lois*, 1748 (*The Spirit of the Laws* 1777).[10] The importance of the theory of climate for her literary criticism and history is obvious. The characteristics of a literary work of art – its aesthetic value, the superiority of the author or the literary style, certain themes, etc. – are all due to the geographical location and belonging of the author, and not to a certain creative genius. The value of a literary work of art is not related to the author's capability of creating and inventing, but to his – or more seldom her – capability of describing the surrounding nature, events, emotions etc. The literary work is, in other words,

10   For elaboration of Montesquieu's theory of climate, see the article by Jesper Hede in this volume.

strongly connected to location – to place. Therefore the literature of the South and the literature of the North differ: The climate, the sky, is probably – Mme de Staël argues – one of the most important reasons for differences between the images, which are enjoyed by northern people, and those which the southern people love to imagine. She elaborates this:

The poets of the South constantly mix the image of freshness, of leafy forests, of clear streams with all the emotions of life. They do not even represent the pleasures of the heart without involving the beneficial shade, which protects them against the burning sun. The vivid nature which surrounds them excites movements in them rather than thoughts. [...] The people of the North are less occupied with pleasures than pain, and their imagination is only more fertile. The spectacle of nature makes a strong impression on them; it seems like it is in their climate, always sombre and nebulous. (Ibid.: 253)

The northern literature is based on an imagination that thrives on the seashore, amid the howls of winds and on the dissolute moors. The melancholic mood of the northern people, Mme de Staël argues, makes their literature more philosophic than the southern literature, since melancholy makes emotions and thoughts sink deeper into the human character and destiny than any other emotion. Due to this tendency towards philosophy, Mme de Staël declares that all her thoughts lead her towards the Nordic literature (ibid.: 253). Writers from the northern countries have succeeded in depicting all that is beautiful, sublime, and touching in the darkish nature. These verbal images give rise to noble and pure feelings, create thoughts and have an instant emotional effect (ibid.: 197). The philosophical thoughts seem to be connected with the dark images of nature. Their poetry, more than the one from the southern countries, is in accordance with the spirit of a free people, and another reason for the sensitivity, which is characteristic of the Nordic literature, is the deference to women in the Nordic countries, which gave them an independence, unknown in other places (Ibid.: 254-55).

While the Nordic literature is thoughtful, melancholic, sombre, serious and sublime, the literature of the southern countries is described as a "voluptuous poetry [which] almost entirely excludes all ideas of a certain level" (ibid.: 254). Living under a burning sun, Mme de Staël writes, makes all passions flame and draws the mind towards pleasure (ibid.: 247). It ignites the imagination in a far more multifarious and exuberant way than living under the dark misty skies of the northern countries could.

Throughout the book Mme de Staël relates the characteristics of the two kinds of literature to climatic differences, and she consequently relates the differences in social institutions and religions to climatic circumstances as well. Further on, she combines the theory of climatic differences with a theory of language. The spirit of a people has an effect on the character of the language, and – in reverse – the language influences the spirit of the people. The sonorous thunder of the Italian language enables, she writes, neither the author nor the reader to think better, and continues:

even the sensibility is distracted from the emotion by the noisy harmonies. The Italian language is not concise enough for ideas; there is not enough darkness for the melancholic of feelings. It is a language with such an extraordinary melody, which moves you, as chords, without you even giving your attention to the meaning of the words. It moves you as a musical instrument. (Ibid.: 250)

But the linguistic ease is also one of the reasons why even the good Italian writers have difficulties in attaining perfection in style. The English language – which in this context is Nordic – is not, she writes, as harmonious for the ear as the languages in the southern countries, but through its powerful pronunciation it offers great advantages for poetry, since all the stressed words influence the soul, because they seem to arise from a living impression (ibid.: 267). The characteristics of the languages are thus closely related to climatic characteristics of the regions: The southern languages are light and pleasant, and the Nordic languages are harsh and powerful.

Mme de Staël sketches a dichotomous map of Europe. Furthermore, her map is three dimensional. Through her history of European literature, she reveals a cartography which combines place and time. In the intersection point between a specific geographical place – a specific location – and a specific time, space emerges. Metaphorically speaking, her text swells up in these chronotopic points and becomes a hilly landscape. The space is populated through her detailed, though selective, descriptions of living conditions, mentality, religious convictions etc. Through her description the reader looks inside the imagined lives and minds of ancient people. This emphasizes her literary style of writing. She creates and depicts possible worlds for the reader's imagination – takes the reader on a journey. Her version of the European map is written in a dramatized style, featuring protagonists and antagonists, causal relations and a narrative structure similar to basic story telling (good vs. evil etc.) and, with its melodramatic structures, similar to modern novel writing.[11] Her story line is clearly following Tacitus, Gibbon and Mallet's versions, but her plot reverses the idea of the northern countries as primitive – in fact they turn out to be the heroes of her story: After learning about civilization and intellectual refinements from the Southern people, they conquered, they were able to write even better literature, because it was more thoughtful and more philosophic. So the barbaric, primitive northern people end up being superior due to their spatial belonging (the harsh winds, darkness etc.), which in the first place made them barbarians.

The space emerging in the intersection point between time and place is defined by the body being there, as can be seen in the theories of climate, for instance. In other words: the body is the centre of the space. This idea of an embodied being – an embodied human subject – keeps popping up in *The Influence of Literature upon Society*. In Mme de Staël's description of virtue in relation to literature, she emphasizes the "impression" which virtue provokes in the human being, and the "sentiment" which is experienced with all that is "sublime" – in art as well as in nature (ibid.: 200). The human subject is *im*-pressed when confronted with the surroundings – is marked with impression and emotion, when meeting a virtuous human being, art, or nature. In other words: The human subject is sensitive and is interacting with the surrounding world. And the impression is bodily: The masterpieces of world literature provoke "a kind of moral and physical shaking" (ibid.: 201) and eloquence can provoke trembling (ibid.: 205). Reading has an effect on not only the mind but the body as well: "The eloquence, the poetry, the dramatic situations, the melancholic thoughts move the organs even though they address reflection." (ibid.: 201). Even though she rhetorically differentiates between body and mind, she does regard body and mind as dependent on each other. The idea of body and mind as an interconnected unit is further elaborated on in her thoughts about the influence of literature upon the human being. Her somatic rhetoric emphasizes the embodied subject as sensitive and interacting, and as a unique individual with personal, subjective experiences: "*Every one of us is shaken* by their [the literary works] beauties in different époques and *individually receives the impression* which they must produce." (Ibid.: 201 – my italics).

This reference to an embodied being and the use of somatic metaphors is extended to her cartography. The influence of the colour of the sky or the temperature is related to the body, and it is, she says, the ability to communicate a sensuous

---

11   Peter Brooks argues in *The Melodramatic Imagination* (1976), that the modern novel has melodramatic features: for instance the expressive body, the excessive style, the intention to say everything and to outline a moral order, the oppositional structure of forces and consequently a fixed list of characters. Several of these features can be detected in various forms in the contemporary travel literature as well. As characteristic rhetorical tropes in travel literature, Chard mentions hyperbole, digression, allegory, opposition among others (Chard 1999).

and spontaneous impression which generates good literature (ibid.: 209). Homer's genius was, according to Mme de Staël, his ability to make the reader see what he had seen himself. The reader senses, in other words, through the author (ibid.: 211). She reveals an idea of a connection between the physical, phenomenological world, *and* body, language, and soul. To be able to depict the experienced, the sensed, is described as the supreme good (ibid.: 253), so in the centre of the making of a literary work is the individual's experience of and sensibility towards the world, and his or her ability to communicate this to the readers. The connection she inscribes between world, body, language and soul, is circuitous and interdependent. The author has to be 'marked' bodily by the surrounding world, and – the other way round, the reader reacts bodily on reading literature. The importance of the writer's spatial placement and the transformation of this into language can also be seen in travel writing from the same period. As Chloe Chard points out, travel writings are closely concerned with "the task of finding the forms of language to translate the topography into discourse" (Chard 1999: 9). In the same line of thought, I will argue, is the problematic of the writer as an eye-witness, which Chloe Chard also deals with:

One rhetorical task that travellers accomplish, when they utter hyperboles of indescribability, is that of affirming their own status as eye-witnesses, who have encountered the objects of commentary in person, and undergone an experience beyond the imaginative grasp of those who know these objects only through the mediation of literature and art. It is the eye-witness alone, such hyperboles suggest, who is capable of experiencing the sense of uniqueness that supplies the precondition for wonder. (Chard 1999: 85)

To have been on the spot – or maybe even writing while being there – gives the writer an authority which seems to be closely connected to both body and modern subjectivity: The importance of being somewhere bodily, and being able to translate that experience into a language which shapes the subject, by giving it a verbal form – that is the transformation of body into language.

Corinne, or Italy

The cartography in *The Influence of Literature upon Society* is expressively gendered and dramatized in Mme de Staël's novel *Corinne, or Italy*. The novel is a travel itinerary and a cultural map in the shape of a love story. The narrative is staged by the conflict between cultural differences and love: Will the love between the protagonists, Lord Nelvil and Corinne, survive the differences caused by their different nationalities, cultural conventions and natures? The young Lord Nelvil (Oswald), is in Italy to recover his health after the death of his father. Deeply immersed in sorrow, he does not notice anything around him, until he witnesses the crowning of Corinne at the Capitol. She is praised for her talent for improvisation, and when she notices Oswald, she spontaneously adds stanzas to her song. The next day he gets the chance to visit her and attend her salon, and predictably they fall in love. To convince Oswald, who is quite an Anglophile, of the glory and beauty of Rome and Italy, Corinne takes him on several excursions in the city and the countryside. Later on they go to Naples and Venice. The descriptions of these journeys closely resemble travel writing: The listing of sights, the views from the carriage, the temperature, the local peculiarities etc. – all wrapped in the learned voice of the heroine. As the letter quoted in the beginning of this article reveals, Mme de Staël intended to combine prose fiction and travel writing in her novel. The combination is quite clear in the novel's headlines, for instance: "Vesuvius and the Naples countryside", and "The farewell to Rome and the journey to Venice". Furthermore, the role of the narrator emphasizes features in the travel writing. The narrator's addressing the reader directly and mentioning her-/himself as an "I" makes the reader a travel companion and gives the narrator an individual personality. The combination of two genres seems to have worked: The novel was read as literature, and according to Chloe Chard it was also actually used as a guide for travellers on the Grand Tour (Chard 1999: 16).[12]

The cartography of the novel

In *Corinne*, Mme de Staël sketches a cartography that is largely similar to the one she presents in *The Influence of Literature upon Society*. However, she nuances it and elaborates it by gendering the geography. The cartography is depicted on two levels in the novel. It is articulated directly in the novel's discourse: Partly through the narrator's comments, which are reflecting on the differences between North and South, partly through the dialogue, which is both relating and reflecting. And it is staged in the narrative due to the list of characters and the main plot – that is, in a less reflective and more dramatic way.

---

12   *Corinne*'s popularity was immense, both as literature, and as role model: "Corinne's popularity was immediate and astounding: the journalist and critic Saint-Beuve called her 'the ideal of all celebrated women' in the 1820s. Her fame spread across Europe and to England and America. […] Portraits of the heroine appeared on biscuit boxes, and Mme. de Staël herself was hailed as 'Corinne' everywhere she went." (Folkenflik 1987: 25). Linda M. Lewis also emphasizes Mme de Staël's and *Corinne*'s importance for contemporary readers and writers. She describes the novel, together with George Sand's *Consuelo* (1842) as "the reference points for woman-as-artist fictions of the entire second half of the century." She describes Staël and Sand as "models as women who dared to publish", and as inspirators for nineteenth-century English women writers "by their personal courage, their uniqueness and vivacity, and their commitment to *liberté* in art and politics." (Lewis 2003: 13)

An example of the cartographic reflections is passages about language. Corinne explains that she uses one or another language according to the feelings she wants to express (Staël 1998: 38). Language and mentality are linked, and so is language and literary style, as Mme de Staël argues in *The Influence of Literature upon Society*. In the novel she lets Corinne explain why improvisation is well suited to the Italian language:

'The talent for improvisation is not more unusual in the languages of the South than political oratory or brilliant, lively conversation is in other languages,' replied Corinne. [...] 'It is not only to the gentleness of Italian, but more to the strong, pronounced resonance of its sounds, that the supremacy of poetry with us must be attributed. Italian has a musical charm so that there is pleasure in the sound of words almost independent of the ideas; moreover, these words have nearly always something picturesque about them, their sound reflects their meaning.' (Ibid.: 44-45)

In contrast the English elocution "is more suited than any other to move the heart when a fine talent makes one appreciate the force and originality of the words." (ibid.: 328). As in *The Influence of Literature upon Society* Mme de Staël – here through Corinne – articulates an idea of literary style, genre etc. being closely connected to the characteristics of a specific language, which again is formed in accordance with the cultural context and the climatic circumstances.

The narrator's reflections on the climate are similar to those expressed in *The Influence of Literature upon Society*. The central idea is the human subject being situated in and interacting with a specific space:

In our climate nothing is like the southern perfume of the lemon trees in the open countryside. It has almost the same effect on the imagination as melodious music; it makes you poetically inclined, stimulates the talent, and intoxicates it with nature. [...] In our northern climates all man's links are with society. In hot countries, nature relates us to external objects, and feelings expand gently outwards. It is not that the South does not have its melancholy aspects; in what places does man's destiny not give that feeling? But in that melancholy there is neither anxiety nor regret. (Ibid.:188-190)

Climatic circumstances determine the temper and mentality of the inhabitants, the literary expressions and social behaviour. But the interrelation between climate and human beings goes the other way as well, at least metaphorically: Near the end of the novel Oswald feels how "all the sensations coming from external conditions, seemed to increase the shudder in his soul." (ibid.: 400). An earlier scene in the novel clearly shows the melodramatic potential in this interdependence between weather and people: When Oswald decides to go back to England without Corinne, her emotional condition is mirrored by a climatic outburst: "Then a terrible rainstorm began; a most violent wind could be heard, and the house where Corinne was staying shook almost like a ship in the middle of the sea." (Ibid.: 303).

National personifications

As the allegorical title indicates the protagonists in the novel, Corinne and Oswald, are countries as well as persons, made concrete by their looks: Corinne is dark and beautiful, and Oswald is described as light, distinguished and handsome. Corinne and Oswald each merge with their respective country in the novel's cartography. Their behaviour, attitude and morality are complemented by comments and passages of discursive reflections on the different countries.[13] The antagonists here are specified in relation to their nationalistic – not regional (North – South) – belonging (England – Italy). Even though Corinne and Oswald each present and defend their national preference, the over all cartography in the story is clear, and does not differ much from the narrator's commenting passages. Their different opinions are even reflected upon by the narrator:

Oswald and Corinne had different opinions on this matter [the masterpieces of painting assembled in Rome], but their disagreement, like all those existing between them, had to do with the differences between nations, climates, and religions. (Ibid.: 143)

The dichotomously formed description does, however, give a more nuanced picture – for instance Oswald describes England as a "haven of modesty and sensitivity", and praises the love and domestic happiness of English living (ibid.: 95), while Corinne does not thrive in England due to boredom, isolation from the rest of the world, and the missing appreciation of the arts and literature (ibid.: 253). In her view England is barren and lacks spiritual life. Oswald, for his part, disapproves of the Italian way of living – in short, the Italian culture is too informal, too lively, too artistic, too decorated instead of being moral, severe and silent. On the dramatic level of the novel, he feels sad and gloomy when he returns to England, without clearly understanding why. It is implied that the melancholic feelings are connected to the country and the climatic conditions, which corresponds to his characteristic of English virtues and to Corinne's experience of being in England.

---

13   Mme de Staël indirectly raises a criticism of the contemporary situation in France through her story dealing with other nationalities. However, she only directly mentions the contemporary situation and the consequences of it in other countries a few times in the novel.

MARIANNE RAAKILDE JESPERSEN

When Oswald leaves Corinne to go back to England, it is as if he is returning to his true self after being deluded by the lure of Italy:

He found his former self again, and although the sorrow of being separated from Corinne prevented him from having any feeling of happiness, he nevertheless returned to a certain rigidity in his ideas that *the intoxicating wave of the arts and Italy* had washed away. *As soon as he set foot in England*, he was struck by the order and prosperity, by the wealth and industry, that greeted his eyes. [...] Oswald thought of Italy to pity it. (Ibid.: 304 my italics)

The North is described as well ordered, noble, wealthy, productive, efficient, and moral; and Italy – the South – is, in short, the complete opposite. Being physically in England, Oswald is released of the dangerously intoxicating powers of the South – he is cleansed, so to speak. The North is pure and clean, while the South is a delusion, poisonous and dirty. The determining point of reference is the bodily presence: When physically in Italy, he is intoxicated by the country; when physically in England, he returns to the moral standards, mentality etc. of this country, as if the soil, the weather, the nature etc. affect his body in a specific way. And the same goes for Corinne when she does not thrive in England. In the novel, being bodily connected to a (native) country seems to be the determining factor for the constitution of the human subject. The modern subject is, in other words, closely tied to the surrounding topography.

A gendered geography

With an English father and an Italian mother, Corinne personifies the perfect combination of the two distinctive cultures, but as the novel unfolds – and ends – it becomes clear that the combination is utopian: Corinne dies. The North-South dichotomy is, in other words, presented as unsolvable. Corinne's dual nationality points towards a problematic of gender, which is staged almost melodramatically in the question of her identity, and at the same time discursively in the novel's cartography. This reveals, I will argue, a gendered geography: The northern and southern hemispheres are, respectively, masculine and feminine.

The gender notion is clear in the novel's outline: Corinne is Italy and Oswald is England. While she is sensitive, imaginative and open to other points of view, he is inflexible and sharply nationalistic. We hear only about Oswald's father. His mother is scarcely mentioned. Oswald has fled from England to recover from his father's death. He cannot marry Corinne, because his father, before dying, decided whom Oswald was to marry. At first this was actually Corinne, until his father discovered, that she would not be happy living in England. Then he chose her half sister instead.

Colour-wise, she is Corinne's contrast: fair hair, blue eyes, pale complexion (ibid.: 306). Oswald will not go against his father's will, and is confirmed in this when he returns to England. This is indeed his Father-land: "He felt strong enough to defy the disapproval of any other country, but the memory of his father was so closely linked in his thoughts with his native land that the two feelings enhanced each other." (ibid.:107). The gendered geography is expressed directly in his reflections upon returning:

But he was exchanging the vague desire of romantic happiness for pride in the true goods of life, independence, and security; he was returning to the life suited to men, action with a goal. Reverie is more for women, beings who are weak and resigned from birth. (Ibid.: 304)

Living in Italy, with Corinne, is an unrealistic romantic dream, not for real men, and from Oswald's point of view the Italian men are not real men:

In Italy, the men are worth much less than the women, for they have the women's faults as well as their own. […] men inspire no kind of respect in women, who are not at all grateful to them for their submissiveness, because the men have no strength of character and no serious occupation in life. For nature and the social order to be revealed in all their beauty, man must be the protector and the woman the protected. (Ibid.: 97)

The values related to northern mentality and culture are also those attached to masculinity: Courage, action, and reality. The connection of the North with fatherland and masculinity, is reiterated in Corinne's story. Her mother was Italian, her father – the friend of Oswald's father – was English. She grew up in Italy, and when she at the age of ten lost her mother, she stayed with an aunt until she went to stay with her father in England at the age of fifteen. Her father died, and at 21 she got her inheritance from her father and mother and decided to leave her English home. She took the name of Corinne, inspired by the Greek and thereby renounced her father's name. She had no longer any rights and her stepmother announced her death. Again the cartography is very explicit: North is connected to the father, masculinity and death (no middle way, no life), and South is connected to the mother, femininity, independence, and life (no father-name, names herself).

The same gendered geography can be detected in the novel's passages on art and aesthetics. These passages closely resemble descriptions from travel writing in their enumeration of masterpieces of art. The statues Niobe and Laocoön, which play a major role in the aesthetic discussions of the time, are mentioned almost

MARIANNE RAAKILDE JESPERSEN

en passant, and in the novel's reflections on art and literature, and in the descriptions of statues Mme de Staël obviously, but indirectly, refers to among others Edmund Burke, Gotthold Ephraim Lessing, and Johann Joachim Winckelmann. This is explicit, when the narrator uses expressions as "tranquillity in strength" (ibid.: 62) and "beautiful and calm" (ibid.: 63) about sculptures and statues, and "calm beauty", "simple expression", and "noble attitude" (ibid.: 152), when talking about what produces the effect in paintings. These expressions are similar to key terms used by Winckelmann in *Gedanken über die Nachahmung der griechischen Werke in der Malerei und Bildhauerkunst*, 1755 (*Reflections on the Imitation of Greek Works in Painting and Sculpture* 1765), and are common in mid/late eighteenth and early nineteenth century discussions on aesthetics.

When visiting her house in Tivoli, Corinne guides Oswald through her gallery of paintings, which in genre and style fit the contemporary ideals of art:

Her collection was made up of historical pictures, pictures on poetic and religious subjects, and landscapes. There were none which contained a very large number of human figures. That kind of painting no doubt presents great difficulties, but it gives less pleasure. Its beauties are too confused or too detailed, and unity of interest, the principle of life in the arts, as in everything, is of necessity broken up. (Ibid. 150)

The passage reflects the mid/late eighteenth century hierarchy of genres in painting, and the general idea and fascination of unity, which for instance is visible in tableaux in paintings, on the stage, and in the art of attitudes and tableaux vivantes.

On their tour through her gallery Corinne comments every single painting:

The human countenance is undoubtedly a very great mystery, but fixed in a picture, it can barely express the depth of a single feeling. Indeed, contrasts, struggles, events belong to dramatic art. It is difficult for painting to convey the succession of events; in that art there is neither time nor movement. […] But is that not a proof that there is always such a difference between poetic subjects and subjects suitable for painting that it is better for poets to write about pictures than for artists to paint pictures about poems? (Ibid.: 153)

Her reflections on the subject matter of poetry and painting are in line with contemporary German discussions about aesthetics and arts, and do closely resemble Lessing's semiotic of arts, according to which painting should not represent action, since the signs in painting are static, and poetry should not represent description, since the signs in poetry are consecutive.[14]

The beautiful South and the sublime North

Mme de Staël in her novel refers to and takes part in the already old debate about the sublime versus the beautiful, both directly through the dialogue, and indirectly through recounts of experiences and feelings. When Corinne takes Oswald to see the dome of Saint Peter's she instructs him to stand in a certain place, and look a certain way in order to get a certain experience: "Stand here," Corinne said to Lord Nelvil,

near the altar, directly beneath the dome. Through the iron grating you will see the church of the dead beneath our feet, but when you raise your eyes you will barely be able to see the top of the vault. Even seen from below, the dome *arouses a feeling of terror*. Abysses seem to be suspended over one's head. Everything beyond certain proportions inspires in man, in that limited being, an unconquerable terror. (Ibid.: 60 my italics)

Instructions and self staging, is needed to have the ultimate experience when seeing 'musts' on the journey – just looking is not enough. Following the instructions, though, the beholder can get a sublime experience of the architectonic masterpiece – an experience of the unlimited which causes a feeling of terror in its potential destruction of the self, but which is delightful due to the distance it is observed from. Another moment of terrifying sublimity is related to the English nature. When Corinne recounts her stay in England she explains: "Everything around me was drab and dismal, and what dwellings and inhabitants there were, were only of use in depriving solitude of the *poetic horror* which makes the heart tremble quite pleasantly." (Ibid.: 255, my italics). It is implied that nature would cause a feeling of poetic horror, if undisturbed by the inhabitants, and that this feeling is pleasant though terrifying – in other words: Undisturbed nature causes an experience of the sublime. In this description Mme de Staël stages Burke's theory on the sublime and the beautiful. Due to its religious belonging the church also initiated a sublime experience. Corinne and Oswald's visit to the Vatican gallery, however, depicts the south as, generally, much more pleasing through the narrator's comments:

14   In her notes to the novel, Mme de Staël relates this discussion to another German thinker: "In a journal called *Europe* there are some remarks full of depth and shrewdness on the subjects which are suitable for painting; I have drawn from them several of the thoughts just given in the text; their author is Mr Friedrich S chlegel. This writer is an inexhaustible source of wisdom, as are German thinkers in general." (Staël 1998: 407 – note 20).

Unlike Christianity, the Greek religion was not the consolation of the unhappy, the wealth of the poor, the future for the dying. It wanted fame and triumph; it formed, as it were, man's apotheosis. In this worship of the perishable, beauty itself was religious dogma. [...] But statues in sleep, or only in a pose of complete rest, present an image of eternal calm that harmonizes marvellously with the general effect of the South on mankind. There, it seems, the arts are peaceful spectators of nature, and genius itself, which in the North disturbs the soul, under a fine sky is but one more harmony. (Ibid.: 141)

The south is connected to beauty, pleasure and harmony, and the North is – with Oswald, nature, moral standard, and melancholy etc. in mind – related to the sublime.[15]

A similar gendered geography is visible between the lines in *The Influence of Literature upon Society*. The South and the literature of the South is characterized by pleasure, harmony, vivacity; it is imaginative – that is pleasing in its innovation, while the northern literature can be hard in its depiction of nature etc. In contrast to the beauty and pleasure of South, North is characterized by discipline, physical strength, control of pain, endurance, honour, melancholy, nobility, and purity. In short: The beautiful feminine South and the sublime masculine North.[16] With the cartography of *The Influence of Literature upon Society* and *Corinne, or Italy* in mind, it is quite obvious, that Corinne has to die: Her dual nationality is, symbolically, the worshippped, but impossible androgynous ideal, lent from Antiquity and refreshed in Neoclassicism. She is both in one – south *and* north.

---

15 An analogy between melancholy and the sublime is not a new idea at the beginning of the eighteenth-century, but is known from the philosophers of the Renaissance a.o. Burke, however, stresses the analogy by pointing to a basic dual structure in the sublime of pain, fear of death *and* the delight of relief. This structure goes for melancholy as well, Elin Andersen argues in *Kroppens sublime tale* (2004: 303). The link between sublimity and melancholy, thus, emphasizes my argument about an aesthetic cartography.

16 Part of this argument I owe to W.J.T. Mitchell, who proposes a link between gender and beauty/sublimity in Lessings *Laocoon*: "The decorum of the arts at bottom has to do with proper sex roles." The link between gender and genre relates femininity to painting, and further on to beauty, and masculinity to poetry and hence sublimity. (Mitchell 1987: 109-110). I, however, propose a geographical application to this link.

References

Andersen, Elin 2004: *Kroppens sublime tale. Om tableau og levende billede hos Diderot, Lessing og Lenz.* Aarhus: Aarhus Universitetsforlag.

Barton, H. Arnold 1998: *Northern Arcadia. Foreign Travelers in Scandinavia, 1765-1815.* Carbondale and Edwardsville: Southern Illinois University Press.

Brooks, Peter 1976: *The Melodramatic Imagination. Balzac, Henry James, Melodrama, and the Mode of Excess.* New Haven and London: Yale University Press.

Burke, Edmund 1998 (1757): *A Philosophical Enquiry into the Origin of our Ideas of the Sublime and Beautiful.* Oxford and New York: Oxford University Press.

Chard, Chloe 1999: *Pleasure and Guilt on the Grand Tour. Travel writing and imaginative geography 1600-1830.* Manchester and New York: Manchester University Press.

Chard, Chloe 2000: Comedy, Antiquity, The Feminine and The Foreign: Emma Hamilton and Corinne: Clare Hornsby (ed.): *The Impact of Italy: The Grand Tour and Beyond.* London: The British School at Rome 147-169.

Folkenflik, Vivian 1987: *An Extraordinary Woman. Selected Writings of Germaine de Staël.* New York: Columbia University Press.

Fjågesund, Peter and Ruth Symes 2003: *The Northern Utopia. British Perceptions of Norway in the Nineteenth Century.* Amsterdam and New York: Rodopi.

Hansen, Robert L. 1973: Forord: de Staël: *Litteraturen og samfundet.* København: G-E-C Gad.

Lessing, Gotthold Ephraim 1854 (1766): *Laokoon oder über die Grenzen der Mahlerey und Poesie.* Leipzig: G.I. Göschen'sche Verlagshandlung.

Lewis, Linda M. 2003: *Germaine de Staël, George Sand, and the Victorian Woman Artist.* Colombia and London: University of Missouri Press.

Mitchell, W.J.T. 1987: *Iconology. Image, Text, Ideology.* Chicago and London: The University of Chicago Press.

Staël, Anne-Louise-Germaine de 1803: *A Treatise on Ancient and Modern Literature. Illustrated by striking references to the principal events that have distinguished the French Revolution.* From the French by the Baroness Staël de Holstein. London: G. Cawthorn.

Staël, Anne-Louise-Germaine de 1812: *The Influence of Literature upon Society.* Second edition. To which is prefixed a memoir of the life and writings of the author [by D. Boileau]. London: H. Colburn.

Staël, Anne-Louise-Germaine de 1844: *De la littérature considérée dans ses rapports avec les institutions sociales* (1800) & *Corinne, ou l'Italie* (1807) in *Ouevres Complétes De Madame de la Baronne De Staël-Holstein,* Tome Premier. Paris: Firmin Didot Fréres, Libraires-Éditeurs, Imprimeurs de l'Institut de France et Treutel et Würtz, Libraires.

Staël, Anne-Louise-Germaine de 1970 : *Madame de Staël, ses amis, ses correspondants. Choix de lettres (1778-1817).* Présenté et commenté par Georges Solovieff. Paris: Éditions Klincksieck.

Staël, Anne-Louise-Germaine de 1998: *Corinne, or Italy.* Translated and Edited by Sylvia Raphael. Oxford and New York: Oxford University Press.

Winckelmann, Johan Joachim 1991 (1755) : *Gedanken über die Nachahmung der griechischen Werke in der Malerei und Bildhauerkunst.* Stuttgart: Reclam.

Original Quotes

Madame de Staël, ses amis, ses correspondants. Choix de lettres (1778-1817). Présenté et commenté par Georges Solovieff. Paris 1970 : Éditions Klincksieck : J'ecrirai une sorte de roman qui serve de cadre au voyage d' Italie et je crois que beaucoup de pensées et de sentiments trouvent leur place là. (Rome, april 9, 1805) 306

The page numbers after the following quotations are referring to:

Ouevres Complétes De Madame de la Baronne De Staël-Holstein, Tome Premier: Paris, 1844 : Firmin Didot Fréres, Libraires-Éditeurs, Imprimeurs de l'Institut de France Et Treutel et Würtz, Libraires

De la littérature chez les anciens et chez les modernes

De l'état actuel des lumières en France, et de leurs progrès futurs

chaque siècle, chaque pays

Je me suis proposé d'examiner quelle est l'influence de la religion, des moeurs et des lois sur la littérature, et quelle est l'influence de la littérature sur la religion, les moeurs et les lois. : 199

J'essayerai de montrer le caractère que telle ou telle forme de gouvernement donne à l'éloquence, les idées de morale que telle ou telle croyance religieuse développe dans l'esprit humain, les effets d'imagination qui sont produits par la crédulité des peoples, les beautés poétiques qui appartiennent au climat, le degré de civilisation le plus favourable à la force ou à la perfection de la littérature, les différents changements qui se sont introduits dans les écrits comme dans les moeurs, par le mode d'existence des femmes avant et depuis l'établissement de la religion chrétienne; enfin le progress universel des lumières par le simple effet de la succession des temps […] : 207

Les peuples du Nord n'attachaient point de prix à la vie. Cette disposition les rendait courageux pour eux-mêmes, mais cruels pour les autres. Ils avaient de l'imagination, de la méencholie, du penchant à la mysticité, mais un profound mépris pour les lumières, comme affaiblissant l'esprit guerrier: les femmes étaient plus instruites que les hommes, parce qu'elles avaient plus de loisir qu'eux. Ils les aimaient, ils leur étaient fidèles, ils leur rendaient un culte; ils pouvaient éprouver quelque sensibilité par l'amour. : 237

Les poëtes de Midi mêlent sans cesse l'image de la fraîcheur, des bois touffus, des ruisseaux limpides, à tous les sentiments de la vie. Ils ne se retracent pas meme les jouissance du Coeur sans y mêler l'idée de l'ombre bienfaisante qui doit les preserver des brûlantes ardeurs du soleil. Cette nature si vive qui les environne excite en eux plus de mouvements que de pensées. […] Les peoples du Nord sont moins occupés des plaisirs que de la douleur, et leur imagination n'en est que plus féconde. Le spectacle de la nature agit fortement sur eux; elle agit comme elle se montre dans leurs climates, toujours sombre et nébuleuse. : 253

la poésie volupteuse exclut presque entièrement les idées d'un certain ordre. : 254

la sensibilité même est distræte de l'émotion par des consonnances trop éclatantes. L'italien n'a pas assez de concision pour les idées; il n'a rien d'assez sombre pour la mélancolie des sentiments. C'est une langue d'une mélodie si extraordinaire, qu'elle peut vous ébranler, comme des accords, sans que vous donniez votre attention au sens meme des paroles. Elle agit sur vous comme un instrument musical.: 250

une sorte d'ébranlement moral et physique: 201

L'éloquence, la poésie, les situations dramatiques, les pensées mélancoliques agissent aussi sur les organs, quoiqu'elles s'adressent à la réflexion.: 201

chaucun de nous est frappé de leurs [the literary works] beautés à des époques différentes, et reçoit isolément l'impression qu'elles doivent produire. : 201

Le Vésue et la campagna de Naples : 770

Les adieux à Rome et la voyage à Venise : 790

Ce talent d'improviser, reprit Corinne, n'est pas plus extraordinaire dans les langues du Midi, que l'éloquence de la tribune, ou la vivacité brillante de la conversation, dans les autres langues. […] Ce n'est pas uniquement à la douceur de l'italien, mais bien plûtot à la vibration forte et prononcée de ses syllabes sonores, qu'il faut attribuer l'empire de la poésie parmi nous. L'italien a un charme musical qui fait trouver du plaisir dans le son des mots, presque indépendamment des idées ; ces mots, d'ailleurs, ont presque tous quelque chose de pittoresque, ils peignent ce qu'ils expriment. : 674

La déclamation anglaise est plus propre qu'aucune autre à remuer l'âme, quand un beau talent en fait sentir la force et l'originalité. : 823

Rien ne resemble, dans nos climats, au parfum méridional des citronniers en plein terre : il produit sur l'imagination presque le même effet qu'une musique mélodieuse ; il donne une disposition poétique, excite le talent, et l'enivre de la nature […] Tous les rapports de l'homme dans nos climats sont avec la société. La nature, dans les pays chauds, met en relation avec les objets extérieurs, et les sentiments s'y répandent doucement au dehors. Ce n'est pas que le Midi n'ait aussi sa mélancolie ; dans quels lieux la destinée de l'homme ne produit-elle pas cette impression ! Mais il n'y a dans cette mélancolie ni mécontentement, ni anxiété, ni regret. : 751

toutes les sensations extérieures semblaient augmenter le frisson de son âme. : 861

Une pluie terrible commençait alors; le vent le plus violent se faisait entendre, et la maison où demeurait Corinne était ébranlée, presque comme un vaisseau au milieu de la mer. : 811

Oswald et Corinne différaient d'opinion à cet égard; mais cette difference, comme toutes celles qui existaient entre eux, tenait à la diversité des nations, des climats et des religions. : 727

sanctuaire de la pudeur et de la delicatesse : 701

17 : Il se retrouvait lui-même; et, bien que le regret d'être séparé de Corinne l'empêchât d'éprouver aucune impression de bonheur, il reprenait pourtant une sorte de fixité dans les idées, que le vague enivrant des beaux-arts et de l'Italie avait fait disparaître. Dès qu'il eut mis le pied sur la terre d'Angleterre, il fut frappé de l'ordre et de l'aisance, de la richesse et de l'industrie qui s'offraient à ses regards […] Oswald pensait à l'Italie pour la plaindre. : 811

Il se sentait fort contre celle de tout autre pays; mais le souvenir de son père était si intimement uni dans sa pensée avec sa patrie, que ces deux sentiments s'accroissaient l'un par l'autre. : 707

[…] mais il échangeait le désir indéfini d'un bonheur romanesque contre l'orgueil des vrais bien de la vie, l'indépendance et la sécurité. Il rentrait dans l'existence qui convient aux homes, l'action avec un but. La reverie est plutôt le partage des femmes, de ces êtres faibles et résignés dès leur naissance […] : 811

Les hommes, en Italie, valent beaucoup moins que les femmes, car ils ont les défauts des femmes, et les leurs propres en sus. […] les hommes n'inspirent aucun genre de respect aux femmes; elles ne leur savent aucun gré de leur soumission, parce qu'ils n'ont aucune fermeté de caractère, aucune occupation sérieuse dans la vie. Il faut, pour que la nature et l'ordre social se montrent dans toute leur beauté, que l'homme soit protecteur et la femme protégée […] : 702

la tranquillité dans la force : 684

belle et calme : 684

beauté calme; d'une expression simple; d'une attitude noble : 732

Sa galerie était compose de tableaux d'histoire, de tableaux sur des sujets poétiques et religieux, et de paysages. Il n'y en avait point qui fussent composés d'un tres-grand nombre de figures. Ce genre présente sans doute de grandes difficultés, mais il donne moins de plaisir. Les beautés qu'on y trouve sont trop confuses ou trop détaillées. L'unité d'intérêt, ce principe de vie dans les arts, comme dans tout, y est nécessairement morcelée. : 731

Sans doute la physiognomie de l'homme est le plus grand des mystères; mais cette physiognomie, fixée dans un tableau, ne peut guère exprimer que les profondeurs d'une sentiment unique. Les contrastes, les luttes, les événements enfin appartiennent à l'art dramatique. La peinture peut difficilement render ce qui est successif: le temps ni le movement n'existent pas pour elle. […] mais n'est-ce pas un preuve qu'il y a toujours une telle différence entre les sujets poétiques et les sujets pittoresques, qu'il vaut mieux que les poëtes fassent des vers d'après les tableaux, que les peintres des tableaux d'après les poëtes ?: 732

Dans un journal intitulé *l'Europe*, on peut trouver des observations pleines de profondeur et de sagacité sur les sujets qui conviennent à la peinture ; j'y ai puisé plusieurs des réflexions qu'on vient de lire. M. Frédéric Schlegel en est l'auteur : c'est une mine inépuisable que cet écrivain, et que les penseurs allemands en général. : 727, note

Placez-vous ici, dit Corinne á lord Nelvil, près de l'autel, au milieu de la coupole, vous apercevrez à travers les grilles de fer l'église des morts qui est sous nos pieds, et, en relevant les yeux, vos regards atteindront à peine au sommet de la voûte. Ce dôme, en le considérant même d'en bas, fait éprouver un sentiment de terreur. On croit voir des abîmes suspendus sur sa tête. Tout ce qui est au delà, d'une certaine proportion cause à l'homme, à la créature bornée, un invincible effroi. : 682

Tout était terne, tout était morne autour de moi, et ce qu'il y avait d'habitations et d'habitants servait seulement à priver la solitude de cette horreur poétique qui cause à l'âme un frissonnement assez doux. : 785

La religion grecque n'était point, comme le christianisme, la consolation du malheur, la richesse de la misère, l'avenir des mourants ; elle voulait la gloire, le triomphe ; elle faisait, pour ainsi dire, l'apothéose de l'homme. Dans ce culte périssabe, la beauté même était un dogme religieux. […] Mais les statues dans le sommeil, ou seulement dans l'attitude d'un repos complet, offrent une image de l'eternelle tranquillité, qui s'accorde merveilleusement avec l'effet général du Midi sur l'homme. Il semble que là les beaux-arts soient les paisibles spectateurs de la nature, et que la génie lui-même, qui agite l'âme dans le Nord, ne soit, sous un beau ciel, qu'une harmonie de plus. : 725-26

A Nationalist Controversy about Language: Were the Languages in the Nordic Countries Nordic?

This chapter discusses the construction of language history by German and Danish scholars, from their encyclopaedic endeavours in the eighteenth century to their attempts at establishing a connection between language, ethnicity and nationality as a means of creating national myths of origin in the nineteenth century. In the wake of developing nationalisms linguistic theories became the object of heated controversies.

In the eighteenth century the political concept of the Nordic countries was based on a north-south division of Europe and typically included Denmark (with Norway and Iceland), Sweden, Poland Russia, and sometimes Prussia.[1] Focusing on language, the concept in this contribution is narrowed down to Denmark, Iceland, Norway and Sweden. The crucial question for scholars of historical comparative linguistics, which began developing as a scientific discipline in the late eighteenth century, was whether the Nordic languages ought to be perceived as an ancient independent branch of the Germanic languages or should be subsumed under Low German.[2] Their aim was to discover the truth about the origin and position of the nordic languages and to create a terminology that would communicate this truth appropriately.

Johann Christoph Adelung, an eighteenth century scholar

Johann Christoph Adelung (1732-1806) studied theology, but earned his living as a grammar school teacher, journalist, proofreader, translator, and finally as chief librarian at the Saxon Elector's library in Dresden. As a true eighteenth century

---

1 See the contribution by Hendriette Kliemann-Geisinger in this volume.

2 I use the English term German as a translation of the German word deutsch and the Danish word tysk. The English term Germanic is used as to translate the German term germanisch and the Danish terms germanisk and germansk. The semantic ambiguities of both German and Germanic are explained when they occur. What is lost in the English translation is the etymological difference that is preserved in both German and Danish: that deutsch and tysk are Germanic words whereas germanisch, germansk and germanisk are derived from Latin.

FIG. 10:

Johann Christoph Adelung was firmly rooted in eighteenth century scholarship. His survey of the world's languages in Mithridates became the stepping stone for a younger generation.

scholar he had widespread interests and published in many fields: history, pedagogy, science, and first and foremost linguistics (Strohbach 1984: 1). Adelung became extremely influential in his own time because of his systematic descriptions of the lexicography and grammar of the contemporary German language. Modern for Adelung's time is his notion that the correct use of German should be derived from actual good usage and not be based on learned constructions.

Adelung's endeavours were typical of eighteenth century cultural patriotism (Hobsbawm 1990: 61). His interest was in "good taste" (Adelung 1782-1783, 1: 85 and passim) in language and literature. He understands his work as contributing to the purity and the correctness of the German language, helping to bring it on a level with other civilized languages such as French and English and make it suitable for all cultural and scholarly purposes, a tool for civilized conversation (Finsen 2001) across the conglomerate of fairly independent principalities that made up the German Empire.

In the introduction to the first of five comprehensive volumes of his pioneering work on contemporary High German[3] usage, *Versuch eines vollständigen grammatisch-kritischen Wörterbuches der Hochdeutschen Mundart, mit vollständiger Vergleichung der übrigen Mundarten, besonders aber der Oberdeutschen* (Grammatical critical dictionary of the High German dialect including a complete comparison with the other dialects, in particular Upper German. An attempt) from 1774 Adelung says:

The German language is divided into two main dialects that differ very clearly, Upper German and Lower German […] The ancient dwellings of the peoples who came into Germany along the Danube are likely to have been very far away from the dwellings of those who chose the more northern route. Language itself proves it. All the peoples who chose the southern route along the Danube, and before that probably lived in or near mountainous areas, are more or less similar in their high language, their full mouth, in their propensity for breath letters and rough double sounds, and in their hissing and rattling, their magnificent words, copious expressions, and favourite figures of speech; just as all the northern peoples who no doubt originally inhabited an even and flat fatherland have completely opposite qualities in their language and manner of speech. (Adelung 1774-86, 1: 6-7)

What is particularly interesting in our context is that Adelung presents letters (today we would say phonetic features) as constitutive of a group of languages.[4] Adelung continues to argue that the languages of the Nordic countries belong to the northern, i.e., Low German, group because of geographic criteria and "letters".

In his dictionary, Adelung uses the word German in two senses, the entry words are, in fact, what we would today call German. But in his remarks on the origins and dialects of the German language quoted above, he uses German as the inclusive name for a wider group including both German and the Nordic languages.

---

3   High German, Hochdeutsch, is the term for the educated written and spoken language in Germany (Bach 1965 (1938): 337ff.).

4   Adelung never exemplified the phonetic features of Upper German, but he must be referring to such examples as the Upper German p̲fund, schi̲ff, ha̲us, me̲in (pound, ship, house, my) versus the Low German p̲und, skip, hu̲s, mi̲n. For a complete survey of such features, see Bach 1965 (1938): 101ff., 227.

The origin of language

In his speculations on language history and language relationships that accompanied his work on contemporary German and were also published independently (Adelung 1781, 1971, (1806) 1806-1816), Adelung was firmly rooted in eighteenth century scholarship. His contributions to the origin and development of language and to the relationships between the world's languages were based on the philosophical debates in the discipline of general grammar. General grammar was the study of language as a phenomenon: the function of language in the development of the human race, the interrelationship of language and cognition, and the nature of representation as noted by Foucault (1994 (1970): 83 ff.). A favourite subject was the origin and development of language.

Adelung's main sources for his work in this field were prize treatises published by contemporary scholars. Prize questions had become important tools for the learned societies that originated in England and France and were getting established in many European countries from the early eighteenth century. By posing prize questions in fields they wished to develop, those societies set the agendas for scholarly work, not just in their own countries but throughout Europe, thus contributing substantially to the scholarly development from universal scholarship to disciplinary specialization in the eighteenth and nineteenth centuries (Harnack 1900).

In 1770, the Prussian Academy announced a prize paper competition: *En supposant les hommes abandonnés à leurs facultés naturelles, sont ils en état d'inventer le langage et par quels moyens deviendront-ils d'eux mêmes à cette invention?* (Assuming humans are left to their natural capacities, are they able to invent language, and by which means will they arrive at this invention by themselves?). More than thirty papers were received in answer to the question (Arens 1969: 121), an indication of the enormous popularity of the issue. Adelung's younger contemporary, the German theologian Johann Gottfried Herder (1744-1803) won the award with his treatise *Über den Ursprung der Sprache* published in 1772 (*Essay on the Origin of Language* 1966).

Like the Swiss philosopher Jean Jacques Rousseau, Herder believed that humans, and not God, had invented language (Irmscher 2001: 42). Before the existence of any language humans had instinctive cries and sounds in common with the animals (Herder 1891 (1772): 9f.). Language developed along with the need to communicate by naming objects. Herder agrees with Rousseau that the difference between animals and humans in their natural state is the human free will, but he also introduces another element "Besonnenheit," i.e., reflection.

According to Herder, language and reason develop alongside each other. Due to their ability to reflect humans are able to notice and remember characteristics of objects and name these objects accordingly. A famous example is the sheep that is remembered by its bleating and therefore named "the bleating one." Such imitations of sounds were believed to have been the origin of the roots that would become the base of rudimentary words.

Adelung adopted Herder's ideas. But in one respect he did not agree with Herder. Herder assumed a golden age, i.e., an early stage in language, full of youth and freshness (Herder 1891 (1772): 16-17). In Adelung's view such early stages remained raw and primitive, and he calls the germanic tribes in the era of the great migrations "rude barbarians" and "beasts of prey" (Adelung 1782, 1: 26f.). To Adelung, the absolute peak of the development remained mid-eighteenth century German (Adelung 1782, 1: 68f.).

Language relationships

A consequence of eighteenth century theories about the origin of language such as Rousseau's and Herder's was the hypothesis that all the languages of the world had developed from a very small group of roots that due to their onomatopoetic origin might have come into being independently of each other in different parts of the world (Foucault 1994 (1970): 109). Etymology, i.e. the tracing of such roots vertically from the words of a contemporary language back to the bleating sheep, with the meaning as the constant element, became popular. Adelung e.g. assumed that the word for the colour red (German rot) is derived from the word for horseback riding (German reiten), a root that even existed in Arabic, red being "the most vehement and sensitive of colours" and horseback riding being a "vehement movement" (Adelung 1781: 32).

Ideas about genealogical relationships among languages were sporadic and intuitive. For example, in Versuch einer critischen Dichtkunst (A critical poetics. An attempt) from 1751, the German playwright and critic Johann Christoph Gottsched lists several similar words in German and the language of the Edda, the famous collection of Old Icelandic poetry which he believed to be Old Swedish. Like the Swiss scholar Paul Henri Mallet (1755), Gottsched assumed that both languages were daughters of the ancient Celtic language (Strohbach 1984: 165). Referring to antique sources, Adelung disagreed with this view: "Caesar himself found in the present France at least three peoples of different origins and languages; Ariovist, a German, had to thoroughly learn Gallic"[5] (Adelung 1782, 1: 12).

Adelung's main source for the idea about the two German dialects and the differences between them was yet another prize treatise, this time by the German

---

5   I.e. a Celtic language.

pastor Friedrich Carl Fulda, who had been awarded the prize of the Royal Academy of Sciences in Göttingen in 1771 (Strohbach 1984: 170ff.). Like their contemporaries, Fulda and Adelung believed linguistic change and development to be caused by climatic, geographic, ethnographic and cultural factors – i.e., factors external to language. They tried to make sense of antique Roman and Greek sources about the tribes north of the Alps, reinterpreting as ancestors those tribes that were considered as enemies and barbarians by Romans and Greeks. Language development from the initial rough and primitive stage to a modern civilized language was also believed to be caused by external factors such as further migrations leading to the mixing of dialects, and by the development of civilization and culture, first and foremost the development of cities and the changes in material production (Adelung 1782, 1).

According to Adelung (1782, 1: 16), those tribes that migrated into Europe in all probability did not have a name for themselves in common. Some of them were referred to as germanics by the Celts and the Romans, and this became the common name for them used by foreigners, whereas they called themselves by the indigenous name Germans, the word that Adelung also prefers in most of his works.

A survey of the world's languages

The culmination of Adelung's work in language history was a survey of the world's languages in four volumes, *Mithridates oder allgemeine Sprachenkunde mit dem Vater Unser als Sprachprobe in bey nahe fünfhundert Sprachen und Mundarten*. (Mithridates or a general handbook of languages with the Lord's Prayer as an example in nearly five hundred languages and dialects). The first volume was published in 1806. Adelung died shortly afterwards while volume two was under preparation, and the work was finished posthumously by his pupil Johann Severin Vater.

This survey of the world's languages is typical of the eighteenth century's encyclopaedic endeavours. A more comprehensive knowledge of languages had come about by an increasing amount of reports by explorers and missionaries. One famous example is Peter Simon Pallas' *Linguarum totius orbis vocabularia comparativa, Augustissimae cura collecta* (A comparative vocabulary of the languages of the whole world collected by the ordinance of the most august Empress) which in its final version in 1791 published word lists from 272 languages. This work was created on the initiative of the Russian empress Katarina II, who personally set up lists of words that had to be translated into as many languages as possible (Arens 1969 (1955): 134-135). Underlying Katarina's word lists for translation and Adelung's use of the Lord's Prayer as language material for *Mithridates* was the eighteenth century assumption that language is identical to naming, which we have already seen above in theories about the development of language. Meaning was believed to be constant across languages and just named differently in different languages (Foucault 1994 (1970): 233f.).

The languages listed in *Mithridates* appear in geographical order starting with the Asian languages in the first volume. In the second volume of *Mithridates*, Adelung turns to the languages in Europe.[6] He still sticks to his original geographic and ethnographic idea about the two German tribes with an upper and a lower language, respectively, considering the Netherlands and the Nordic countries as belonging to the lower tribe.

But, rather self-contradictorily, he also introduces a new division between a northern, Scandinavian tribe and a southern tribe bordered by the Baltic Sea and the river Eider. Adelung's reasons for establishing a Scandinavian main stem and another – German – main stem is the idea that the languages in Sweden and Norway display a mixture of low and high features that he believes to have been caused by migrations in the area. But Danish, Adelung maintains, "connects immediately to Frisian and Saxonian, the old Low German dialects" (Adelung 1806-1816, 2: 297). Icelandic, in Adelung's view, is identical to the Norwegian language, as the Icelanders originally came from Norway (Adelung 1806-16, 2: 305). Adelung chooses the inclusive name germanic for the Scandinavian and German main stems and English.

Adelung's *Mithridates* became the point of departure for the new generation of language scholars in the first half of the nineteenth century.

A critical review by Rasmus Rask

Rasmus Rask (1787-1832) grew up in a rural family in Denmark. He was sent to grammar school, where he started teaching himself Old Icelandic. After graduating in 1807 he studied theology at the University of Copenhagen, aided financially by several patrons. But, in reality, he devoted most of his time to linguistic studies.

Rask enters the scene in 1809 with an extremely critical assessment of Adelung in a review of the second volume of *Mithridates* written in German. His most important point is that Adelung's inclusion of the Nordic languages in Low German is wrong on linguistic grounds (Rask 1932-1935 (1809) 2: 108). In the aggressive and ironic tone that would become his trademark in scholarly debates, Rask offers his

---

6   Starting on page 270 the volume is continued by Vater, based on Adelung's notes. However, I shall continue referring to it in Adelung's name since the section that interests us here is obviously still his work.

suspicions: "I don't know if one must seek the cause in unrightful nationalism or in the unforgivable lack of knowledge of the Nordic languages, particularly in someone like Adelung." He continues polemically: "However, the author confesses that Swedish and Norwegian may no longer be included in *'the pure lower language'*, so he must consider Danish and Icelandic pure Low German!" (Rask 1932-1935 (1809) 2: 111. Rask's emphasis). That this passage occurs in a chapter where Adelung tentatively presents the Nordic languages as a separate main stem is ignored by Rask. Then follows Rask's own hypothesis that, first, the languages are divided into "two main groups, the *Nordic* (Scandinavian) and the *German* (Germanic), and then the latter is divided into two sub-species, Lower and Upper German [...]." (Rask 1932-1935 (1809) 2: 113. Rask's emphasis).

Consequently, Rask also believes that the Nordic countries were not inhabited by people of a Low German tribe, but by people of another, related tribe. The language of this people is, in Rask's view, identical to the Old Icelandic language, which is still preserved nearly unchanged in modern Icelandic. Rask believed this language to be the ancestor of Danish and Swedish.

In his review, Rask criticizes Adelung for lack of knowledge and dishonesty, suspecting him of nationalist motives for "reducing ancient Nordic literature and history in every manner imaginable" (Rask 1932-1935 (1809) 2: 120).

Rask is obviously right in his criticism that Adelung's knowledge of the Nordic languages and Nordic literature was limited – or even non-existent. But there is nothing to be found in *Mithridates* that would justify Rask calling Adelung "the most ardent adversary in Germany against everything Nordic" (Rask 1932-1935 (1809) 2: 123). In the section of *Mithridates* that is so heavily criticized by Rask, Adelung even praised the good quality of ancient Nordic literature.

Rask's Old Icelandic Grammar

Rask's review of Adelung contains an outline of the views that he elaborates in *Vejledning til det Islandske eller gamle Nordiske Sprog* published in 1811 (*A grammar of the Icelandic or Old Norse Tongue* 1843).

The introduction to the Old Icelandic grammar is typical of nineteenth century attitudes towards language and nationhood:

At a time when the patriotism and self-esteem of the Danish people seems to be doubling, when so many distinguished scholars are trying to place the deeds, institutions and ideas of our fathers in the light they deserve, when even the greatest poets in Denmark are praising the ancient acts of the fatherland in immortal works, when the Danish language has attracted so much attention and is cultivated with so much diligence, when, indeed, the government is ardently attending to the antiquities of the fatherland, their preservation and interpretation,[7] there is hardly any need of long excuses for an attempt to present the structure and organization of the ancient Nordic language of our fathers, in other words, an Icelandic grammar. [...] The language itself needs but to be known in order to inspire respect for our fathers, whose whole spirit appears so favourably in it, as in a mirror. (Rask 1811: V)

Like Adelung and his contemporaries, Rask constructs the tribes of the great migrations as ancestors, and, like Adelung, Rask speaks of patriotism as the incentive for his work. However, a lot more than making language a tool for civilized conversation is at stake here. Rask idealizes the ancient language as a historical relic. The ancient language has a value of its own and is not just seen as a means of understanding the modern language. Finally, speaking of the spirit of the ancestors emerging in the language as in a mirror shows that Rask shares the ideas that had become modern in the late eighteenth and early nineteenth centuries, emphasizing the deep, intimate connection between an ethnic group and its language.

Whereas Adelung had decided on the name Germanic for the whole language group, Rask suggests the name Gothic:

[Gothic] seems particularly well suited for denoting the whole large language stem that includes the German (Germanic) and Nordic (Scandinavian) languages which the Germans (Adelung in particular) not too correctly or modestly have begun to call Germanic. But we have never heard about Germanics in the North, and even the ancient Romans who used the name explicitly limited it to the Germans, or even a single tribe among them. Goths, however, are the only important people of whom reliable traces are found both in the Nordic countries and the south and whose language on both sides is known to have been genuine branches of that large language stem; it therefore seems to be the only convenient point of unification from which a common name may be taken. (Rask 1811: VII-VIII, footnote.)

This quotation reveals the core of Rask's theory and terminology. For the rest of his life he stuck to Gothic as the inclusive name of the whole language group.

In his work Rask uses the image of the genealogical tree, which has several stems and branches, to represent the common descent of languages and their gradual diversification. He also uses family terms about language relationships, speaking of Danish as a "sister of Swedish" descending from "the mother language of Icelandic" (Rask 1811: XVI). In Rask's opinion, Icelandic exceeds most West

---

7   Rask must be referring to the establishment of *The Royal Committee for the Preservation and Collection of National Antiquities* in 1807. See the contribution by Karin Sanders in this volume.

FIG. 11:

In his prize thesis Rasmus Rask formulated principles of historical comparative linguistics that are still considered relevant. Lithograph from 1844.

European languages, if not all of them, in purity and originality, "this sweet quality that is to language what independence is to the state" (Rask 1811: IX). Those scholars who disagree (Rask mentions Adelung) are rejected as "envious" and "enemies" (Rask 1811: XXXII, footnote).

Rask bases his argument on the Icelandic sagas, which only mention one language in the Nordic countries, called Danish or Norse, as well as on names of people and places in the Nordic languages and on inscriptions on runic stones. Like Herder and the Brothers Grimm (see below), Rask claims that ancient literature is fit to serve as an inspiration to modern writers:

We certainly [need not ...] abduct the Muses from Parnassus in order to write beautiful and uplifting literature and poetry here in the Nordic countries; in other words, we need not shape everything according to Greeks and Romans since we can find much that is worthy of imitation in our own venerable fathers. (Rask 1811: XIV)

Although Rasmus Rask was a great traveller, his aim was not to discover the world but solely to study languages and establish contacts with fellow scholars. He visited Sweden and Norway in 1812 and spent about two years in Iceland from 1813 to 1815, briefly visiting Scotland on his way home. Later, from 1816 to 1823, he went on a great and extremely strenuous journey to India through Sweden, Finland, Russia and Persia to study languages and buy manuscripts. He was supported economically by the Danish King and other patrons (Rask 2002).

Throughout his life, Rask corresponded with other scholars from the Nordic countries and Europe, as was typical of the European scholarly community in the nineteenth century. What interests us here is his correspondence with the Brothers Grimm in Germany, conducted at irregular intervals from 1811 to 1828. They corresponded first and foremost about scholarly issues and also kept each other posted on interesting new publications in their fields, and at a time when communication was still quite complicated, they provided each other with books. The debates between Rask and the Grimms were not just conducted in their correspondence but also in their works and in the reviews that they wrote of each other's books.

Jacob (1785-1863) and Wilhelm (1786-1859) Grimm both studied law, but through their professor Friedrich Karl von Savigny, they became interested in philology. Both brothers worked for several years at the Elector's library in Kassel, and in 1829 they moved to Göttingen, where Jacob became a professor and librarian, and Wilhelm became an assistant librarian and later also a professor. For many years they shared their household, working separately and together on language history and lexicography and editing ancient German and Nordic texts, among others the Old Icelandic *Edda*. In wider circles they are probably best known for their collection and publication of German folk tales. As a specialist on language history, Jacob Grimm was the one who had most in common with Rask, and the correspondence increasingly took place between the two of them.

In his first letter to Wilhelm Grimm in 1811, Rask enclosed his Old Icelandic grammar, asking Grimm's opinion about it. Here Rask, whose German is excellent with only minimal errors, apologizes for his lack of training in German. He asks for Grimm's indulgence, promising that he will be indulgent himself if Grimm would like to try writing in Danish (Hjelmslev 1941, 1: 51). Thus, Rask elegantly places Danish, a language then only spoken by about a million people, on a level with German, which was spoken in a large part of Europe. It soon appears that the Grimms have no difficulty understanding Danish, so the correspondence continues with Rask writing in Danish and the Grimms writing in German.

Both Jacob and Wilhelm Grimm are full of praise for the Icelandic grammar, with Jacob going into detail on this in a (lost) letter to Rask. Its contents may be inferred from the review of the Old Icelandic grammar that Jacob Grimm published one year later:

[…] Mr. Rask has written a necessary book in a very pleasing and interesting manner, displaying the greatest familiarity with his topic […]. His manner of writing is easy, clear and, justly enough, in his mother tongue; no obstacle at all to Germans, because whoever studies Icelandic cannot possibly ignore Danish. (Grimm 1869 (1812): 67)

After this initial praise, Grimm presents his main objection. Like the late Adelung, Grimm believes that the term Germanic should be used to name the whole language group, including Icelandic. As an alternative to Germanic, Grimm considers the word German.

Jacob Grimm and Rask had the notion of a genetic language relationship in common, but their disagreement was not just over names; Grimm also stressed the basic unity of the whole language group more heavily than Rask, who believed that the language group might never have been a unity and wanted to establish the Nordic languages as an ancient independent stem.

But just as Rask accuses Adelung and other Germans of nationalism in his Old Icelandic grammar, Grimm now directs the same accusation at Rask for his evaluations of the Danish and the German language. Grimm accepts Rask's point that Danish is linguistically close to Icelandic and not at all to German, but in the following sections of the review, he implies that Rask compares Danish and German to the disadvantage of the latter. Grimm reverses the argument stressing the advantages of German:

[…] in general, Danish compares unfavourably with German; even in comparison with Icelandic German has some advantages, and Old German has remarkable similarities with Old Nordic which are still reflected in our German but are extinct in Denmark. (Grimm 1869 (1812): 69)

Grimm elaborates his criticism of contemporary Danish stating how "disgusting […] Danish endings, e.g. the very frequent 'else', are to our ears […]" (Grimm 1869 (1812): 72).

Any reader of Rask's Old Icelandic grammar would have been thoroughly puzzled. Rask was often very polemic, but in the case discussed here, he just quite soberly offers linguistic evidence that Danish cannot be derived from Low German. An explanation may be found in a subsequent section of the review:

FIG. 12:

The two brothers Jacob and Wilhelm Grimm, who worked together for most of their lives, are seen today as the founding fathers of Germanic philology. German engraving from 1840.

[I]t must have been painful to any German, particularly now, to discover from a recently issued decree by the Danish government that the German language will gradually be put under pressure and probably be oppressed in the German-speaking countries belonging to Denmark. Is it not just, O German, that the language that you imbibed in the cradle from your mother's sweet talk, together with the milk, is held dear and worthy by you! (Grimm 1869 (1812): 73)

What is at stake is Danish language policies in the duchies of Schleswig and Holstein under the Danish Crown. In Holstein the population was German-speaking, and in Schleswig part of the population spoke Danish and the other part German. In 1810, a Royal Ordinance was issued decreeing that the language in schools, church and court must be Danish instead of German in the districts of Schleswig where Danish was "the language of the ordinary man". Similarly there were thoughts about introducing Danish alongside with German in Holstein.[8]

In a letter to Jacob Grimm of 28 August 1811, Rask refers to Grimm's criticism of Danish by stating that he does not want to give Danish priority over German, nor German priority over Danish (Hjelmslev 1941, 1: 70).

In a letter written to Wilhelm Grimm on the same day Rask elaborates on the term germanic, claiming that in its present use in Danish the word is synonymous with German (Sørensen 1997, 421):

In spite of the reasons provided [I can] not quite excuse the egotistical or far too patriotic use of the word germanic. If this refers to ancient times when the languages had not yet separated, then it is *superfluous*, at least there are no traces of such an object, which probably never existed. If it is meant to denote the always different but also always related languages belonging to this class [...], then it becomes *incorrect*, because it clearly expresses one single branch of the same and according to its present use is quite identical with *German*. Who would include the Nordic countries under Germania? The whole difference is that one word (German) is local, the other (Germanic) foreign. (Hjelmslev 1941, 1: 73f. Rask's emphasis)

Both Rask and Grimm argue passionately, accusing each other of exaggerated nationalism but so far keeping a civilized tone. Grimm brings forward his criticism "sincerely, honestly, and mildly" (Grimm 1869 (1812): 67), and Rask apologizes for his polemic tone, which "so easily comes about when someone speaks his case with warmth" (Hjelmslev 1941, 1: 73f.).

Rask's prize treatise

In 1811, the Royal Danish Academy of Sciences and Letters posed a prize question that reads as follows: *Med historisk Critik at undersöge og med passende Exempler at oplyse, af hvilken Kilde det gamle skandinaviske Sprog sikkerst kan udledes; at angive*

---

8   These ideas were not carried out in practise, probably because of internal disagreement in the Schleswig-Holsten Chancellery. The only results were a couple of ordinances from the following year decreeing that everybody applying for office and all lawyers in Schleswig had to prove that they mastered the Danish language (Skautrup 1944-70, 3: 118f.)

Sprogets Character og det forhold, hvori det fra ældre Tider og igiennem Middelal-
deren har staaet dels til nordiske, dels til germanske Dialecter; samt nöiagtigen at
bestemme de Grundsætninger, hvorpaa al Udledelse og Sammenligning i disse Tunge-
maal bør bygges.[9] That the learned men of the Academy had Rask in mind may be
inferred from their distinction between the Nordic and Germanic dialects (Rask
1932-35, 3: 3).

Due to his travels in Iceland, Rask was not able to hand in his paper until 1814.
But he won the gold medal of the Royal Society, and his treatise was published in
1818. The first main chapter is about the principles of etymology, a novelty that
inaugurates a stricter theoretical and methodical attitude to the investigation of
language relationships than had existed in the eighteenth century. Meaning based
on similarity among some roots is not enough; what counts are first of all the
formal properties of a language. Rask points to "letter transitions" and systematic
similarities in grammar, i.e. inflectional endings, a level that had hardly been considered in the eighteenth century (Rask 1932-35 (1818) 1: 49-51).

In his treatise, Rask elaborates what we have come to know as his ideas about
the Nordic and Germanic languages and partly reproduces the debates between
himself and Jacob Grimm. What is new in the history of linguistics at this stage,
however, is his systematic comparison between Old Icelandic and several other
languages. Rask discovered the regularity in "letter transitions" between series of
consonants in what he had chosen to name the Gothic languages and several other
European languages.[10] On these grounds he was able to clearly determine which
languages belonged to the Gothic group, and he also established the relationship
between the Gothic group and Latvian, Latin, Greek and the Slavonic languages.
Rask did not assume that Icelandic derived from any of those languages, but he
found so many basic similarities that he believed all these peoples and languages
to have a common ancestor, which he chose to name Thracian. At this point, Rask
did not yet know Persian and Sanskrit,[11] languages that he was to study during his

9   Through the use of historical criticism and appropriate examples to examine and illustrate the source
    from which the old Scandinavian language most likely derives; to indicate the character of the lan-
    guage and its connections to the Nordic and Germanic dialects from ancient times through the Mid-
    dle Ages; and also thoroughly to determine the principles on which all derivation and comparison in
    these languages should be based. The prize question was issued in both Danish and Latin (Pedersen
    in Rask 1932-35, 1: XV), which had been the practice of the Royal Danish Society since the first prize
    questions on record in 1768 (Molbech 1843: 559ff.).

10 These regularities, e.g., Latin p̲ater = English f̲ather, Latin tenuis = English t̲hin, Latin c̲ornu = English
    h̲orn are known today as the Germanic consonant shift. For a complete account, see e.g. Bach 1965
    (1938): 58ff..

11 Similarities between Sanskrit and the European languages had been noticed by a few European of-
    ficials, scholars and missionaries in India in the course of the eighteenth century, not least William
    Jones in 1788. The first systematic comparison between Sanskrit, Persian, and the European languages
    (contributing to the notion of an Indo-European language group) was published in 1816 by Rask's
    German contemporary Franz Bopp (1791-1867) (Arens 1969 (1955): 146, 175).

great journey, so he is rather unclear about possible relationships between these languages and Thracian.

Deutsche Grammatik by Jacob Grimm

In the meantime in 1819, Jacob Grimm published the first volume of his *Deutsche Grammatik* (direct translation: German grammar, published in English as *Germanic Grammar* 1893). This was an extremely ambitious historical comparative grammar starting with the oldest sources of Gothic, Old Upper German, Old Saxonian, Anglo-Saxon, and Old Icelandic. Grimm now chose to term these languages German dialects, using German as the inclusive name for the whole language group.

Similar to Rask, Grimm also had a nationalist purpose. His dedication to Savigny, his old professor, echoes Herder and the late eighteenth century. Like Rask, Grimm distanced himself from those who think that only classical literature is worthwhile as opposed to "the supposedly boorish ways of our own past":

I firmly believe that even if the value of our national ideas, antiquities and customs might be considered much poorer than we justly and modestly dare assume, the knowledge of the local is nevertheless most worthy and healthy to us and ought to be preferred over all foreign scholarship. By nature we are dependent on the fatherland and with our inborn gifts we are not able to learn to understand anything else as clearly and to such an extent. (Grimm 1819: without page)

In "we", "fatherland", and "our inborn gifts" the essential unity of nation, people and culture, including language, is taken for granted.

Grimm did not subscribe to the eighteenth century theory that language development and change was caused by external factors. In his view, language assumes a mysterious quality as an "unacknowledged, subconscious secret" with a life of its own:

[…] an indefatigable creative language spirit that like a brooding bird builds its nest anew when the eggs have been taken away; poets and authors feel its invisible influence in their enthusiasm and their emotions. (Grimm 1819: XV)

Rask, who in the course of his life learned fifty-five languages (Rask 2002: 15), would hardly have accepted Grimm's theory that a foreign language cannot be learned properly, but they never discussed this. Altogether Rask took a more rationalist view on language, comparing it to an object in nature. True language philosophy must be similar to natural history – Rask refers to Linné and Newton – the object of study being what Rask calls "the system and the physiology of language" (Rask 1932-35 (1830) 2: 377).

In his introduction to the first volume of the German grammar Grimm praises Rask, whose prize treatise was published so late that Grimm was not able to use it for his own work. Grimm says that his own results concerning the ancient German languages are in agreement with Rask's, and that he himself has learned a lot from Rask about the connections between the European languages (Grimm 1819: XVIIIf.). The central issue in the correspondence between Rask and the Brothers Grimm, namely, how to name the language group, is at this point only given a footnote:

As everybody will notice, I am using the term *German* in the general sense so that it also includes the Nordic languages. Many would have preferred the word Germanic and subsumed German and Nordic as special cases under its generality. However, as Nordic scholars recently have protested formally against the idea that their race is Germanic, the participation in this name, honourable since Roman times, should not be forced upon them. But *Gothic,* the name suggested by them, is not acceptable either. The Goths are a particular tribe, and other tribes cannot possibly be named after them. *German*, consequently, remains the only general term that does not denote one single people. (Grimm 1819: XXXVIII, footnote. Emphasis by Grimm)

In spite of this very clear statement, Grimm's own practice remains ambivalent. He uses German both as the inclusive name for the whole language group and also quite narrowly about the German language.

What seems to have interested Grimm more than Rask's terminology, was Rask's analysis of the letter transitions. Rask's observations led Grimm to revise the first volume of his German grammar before publishing the next three volumes. The second edition appeared in 1822. Using Rask's prize treatise as his model, Jacob Grimm added a long initial chapter about "the letters." In this chapter, Grimm presents and systematizes the letter transitions discovered by Rask, coining the term "Lautverschiebung," i.e., sound shift but without mentioning Rask at this particular point. As a consequence, even today this phenomenon is often referred to as Grimm's law.

The final rupture

For the rest of their lives, Rask and Grimm each stuck to their own ideas. Their passionate attitudes in the debate may be explained by their respective nationalist interests. In "a nationalist dilation of time" (R. Burger, quoted in Wodak et al. 1999: 1), they claim the same territory for the construction of different myths of origin. Rask's aim is to establish an independent and direct Nordic tradition from the Old Icelandic language and literature until modern times. The interest of several German scholars in the same material, among them first and foremost the Grimms, must be understood as part of *their* search for a national identity (Sørensen 1997). By appropriating the Nordic cultural tradition and the Nordic languages as sources for their own ancient German studies, and stressing the original linguistic unity in the whole area, they were able to include the Nordic past in the construction of a German myth of origin.

What eventually caused the rupture between Rask and Jacob Grimm was not this nationalist controversy but disagreements about principles of grammar and philology, which were important scholarly issues in the early decades of the nineteenth century when historical comparative grammar was being institutionalised as a discipline.

Their debates on such issues are carried out in letters, book reviews and rebuttals, and in introductions and footnotes in a number of texts during the years 1825-27. In 1826 Grimm's review of Rask's Old Frisian grammar, published in 1825 (Grimm 1869 (1826)), made Rask so furious that he wrote a lengthy and pedantic rebuttal (Rask 1834-38 (1826)) accusing Grimm of ill will, stubbornness, pettiness, and lack of knowledge. This repudiation would be the last straw for Grimm: in a letter to the Danish scholar Christian Molbech, Grimm writes that Rask's attacks are of such a character that he is not going to answer them (Bjerrum 1968, 1: 240). Rask and Grimm never reconciled.

End of story?

This story may be continued in several ways:

1. The similarities between Rask's and Jacob Grimm's methods and attitudes are much greater than their differences. But Grimm published his works in a more widespread language. In addition, he had a secure social position for most of his life, and he lived to be nearly twice as old as Rask. Not until 1831 was Rask offered a professorship in oriental languages at the University of Copenhagen that would give him the time and money necessary to pursue his studies. He is reported to have said, "I fear it is too late!" (Rask 2002: 225); he was already suffering from tuberculosis and died in 1832, only forty-four years old.

2. Posterity has wondered about Rask's personality. He got into quarrels with numerous colleagues, and during his great journey he suffered from hallucinations and compulsive ideas (Rask 2002). After his return, Rask gradually devel-

oped into an odd figure and became a disappointment to fellow scholars who had high expectations of his work. Apart from his seminal work on Iranian philology from 1826, *Om Zendsprogets og Zendavestas Ælde og Ægthed* (About the antiquity and authenticity of the Zend language and the Zend Avesta), he devoted his time to minor works and not least to a reform of Danish orthography and fierce and lengthy quarrels with other Danish scholars on this matter.

3. Rask tried to take revenge on Jacob Grimm. In 1830, he published an anonymous review of the first and second volumes of Grimm's *Deutsche Grammatik* in English (Rask 1834-1838 (1830)). In this review Rask compares the first two volumes of Grimm's work with a prize treatise on the history of the Danish, Norwegian and Swedish languages by N.M. Petersen, who, incidentally, was Rask's life-long friend (Rask 2002). The reviewer positions himself as an unspecific "we", an anonymous, disinterested but very well-informed scholar from outside who is objectively able to compare the advantages and disadvantages of "Professor Rask's", "Mr. Petersen's" and "Dr. Grimm's" approaches – to the absolute advantage of Rask and Petersen. By referring to Rask as "Professor Rask" a year before his actual appointment and reducing professor Grimm to "Dr. Grimm", the anonymous author elegantly constructs a higher status for Rask.

4. Jacob Grimm was a strong advocate of a united Germany, and from the early 1840s he based nationalist territorial claims on his own theories about language history. He propagated the view that the partly German-speaking duchies of Schleswig and Holstein must rightfully become part of a united Germany together with the Danish peninsula of Jutland since, in his view, the language of Jutland had originally been a Low German dialect (Sørensen 1997). Dying in 1863, however, Grimm did not live to see the conquest of Schleswig and Holstein by Prussia and Austria in 1864.

5. Rasmus Rask's and Jacob Grimm's work became the starting points for a systematic, empirically based historical comparative linguistics that would occupy scholars throughout the rest of the nineteenth and the greater part of the twentieth century. Returning to the truth about language history and language relationships, which was the major issue of concern to Adelung, Rask, and the Grimms, modern language history, after debates lasting well over 150 years, now follows Rask in constructing the Nordic languages as an old separate branch. But Germanic is now the unanimously accepted inclusive name for the whole language group.

References

Adelung, Johann Christoph 1774-1786: *Versuch eines vollständigen grammatisch-kritischen Wörterbuches der Hochdeutschen Mundart, mit beständiger Vergleichung der übrigen Mundarten, besonders aber der oberdeutschen.* Leipzig: B. Chr. Breitkopf und Sohn.

Adelung, Johann Christoph 1781: *Über den Ursprung der Sprache und den Bau der Wörter, besonders der Deutschen. Ein Versuch.* Leipzig: J.G.I. Breitkopf.

Adelung, Johann Christoph 1782: *Umständliches Lehrgebäude der Deutschen Sprache, zur Erläuterung der Deutschen Sprachlehre für Schulen 1-2.* Leipzig: J.G.I. Breitkopf.

Adelung, Johann Christoph 1782-1783: *Magazin für die Deutsche Sprache.* Leipzig: No publisher.

Adelung, Johann Christoph 1971 (1806): *Aelteste Geschichte der Deutschen, ihrer Sprache und Literatur, bis zur Völkerwanderung.* Hildesheim, New York: G. Olms.

Adelung, Johann Christoph 1806-1816: *Mithridates oder allgemeine Sprachenkunde mit dem Vaterunser als Sprachprobe in bey nahe fünfhundert Sprachen oder Mundarten 1-4.* Berlin: Vossische Buchhandlung.

Arens, Hans 1969 (1955): *Sprachwissenschaft. Der Gang ihrer Entwicklung von der Antike bis zur Gegenwart.* Freiburg/München: K. Alber.

Bach, Adolf 1965 (1938): *Geschichte der deutschen Sprache.* Heidelberg: Quelle & Meyer.

Bjerrum, Marie, 1968: *Breve til og fra Rasmus Rask 3, 1., 2. Halvbind. Brevkommentar og håndskriftkatalog.* Copenhagen: Munksgaard.

Finsen, Hans Carl 2001: *Die Rhetorik der Nation. Redestrategien im nationalen Diskurs.* Tübingen: Attempto.

Foucault, Michel 1994 (1970): *The Order of Things. An Archaeology of the Human Sciences.* London: Routledge.

Grimm, Jacob 1819: *Deutsche Grammatik I.* Göttingen: Dieterische Buchhandlung.

Grimm, Jacob 1822-1837: *Deutsche Grammatik 1-4* (1 = Second edition). Göttingen: Dieterische Buchhandlung.

Grimm, Jacob 1869, 1884 (1812): Vejledning til det islandske eller gamle nordiske sprog, af Rasmus Kristian Rask. (Anleitung zu der isländischen oder altnordischen Sprache, von R. Chr. Rask.): Jacob Grimm: *Kleinere Schriften.* Berlin: F. Dümmlers Verlagsbuchhandlung. Harrwitz und Gossmann, 4: 65-73, 7: 515-530.

Grimm, Jacob 1869 (1826): Frisisk sproglære, udarbejdet efter samme plan som den islandske og angelsaksiske af R. Rask, prof. i literærhistorien og underbibliothekar: Jacob Grimm, *Kleinere Schriften.* Berlin: Ferd. Dümmlers Verlagsbuchhandlung. Harrwitz und Gossmann, 4: 361-376.

Harnack, Adolf 1900: *Geschichte der Königlich Preussischen Akademie der Wissenschaften zu Berlin.* I. Berlin: Reichsdruckerei.

Herder, Johann Gottfried 1891 (1772): *Abhandlung über den Ursprung der Sprache.* Bernhard Suphan. Ed.: *Sämtliche Werke. 5.* Hildesheim, New York: G. Olms/Triesenberg. Weidmann: 1-148.

Hjelmslev, Louis Ed. 1941: *Breve til og fra Rasmus Rask 1-2.* Copenhagen: Munksgaard.

Hobsbawm, E. J. 2002 (1990): *Nations and Nationalism since 1780.* Cambridge UK: Cambridge University Press.

Irmscher, Hans Dietrich 2001: *Johann Gottfried Herder.* Stuttgart: Reclam.

Mallet, Paul Henri 1755: *Introduction à l'Histoire de Dannemarc ou l'on traite de la Réligion, des Loix, des Moeurs & des Usages des Anciens Danois.* Copenhagen: No publisher.

Molbech, Christian 1843: *Det Kongelige Danske Videnskabernes Selskabs Historie i dets første Aarhundrede 1742-1842.* Copenhagen: På Selskabets Bekostning.

Rask, Kirsten 2002: *Rasmus Rask. Store tanker i et lille land.* Copenhagen: Gad.

KIRSTEN GOMARD

Rask, Rasmus 1811: *Vejledning til det Islandske eller gamle Nordiske Sprog*. Copenhagen: Hofboghandler Schubothes Forlag.

Rask, Rasmus 1834-1838 (1826): Modbemærkninger ved Anmældelsen af min frisiske Sproglære: H.K. Rask Ed: *Samlede til dels forhen utrykte Afhandlinger af R.K. Rask. Udgivne efter Forfatterens død 1-3*, 3: 198-234.

Rask, Rasmus 1834-1838 (1830): Om Grimms Deutsche Gramm. Gött. 1822-26; og om Det danske, norske og svenske Sprogs Historie, af N.M. Petersen. Copenhagen. 1829: H.K. Rask Ed.: *Samlede til dels forhen utrykte Afhandlinger af R.K. Rask. Udgivne efter Forfatterens død 1-3*, 2: 442-462.

Rask, Rasmus 1932-1935: *Udvalgte Afhandlinger 1-3*. Ed. by Louis Hjelmslev. Copenhagen: Levin & Munksgaards Forlag.

Rask, Rasmus 1932-1935 (1809): Bemerkungen über die skandinavischen Sprachen, veranlasst durch den zweiten Theil des Adelungschen Mithridates: Rasmus Rask 1932-1935, 2: 102-125.

Rask, Rasmus 1932-1935 (1818): *Undersøgelse om det gamle Nordiske eller Islandske Sprogs Oprindelse*: Rasmus Rask 1932-35, 1.

Rask, Rasmus 1932-35 (1830): En Forelæsning over Sprogets Filosofi: Rasmus Rask 1932-35, 2: 373-378.

Skautrup, Peter 1944-70: *Det danske sprogs historie 1-5*. Copenhagen: Gyldendalske Boghandel Nordisk Forlag.

Strohbach, Margrit 1984: *Johann Christoph Adelung*. Berlin, New York: De Gruyter.

Sørensen, Bengt Algot 1997: Wissenschaft und Ideologie. Deutsch-Dänische Streitgespräche im 19. Jahrhundert: Arndal, Steffen Ed.: *Bengt Algot Sørensen. Funde und Forschungen*. Odense: Odense Universitetsforlag: 411-429.

Wodak, Ruth et al. 1999: *The Discursive Construction of National Identity*. Edinburgh: Edinburgh University Press.

Original Quotes

Die deutsche Sprache theilet sich in zwey Hauptmundarten, welche sehr merklich voneinander unterschieden sind, in die *oberdeutsche* und die *niederdeutsche* […] Es ist wahrscheinlich, daß die ältern Wohnsitze derjenigen Völker, welche längst der Donau nach Deutschland gekommen sind, von den Wohnsitzen derjenigen, welche den mehr nördlichen Weg erwähleten, weit entfernt gewesen sind. Ihre Sprache selbst beweiset es. Alle Völkerschaften, welche den südlichern Weg an der Donau einschlugen, und ehedem vermeintlich An- und Einwohner gebirgiger Gegenden waren, kommen in der hohen Sprache, in dem vollen Munde, in der Neigung zu den Hauchbuchstaben und den rauhen Doppellautern, in dem Zischen und Rasseln, in dem Wortgepränge, in weitschweifenden Ausdrücken und manchen Lieblingsfiguren mehr oder weniger miteinander überein, so wie alle nördlichen Völkerschaften, welche ursprünglich ohne Zweifel ein ebenes und flaches Vaterland hatten, in ihrer Sprache und ganzen Mundart den vorigen ganz entgegen gesetzte Eigenschaften haben.

Caesar fand schon zu seiner Zeit in dem heutigen Frankreich wenigstens drey Völker von verschiedener Herkunft und Sprache; Ariovist, ein Deutscher, mußte das Gallische ordentlich lernen.

schließt sich unmittelbar an die alten Niederdeutschen Mundarten, das Frisische und Sächsische an, welchem es unter den Scandinavischen Mundarten am nächsten verwandt ist.

Ich weiss nicht, ob man die Ursache dazu in dem falschen Nationalismus oder in einer, vorzüglich bei einem Adelung, unverzeihlichen Unkunde der nordischen Sprachen suchen soll […] Doch gesteht der Verfasser, dass man nicht mehr Schwedisch und Norwegisch "*zu der reinen nie-*

dern Sprache" rechnen könne; demnach ist wohl Isländisch und Dänisch reines Plattdeutsch!

Z[…] zwei Hauptclassen, die *nordische*, (skandinavische,) und *deutsche*, (germanische,) demnächst theilt sich letztere in zwei Unterarten, Nieder- und Oberdeutsch […].

der eifrigste Gegner in Deutschland gegen alles Nordische.

Paa en Tid, da Dannefolkets Fædrenelandskjærlighed og Selvfølelse synes at fordoble sig, da saamange fortræffelige Lærde søge at stille vore Fædres Bedrifter, Indretninger og Begreber i det fortjente Lys, da selv Danmarks største Digtere besynge Fædrenelandets gamle Handeler i udødelige værker, da det danske Sprog har tiltrukket sig saa megen Opmærksomhed, og dyrkes med saa megen Omhu, ja da Regjeringen endog tager sig med Iver af Fædrenelandets Oldsager, deres Bevaring og Udtydning; behøves vel neppe lang Undskyldning for et Forsøg til at fremstille vore Fædres det gamle nordiske Sprogs Bygning og Indretning, med andre Ord, en islandsk Sproglære.[…] Sproget selv behøver blot at kjendes for at opvække Ærbødighed for vore Fædre, hvis hele Aand saa fordelagtig viser sig deri, som i et Spejl.

[Gotisk] synes særdeles fortrinlig skikket til at betegne den hele store Sprogstamme, som indbefatter de tyske (germaniske) og nordiske (skandinaviske) Sprog, hvilken Tyskerne (især Adelung) ikke alt for rigtigen eller beskjedent have begyndt at kalde den germaniske. Men Germaner i norden have vi aldrig hørt tale om, og selv de gamle Rommere, som brugte Navnet, indskrænkede det udtrykkelig til Tyskerne eller endog en enkelt Stamme af dem. Goter derimod er det eneste betydelige Folk, hvoraf vi finde sikre Spor baade i Norden og Syden og hvis Sprog vi paa begge sider vide at have været ægte Grene af hin store Sprogstamme; det synes derfor den eneste bekvemme foreningspunkt, hvoraf et fælles Navn kan tages.

denne søde Egenskab, der i Sproget er, hvad Selvstændighed er i Staten.

vi [behøve] ingenlunde […] at bortføre muserne fra Parnas, for at skrive og digte skjønt og opløftende her i Norden; med andre Ord, vi behøve ikke at forme alt efter Græker og Rommere, da vi hos vore egne ærværdige Fædre kan finde saa meget efterlignelsesværdigt

[…] hr. Rask hat ein nothwendiges buch auf eine recht erfreuliche, anregende weise zu geben gewußt, er zeigt vor allem vertrauteste bekanntschaft mit seinem gegenstand […]. Seine schreibart ist leicht, klar, und wie billig und recht, in seiner muttersprache; für deutsche gar keine erschwerung, weil, wer das isländische studirt, das dänische nie vorbeigehen kann.

[…] im großen aber kann das dänische mit dem deutschen keine vergleichung aushalten, sogar vor dem isländischen hat das letzte einzelne vorzüge, und mit dem altnordischen hat das altdeutsche hervorleuchtende ähnlichkeiten, von denen noch strahlen auf unser deutsch fallen, die in Dänemark vergangen sind.

wie widrig unsern ohren […] dänische endungen, z.b. die so häufige auf else dünken […].

[…] es hat jedem Deutschen schmerzhaft sein müssen, zumal jetzt, aus einer neulich erschienenen, öffentlichen verordnung der dänischen regierung zu ersehen, daß in den ihr untergebenen deutschredenden ländern die deutsche sprache nach und nach gedrückt und wohl unterdrückt werden soll. Ist es nicht billig, du Deutscher, daß die sprache, welche du in der wiege aus dem süßen vorgeschwätze deiner mutter sammt der milch eingesogen, bei dir lieb und werth gehalten werde!

[Jeg kan] uagtet de anförte Grunde ikke ganske undskylde for [Adelungs og andres] egoistiske eller alt for patriotiske Brug af ordet *germanisk*. Skal derved betegnes den allerældste Tid, da Sprogene endnu ikke havde adskilt sig, da er det *overflödigt*, i det mindste haves ingen Spor til en saadan Gjenstand, som rimeligvis aldrig har været til. Skal det derimod […] udtrykke de vel stedse forskjellige, men dog og stedse beslægtede Sprog som höre til denne Klasse, da bliver det *urigtigt*, fordi det bestemt udtrykker en enkelt

Gren af samme og er efter dets nuværende Brug ganske entydigt med *tysk*. Hvem indbefatter vel Norden under Germanien? Hele Forskjellen er at det ene Ord (tysk) er indenlandsk det andet (germanisk) fremmed.

das vermeintlich bäurische Wesen unserer eigenen Vorzeit.

Ich bin des festen Glaubens, selbst wenn der Werth unserer vaterländischen Güter, Denkmäler und Sitten weit geringer angenommen werden müsste, als wir ihn gerecht und bescheiden voraussetzen dürfen, dass dennoch die Erkenntnis des Einheimischen unser die würdigste, die heilsamste und aller ausländischen Wissenschaft vorzuziehen wäre. Auf das Vaterland sind wir von Natur gewiesen und nicht anderes vermögen wir mit unseren angeborenen Gaben in solcher Maaße und so sicher begreifen zu lernen.

[…] unermüdlich schaffenden Sprachgeistes, der wie ein nistender Vogel wieder von neuem brütet, nachdem ihm die Eier weggethan worden; sein unsichtbares walten vernehmen aber Dichter und Schriftsteller in der Begeisterung und Bewegung durch ihr Gefühl.

Ich bediene mich, wie jeder sieht, des Ausdrucks *deutsch* allgemein, so dass er auch die nordischen Sprachen einbegreift. Viele würden das Wort *germanisch* vorgezogen und unter seine Allgemeinheit das Deutsche und Nordische als das Besondere gestellt haben. Da indessen nordische Gelehrte neuerdings förmliche Einsprache dawider thun, dass ihr Volksstamm ein germanischer sey, so sollen ihnen die Theilnahme an diesem seit der Römerzeit ehrenvollen Namen so wenig aufgedrungen worden, als der von ihnen vorgeschlagene allgemeine, *gothisch* gebilligt werden kann. Die Gothen bilden einen sehr bestimmten Stamm, nach dem man unmöglich andere Stämme benennen darf. *Deutsch* bleibt dann die einzige allgemeine, kein einzelnes Volk bezeichnende Benennung.

II: Travels
– Encountering and Experiencing the North

ANTJE WISCHMANN

The Library at Lövstabruk: A Utopia

Lövstabruk, a city-like ironwork settlement with a comprehensive library may be seen as a monument to Swedish and European Enlightenment culture. This article analyses the historical, topographic and cultural aspects of this industrial settlement in Uppland, Sweden, in the middle of the eighteenth century, and focuses on the spatial order of the location and the illustrious character of the book collection in the private library.

Lövstabruk dates back to the Swedish pre-industrialization period in the early seventeenth century. In the 1720s, the settlement was practically rebuilt after having been demolished by Russian troops in 1719. The community consisted of Calvinist immigrants who came from French-speaking Walloonia, a region that is now part of Belgium, in the first decades of the seventeenth century.

Charles De Geer* (1720-78), the fourth patron of the settlement, owned not only the industrial buildings but also the workers' housing as well as the infrastructure of the town.[1] While De Geer's* utilitarian beliefs are illustrated in the economic success of the ironworks, the manor house, the library and the natural history museum represent his aesthetic and scholarly ambitions. The settlement had several characteristics of a colony: its isolated location in a forest in the countryside, the inhabitants' French language, their Calvinistic religion and their professional training in European ironwork techniques, all contributed to the uniqueness of the community.

Lövstabruk can be seen as a Swedish colony of Walloonia, but also as a mercantilistic Utopian ideal of a well-planned society where utilitarianism and beauty make a desirable whole, or a kind of best possible world. The original settlement can be perceived as a homotopy, a concrete place similar to an existing foreign place, according to Foucault's concept of "other places" (Foucault 1967: 34-46). However, Lövstabruk can also be perceived as a heterotopia, an ideal "unreal space" (utopia) according to Foucault's concept because it is "perfecting the society" as a

---

1   In this article I will mark the protagonist with an asterix * because of the complicated De Geer genealogy (Douhan 1996: 45).

kind of partly realized Utopia (ibid. 39). Lövstabruk, the newly started colony, may even have had more obvious religious ideals and economic efficiency than Walloonia itself. There were enormous contrasts to the surrounding Swedish majority in Uppland, for example with regard to social care. Because of its function as a heterotopia, the settlement could be seen as representing a Calvinistic Utopia, a diligent life of hard work and obedience in daily life.

If we adhere to this model, the library of Charles de Geer* appears to be a smaller heterotopia inside a larger heterotopia. The library collected literary and scientific texts, maps and pictures from the public sphere and the outside world, in the inside of a private building. The modest library pavilion was (as well as the natural museum pavilion) placed by the canalized River Risforså. The location of the library and its architecture resembled a cargo ship. Foucault described the ship as the epitome of a heterotopia (ibid. 46). The library could be seen as a floating archive, a part of the circulation of books and journals from the European Enlightenment.

History and topography of a colony

Charles De Geer* (1720-1778) was born in Finspång in Östergötland. He moved to Utrecht at the age of three and spent his formative years in a French-Dutch cultural context. He arrived in Lövstabruk in 1739 and brought with him several colonial ideas: firstly, capital and the famous De Geer-family tradition of business and entrepreneurship; secondly, his French education; and thirdly, the initial book delivery for his private library. His family had connections to the Dutch overseas trade and the commercial exploitation of the colonies. Although these activities took place far away from the ironwork settlement, they still had an impact on it, especially with regard to the transfer of knowledge and skills. Bar iron was exported from Lövstabruk to England and Holland, and books from Leiden and goods from the colonies were delivered from Amsterdam in exchange.

From 1611-1718 when Sweden was a great power (*stormaktstiden*), Uppland's iron industry became profitable by producing canons that were used in the wars of continental Europe. At that time, Louis De Geer de Brialmont (born in Liège in 1587, died in Amsterdam 1652, elevated to the Swedish nobility in 1641) had taken over the ironworks from his father, Louis De Geer de Gaillarmont (1535-1602) and entered into business with Gustav II. Adolf. De Geer de Brialmont had leased and managed two small ironworks in Lövstabruk since 1627. He bought them in 1643, together with Willem de Besche from Amsterdam, and expanded them to become the largest ironworks of Sweden. This partnership can be seen as the beginning of Swedish industrialisation. Pig iron was manufactured at Lövstabruk until 1750 and

ANTJE WISCHMANN

bar iron (*vallonjärn*) until 1926. The iron was shipped to Stockholm, for further transport to England and Holland, from the port of Angskär on the Baltic Sea.

At the beginning of the seventeenth century, Walloons from the area of Liège and Namur were recruited to work in the Swedish ironworks because they were well-trained and experienced charcoal burners, blacksmiths and metalworkers.[2] These guest workers became a well-known minority in Sweden and comprehensive research exists about them (Florén and Ternhag 2002). Approximately 760 Walloon workers came to Lövstabruk. The development of a distinct social infrastructure was intended to keep the workers at the plant on a long-term basis. In this way, the patrons could avoid losing their 'experts' to other companies. The procedure for iron manufacturing was even kept secret. As the Calvinists became assimilated into the local settlement the characteristic of a religious colony became less striking, but the difference between the minority in the small town enclave and the population in the surrounding rural area remained.

Compared with other ironwork settlements where terms such as 'Walloon iron,' 'German smith' or 'French blast furnace' were used to name equipment and procedures, the term 'Walloon' in Lövstabruk had a special ethnic connotation. (The French spelling 'Leufsta(d)' is still used parallel to the recent Swedish spelling.) The inhabitants were isolated from the majority of the population in terms of language, ethnicity and religion. The architectural historian, Fredric Bedoire, even sees a causal connection between the status of members of the Protestant Reformed Church in Belgium, France and Sweden, and the concept of Lövstabruk as an ideal city. According to Bedoire, foreign businessmen who had emigrated to Sweden, such as the De Geer family, did not follow the local aristocratic tradition with regard to architecture. They had their own architectural style that originated from the Protestant Reformed Church buildings (Bedoire 1995: 161). Bedoire assumes that the eighteenth century design of *bruk* (ironworks) was influenced by Huguenot architecture and that the two Swedish architects, Carl Hårleman (1700-1753) and Jean Eric Rehn (1717-1793), who were involved in numerous projects, were familiar with Huguenot ideas via their study trips and contacts with international colleagues. Bedoire mentions the union of religion and work ethic, and the architectural concept of a utilitarian view of life as characteristic of Huguenot town planning.

The closed and compact impression of the settlement, in other words its unity and density, can be explained by the fact that Lövstabruk was completely rebuilt

---

2   For the different professions and qualifications see Haggrén 2001: 98-137.

after 1719.[3] It was either the architect, Johan Hårleman, who was responsible for the master plan when he was put in charge by the third owner of Lövstabruk, *landshövding* (county governor) Charles De Geer (1660-1730), or Nicodemus Tessin the Younger (1654-1728) (Selling 1980: 56-58). Most probably, Tessin carried out the basic plan whereas Hårleman was responsible for the detailed planning (Sandström-Hanngren/Edling 1981:19-20).

Apart from the fact that the street with the archive building at the end is not directly opposite the main street, the plan for the baroque garden was carried out consistently and still exists today. The houses and workshops were finished in 1723. The manor house, originally constructed in timber, was rebuilt in stone in 1744.[4]

To visit Lövstabruk is to take a journey back in time or to walk into a historical painting because entering Lövstabruk means experiencing a notion of harmony and efficiency. The temporal and spatial experience is to some degree predetermined because the views of the park routes have been planned. The tour round the lake is an easy walk, including some rest places where visitors may enjoy the view. The balanced shaping of the landscape with respect to the arrangement of the buildings, the garden of the manor house and the park does not entail a distancing from nature. Rather, it provides a feeling of distance from the overall plan of the settlement. This impression is increased when visitors appreciate that the site was chosen on the basis of technological considerations and after the marshland had been reclaimed. The lake shore and the river banks are integrated elements in the scenic arrangement.[5]

The settlement has several urban characteristics, for example the grid pattern, the main street, building materials of stone, and facades in Belgian yellow. Within the area of the *bruk*, the distance of each building to the manor house is a system representing social status. The church, the house of the manager and the *brukskontor* (with the function of a bank and a depot) are nearest to the manor-house site, whereas the poor house is far away from it. The church (with a well-known baroque organ from 1727) and the manager's house have the same roof height and exterior proportions reflecting how both religious and mercantile values are equally important.

The pavilion-like, archive building is located opposite the manor house. Contracts, promissory notes and accounts of the workers' wages were found in the

---

3   The earliest geometrical masterplan of Lövstabruk from around 1640 corresponds with the chequered pattern of the town Gävle (about 50 km away from Lövstabruk), designed by Nicodemus Tessin the elder in 1646.

4   Either was J.G. Destain (or Destin) the architect of the manor-house, because he designed a similar plant in Södermanland (Björksundsherrgård) (Unnerbäck 2000: 9) or it was Göran Josua Adelcrantz, assistant of Nicodemus Tessin the younger (Sandström-Hanngren/ Edling 1981: 23-24).

5   For theories of the picturesque see Stephanie Buus, 2002.

ANTJE WISCHMANN

Lövstabruk. Utsikt från Norra Hammaren mot Herrgården. Elias Martin, 1790.

archives and in the *brukskontor*. The workers usually received their wages as paper accounts detailing the money spent on grain, clothes or school books etc. From the workers' perspective, the archives and the *brukskontor* represented a powerful bureaucracy, regulating their everyday life e.g. which families could claim a portion of free grain because of the birth of a child, whose dept repayment would be adjourned because of a husband's or father's sickness. Lövstabruk had its own jurisdiction, with the patron and the manager acting as the Court of Appeal.

The school is located between the church and the archives pavilion, and the hospital is between the manager's house and the archives. The manager, priest, teacher, physician, organist and the higher craftsmen belonged to the rising middle class of the town who profited from the social system. One organist's son received a scholarship from the patron to study medicine at Uppsala where he gained his doctorate under the supervision of Linné. Later on, this professional training enabled him to be employed as the physician of Lövstabruk. Such investments were not always successful because some of the specialists moved to Gävle, the largest town nearby, or to Stockholm or even to St. Petersburg.

The smiths' houses are situated on the 800 m long main street, on the opposite side and separated from the manor house. The western part of Lövstabruk, with the most important settlement buildings, is enclosed between the two larg-est side streets. The church, school and both warehouses are situated in a square section, from which other small lanes branch off. The 'workers' half' of the set-tlement, geometrically and symmetrically sectioned, constitutes a counterpart to the geometrical garden and the symmetrical arrangement of the site of the manor house. The earliest map from 1687 emphasizes the basic feudal orientation of the manor house, because the main entrance and the yard do not face the garden and the 'center of the town' but face a French style avenue leading to an open landscape (Thörnvall 1985: 68). The contact between the patron and the workers was always dealt with by the manager (*bruksdirector*) or his staff.

The partitioning of the area into zones can be seen very clearly on the map 'Grund=Ritning öfwer Leufsta bruk' (ground plan of Lövstabruk) by Olof Gerdes (1735). The separation of the patron's side and the subordinates' side, including the main production zone, attracts attention because the water line is drawn in a strik-ing way. Only the smithy including the lower hammer with the coal house and the *labby* (a little hall where the workers could take their four-hour rest between shifts) are located quite near to the library by the canal because of the need for water during the manufacturing process. Thus one might speculate whether the library's location by the canal really was planned in order to emphasize the architectural ship analogy. The library must after all have been a noisy place on working days.

The lattice fences and the stone wall can be recognized on Gerdes' map as well as the exact partitioning of all the smiths' properties. The map depicts exactly the rows of trees on the three major streets and on the three large park avenues, and thereby stresses the calculated internal and social boundaries within the set-tlement.

The presentation of Lövstabruk in documents from the eighteenth century

How the visitors to Lövstabruk, many of them artists and writers, express their opinion about the settlement depends mainly on their attitude towards both the artificial notion (skilfulness) and the subjugation of nature (monumental rule). Of course the authors and painters who appreciate Lövstabruk have another focus than those making critical or distanced comments but nearly all of them notice that the architecture expresses social order.

The topographic painting of an ironwork settlement (*bruksbild*) constitutes a subgenre of its own in eighteenth century Swedish painting. In an anonymous painting from 1710, the viewer is provided with a panoramic view where the buildings dominate and the landscape, as well as the garden, are almost missing (Ahlund 1996: 82-83). Olof von Dalin's ink sketch *View over the Lake towards Lövsta-*

bruk's Manor House (1745) partly follows the topographic tradition, although from a perspective closer to ground level and not when viewed from above. Thus, the reflecting water surface occupies a big part of the painting. On the right hand, a part of the main street can be seen, but only the central crossing of the town is comprehensible. The sketch pays homage to a festive and contemplative Lövstabruk; only the tops of two chimneys emitting smoke in neat ornamental forms are a reminder of industrial activity.

Concurrently with Dalin's sketch, the painting of Elias Martin from 1790 (Fig. 13) focuses on the characteristics of the park by describing the park landscape and the manor house in detail. The form of the trees, spreading their branches and the reflection of the summer clouds on the lake's surface are more important than the main street and other buildings which are nearly covered by trees. The painter's interest in the partly wild and partly tamed landscape is obvious and can be explained by Martin's interest in the architecture of English parks. The focus of the composition and the preferred use of pastel colours are typical traits of the 'Gustavian' style of painting (Ahlund 1996: 97-98). This picture is not intended to give a topographic overview. The decorative human figures seem at first glance to be tourists going for a walk, but their nice clothes are deceiving. The figures represent the different social groups and professions of Lövstabruk inhabitants, as one can see from their clothing, attributes and wagons. They are characterized positively and picturesquely and their every day life seems to be free of labour and social conflicts. Elias Martin's picture hints at some characteristics of the social ideal, *brukssamhälle,* as a model society and he presents a romantic ideal of a noble rural town with a distinguished culture.

Christer Berch, who also wrote a thesis about metal making, describes both the landscape and makes detailed observations about Lövstabruk in 1753 (Thörnvall 1985: 167-172). A young herdsman's payment is the first piece of information about Lövstabruk. "Starting from the forest there is a straight path to the plant, where a boy, who works as a gatekeeper and prevents pigs from leaving the area, opens the gates; for this job he gets 12 öre a day from the chamberlain" (ibid. 167). The economic and hierarchical interaction between the patron and the workers is important. Berch notices the wrought-iron lattice fences as well, but interprets them as elements, which have been imported from the Netherlands and confirm the splendour and the urban appearance of the ironwork settlement. He concludes that, "this place should have the status of a city" (ibid. 168). In Berch's opinion the city-like character of the settlement derived from the size of some architectural elements (i.e. the streets and the fences) and from the owner's ancestry, and these made the European connection in Lövstabruk noticeable. According to Berch, the variety of the workshops could compete with other Swedish cities (ibid. 179). It is quite remarkable that Berch proposes that people living in Stockholm should use similar trolleys for shopping as those used by the workers' wives in the settlement, as this would reduce the need for physical strength and the need for horses. When describing 'street life' in the settlement, Berch uses a typical metaphor for big cities, the ant hill: "[the workers' wives] were crawling like ants, forward and back again, the streets were filled with their trolleys" (ibid. 171). By emphasizing the economic and transport structures, this 'urban' image in literature differs quite a lot from the pastoral paintings.

One of the most famous statements about Lövstabruk comes from Crown Prince Gustav III who, after a visit to Lövstabruk in 1768, wrote to his mother Lovisa Ulrika, "However, I must say my dear mother you have not seen anything of Sweden, if have not seen Leufstad" (Anfält 1991: 197). This quotation expresses the idea that Lövstabruk could be seen as a metonymy representing the ideal of a prospering and orderly state – even in a politically unstable period.

Jonas Carl Linnerhielm (1758-1829) provides his readers with a detailed description in his travel letters from 1797 in which his own aesthetic experience is given priority. His first impression on arrival on a summer's evening is that of a medieval atmosphere, with the grazing horses having been left behind by knights. This atmosphere suggests a poetic mood, "filled with imaginations from the old bards' world" (Linnerhielm 1985: 10). He is very surprised about the size and the spatial-visual proportions of the ironwork settlement, which is increased by the use of the adjective "frapperad" (striking). He observes that the visitor's gaze is directed at the architecture and interprets this gesture as proof of the patron's power and the way nature has been tamed.

You arrive at this place passing a beautiful pine wood, which is followed by a lush elder tree grove and, in the end, by a long tree-lined walk, all in one line. The river can be seen constantly and the buildings are reflected in the water. Although a straight line is unpleasant for the person who is hiking for pleasure or for the lover of nature, one has to admit that this line makes a great impression. This is a very natural consequence. The thought is telling you immediately that there must be a mighty owner of this place who is able to overcome all obstacles within this settlement. However, is great and beautiful really the same? And which of these results in discomfort? (Ibid. 10-11)

Linnerhielm dislikes the geometrical organization of the settlement in that nature is being tamed and restrained. He critically wonders whether the main intention really is aesthetic, hinting that the pragmatic and representative intentions might be more important. A critical tone is also obvious when Linnerhielm describes the numerous wrought-iron fences which are extremely expensive. At the same time he snubs the French garden where "nothing seems to be attractive to me" (ibid. 11). The manor house is mentioned because of its distinguished wings and inner courts but "the building could also be an expression of force" (ibid. 11). Thereby, he characterizes the architectural style as rationalistic and disciplining. Obviously, Linnerhielm did not visit the library but reports that it contained 7,500 volumes. His report closes with some mercantile details: the output of the ironworks, the number of employees (1,900) and the removal of the blast furnace. The last impression, in contrast with the mild atmosphere in the beginning, is the industrial noise from the working machinery. "A sanding machine to grind big anvils and the mill with its six millstones increase the motion and also the noise on the river, which apart from that is flowing gently" (Ibid. 12).

Four years later, Johan Erik Forsström also critically describes Lövstabruk in his travel diary (Thörnvall 1985: 188-189). Visiting the settlement from 27-28 June 1801, he remarks that it is characterized by a lack of art and craftsmanship, and notices that some buildings have been neglected. Similar to Linnerhielm, he comments on the excessive state of the wrought-iron fences and criticizes the treatment of the natural landscape. "The place is more boring than Forsmark [bruk], where craftmanship is also used to parcel up nature" (ibid. 188). The contrast between the careful design of the fences, which mark or protect the most valuable buildings, and the dilapidated areas, makes Forsström indignant. He notices the social demarcation of areas and emphasizes the excluding effects of the boundaries (Ibid. 188).

None of the travel texts I have read describes an encounter between the production sphere and the patron's sphere. However, Forsström indicates that the education and the customs of the occupants of the manor house were not very distinguished. After having given a respectful description of the private library he comments on the informal or maybe rustic behaviour of the De Geer family. "After we had returned from the library we were surprised to meet the baron's wife, who was in the company of a few other women and was sitting in a beautiful negligé in order to eat sausages for breakfast." (Ibid. 188-189)

The library and its owner

The library pavilion was designed by Jean Eric Rehn in 1756 and comprises a hall with five windows and two small rooms (which can be heated). The interior is in Rococo style with doors, shelves and several low closets painted in bluish pearl grey and decorated with gilt edges. The numerous windows and the white ceiling give the room an atmosphere of ease and openness although the shelves are packed with books. On the hall's parquet floor, a work table and a wood file for maps and posters are placed. Numerous maps and additional bookshelves can be found in the rooms, and De Geer's carefully written library catalogues emphasize how the book collection is systematically classified.

Looking from the bridge, which crosses the canal and connects the manor house with the garden, the visitor will probably get the impression of the library building as a ship ready to embark. The canal's waterfront right behind the pavilion is not visible and the library seems to stand on water rather than on the ground (Fig. 14). In the middle of the eighteenth century the pavilion was completely surrounded by water and only accessible by a tiny bridge (Ahlund 1996: 92). The library was probably meant to look like a ship.

The reflection of the library, the museum pavilion and the manor house in the water is intended to enlarge the buildings optically, a method which was adopted from continental architecture. Many paintings and engravings picture this reflection of the interaction between water and sunlight. If a visitor today spends some time in the library, he/she will see an idyllic situation when looking out of the windows. During the light seasons, the sun reflects on the water and may be mirrored on to the white ceiling, whirring and shimmering. The golden spines of the books reflect the sunlight floating in through the windows. Nowadays, the silence in the library makes the visitor forget the noise of the blacksmiths' hammers that once could be heard.

If we adhere to Foucault and see the ship as a heterotopia, with a proverbial "imagination arsenal" (1967: 46), possibly referring to several 'other spaces', i.e. well-known countries or harbours and unknown imagined places, which sometimes can only be reached and discovered with the special equipment on board – such as and including the books. The ship-like pavilion is characterised by a spatial, metaphorical, 'textual' and material dimension. It is a 'heterotopian' reservoir of both temporal and spatial units (places), which might be accessible for the users of the library by reading certain texts. However, it is material proof of mercantile circulation and trade as well.

Taking into consideration De Geer's* individual interests, his library may be regarded as an ideal library for a scholar of the Enlightenment period:

Typical characteristics: [...] apart from a general openness towards the contemporary philosophical developments, and the history of science and literature, the following tendencies can be noted: 1. The main publications and main authors of the epoch are present. 2. The Latin Language loses its dominant position. On the continent, French, to a large extent, takes over the former role of Latin. From the middle of the eighteenth century, the influence of English greatly increases. 3. The decrease of theological papers must be noticed as a constant. 4. The predominance of the history section is very obvious. (Adam 1995: 66-67)

The only deviation from Wolfgang Adam's criteria is the dominance of scientific works, which can be explained by De Geer's* personal research. Theological writings are obviously superseded by scientific and literary books and magazines.

The *landshövding*, Charles De Geer, had already established a solid and well sourced library at Lövstabruk (Katalog 1907: 259-262). Before the young baron, Charles De Geer* arrived in 1739, the manager, Erik Danielsson Touscher, had bought an impressive selection of books for the new owner, although the pavilion was not completed until 1758. It was the manager's opinion that the baron should be educated in a patriarchical 'gothicist' spirit (*göticism*), which is why he bought relevant works i.e. *Atlantica* of Olof Rudbeck the Elder, and works of Johannes Messenius, Georg Stiernhelm, Johannes Schefferus, Olof Verelius and Johan Fredrik Peringskiöld (Anfält 1987: 2).

From his home in Utrecht, the young De Geer* brought the following books: *Dictionnaire historique et critique* (Historical and Critical Dictionary 1702) by Pierre Bayle, Louis Moréri's *Le Grand Dictionnaire Historique* (Big Historical Dictionary 1724), and Bernard Le Bovier de Fontenelle's *Entretiens sur la pluralité des mondes* (News about the Variety of the World 1701, Anfält 1993: 253). The children's room at the De Geer's manor house 'Rijnhuizen' in Utrecht had a library containing the scientific magazines, *Acta eruditorum* (Erudite Records) from Leipzig (Anfält 1995a: 332). In 1739, De Geer* acquired Voltaire's *Lettres philosophiques* (Philosophical Letters 1729, Anfält 1995b: 272). From Lövstabruk, he ordered one of the most famous publications of the Enlightenment, *Encyclopédie ou dictionnaire raisonné* (Encyclopaedia and Dictionary 1752) by Denis Diderot and Jean le Rond d'Alembert. This marks his ambition to have a library representative of the time and meeting the latest scientific standards.

Lövstabruk library's nominal catalogue from 1907 and the catalogues about engravings and art reproductions, as well as De Geer's* musical collection, reflect his curiosity, educational interests and scientific ambition as a scholar. According to Tomas Anfält's research, it is possible to deduce De Geer's* reading habits[6] and to speculate about the characteristics of the "interpretive community" (Chartier 1992: 34) of the De Geer-family. As the library was owned by an active research scientist, a quarter of the book collection consists of scientific publications, with a focus on entomology and biology: for example René Antoine Réaumur's, Carl von Linné's and Olof Rudbeck's (the Younger and the Elder) publications and refer-

---

6   To maintain an overview about the large amount of texts, De Geer* put on reference registers and lists. Anfält reconstructs even individual order procedures by the correspondence: For example received De Geer* Jean-Jacques Rousseau's *La nouvelle Heloïse* (1761) in February 1762, after having read a review in August 1761 (Anfält 1991: 208).

FIG. 14:
Above: The library pavilion seen from northwest direction (on the right-hand side of the Manor House); Below: The library pavilion seen from southwest direction from the channel bridge. Photographs by AW.

ANTJE WISCHMANN

Book examples from the library on the windowsill. Left: The natural history by August Johann Rösel von Rosenhof: Historia naturalis ranarum nostratium. Nürnberg 1758. Right above: Olof Rudbeck the elder: Atlantica. Right below: Denis Diderot's and Jean Le Rond d'Alembert's Encyclopédie (1751-72).

ence books on 'natural history' as this interdisciplinary subject was called at the time.[7] Examples of scientific reference literature are Mark Catesby's *The natural history of Carolina, Florida and the Bahamas* (1731-43), and Georg Louis Leclerc, comte de Buffon's *Histoire naturelle* (Natural History 1749-75, Anfält 1993: 256). Even two publications of the famous Dutch entomologist Maria Sibilla Merian are available: *De generatione et metamorphosibus insectorum Surinamensium* (About the Metamorphosis of Insects from Surinam 1726), and *Histoire des insectes de l' Europe* (Natural History of European Insects 1730).

7   Also philosophy, meant to be a very broad discourse, often associated with political criticism or polemic.

During his studies in Uppsala 1738/39, De Geer bought parts of the famous library of Olof Rudbeck the Younger. The value of those volumes increased in 1702 after a fire in Uppsala destroyed Rudbeck's library including the wooden printing plates for the famous botanical work, *Campus elysii* (Elysian Fields). De Geer* also bought several manuscripts by Carl von Linné i.e. *Catalogus plantarum rariorum* (Catalogue of Rare Plants), and *Dissertatio de nuptiis et sexu plantarum* (Thesis about the Reproduction and the Sex of Plants), *Hortus uplandicus* (The Garden of Uppland). For most visitors, the main book attraction today is *Fågelboken* (Book of Birds 1739) with drawings by Olof Rudbeck the Younger and Anders Holtzbom because of its detailed life-sized illustrations of birds. This naturalistic method of illustrating animals was an innovation. Before the empirical turn in natural history, drawings were drawn using written descriptions from different sources of natural history. In contrast, the illustrations in *Fågelboken* demonstrate a kind of 'visual autopsy'. For example, the illustration of the wood grouse not only shows the pattern of the plumage in exact detail but also the tiny insects near the dead bird's body which have been attracted by the odour of the carcass.

De Geer* did not use his library primarily for show but as a scholar's working room. He carried out his entomological research here and this resulted in a publication consisting of eight volumes which he illustrated himself: *Mémoires pour servir à l'histoire des insectes* (Thesis about the Usefulness of Insects 1752-78). This work leans strongly on Charles Bonnet and Réaumur's work with the same title and it proves that even insects are useful beings within God's creation. De Geer* was not only interested in insects' form and anatomy, but also in their behaviour. Despite his friendship with Carl von Linné, whom he had become acquainted with during his studies in Uppsala from 1738 to 39, De Geer* did not use Linné's scientifically innovative topical terminology in the first volumes, but respectfully followed Réaumur's system, which underlines De Geer's* French orientation at that time.

The publications of *Kungliga Svenska Vitterhetsakademien* (Royal Swedish Academy of Science) of 1755, to which De Geer* himself contributed, are also still in the library as is his correspondence with contemporary scientists i.e. Linné and Réaumur, his mentor in entomology.

The book collection gives examples of the specialization as well as the popularization of scientific discourse, a contradictory dynamic relation involving broad 'natural history,' divided into several sections and special discourses, on the one hand, and entertainment and educational intentions i.e. Francesco Algarotti: *Le Newtonianisme pour les dames* (Newton's Research, for Female Readers 1739), and August Johann Rösel von Rosenhof: *Insectenbelustigungen* (Insects for Your Pleasure 1761), on the other hand. An encyclopaedia of the reformed pastor, François

ANTJE WISCHMANN

Valentijn, demonstrates how discourses could overlap and interact. *Oud en nieuw Oost-Indiën* (Old and New East India 1726), published in Amsterdam, deals with politics, everyday life, culture and religion in this group of islands. From a Dutch point of view the readers could imagine 'other places' as possible worlds or cultures to participate in. This also contributed to their 'colonial consciousness,' making them aware of the living conditions of the inhabitants of the colonies.

Furthermore, technical literature and literature about the iron industry was of interest to De Geer*. These books were typical contributions to the discourse of technical progress, remarkably often imported from German which was a source of important engineering innovations at the time. Some illustrative examples are: *Propempticon inaugurale de ortu venarum metalliferarum* (Thesis about the Origin of Metal Seams 1700) by Georg Ernst Stahl, *Acta et tentamina chymica* (Chemical Documentation and Experiments 1712) by Urban Hiärne, *Allgemeines Handlungs- Kunst- Berg- und Handwerckslexicon* (General Encyclopaedia about Business, Manufacturing, Mining and Trading 1722) by Adran Beier, *Kort beskrivning om eld- och luftmaskin vid Dannemora Gruvor* (Short description of the fire and ventilation engine at Dannemora mine 1734) by Mårten Triewald, *Gründlicher Unterricht von Hütte-Werken* (Thorough Instructions about Ironworks 1738) by Christoph Andreas, *Erzstufen und Bergarten* (Ore Levels and Rock Sorts 1753) by Casimir Christoph Schmiedel.[8]

The travel literature in the library, mainly written in French, has hardly been investigated, which should encourage future research projects on this subject. One group of books deals with the topic in the Nordic region: Cornelis Gijsbertsz Zorgdrager: *Bloeyende Opkomst der aloude en heedendaagsche Groenlandsche visschery* (Development of Early and current Fishing in Greenland 1720), Arvid Ehrenmalm: *Resa igenom Wäster-Norrland* (Travel through West-North Sweden 1743), Carl Hårleman: *Dag-bok öfwer en ifrån Stockholm igenom åtskillige rikets landskaper gjord resa* (Diary about a Journey from Stockholm to Different Areas of Sweden 1749), Uno von Troil: *Bref rörande en resa til Island* (Letter about a Journey to Iceland 1777) and a travel diary manuscript about a journey through Sweden by Emanuel De Geer and Adolf Fredrik Barnekow from 1768. Also the collected papers, *Recueil de voyages au Nord* (Collected Papers about Journeys in the North 1731-38) by Jean-Frédéric Bernard in ten volumes should be mentioned. And the 27 volumes describing various journeys and memoirs (1728-42) by the Dominican missionary and early ethnographer, Jean-Baptiste Labat, indicate that these texts were popular reading. Although De Geer* did not do any travelling himself, sev-

8   The catalogue's (*Leufsta bruks gamla Fideikommissbibliotek* 1907, according to De Geer's* manuscript catalogues) spelling of titles and authors was corrected by the online catalogues copac.ac.uk and www.gbv.de (available 2 january 2005).

eral travel guides about European countries and cities were ordered. He preferred to travel in his mind and tried to learn about 'other places' by cultural orientation as well as imagination. The library made this kind of travel possible.

There was a curiosity about foreign countries and colonies in the far away country of Sweden. Through texts, a colonial perspective was transferred from the Dutch centre of global trade to the Swedish periphery. These texts contributed to the discourse of progress, by discovering, naming and mapping the world.[9] Willem Bosman: *Voyage de Guinée* (Travel to Guinea 1705), Abraham Bogaert: *Historische reizen door d'oostersche deelen van Asia* (Historic Travels through Eastern Parts of Asia 1731), l' Abbé Boulet: *Histoire de l'Empire Chérifs en Afrique* (History of the Empire of Morocco 1733), Frederik Ludvig Norden: *Voyage d'Egypte et de Nubie* (Travels to Egypt and Nubia 1755), Pehr Osbeck: *Dagbok öfver en ostindisk resa* (Diary about a Journey to East India 1757), Thibault de Chanvalon: *Voyage à La Martinique* (Travels to Martinique 1763), Carsten Niebuhr: *Beschreibung von Arabien* (Description of Arabia 1772), Anders Sparrman: *Resa till Goda-Hopp-sudden* (Journey to the Cape of Good Hope 1783). Cultural geography and historical trade routes are interdependent and are part of the same mapping process that visualizes the hierarchy between the 'colonising' and the 'colonised'. The history of consumption and the history of the distribution of knowledge belong intimately together.

De Geer* subscribed to about 100 periodicals and magazines informing him about European and worldwide culture from a French Enlightenment perspective. He ordered books and other publications translated into French from the Dutch bookseller, Luchtman, in the university city of Leiden. The first package of books was sent from Leiden to Lövstabruk in 1746, and contained the Dutch magazine, *Bibliothèque raisonnée* (Profound Collection 1728-53). In spite of the fact that the contributors to this magazine were Huguenots (Anfält 1995a: 333), it contained scientific and literary articles without taking political or religious borders into consideration. In 1751, De Geer* ordered 150 volumes of *Journal des Savants* (Scholarly Journal) from Holland, in a large wooden case. *Journal des Savants*, also advertised travel literature, and *Philosophical Transactions* were early scientific magazines with a broad scope and covering different special discourses in order to present different fields of research typical of the time. From 1748, De Geer* also subscribed to another magazine, *Mercure historique et politique* (Historical and Political Mercure), which was about the European political situation but was also entertain-

9   The Dutch commercial properties or colonies were for example located in East India (i.e. Sumatra, Java) (map in Schmitt 1988: 91), that was called Dutch-India; further in South America (i.e. Dutch Guayana = Surinam) and on the Caribbean Islands (West India; i.e. Martinique, Jamaica) and in North-America (called New Netherlands).

ANTJE WISCHMANN

ing with unusual reports. The magazines, *Amusements the dames* (Amusement for Ladies) and *Bibliothèque choisie et amusante* (Selected Papers and Entertainment), were at the time not only reading for entertainment value but for cultural orientation as well.

Tomas Anfält found several publications, which were forbidden in France, but could be exported to Sweden by misleading the censors, for example by using false covers and false addresses for the publishers. Provocative political and literary texts, satirical papers mocking monarchs and priests, and 'immoral' literature, which was often published in the Swiss town of Neuchâtel, belonged to this group of publications. These provocative texts were officially called "livres philosophiques" (Anfält 1995b: 274). An example of popular literature is the novel: *Der durch die Printzeßin von Ursinis Besessen gewesene […] Philippus V* (Philipp V, Formerly Obsessed with the Princess of Urbini 1771), the original in German by David Fassmann from 1719. Probably not all the literary publications were bound as separate books, but disintegrated after they had been read by many people. This notion comes partly from the following publication which combines two very different texts in one volume: firstly the alchemist publication *Des Englischen Grafens von S*** experimentirte Kunst-Stücke* about producing gold (The Elaborate Experiments of the English Count of S*** 1731) and secondly I.I. Rembold's tract about grasshoppers (probably from 1748). This is once again an example of how several (at that time) undifferentiated discourses were combined even on the material level.

Anfält uses Robert Darnton's research about forbidden bestsellers in pre-revolutionary France as a starting point for his examination of the book collection. He concludes that the De Geer-family bought 108 out of a total 700 books listed as provoking titles by Darnton (1995b: 173). He gives some examples of 'immoral' titles, which were published anonymously including *Thérèse Philosophe*, *Anecdotes sur Mme la comtesse du Barry*, and *Vie privée de Louis XV* (Philosophic Thérèse, Anecdotes about the Countess of Barry, The Private Life of Louis XV, Anfält 1995b: 273).[10] The report about Louis XV describes the prodigality and the love affairs of the King. It is a kind of sensational literature that possibly contributed to increase scepticism towards the monarchy (Anfält 1995b: 275). The title of *La Chronique Scandaleuse, ou Paris ridicule* (Chronicle of Scandals or Ridiculous Paris 1668) by Claude le Petit indicates a devaluation of the urban customs and

---

10   See also Darnton 1995: 249-299 about *Thérèse Philosophe* (probably 1748 by Jean-Baptiste de Boyer, marquis d'Argens) and Darnton 1995: 337-390 about *Anecdotes sur Mme la comtesse du Barry* (probably 1775 by Mathieu François Pidansat de Mairobert). Also the famous libertine novel *Les liaisons dangereuses* 1782, [*Dangerous Connections*, 1784] by Choderlos de Laclos is a part of the Lövstabruk book collection.

a decline in urban life. Another publication of a libertine author that could circumvent the French censors was the thesis, *L'anti-Babylon* (Anti-Babylon 1759), by Louis Charles Fougeret de Monbron using a pen name, criticizing decadent city life and apparently (!) published in Bagdad (Anfält 1993: 257). The second part of the publication, *La Capitale de Gaules ou La nouvelle Babilonne* (The Capital of Gallia or the New Babylon 1760), by the same author is part of the Lövstabruk collection.

The French language dominated, in both correspondence and conversation, although De Geer* did not cultivate any direct contacts with France. The central role of the French culture is confirmed by the fact that De Geer* first ordered the magazine, *The Spectator,* in English, but acquired it later in French too. After De Geer's* marriage in 1743 to Catharina Charlotta Ribbing, his Swedish assimilation was confirmed, and the French orientation gradually weakened.

From the age of twenty, De Geer* had been a member of *Kungliga Vetenskapsakademien* in Stockholm, which was founded in 1739 in order to promote mathematics and natural sciences. In 1749 he became a member of the Royal Academy of Sciences in Paris. However, he did not enjoy his visits at *Riddarhuset* (House of Knights) or *Stockholms Slott* (Stockholm Palace) and carried out his official and social duties in the capital with a touch of aversion. In spite of this, he was appointed a royal marshal and was later elevated to the rank of baron. Although De Geer's* family had friendly relationships with the circles around Gustav III, De Geer* maintained a sceptical attitude towards the big city of Stockholm which in his eyes was characterized by a decline in moral standards. His activities for education and edification, which even influenced the daily life of his increasing family of ten, seemed to be his main and most meaningful task. De Geer's* research and the book collection became another task of life, which his son Charles De Geer the Younger (1747-1805) continued after 1778, even if less ambitiously. He was especially interested in travel literature and, unlike his father, made many journeys himself, but he did not share his father's passionate interest in magazines and he ended nearly all subscriptions. In 1805, the library contained about 8,500 books, and both the interior and the stock of books was hardly changed until 1907.

The unchanged condition of the library is one of the reasons why the settlement, as a whole, appears to be a monument to the Enlightenment. Its completeness proves, once again, that the colony as a heterotopia, refers not only to the best world possible, but also to the encyclopaedia of the Enlightenment. The settlement combines both the production and consumption of goods with the development of culture and knowledge in a well thought out way. The life of the colony's inhabitants was rather privileged compared with general conditions in Sweden at the time, and visitors considered it to have urban characteristics. From different cul-

ANTJE WISCHMANN

tural perspectives i.e. architectural, infrastructural, social, linguistic and religious, its island status is confirmed. The mutual influences between the economic sphere and cultural-scientific sphere were intense, mostly for the De Geer family but to a lesser degree for the workers. The guiding principle both for the ironworks and the cultural consumption was 'prodesse et delectare' combining an edifying life as an entrepreneur with an edifying occupation.

References

Adam, Wolfgang 1995: Bibliothek, Schneider, Werner ed.: *Enzyklopädie der Aufklärung. Deutschland und Europa.* München: Beck: 66-67.

Ahlund, Mikael 1996: Svenska bruksbilleder under 1700-talet, Stiftelsen Leufsta: *Vallonerna*: 81-112.

Anfält, Tomas 1987: The Old Library at Leufsta, *Uppsala Newsletter, History of Science*, 7: 1-4.

Anfält, Tomas 1991: Consumer of Enlightenment. Charles De Geer – Savant and Book Collector in Eighteenth-Century Sweden, 2: 197-210.

Anfält, Tomas 1993: Från nytta till nöje. Ett svenskt Herrgårdsbibliotek, Grate, Pontus et al. eds.: *Solen och nordstjärnan. Frankrike och Sverige på 1700-talet.* Stockholm: Nationalmuseet/ Bra Böcker: 252-257.

Anfält, Tomas 1995a: Baronen och 1700-talets informationssamhälle, Lars Höglund ed.: *Biblioteken, kulturen och den sociala intelligensen.* Borås/Göteborg: Publiceringsföreningen för institutionerna Bibliotekshögskolan Borås och Centrum för biblioteks- och informationsvetenskap: 330-339.

Anfält, Tomas 1995b: Bad Books and Barons. French Underground Literature in a Swedish eightteenth Century Private Library, Sten Hedberg ed.: *Serving the Scholarly Community. Essays on Tradition and Change in Research Libraries.* Uppsala: Uppsala Universitet: 271-279.

Anfält, Tomas 1996: Herrgård och bruk. Om livet på Leufsta på 1700-talet, Stiftelsen Leufsta ed.: *Vallornerna.* Lövstabruk: 48-80.

Anfält, Tomas 1997: Offentlighet och privatliv. Om livet på Leufsta herrgård på 1700-talet, Erik Kjellberg ed.: *Herrgårdskultur och salongsmiljö. Rapport från en nordisk konferens på Leufsta bruk 12-14 maj 1995.* Uppsala: Institutionen för musikvetenskap: 3-14.

Anfält, Tomas 2002: Bilden av ett bruk. Bruksbor och brukspatroner i vallonbruket Lövsta under 1700-talet, Florén och Ternhag: *Valloner*. 95-106.

Bedoire, Fredric 1995: Kyrka, herrgård och bruk. Den fransk-reformerte kapitalisten som byggherre och kulturförmedlare i det svenska 1700-talet, *Konsthistorisk Tidskrift*, 3: 147-162.

Chartier, Roger 1992/1995: *Böckernas ordning. Läsare, författare och bibliotek i Europa mellan 1300-tal och 1700-tal.* Stockholm: Anamma.

Darnton, Robert 1995: *The Forbidden Best-Sellers of Pre-Revolutionary France.* New York/ London: W.W. Norton Company.

Douhan, Bernt 1996: Louis De Geer, Stiftelsen Leufsta: *Vallonerna*: 32-47.

Florén, Anders and Gunnar Ternhag eds., 2002: *Valloner – järnets människor.* Hedemora: Gidlund.

Forsström, Johan Erik 1801/1917: *I Norrlandsstäder och Lapplandsbygd år 1800. Johan Erik Forsströms dagbok öfver resan i Norrland och Finnmarken 1800 och i Roslagen 1801.* Stockholm: Nationalförlaget.

Foucault, Michel 1967/1990: Andere Räume, Karl Heinz Barck et al. eds.: *Aisthesis. Wahrnehmung heute oder Perspektiven einer anderen Ästhetik.* Leipzig: Reclam: 34-46.

Haggrén, Georg 2001: *Hammarsmeder, masungsfolk och kolare. Tidigdindustriella yrkesarbetare vid provinsbruk i 1600-talets Sverige.* Stockholm: Jernkontoret.

Katalog öfver Leufsta Bruks Gamla Fideikommissbibliothek, 1907, Nominalkatalog. Uppsala: Almqvist och Wiksell.

Knapas, Rainer 2003: Biblioteket – en värld i böcker, *Monrepos. Ludwig Heinrich Nicolay och hans värld i 1700-talets ryska Finland.* Stockholm: Atlantis: 101-113.

Linnerhielm, Jonas Carl 1797/1985: *Bref under resor i Sverige 1797.* Stockholm: Rediviva.

Salvius, Lars 1741: *Beskrifning öfver Sveriget. Första tomen om Uppland.* Stockholm: Salvius, Horrn, Roepke.

Sandström-Hanngren, Marianne and Barbro Edling, 1981: *Bruksseminariet. Kompendium Nr. 5. Leufsta bruk.* Stockholm: Konstvetenskapliga Institutionen vid Stockholms Universitet.

Schmitt, Eberhard et al. eds. 1988: *Kaufleute als Kolonialherren. Die Handelswelt der Niederländer vom Kap der Guten Hoffnung bis Nagasaki 1600-1800.* Bamberg: Buchners Verlag.

Selling, Gösta 1980: De tre herrgårdarna på Leufsta, *Uppland. Årsbok för medlemmarna i Upplands fornminnesförening och hembygdsförbund*: 41-78.

Thörnvall, Folke 1985: *Leufsta – ett gammalt upplandsbruk. Käll- och litteraturstudier.* Tierp: Löjdquist tryckeri.

Unnerbäck, R. Axel, 2000: *Leufsta bruks kyrka.* Ed. by Uppsala stift and Bengt Ingmar Kilström. Uppsala: Ågerups.

Original Quotes

Linnerhielm: "Uppfylld af föreställningar om Skaldernas verldar".

Man ditkommer genom en skön Tall-skog, som succederas af frodiga Al-lundar och slutligen af en lång planterad Allée, alt i en linea. Ständigt synes den vackra åen, i hvilken byggnadarne nu speglade sig. Så obehagligt en rätt linea är för Lustvandraren eller för älskaren af den fria Naturen, måste man dock medge att den hyser någon ting stort. Detta är en helt naturlig följd: Tanken säger genast, att det måste vara en mägtig ägare för att öfvervinna alla hinder vid anläggningen. – Men är det stora och det sköna ett och det samma? Och hvilket åtföljes snarast af ledsnaden?

dit ingen ting låckade mig:

kanske dock altid åtföljdt af tvånget.

En Slipinrättning till stora Städs slipande och Mjölqvarnen med sex par stenar öka rörelsen och tillika bullret i den annars sakta flytande åen.

Forsström: "Stället tycktes vara mera trist än Forsmark, också var mycket konst använd härstädes för att embellera naturen."

Efter återkomsten från biblioteket öfverraskades oförmodligt uti informatorns kammare barons mamsell, som i sällskap med några andra fruntimmer uti allsköns negligé därstädes nedsatt sig att dejunera korf.

Berch: "uti denna Skog var en rätt väg gjord ända fram till bruket, der en gåsse, som är grindsvaktare och afhåller svinen att komma in i Bruket, uplåter grindarna, för hvilken syssla han får af Cammarherrn 12 % [öre] om dagen"

och vi tyckte oss önska, at denna ort måtte få Stadsfrihet […].

[qvinnfolken] krälade som myror, fram och tillbaka, och gatorna voro uppfylte med kärror

Christendomsvärk, som hos de fläste är sällsynt

ANTJE WISCHMANN

Wolfgang Adam: "Bibliothek": "Als typische Merkmale […] lassen sich neben der generellen Offenheit für zeitgenössische Entwicklungen in der Philosophie, der Wissenschaftslehre und der Literatur folgende Tendenzen festhalten: 1. Die Leitwerke und die Leitautoren der Epoche sind präsent. 2. Die lateinische Sprache verliert ihre beherrschende Stellung, auf dem Kontinent übernimmt weitgehend das Französische diese Rolle, ab Mitte des 18. Jahrhunderts wird der englische Einfluß immer stärker. 3. Der Rückgang des theologischen Schrifttums ist als Konstante zu bezeichnen. 4. Der dominierende Rang der historischen Abteilung ist unübersehbar.

BJARNE ROGAN

Travelling – Between Materiality and Mental Constructs: Encounters in Norway in the Eighteenth and Nineteenth Centuries

Travelling has certain material foundations which tend to be understated, or often totally ignored, in studies of the history of travelling – notably the fact that any traveller needs conveyance, lodging and food. These are fundamentals of the journey, which are too often overlooked, and all the more so as the travellers themselves often have omitted them in their travel accounts, especially if the accounts are written as essays rather than as diaries. There is however a very close relation between this material basis of the journey and the representational sphere that may easily be observed, even by historians who are not normally concerned with materiality.

Travelling in Norway in the eighteenth and nineteenth centuries meant travelling in a peculiar manner. The national mode of conveyance was exotic to foreigners, as was the lodging system. The lodging and the conveyance – in Norway and partly also in Sweden – brought the tourist traveller into exceptionally close contact with the indigenous population. We see this most clearly through the eyes of foreign visitors – who in those centuries belonged almost exclusively to the upper classes – when they came in contact with Norwegians, whether common farmers or the elite.

My assertion is that the special way of travelling and the close contact with common people and a (supposedly) original and uncorrupted rural farming culture were among the most important attractions of travelling in Norway, perhaps just as important as the country's nature and wilderness and its fjords and waterfalls. Or rather, all these aspects seem to have played together in an intricate way. I want to discuss how practical and material conditions and intellectual assumptions interfered and contributed to turn the journey in Norway into a special cultural encounter – an encounter that in itself might be a motivation for the visit.

Travel accounts are always incomplete and unreliable; you can verify this by travelling yourself. And if you want to relate your story, you will fall into the same pitfall; from a distance everything is forgotten – or idealized: you see only the luminous points. (Sainte-Beuve [1839] 1945: 29)

The nineteenth [of May, 1787]. Dined, or rather starved, at Bernay, where for the first time I met with that wine of whose ill fame I had heard so much in England, that of being worse than small beer. (Young 1915: 7-8)

Being familiar with travel accounts from Norway, I have been struck – when reading similar accounts from France, the Netherlands, the Italian states, etc. – by the fact that information on travelling modes, on lodging and other practical issues, is very scarce, at least in the latter half of the eighteenth and in the nineteenth century, compared to corresponding accounts from Norway. With the exception of references to border controls, especially in Italy, with passport and visa problems, customs and luggage ransacking, money exchange and bribes to countless numbers of border officers, the journey itself is often invisible, almost non-existent.

To illustrate this phenomenon, we shall first take a look at a travel account from late eighteenth century France: *Young's Travels in France During the Years 1787, 1788, 1789*, written by the Englishman Arthur Young, will serve as a contrastive case-study. I will then proceed to a description of travelling modes and accommodation in Norway in the eighteenth and nineteenth centuries, and discuss these as integral parts of the travel experience.

Young crossed France on three long journeys in the 1780s, with the aim of studying the state of agriculture in the French provinces. Young excuses himself in the foreword for choosing the diary form, an excuse that is typical for the genre, serving to demonstrate the (assumed) modesty of the author and warranting the authenticity of the tale. His text is – as he states himself – full of small-talk and details that may bore the reader. Actually, the form of the account is that of a diary, combined with reflections and a summarization towards the end of the three journeys.

Small-talk or not, the practical information Young gives on travelling in France in the eighteenth century is remarkably sparse. During a whole month of travel, Young mentions twice, and only incidentally in order to explain other events, that he brought from England his own horse and a chaise. To let his horse recover from a cold, he takes a stage-coach (Fr. *diligence*) the last part of his journey to Paris. With one sentence only, he criticizes the French stage-coach system for high costs and low frequency, compared to England; in another sentence he mentions that traffic is low around Paris, compared to London; in a third, that a river ferry is better and less expensive than in England. But these are all very brief remarks, presented at long intervals, on the few travel experiences that differ radically from what he is used to in England. Young travels for weeks before he makes a remark about the inns; he never tells the reader how he passes the nights, unless when he stays in some local nobleman's house. Not until he has travelled for almost one month and has arrived in southern France, does he make a general and summarizing comment on the inns and the food. His epitaph quotation on the bad French wine is one of the few exceptions I have found – the exception that proves the rule and confirms that comparison lurks behind most statements. But the main conclusion remains valid: even if there were differences in details, the travel experience, at least as late as the end of the eighteenth century, seems largely identical in France and in England. Consequently it was not worth writing about.

At the end of his third journey, however, when he passes into Nice and Savoie – districts which belonged to Italy, the material conditions for travelling change radically. As there were no longer roads to drive on he had to sell his horse and chaise. From then on he was forced to hire mules and local peasants to guide him, peasants with whom this French-speaking Englishman could hardly communicate, having no language in common. Almost all his contacts so far in France seem to have been with people from the upper classes of society, his peers or above. A few comments on the common people – mainly of the type: "The women did not wear stockings" – do not change this impression.

Young was interested in agriculture, but not in those who cultivated the soil; he was interested in the cultivated landscape, but not in the culture of its cultivators. He had hardly ever entered a peasant's abode. The much closer physical contact with common people during the last stage of his journey – caused by difficult travel conditions – was to him a new experience.

From this part of the journey he gives more detailed descriptions, for instance of how people travelled on sledges on the snowy mountain slopes. Or as he states himself: "Here I am, then, in the midst of another people, language, sovereignty and country – one of the moments of a man's life that will always be interesting, because all the springs of curiosity and attention are on the stretch" (1915: 271-72). The journey had suddenly become exotic, very different from what he was used to from his own country, and the travel account becomes correspondingly different.

There is nothing remarkable in the fact that Young did not communicate to his readers things that did not interest him. The point is that this journey, like very many other journeys in central parts of Europe in the eighteenth and nineteenth centuries, did not offer radically different conditions for the traveller. It was not the material conditions encountered that were the "luminous points" of the voyage, to paraphrase Sainte-Beuve. In this respect, the Nordic countries represented an exotic alternative – so exotic that travelling tended to become an attraction and a purpose in and of itself.

The Norwegian posting system – the skyss

The Norwegian peasant, in fact, is a very stubborn animal: but he seems to possess so free, so firm, so independant a spirit, that it cannot but strike those, who have been born themselves in a land of liberty. (Brooke 1823: 179)

The great difference between Young's account from France and most travel accounts from Norway is the detailed descriptions in the latter on how to travel and how travellers were lodged. These two elements of the transport infrastructure – to use a modern term – were closely related, as both depended to a large extent upon local peasants. We shall follow the structure of the descriptions of the guide books and the travelogues, which means starting with the conveyance.

The mode of conveyance – the *skyss* – was so special that most travel accounts contain an introductory description. The reason was twofold. The majority of authors thought such descriptions necessary for the readers to contextualize the scenes and to understand the travel experience. But it was also felt to be an inseparable part of the travel experience in itself, and as such well worth relating.

The *skyss* was a 'posting system' for the conveyance of people that was based on the obligatory work of peasants (i.e., an obligation to contribute one's labour to the Crown). It was the only public conveyance system in Norway for several centuries, until the latter half of the nineteenth century when the era of horses came to an end and steamers and trains began to take over. Broadly speaking, Norway never had a stage-coach system, like England and several countries on the Continent. The *skyss* system was peculiar to Norway and Sweden, and it is not found elsewhere in Europe.

Descriptions of the *skyss* abound in accounts from the eighteenth and nineteenth centuries, and also earlier, as the system was basically the same from around 1650 until the 1850s, when it changed quite rapidly over most of the country. In peripheral regions, however, it remained unchanged until the first years of the twentieth century. It is interesting to note that even well after the time when the system had been abolished in most places, it was still felt necessary by some authors to start their travellogues with a *skyss* episode. Thus the tourists continued to read the descriptions handed down by their forerunners, and a *skyss* trip was still part of the expected travel experience in Norway. Reality was changing, but the old myths survived in the travel expectations. That is why we can find a description

FIG. 16:

Scene from a skyss station, where the travelling townsman waiting for a horse encounters the farm people. Even as late as in the 1850s-60s, the visit of a townsman might raise curiosity, at least in districts away from the main roads. Drawing by Carl Frederik Diriks (1814-95).

like the following one in an account of a visit to Norway around 1900 – notably to a remote part of the country – made by a British couple. The opening chapter of Jungman's travel account, entitled "Precarious Travel", complies with the requirements and expectations of the genre:

It was at Hell that we had our first experience of the stolkjærre [a cart]. […] after waiting some three hours …] appeared the plumber's handcart […] and in it a very diminutive boy, who manly tackled the luggage […]

At length we reached a lonely farmhouse […] and we paid him his little bill, with the addition of a small *pourboire*. He shook hands very gravely with Nico, and, looking again at his money, […] shook hands with me too. […] Soon an old woman appeared at the door of the house, and beckoned us in. I explained as well as I could, with the help of a phrasebook, that we wanted a horse and stolkjærre as quickly as possible. This seemed to amuse the old lady immensely. She laughed until the tears came into her eyes, and, taking the book from my hands, examined it intently upside down. As it was getting late and we had still a long way to go, Nico tried what could be done by a pantomimic display. Sitting astride a chair, he tied his handkerchief to represent the reins, and supplemented the performance with encouraging noises addressed to an imaginary steed. This tickled the people of the house; but I realized that we were no nearer our object, and I decided to forage for myself.

I boldly ascended the steep incline of logs that led from the yard to a very dark stable. I found no horse ; but there was a stolkærre without the ghost of a spring. I appealed again to the old lady , who had followed me, for a horse. She merely patted me, and, I think, urged me to be calm. Just at this moment another boy appeared on the scene, and inquired whether it was really a horse that we wanted. Knowing the Norwegian for *horse*, I nodded vigorously. He smiled indulgently, but took no step. After another half hour's alternate shouting and periods of calm, roused himself to action and went off, while the old lady, who, I believe , was really kind and interested in us, took me to the kitchen and made up the fire, as she discovered that my hands were cold. I suppose she knew what we wanted all the time, and that we ought to have taken things more easily; but at that time I knew nothing of the unwritten laws with regard to posting in Norway. (Jungman 1905: 11-14)

A description of the coaching system was more or less obligatory in travel accounts from Norway. These texts varied from plain, informative and technical descriptions to elaborated and dramatized tales – or both, as was the case with Jungman's account. They were part of the genre. But whether the descriptions were exaggerated (as Nico Jungman's certainly was) or not, whether they developed into more or less stereotyped forms, their presence is in itself proof of an exotic experience, or at least of an anticipated exotic experience.

The conveyance – a cultural and social encounter

[…] in my young days you could not think of Norway without having a carriole in the background of your thought; the idea of it suggested itself as naturally as that of meals or a bed. [...] It has been described by, say, a hundred writers, which shall not deter me from being, say, the hundred and first to do so. [...] never has the ingenuity of man evolved anything more admirably adapted for its purpose in life, more efficient and convenient, more flawless in arrangement. (Pottinger 1905 I: 43-45. Pottinger was a regular visitor to Norway from the 1850s onwards.)

The peculiarity of the Norwegian posting system resided primarily in the obligation imposed on the farmers to procure horses and carts at the stages – which were ordinary farms – whenever travellers required conveyance. No farmer could refuse to convey a traveller who turned up at the stage.

How was the system organised? Along the main roads there were stages every 15 to 20 kilometers. These stages were ordinary farms. A team of local farmers was

Torfe mei da! no er alt Vondt ut aa gaa i Morrafoli—
Forfte Møde om Morgenen, en gammel Kone og en Hare der løber over Veien,
betyde hver for fig Vanheld paa Reifen.

FIG. 17:

A skyss scene, probably from the 1830s or 1840s, showing the close, even physical, contact between traveller and peasant, and the transmission of rural culture. The traveller (with the cap, to the right) holds the whip and the reins. The peasant (with the hat), shoulder to shoulder with him on the cart seat, exclaims: "Oh, bless my soul! All evil things come our way in the morning sun." And the text below explains: "The first meeting in the morning, an old woman and a hare running across the road, are both bad omens for the journey." Drawing by Johannes Flintoe (1787-1870).

organised around every stage. All farmers living within a radius of 10-12 kms from the stage belonged to the team. The team could consist of c. twenty right up to several hundred members. Taking turns in a rotation system, these farmers were obliged to do the conveyance. When a traveller arrived at the stage, which might also serve as an inn, the farm owner went out to look for the farmer whose turn it was to conduct the traveller – i. e. not the nearest farmer, but the one whose turn it was, according to a complicated roll.

Meanwhile the traveller had to wait at the farm, normally from one to three hours, before the farmer in question arrived with a horse and cart. It is this waiting scene that we got a glimpse of through the lenses of the two English tourists just quoted above. For centuries, travelling in Norway meant passing approximately half of the day at local farms, waiting for the conveyance to turn up. During these long waiting hours at every stage farm along the route, the foreign travellers came into close contact with Norwegian farmers. They normally waited in the kitchen, which was also the living room, or they strolled around, inspecting the farm and observing the farmers' everyday lives.

When the farmer finally turned up with his horse and a cart, he accompanied the traveller to the next stage, which might be a couple of hours' ride away. During the ride, the farmer was seated side by side with the traveller on the cart, or just behind him, or he would walk or run beside the cart – but always in very close contact. Since the farmers' carts had no springs, the tourists also had close contact with 'the real' Norway. "I have felt on my body every pebble and every hole in the road", is a typical comment.

The Norwegian farmers were reputed to be talkative, asking questions and readily answering back – in a mixture of English and Norwegian. The travellers have described the curiosity of the farmers, all their questions, their handshaking, and their candidness. Even an English lord or a French marquis had to accept hand-shakes with farmers and incessant questions like "What is your name?", "Where do you come from?", "What are you doing in Norway?", "Are you married?", "How many children do you have?", etc. Upon arrival at the next stage farm, the farmer returned home with his horse, the owner of the stage farm left to find a new farmer conveyor, and for the tourist there were additional waiting hours in a new farmer's kitchen or another farmyard.

Why did Norway have such a peculiar mode of public conveyance? A network of stage-coach routes, after the English and Continental model, was impossible. The main obstacles were the topography of the country and the state of the roads, and even more important: a sparse and dispersed settlement pattern – there were no villages in Norway, only isolated farmsteads in the countryside.

This conveyance system, where the farmers had to do the work *in natura* – comparable to, for instance, military service and other duties – was a tax. Every farmer had to perform this duty, in relation to the size and tax value of his farm. *Skyss* was an in-kind tax (in this case consisting of a specific quantity of the tax-payer's labour time and use-value of his horse and cart) levied on property in a pre-industrial society with a predominantly non-monetary subsistence economy.

What did the farmers think of this system? This is not our topic here, but a short answer could be that during some periods it was regarded as slavery, at other times it was very popular; after 1784 it became a source of revenue for the farmers (even if it was still a duty, each traveller had to pay a charge to each farmer, after varying tariffs) and it offered a possibility of getting away from the daily toil at the farm and meeting the outside world.

What did the travellers think? The great majority of foreigners appreciated this mode of conveyance. There was some grumbling over all the waiting hours and the uncomfortable farmer carts. But foreigners marvelled at seeing small boys, sometimes even young girls, driving the horses to the stage. The tourists were allowed – and even supposed – to drive themselves, and to most of them it was a new and thrilling experience to hold the reins. Many foreign tourists had little or no experience with driving horses, being used to stage-coaches with coachmen. This lack of experience sometimes resulted in driving the horses too hard, a situation that not infrequently led to quarrels with the horse owners. Even physical fights between tourists and farmers, provoked by the treatment of their horses, have been reported. Sir Henry Pottinger, who from the 1850s visited Norway almost every summer for half a century, gives a vivid and detailed description of a three-round fight with a local horse owner on the Dovre mountains, ending with a bleeding nose for the Englishman and a knocked-out peasant – who luckily had left his knife back home (Pottinger 1905, I: 49-57). The Norwegian attorney general Bernhard Dunker relates from his journey through Telemark in 1852:

In order to get from stage to stage in time, without driving the horses to death and having to fight with every *skyss* peasant, which is very inconvenient, especially when the peasant has the double strength of the traveller – and such cases have been reported, I had all along my way to walk up every hillside. This has a double advantage: the horse endures the trip much better, and you do not have to fight the *skyss* boy, whose heart you will win by such a noble consideration for his horse. (Dunker s. a.: 125-126)

Such episodes were of course not frequent, but their eventuality added to the respect for the common peasants and the thrill of the journey. Another important attraction was the special Norwegian vehicle called *karjol* – carriole, a nineteenth century light and very rapid one-person chaise (cf. the Pottinger quotation above). No wonder foreigners found *skyss* an exotic experience, well worth expanding upon in their travel accounts.

A few foreign travellers disliked the unexpected closeness to common people. There were even a few arrogant Englishmen who found the physical closeness to the horse owners repulsive, making allusions to vermin, etc. But the majority were amused by this novel situation and appreciated the contact; they were amazed by the spirit of equality among Norwegian farmers, and they respected their independence and self-confidence. Foreigners warned their compatriots against hurrying or abusing Norwegian *skyss* conveyors, station masters or post-house keepers, thus running the risk of not being helped, of having to carry the luggage themselves or of not being given a lodging. Arrogant behaviour from the tourist was not tolerated by most farmhouse innkeepers; their best weapon was to say that all rooms were occupied, just as some *skyss* conveyors might deliberately work at

FIG. 18:

A skyss scene, painted by Axel Ender (1853-1920). It was normally the traveller who held the reins in the carriole, while the skyss boy either was running behind or was seated on the luggage, just behind the traveller – from where he could, in emergency cases, grasp the reins. The carriole – a typical Norwegian vehicle, and very popular with the tourists – is of an elderly type, from around 1850.

a slow pace if they disliked the tourist. Or as a late English tourist remarked, with reference to a long tradition:

A Norwegian, whatever his standing may be, is the equal of everyone. Politeness on the part of the traveller is such a necessity that the guide-books mention it. The domineering tourist will meet with difficulties and rebuffs. (Jungman 1905: 81)

We may conclude, so far, that the conveyance system in itself was an exotic experience to foreigners visiting Norway, and it gave an abundance of possibilities for direct, close and even physical contact between the foreign visitor and the Norwegian farmer, i.e., between the upper class tourist and men and women of the people – commoners whose self esteem and sense of liberty did not perhaps differ so much from that of the visitor. Travelling in Norway was indeed a cultural and social encounter, thanks to the *skyss* system, and to many travellers this was one of the 'luminous points' of the journey.

Accommodation and hospitality: Inns and parsonages

I live, to be sure, and so does my horse, in the country manner which is certainly not the English one; but whoever has travelled in the Highlands, or even in the Lowlands of Scotland twenty years ago, has no right to complain of his accommodation here. An Englishman, bred in the midst of that peculiar attention to cleanliness and nicety, which, even now, is almost exclusively English, will find much to horrify him in a Norwegian inn; but such gentlemen are scarcely in a situation to judge the habits of a people.

    (Samuel Laing 1836: 59)

Of the post-houses a very small number are good, others are tolerable, but by far the greater proportion are dirty and wretched, one of our little country inns being superior to the best of them, and less expensive … [As for the prices] imposition must be resisted as it best may …

    The most convenient plan of travelling is to learn something of the language, and then trust to meeting with the clergy, who are always ready to assist the stranger, and may be implicitly depended upon …

    (W. H. Breton 1835: 64, 54)

We shall have a look at another aspect of this cultural encounter. Our peephole is accommodation, and the key word is hospitality. As shown by the above quotations, the two British travellers in the 1830s had had the same experience, but their attitudes were as opposite as could be. Whereas the favourably inclined Samuel Laing accepted the local inns, the more arrogant and critical William H. Breton shunned the inns and sought the vicarages – as most of his compatriotes did, however.

    But let us first lend an ear to a contemporary observer, Gustaf Peter Blom, a Norwegian district governor who made a grand tour of Norway in 1827. In his travel account he wrote exuberantly in praise of Norwegian hospitality:

In no country is hospitality more common and more abundant than in Norway. This is a truth acknowledged by all travellers, and especially commented upon by the foreigner, in whose own country any facility or any convenience is available for money, but – as a result of this – nobody feels any duty towards the traveller […] (Blom 1830: 337)

Much could be said about this patriotic praise. It is a fact, however, that many foreign visitors, in these early years of the nineteenth century, expressed the same opinion – but perhaps in a bit more nuanced way, to be discussed later.

    What were the choices for lodging, in the eighteenth and early nineteenth centuries, before hotels began to develop? In the countryside, there were two ways

FIG. 19:

A scene from a skysstasjon or peasant inn in the 1820s-30s, entitled: "Prejudices do not fill the stomach when travelling". The two urban guests are leaving the table in disgust, whereas the old peasant woman exclaims: "The bowl is nice and the milk is good!" The disgust expressed by the two gentlemen may be due to either the quality of the food served, or to the fact that the milk bowl is – or is very similar to – a night pot. (Milk, fresh or in prepared forms, was sometimes the only thing the traveller could be sure to have in these peasant inns). Drawing by Johannes Flintoe (1787-1870).

of finding a bed and a meal; one was "the peasant solution", the second "the clergy solution". In the towns there might be some inns and even hotels, but for a long time the normal solution was to find boarding in private homes and have meals at the *table d'hôte*.

What I have coined "the peasant solution" originally meant seeking shelter and bed in private farmhouses – a tradition from the Middle Ages that continued far into nineteenth century, mainly though for travellers of lower social status. Around 1650 laws were passed that prescribed inns – which actually meant lodging at *skyss* stages or other farms – along the main routes, but these "inns" were rare before the nineteenth century. From the late eighteenth century the *skyss* stages could normally offer a bed or two. But both inns and stages were of a peasant standard, which was very low in the opinion of the foreigners: beds with straw mattresses, sheep-skins as bedclothes not infrequently infested with vermin, windows that did not open, rooms full of smoke from open fireplaces, and peasant food – sometimes nothing but milk and porridge. In early nineteenth century travel accounts most (peasant) inns are described in terms like "nasty dwelling", "dirty inn", "wretched accommodation", etc. The traveller who sought accommodation at these inns risked another and perhaps less welcome dose of insight into rural life, more concrete and less comfortable than the long waiting hours at the stages.

The best solution, and the one travellers choose whenever possible, was "the clergy solution" – which meant seeking out the farm of a local official or goverment servant, who also lived on isolated farms in the countryside, but these were farms of a much higher standard. These farms sometimes belonged to the magistrate or the doctor, sometimes to an officer, but most often to clergymen.

At a rough estimate, about one thousand government officials and civil servants lived in the Norwegian countryside, outside the towns, at the beginning of the nineteenth century. With their families they represented less than 0.4 % of the population of the rural districts. These thousand families were small oases of culture and civilisation spread out in a barren peasant desert. The clergy were by far the most numerous group among these officials, and the vicarages were normally the farms that were best suited to receive guests. For centuries, these residential farms had had large stables for horses, guest chambers and a special chamber intended for the bishop and his entourage on their regular trips to their religious dominions. The vicarages were the property of the State, and part of the minister's payment was the revenue of the farm.

In northern Norway there were – in addition to the local ministers – a group of rich and comfortably situated merchants who acted more or less like a local nobility, and who kept their doors open for travellers – few as they were in the far North.

Thomas Forester was one among many tourists who quickly discovered the hospitality of the farmers but preferred that of the vicars:

The period is not very remote when since the tourist might be passed, with slight introduction, from house to house, through the remoter districts of Scotland and Ireland […] In the course of time, as travellers multiply, this system becomes burthensome, and houses of entertainment spring up for their accommodation.

In Norway, these [inns] are of rare occurrence. […] The people have not yet generally learnt to make hospitality to strangers a marketable commodity. We soon discovered this amiable prejudice, and […] were careful not to claim entertainment from the farmers upon the strength of our ability and willingness to pay for it. A slight conversation on our route and plans never failed […] to lead to an invitation to enter their houses and take rest and refreshment. […]

On the present occasion we had heard too much of the hospitality of the people of all classes to be under any great uneasiness. The choice seemed to lie between the substantial farm-house on the slope of the hill, and the parsonage, or præste-gaard, which stood near the water's edge. The latter had, on various accounts, the decided preference. (Forester 1850: 53-54)

Forester goes on to describe how his own and his companion's sensibility and modesty prevented them from knocking on the door claiming a hospitality that had to be gratuitous – a conduct "so foreign to our habits and ideas [as] to walk up to a strange gentleman's house and ask for board and lodging" (1850: 55). But the vicar himself, who had discovered the strangers, came to their rescue by claiming his right to invite guests.

Forester's description, as well as that of many other travelogues, leaves no doubt as to why the vicarage was "the decided preference". For the travellers a stay at the vicarage meant good – sometimes even generous – meals, perhaps a glass or two of wine, pleasant company with people of their own kind of breeding and manners, and a comfortable bed. Normally, the ministers and their families could be expected to speak English, German or French, and not all of them had forgotten their Latin – so communication was easier than with the farmers. A stay at the vicarage seldom lasted only one night – it was often extended to two or three days or even more – and the travellers did not pay for the stay. There were hardly any foreign visitors to Norway from the seventeenth century to the first half of the nineteenth who did not take advantage of the vicarages, and numerous travel accounts give enthusiastic descriptions of these stays and of the hospitality of Norwegian ministers.

The practice of taking in travellers at vicarages came to an end after 1850, when the number of tourists rose dramatically in the central parts of Norway. Norwegian ministers were generally not well paid, and we know from several biographies that the stream of visitors might be quite burdensome, not least for the household economy, as the nineteenth century progressed. Only in the most remote districts, where few visitors came, did the practice survive into the 1870s and 1880s.

Why this overwhelming hospitality at the vicarages? The main reason is to be found in their isolated situation. The vicarages were small islands of breeding and refinement in a vast ocean of peasant culture, and they had an important function in importing urban culture into the countryside. On the other hand, the ministers and their families led a life in solitude and isolation – isolation from their peers, from urban culture and from European civilization – and all the more so the further north they were relegated.

Biographies written by ministers abound with descriptions of their lonesome lives; their conversations with the locals were seldom extended beyond chats on the weather, the fisheries or the harvest. A visitor from the outside world was like a gift from heaven; a Norwegian townsman was more than welcome, and a foreigner, who could bring news from far away, was even more welcome. The ministers were well paid for their renowned hospitality – not in money, but socially and culturally – by scarce and valuable company and fresh infusions of cultural capital.

For the foreigners, accommodation at the parsonages meant close contact with another culture – perhaps still rural, but very different from that of the farmers at the stages and in the inns. Even if a few travellers found the manners of the minister somewhat rustic and unsophisticated – and some also found the meals a bit on the heavy side and the drinks too generous – most travel accounts report enthusiastically on this form of accommodation and this totally unexpected degree of hospitality.

Other hosts: The bourgeoisie and the merchants of the North

In no country is hospitality more common and more abundant than in Norway. [...] The northern districts are no exception, as nowhere else in Norway one finds a greater hospitality than just there [...] (Blom 1830: 337)

We shall view the question of attitudes and mentalities through a third peephole, which is the hospitality of the urban bourgeoisie and the merchants of northern Norway.

During the last part of the eighteenth century and the early nineteenth, until the Napoleonic wars put an end to the good times, liberalist trends in European trading laid the foundation of a new Norwegian bourgeoisie, consisting of well-off or even very rich merchants in the towns of southern Norway. This bourgeoisie had close trade relations especially with England, but also with France and other European nations, and they looked to Europe for cultural contacts, trends and fashions. They lived in spacious town houses or in mansions outside the towns, and they acquired the habit of inviting foreign travellers who arrived in town to dinner parties.

A couple of examples will suffice. When the Englishman Edward Daniel Clarke (see A. Ryall's article in this volume) visited Trondheim in 1799, he stated that with a letter of introduction to one family, the traveller was immediately presented to all the other important families of the town; "invitations arrive from every corner of the town, in a number that surpasses the capacity of the visitor" (1977: 64). The German visitor Leopold von Buch states in 1807 that "no traveller

FIG. 20:

The Bogstad mansion, belonging to the Anker family and situated just outside Christiania, in the 1790s. Bogstad was one of the most renowned mansions of the young Norwegian bourgeoisie, where foreign travellers (unexpectedly) were invited to sumptuous dinners. Mary Wollstonecraft probably was here in 1795, Edward Daniel Clarke in 1799, and Alexis Lamotte in 1807. Vue de Bogstad, colour aquatint by Lorentzen & Haas, after Lorentzen's visit in 1792.

leaves this town without feeling enthusiastic about the reception […] This cordial welcome, this conviviality and this warm sympathy seem to be quite natural […] they are displayed in a way that one might have expected only from people of a superior culture and refinement" (von Buch 1810: 108).

The high bourgeoisie of Christiania, the capital city, were renowned for their lavish banquets to which foreign travellers were invited. When Clarke was invited to the mansion of Collett in 1799, he wrote: "The dinner was so lavish that it would hardly be possible for our own king to give a more splendid party. We were offered all the delicious plates of the country and all the wines of Europe." The following day, the scene was repeated at the neighbour's (Anker's) place "with as much splendour as would offer any foreign prince" (1977: 124). Similar descriptions are given by several travellers, among others the Frenchman Alexis Lamotte in 1807.

BJARNE ROGAN

So much for the hospitality and the lavishness of the Norwegian bourgeoisie, as praised by their peers and superiors from other European countries. But were the visitors always so positive? No, not always. Let us, however, first pay a short visit to northern Norway and its well-off merchants.

When the governor Gustav Peter Blom made his grand tour of Norway in 1827, he wrote – as quoted above – exuberantly about Norwegian hospitality as the best in the world. And he added that within the confines of Norway, hospitality was nowhere greater than in northern Norway. Actually, many foreign travellers during the nineteenth century were of the same opinion. The German tourist Friedrich Boie has given one of the most poetic descriptions of northern hospitality, when in 1817 he wanted to pay for his stay in a merchant's house. The hostess, who led him to the window, pointed at the sea in front of the house and the fields around, and allegedly replied as follows: "As long as the soil gives us cereals and the sea gives us fish, no traveller shall have occasion to say that he had to pay [for his stay in our house]!" (Boie 1822: 74). Very many travel accounts tell similar tales. The tourists were seldom if ever allowed to pay for their stay, and as several of them stated: the further north you go, the less use there is for money (Nilsson 1879, Brooke 1823).

Characteristic of this northern hospitality were the generous and even lavish meals, and much drinking, two features that several visitors have commented upon in their travel accounts. We shall see how these remarks triggered a vivid polemic.

The English tourist, explorer and geographer Arthur de Capell Brooke, who toured northern Norway in 1820, wrote enthusiastically about his stay, the hospitality, and the Norwegians he met. This British aristocrat was really impressed by the people he met, whatever their social standing. But in his travel account he did not conceal that he sometimes felt a tone of exaggeration – many meals, among others one offered by the local county governor, from which he detailed descriptions of all the servings – were far too generous for his taste, and he wondered why every visit and every farewell had to be accompanied by glasses of brandy. And he found the local merchants' life during the long, dead winter season rather dull – filled as it was with visits, dinners, smoking and card playing. His criticism – if so it may be called – was mild and benevolent, but the aforementioned governor Blom from southern Norway reacted sharply to these remarks about his colleagues, which he regarded as condescending. Blom, who thought Norwegian hospitality the best in world, counter-attacked the Englishman vigorously by criticizing English drinking habits and idle life in the London clubs, and he claimed that Brooke had misinterpreted these innocent material expressions of hospitality and goodwill. Paradoxically, Capell Brooke started several clubs in England, where one of the main attractions – according to the tradition – were Norwegian style dinners!

Why did the Norwegian governor react so vehemently to these remarks – remarks that were perhaps ironic but by no means malicious? What really wounded Blom the most must have been the allusions to a lack of knowledge, a lack of *savoir-vivre*; immoderation at the table might be interpreted as a moral deficiency amongst the class that was to build the newly independent nation of Norway.

Many of the descriptions of splendid receptions in the bourgeois mansions in southern Norway are tinged with ambivalence. We can often read between the lines a certain reserve, and in a few cases this reserve turns into open criticism of the forms of sociability displayed by the Norwegian bourgeoisie.

The Frenchman Alex Lamotte felt a certain lassitude at the sumptuous dinners during his stay in 1807; the Englishman Clarke sometimes felt alienated in 1799 – at least in the south, where he found the hospitality corrupted by foreign influences, manners and luxury. The English traveller Mary Wollstonecraft felt disgusted with the receptions on her tour in 1795, with the enormous meals, all the drinking, and in general what she found to be a caricature of European civilization. She claimed the farmers – whom she hardly met at all – to be more polite than the upper classes, because they wanted to please the visitor, and not to be admired for their behaviour – a harsh but rather naïve criticism; clearly romantic and intellectualist.

The quest for the Noble Savage and an encounter filled with ambiguity

As a tourist who has done nothing but to follow the beaten track [...] I must once again meditate on the notes that I have put down, day after day, of my travel impressions [...] I must admit that the strange contrasts that struck me even in my very first, picturesque impression of Norway, in the seasonal contrasts, reappear in the physical and moral structure of its people, in the habitus of every individual [...] These people are both better and worse than us. There is no virtue to be found here that is not immediately counterbalanced by decay. [...] I do not claim that it is these contrasts in themselves that characterize the nature of the Norwegians, but rather the extreme exaggerations, the unbalance of the leaps and bounds. (le Roux 1895: 219-21)

Tourism is an encounter in space between different cultures. This encounter can be more or less superficial, more or less profound. But it always takes place in a physical setting or in an arena. The arenas where foreign tourists met the local population in Norway in the eighteenth and the nineteenth centuries were different from most settings elsewhere in Europe. In Norway the most important arenas were the *skyss* system, the peasant stages and peasant inns, the vicarages, the bourgeois mansions, and the northern merchants' homes. These arenas were the

FIG. 21:

Encounter between two cultures. From the 1820s, a vogue of pedestrian tourism brought the intellectual urban elite into the more remote parts of the Norwegian countryside. Here two wandering townsfolk enter a modest peasant abode in Telemark. They can hardly hide their astonishment - or rather amusement ? – when spotting the pig under the kitchen table and observing the peasant woman combing lice from her hair into a tray. The pig in the kitchen of the peasant inn has been reported by more than one traveller, among whom Leopold von Buch (1810) and Friedrich Boie (1822). The latter has described how the pig played with the children of the house and claimed its share of the traveller's breakfast. Drawing from 1842 by Carl Frederik Diriks (1814-95).

material basis for the encounter between different cultures, and also for the social encounter between the upper class foreigner and the indigenous commoner. Such encounters hardly ever took place in countries like England and France, except perhaps on a much more superficial level, because transport and accommodation were organised differently. In the advanced European countries a modern infrastructure was at the traveller's disposal.

I have tried to show how different the contact was between the traveller and the indigenous population in France and in Norway. Admittedly, Arthur Young travelled in France with other aims than learning to know the French, and he never really came close to French rural culture. But many foreigners travelled through

Norway with rather similar aims, in particular to enjoy the nature, to study natural sciences or to sense a mystic Nordic past. But whatever their aim, they all experienced an extraordinarily close contact with the population, thanks to the very special infrastructure of travelling. This contact became an important and integral part of the travel experience.

Some visitors suffered from the close contact with the farmers, some were ambivalent, but the majority seem to have appreciated it. The long waiting hours in the farmers' simple abodes might be regarded as an ordeal, and even the most romantic travellers wished to avoid peasant accommodation at stages and farm inns. A solution was normally at hand: to seek the vicarages instead, or alternatively the homes of rich merchants.

But even the encounter with the Norwegian middle and upper classes was not without ambiguities. The material advantages of these contacts were eagerly sought by the tourists, and the hospitality was highly praised. But we also sense distaste for exaggerated forms of hospitality, which might even lead foreign travellers openly to express criticism of their hosts' lack of refinement.

This ambivalent attitude cannot be understood independently of the interest that foreign travellers took in the character of the Nordic peoples, a theme that we meet again and again in the travel accounts. The visitors in Norway expected to find an uncorrupted nature and to sense the atmosphere of a distant but splendid past. And they expected to see the reflection of this serene nature in an uncorrupted people, just as they wanted to see in every modern Norwegian an echo of the ancient, proud and independent farmer, free from all signs of serfdom, as well as the image of valiant Viking warriors. This romantic conception lasted a long time, from the late eighteenth century until the early years of the twentieth.

The general pattern that can be found through a broad reading of the travel accounts is that the foreigners were more satisfied with the countryside population and their (supposed) qualities than they were with the city population, the idea being that European civilization infected the cities before the countryside. And they were happier with people up north than in the south, for the same reason. The authentic character of the people was supposed to be inversely proportionate to the distance from the European continent and from the cities.

Few travellers expressed this attitude more cogently than did Brooke:

I could not avoid being struck with the great change in the manners of the inhabitants of the northern from those in the more southern parts of Norway. With the latter there always appeared a strong tendency to imposition, and an excessive charge for the most trifling article. An Englishman they seemed to consider as a moving treasury, which at their demand would be immediately opened. How strikingly different from those in the north!

When at Drontheim, they told me, the farther north you go the better you will be treated, and I now found the truth of this assertion. As the traces of roads gradually disappeared, so in proportion did the manners of the inhabitants become more interesting; and when civilization would have been said by most to be left far behind, hospitality, candour, and simplicity became doubly conspicuous. (Brooke 1823: 224-25)

One of the central qualities of the authentic and uncorrupted Norseman was supposed to be genuine hospitality, without pretensions or ulterior motives. As long as hospitality was greater in the countryside than in the cities, and as long as they found more of it the further north they went, the theory was confirmed and the travellers satisfied. But the moment the visitors sensed that the hospitality encountered was corrupted by European civilization, when they felt that it had become exaggerated, pretentious and no longer genuine, they became disappointed, and ambivalent or even critical remarks fill the pages of their travel accounts.

What made the voyage to Norway so extraordinary was that the myths of the ages-old, uncorrupted character of its people could be tested out through the very special material conditions for travel and accommodation. Some travellers found the myth verified and others found it falsified, but that was part of the travel experience.

References

Boie, Friedrich 1822: *Tagebuch gehalten auf einer Reise durch Norwegen im Jahre 1817*. Schleswig: Königl. Taubstummen-Institut.

Blom, Gustav Peter 1830: *Bemærkninger paa en Reise i Nordlandene og igjennem Lapland til Stockholm, i året 1827*. Christiania: Det Wulfbergske Bogtrykkerie.

Breton, William H. 1835: *Scandinavian Sketches or a Tour in Norway*. London: J. Bohn, Schultze & Co.

Brooke, Sir Arthur de Capell 1823: *Travels through Sweden, Norway and Finmark, to the North Cape, in the summer of 1820*. London: Rodwell & Martin.

Buch, Leopold von 1810: *Reise durch Norwegen und Lappland*. Berlin: Georg Reimer.

Dunker, Bernhard s. a.: Reise til Tellemarken og til Arendal. Sommeren 1852. Kristiania: Gyldendal.

Clarke, Edward Daniel 1977 (1819): *Reise i Norge 1799*. Oslo: Universitetsforlaget.

Forester, Thomas 1850: *Norway in 1848 and 1849, containing rambles among the fjelds and fjords of the Central and Western districts*. London: Longman, Brown, Green, & Longmans.

Jungman, Beatrix (Nico) 1905: *Norway by Nico Jungman*. London: A. & C. Black.

Lamotte, Alex 1813: *Voyage dans le Nord de l'Europe, consistant principalement de promenades en Norwège, et de quelques courses en Suède, dans l'année MDCCCVII*. London: J. Hatchard, Ellerton & Henderson.

Laing, Samuel 1836: *Journal of a Residence in Norway during The Years 1834, 1835 and 1836; made with a view to inquire into the moral and political economy of that country, and the condition of its inhabitants*. London: Longman, Rees, Orme, Brown, Green, & Longman.

Nilsson, Sven 1879: *Dagboksanteckningar under en resa från södra Sverige till nordlanden i Norge 1816*. Lund: Fr. Berlings Boktryckeri och Stilgjuteri.

Pottinger, Henry 1905: *Flood, Fell and Forest*, Vol. I-II. London: Edward Arnold.

Rogan, Bjarne 1986: *Det gamle skysstellet. Reiseliv i Norge frå mellomalderen til førre hundreåret*. Oslo: Det Norske Samlaget.

Rogan, Bjarne 1998: *Mellom tradisjon og modernisering. Kapiter av 1800-tallets samferdselshistorie*. Oslo: Novus forlag.

Rogan, Bjarne 1999: Meninger og myter om landet i nord. In: Rogan, Bjarne ed. 1999: *Norge Anno 1900. Kulturhistoriske glimt fra et århundreskifte*. Oslo: Pax.

Rogan, Bjarne 2004: L'auberge du bon secours. In: Montandon, Alain (ed.): *Le livre de l'hospitalité*. Paris: Bayard.

Roux, Hugues le 1895: *Notes sur la Norvège*. Paris: Calman Levy.

Sainte-Beuve 1945: *Voyage à Naples*. Ed. Gabriel Faure. Paris: L'imprimerie de J. Haumont.

Schiötz, Eiler 1970 *Utlendingers reiser i Norge. Itineraria Norvegica. En bibliografi*. Oslo: Universitetsforlaget.

Schiötz, Eiler 1970: *Utlendingers reiser i Norge*. Vol. II Supplement. Oslo: Universitetsforlaget.

Wollstonecraft, Mary 1977 (1796): *Min nordiske reise*. Oslo: Gyldendal.

Young, Arthur 1915: *Young's Travels in France During the Years 1787, 1788, 1789*. Ed. B. Betham-Edwards. London: G. Bell and Sons.

Original Quotes

Sainte-Beuve Les récits de voyage sont toujours incomplets et infidèles; on le vérifie en voyageant soi-même, et à son tour, si l'on raconte, on tombera dans le même inconvénient; à distance tout s'oublie, s'idéalise: on ne voit que les points lumineux. (Sainte-Beuve [1839] 1945)

Dunker For at komme frem til Skifterne til bestemt Tid uden at kjøre Hestene ihjel og slaaes med alle Skydsbønder, hvilket især er ubehageligt, naar Skydsbonden er dobbelt saa stærk som den Reisende, og man har havt Exempler paa, at dette kan være Tilfældet, maatte jeg paa den hele Vei gaae i hver eneste Bakke, hvilket har den dobbelte Fordeel, at Hesten holder meget bedre ud, og at man ikke kommer op at slaaes med Skydsdrengen, hvis Hjerte man vinder ved en saaa ædelmodig Omhu for hans Hest. (Dunker s. a.: 125-126)

Blom 1) Gjæstfriheden er i intet Land almindeligere og større end i Norge. Dette er en Sandhed, som enhver Reisende erkjender, og som især bemærkes af Udlændingen, der i sit Fædreneland, hvor ingen Beqvemmeligheder mangle den Reisende for Penge, men hvor, som en følge deraf, ogsaa enhver troer sig befriet fra nogen Pligt med Hensyn til den Reisende, er vant til at støtte sig selv, uden at blive bemærket. (Blom 1830: 337)

2) Gjæstfriheden er i intet Land almindeligere og større end i Norge […] Nordlandene staa saa langtfra tilbage i denne Punct, at man meget mere ingensteds i Norge finder større Gjæstfrihed end der … (Blom 1830: 337)

Boie So lange noch das Land uns Korn und die See uns Fische gibt, soll uns kein Reisender nachsagen können, dass wir Geldt von ihm angenommen hätten! (Boie 1822: 74)

Le Roux Pour moi qui ne suis qu'un touriste de grande route […] je viens de battre une fois de plus les fiches sur lesquelles, au jour le jour, j'ai noté mes impressions de promeneur […] il me faut reconnaître que les disparates prodigieuses qui m'apparurent tout d'abord dans l'aspect pittoresque de la Norvège, dans l'antithèse de ses saisons, revivent dans la structure physique et morale de la race, dans l'habitude de chaque individu […] ces gens sont meilleurs et pires que nous. Point de vertu chez eux qui ne soit tout de suite payée d'une déchéance. […] Ce ne sont donc point ces antithèses que je signale comme une caractéristique de la nature norvégienne, mais l'excès prodigieux, le déséquilibre de ces sursauts. (Le Roux': 219-221)

ANKA RYALL

A Humbling Place: Tests of Masculinity in Early Nineteenth-Century Travel Narratives from Lapland

The greatest deeds have always been accomplished in high latitudes, because the highest latitudes produce the greatest men.

    Charles Tuttle, *Our North Land*, 1885.

What I have suffered [. . .] I will not fill my letter with; it will be enough to say, I have never had two days of health since I set out for Lapland. I had the melancholy task of telling Cripps how to commit my poor carcass to a grave, and to go home. Once I lost my senses; and, but a few days ago, having crossed the Norwegian Alps with great fatigue, I fancied I had a hole in my throat, and fainted with the chimeras of my own disordered imagination. Now, thank God! I am better, as you see, for I can write. All my illness arose from fatigue, and neglect of sleep, and perhaps from the effect of climate on a constitution unarmed to encounter a frigid zone.

    Edward Daniel Clarke, letter to William Otter, 23 September 1799.

Travel narratives, as the famous German naturalist Alexander von Humboldt points out in the introduction to his *Personal Narrative of Travels to the Equinoctical Regions of America*, have "two very distinct objects: the greater or the less important events connected with the purpose of the traveller, and the observations he has made during his journey". Writing in the early nineteenth century (the 30-volume French original of his great work, *Voyage aux régions équinoxiales du Nouveau Continent*, was published between 1805 and 1834), Humboldt laments what he considers as an unfortunate generic shift of emphasis away from "that part of the traveller's narrative which we may call dramatic" to "dissertations merely descriptive" on such topics as natural history, geography or political economy. In his opinion the best travel writing – that which provides "the most faithful picture of manners" – is subjective and interactive: "The character of savage or civilized life is portrayed either in the obstacles a traveller meets with, or the sensations he feels. It is the traveller himself whom we continually desire to see in contact with the objects which surround him" (Humboldt 1852: xix-xx). As Nigel Leask has noted, his views are one indication of the struggle in both Enlightenment and Romantic travel writing "to integrate literary and scientific discourses" (Leask 2002: 9).

Although it was the perceived scientific value that justified both the production and dissemination of travel narratives, the great popularity of such texts during the eighteenth and early nineteenth century must be explained primarily in terms of their entertainment value. Readers, as Humboldt's introduction indicates, wanted personal anecdotes and dramatic events as well as serious information, and the romance-obsessed young heroine of Jane Austen's *Northanger Abbey* (1818) is probably typical of the period in placing "travels" somewhere between the fiction that she loves to read and the "real solemn history" that she "cannot be interested in" (Austen 2003: 104). The extent to which Humboldt's assumptions were taken for granted by his contemporaries is evident in the geologist Robert Jameson's introduction to the English translation of his German colleague Leopold von Buch's *Reise durch Norwegen und Lappland* (published in 1813 as *Travels through Norway and Lapland, during the Years 1806, 1807, and 1808*). This book virtually effaces the traveller's personal experiences in order to foreground his epistemological authority, but Jameson finds it necessary to remind the reader that they are nonetheless present as a dramatic subtext. "[Buch's] personal fatigues, inconveniences, and dangers, are so slightly touched on," he writes, "that it is only the experienced traveller who can discover, through the veil which he has cast over his relations, his frequent distressing anxiety of mind, the alarming dangers to which he was so often exposed, and the excessive and overpowering fatigue to which he was subjected" (Buch 1813: xi). For Jameson, as for Humboldt, travel writing clearly ought to contain a personal drama as well as "descriptive" elements.

In this article I will take my lead from Humboldt and focus specifically on the dramatic and personal aspects of two other popular and well-known travel narratives of the Scandinavian high north from the period around 1800: the Italian Giuseppe Acerbi's *Travels through Sweden, Finland, and Lapland, to the North Cape, in the Years 1798 and 1799* (published in English 1802) and the British Edward Daniel Clarke's two volumes on Scandinavia in *Travels in Various Countries of Europe, Asia and Africa* (published in 1818 and 1823). Both works deal with journeys undertaken in 1799, and both – in contrast to Buch's *Reise* – use a narrative of personal trials to dramatize the North as an environment in which the traveller's masculinity is promoted, challenged and ultimately humbled.

I will argue that the North as a particular geographical location comes alive more vividly in such aspects of the texts than in the descriptive passages usually cited by scholars using them mainly as historical eyewitness reports. Hence, my reading is less concerned with Clarke's and Acerbi's roles as observers of the landscape and the peoples of Europe's northern periphery than with how the physical

ANKA RYALL

FIG. 22:
The Lapland explorer as voyeur. Illustration from Giuseppe Acerbi's Travels (1802).

and mental impact of this area is registered in their *Travels*. In this sense both accounts are narratives of the self as well as of geographical exploration. Like the texts discussed by Jonathan Lamb in his recent study of the literature of South Pacific exploration in the period 1680 to 1840, they dramatize the struggle for self-preservation in encounters and environments that intensify those "uncertainties that troubled the stability of the European self" during a period of emerging individualism (Lamb 2001: 5). From very different perspectives they highlight both the drama of northern travel and the vulnerability of the metropolitan traveller exposed to extreme natural conditions and alien topographies and cultures.

What counts as the North in late eighteenth-century travel narratives from Scandinavia varies considerably, as H. Arnold Barton has shown.[1] In Mary Wollstonecraft's *Letters Written during a Short Residence in Sweden, Denmark, and Norway* (1796), to cite an influential example, even the southern and populous coastal areas of the Nordic countries are represented as an "abode of desolation" defined by its cold climate and long summer nights (Wollstonecraft 1989: 262). This common image of the cold north as opposed to the warm south is only partly confirmed by Acerbi and Clarke, who are both surprised by the hot summer temperatures within the Arctic Circle. Clarke, for example, reports "feelings that might rather have suited a tropical climate. The deep shade of the forests protected us from the heat; but the sun's rays were very powerful, the weather sultry, and the mercury in *Fahrenheit's* thermometer stood, in the most shaded situation, so high as 68°" (Clarke 1824, 9: 383). Hence the simple opposition between north and south is modified. Still, the area in the far northern periphery of Europe that Clarke and Acerbi visited undeniably represented what Barton calls "the ultimate Nordic experience, expressing the most basic motives for travels in the North: exoticism, primitivism, and escape from Mediterranean classicism" (Barton 1998: 116). In Acerbi's and Clarke's narratives, the act of going there transforms travellers from tourists to explorers of the unknown.

Strange and Untrodden Territory

The territory they explored was an enormous, thinly populated, partly uncharted and almost roadless tract that usually went under the name of Lapland (after the indigenous population, the Lapps, who called themselves Sámi and the land Sápmi). As a geographical area Lapland was not clearly defined; historically the term referred loosely to the northern regions of the Fenno-Scandinavian peninsula and the Russian north-west. However, the area was in the process of being regulated as a result of the border treaty of 1751 between Denmark-Norway and Sweden-Finland. This agreement included the so-called Lapp Codicil, designed to allow the nomadic reindeer Sámi to continue their ancient seasonal movement across the national borders. The early eighteenth-century efforts at describing this area, initated by Olof Rudbeck the younger and followed up by the famous Linnaeus in *Flora Lapponica* (1737), attracted other outside observers. At the same time, because the area was believed to contain rich natural resources, there was a beginning influx of colonizers, that is, settlers from southern Scandinavia who went north

---

1   See also Hendriette Kliemann-Geisinger's article in this volume.

as farmers, missionaries and traders, and whose culture clashed with that of the indigenous population.

Edward Daniel Clarke (1769-1822) and Giuseppe Acerbi (1773-1846) were both in Swedish Lapland during the same year, 1799. They even encountered each other briefly in Oleåborg (now Oulu in Finland) in August. Both were young, Acerbi in his mid-twenties, Clarke just thirty. Whereas Acerbi was wealthy and travelled (at least according to Clarke) with a large entourage, the impecunious Clarke financed his own journey by travelling as the tutor of a Cambridge student named John Marten Cripps. It was the fourth time he in this way was able to satisfy that love of travel which was "the ruling passion of his mind" (Otter 1825, 1: 441). His earlier tours with other rich students had taken him through Britain and to Scotland, as well as on a two-year Grand Tour of France, Germany, Switzerland, Italy and Spain. With Cripps he had started his Scandinavian tour accompanied by two university friends, William Otter and Thomas Robert Malthus, the latter of whom had just published the first anonymous edition of *Essay on the Principle of Population* (1798) and wanted to collect facts that could be used to support his theories. But in southern Sweden the four parted company, and while Malthus and Otter proceeded to Norway, Clarke and Cripps travelled north along the Bothnian coast to Lapland in order to get "as near the pole as possible", as Clarke phrased in an optimistic letter to his mother (Otter 1825, 1: 452).

Originally Clarke and Cripps had only intended to see as much of northern Sweden, Norway and Russia "as could be comprehended within the extended limits of a long summer vacation" (Otter 1825, 1: 114). Instead they continued from Russia to Turkey and the Levant, not returning to England until November 1802, three and a half years after their departure. Clarke then proceeded to make an academic career for himself on the basis of his travels, eventually becoming Professor of Mineralogy at Cambridge (Dolan 2000: 170). Although he and Cripps were referred to as "the Lapland Travellers" by the local press after their return (Dolan 2000: 153), the first and second parts of his *Travels* deal with the later stages of their journey. The first volume of the third part, on Scandinavia, was not published until 1818, that is, almost two decades after the start of his journey. Even though the narrative seems to adhere quite closely to journals that he had kept during the trip, he substantiates and sometimes modifies his own findings by footnote references to several other travel accounts, among them Acerbi's. He also quotes extensively from his travel companion's manuscript journal. The use of such secondary material, together with his emphasis throughout on factual details and accurate observations, signal Clarke's wish to be known as a scientific traveller (Ryall 2002: 25).

On the basis of his *Travels*, Acerbi may be characterized as more of a dilettante, although he too enjoys classifying and taking measurements. Born near

Mantua in Lombardy, he was the son of a lawyer and studied law himself before beginning his career as a traveller in 1796 with a tour to Austria, Germany, England, Holland, Belgium, France and Switzerland. On this trip he started writing a journal, in which he made unsystematic notes about everything from restaurant bills to pictures he had seen in museums, a practice he continued on his subsequent journey to *Grande nord* (Nencioni 2004). Like Clarke he wanted to get as far north as possible and claimed to have been the first Italian to set foot on the North Cape (not knowing or neglecting to mention that his compatriot Francesco Negri had preceded him by over 130 years) (Acerbi 1802, 1: 395). His narrative was completed during a stay in London soon after his Scandinavian journey and published in 1802, the year Clarke and Cripps returned from their long journey. Perhaps with a view to the great popularity of travel books in Britain, it was written in English with the assistance of William Thomson (1746-1817). Thomson was a miscellaneous writer and author of the anonymous *Letters from Scandinavia, on the Past and Present State of the Northern Nations of Europe* (1796), which contains four chapters on Lapland. The exact nature of Thomson's contribution to Acerbi's *Travels* is not known, but although it is doubtful whether he had actually visited Scandinavia himself (Brant 2000), it may be surmised that he was a collaborator rather than simply a translator (Nencioni 2004).

While the Lapland section of Clarke's *Travels* covers only three chapters (chapters IX-XII) of his first volume on Scandinavia, Acerbi made Lapland the main focus of his *Travels*. Approximately half the narrative chapters of the book are devoted to his journey within the Arctic Circle, and the second volume is concluded with a long section titled "General and Miscellaneous Remarks Concerning Lapland". Both, however, wrote on the basis of relatively brief visits. The northbound journey from Uleåborg to the North Cape and back described by Acerbi takes approximately two months: he leaves on 8 June and returns on 11 August. Clarke's chapters on Lapland encompass only half that time, from the beginning of July until the beginning of August. Because there are no roads north of Övertorneå, both have to make their way with their companions by boat along navigable rivers, and both describe primitive accommodation on farms and in Sámi settlements. Among other hardships and inconveniences both emphasize attacks by mosquitoes, which come in thick clouds "clamourous for their prey" (Clarke 1824, 9: 414) or as an "army of insects" (Acerbi 1802, 2: 91). Moreover, for both such challenges are compensated by the excitement and novelty of travel in a region where even "the penetrating eye of Linnæus left something [...] for future discovery" (Acerbi 1802, 2: 129).

Even their personal motives for travelling north are expressed in similar terms, as an ideal combination of exotic adventure and encyclopedian Linnaean knowledge production. In the conclusion of the Lapland section of his *Travels* Clarke formulates his explanation as a response to an imagined sceptical question:

What then are the objects, it may be asked, which would induce any literary traveller to venture upon a journey into *Lapland*! Many! That of beholding the face of Nature undisguised; of traversing a strange and almost untrodden territory; of pursuing inquiries which relate to the connexion and the origin of nations; of viewing man as he existed in a primæval state; of gratifying a taste for *Natural History*, by the sight of rare *animals*, *plants*, and *minerals*; of contemplating the various phænomena caused by difference of *climate* and *latitude*: and, to sum up all, the delight which travelling itself affords, independently of any definite object; these are the inducements to such a journey. (Clarke 1824, 9: 561)

Acerbi, in the preface to his *Travels*, likewise addresses those sceptics who wonder "why a native of Italy, a country abounding in all the beauties of nature, and the finest productions of art, should voluntarily undergo the danger and fatigue of visiting the regions of the Arctic Circle" (Acerbi 1802, 1: vii). The obvious answer, according to Acerbi, is that an encounter with the extreme North provides the southerner with a basis for cultural comparison necessary for the production of new knowledge. But what particularly seems to have drawn him is the challenge of a "hardy" region characterized by the lack of all those soft "luxuries", "allurements of climate" and "temptations to pleasure" that attract travellers to the South. "Journeys in the North will be undertaken by those only who have a just and masculine taste for nature, under every aspect," he concludes (Acerbi 1802, 1: x).

The key word in Acerbi's explanation is "masculine". Underlying the argument of the preface is the dichotomy found, for instance, in Montesquieu's mental cartography, between a fertile, civilized and inviting but effeminate South and a desolate, primitive and forbidding North – a hardy environment both demanding and promoting hardy, masculine qualities. Hence Acerbi, more explicitly than Clarke, conceptualizes the North in terms of a conventional binary (see, for example, Stadius 2004: 235-37 and Niemi 1997: 75). But in both their *Travels* Lapland is imagined as a setting for the unfolding of a heroic masculinity. This form of masculinity is expressed partly through their use of conventional motifs such as the conquest of space, the appropriative survey of landscapes viewed from above, and the crossing of borders between European civilization and non-European barbarism. More interestingly, it is expressed, as I have already indicated, in terms of a narrative of personal trials and dramatic incidents.

The occasions used by Acerbi and Clarke to mark their status as explorers reflect their respective success and failure. As a narrative of a successful expedition, Acerbi's *Travels* culminates in an account of his sublime overview from the desolate North Cape plateau of the ocean and the midnight sun moving along the horizon. Here, at the goal of his expedition, human cares "are recollected as a dream", he states; "the various forms and energies of animated nature are forgotten; the earth is contemplated only in its elements, and as constituting a part of the solar system" (Acerbi 1802, 2: 111). In the encounter with the sublime vastness of the ocean he is humbled by a power much greater than himself, but also elevated by his own ability to encompass in one view the whole universe. Such perceptions, as many critics have pointed out, implicitly gender the sublime; in Anne Mellor's words, it becomes "an experience of masculine struggle and empowerment" (Mellor 1993: 87). Hence, the masculinity of Acerbi's achievement as a traveller is enhanced by the emotional impact of the view of the Arctic Ocean.

Clarke and Cripps, too, had originally planned to get as far north as "the *Icy Sea*" (Clarke 1824, 9: 523), but because Clarke fell ill, they were forced to return south after reaching Enontekis (now Enontekiö in northern Finland). Clarke's *Travels* is therefore an account of his failure to reach the goal he had set himself, and this may explain his more explicit emphasis throughout on the obstacles and hardships of his journey. Even so, his aborted expedition contains some significant heroic moments, particularly the crossing and re-crossing of the Arctic Circle, "the boundary of the *Temperate* and the *Frigid Zones*" (Clarke 1824, 9: 382-83). On the return south they celebrate both their survival and safe return to civilization by standing up in the boat with their hats off while recrossing this boundary: "We looked back towards the regions we had traversed," Clarke writes, "unmindful of the toils, the trials, and the privation, to which we had been exposed" (Clarke 1824, 9: 559-60). Like Acerbi, Clarke has triumphed over the wilderness as well as over himself.

The personal dramas unfolding above and between the lines of Acerbi's and Clarke's narratives are much less predictable. Although both *Travels* are dominated by the cultural attitude that Edward Said labels "flexible *positional* superiority" (Said 1994: 7), both narrators also succumb to moments of ambiguous identification with the local culture. Not only do these moments demonstrate vulnerability rather than conquering heroism, they also result in a confusion that clearly cannot be fully articulated. This is more obvious in Clarke's account of partial failure than in Acerbi's success story. But in both the struggle to preserve the self eventually leads to the paradoxical outcome registered by Lamb in narratives of South Seas travel, that "the self is preserved only by being changed [. . .] into something odd and strange, subject to moods, passions, and corruptions not easily transmitted to a polite audience" (Lamb 2001: 12).

As a first-person narrator Clarke avoids the singular "I", using instead a plural "we" that also encompasses his travelling companions (in Lapland they were an English servant and two local interpreters in addition to Cripps). When referring specifically to himself alone, he consistently does so in the third person, as "he", "the traveller" or "the author". According to Charles Batten, this was a distancing technique commonly used in eighteenth-century travel writing in order to prevent censure for egotism (Batten 1978: 40). Clarke's impersonal empirical orientation is also evident in his focus on factual details such as daily temperatures (including differences between temperatures in the sun and shade), elevations, general lay of the land, distances travelled and distances from the sea and so on, as well as in his attempts to verify and often correct the inadequate maps of the areas they travel through.

None the less, Clarke's textual presence as the protagonist of his own narrative is exceptionally strong, particularly in the Lapland section of his book. The main reason is his frequent emphasis on the many forms of torture he endures on his northbound travels. Lapland manifests itself in external facts and observations, but also in the intimate bodily experience of exposure to extreme conditions, manifested in unpalatable or undigestible food, in the ever-present mosquitoes, in the twenty-four-hour daylight that prevents sleep and is extremely painful to the eyes, and – as a consequence – in increasing debilitation. The rational narrative of geographical observations on the journey north is therefore interwoven with and sometimes undermined by another narrative of self-observations, suffering and loss of control.

Even before the most strenuous part of his expedition, Clarke, as he tells his readers, suffers from failing health. He ascribes it to a combination of exhausting travel and lack of sleep, which has resulted in "a total loss of appetite, attended with symptoms rather of an alarming nature" (Clarke 1824, 9: 357). In spite of this, he is heroically determined to persevere, but becomes so ill after only one day's journey north of Torneå that he finds it necessary to send back there for a physician before continuing. His illness is then diagnosed "to proceed principally from an obstruction of the biliary duct; caused by long travelling, exposed to nightly dews, excessive watchfulness, and a *Swedish* diet of salted provisions". But instead of prescribing either medication or rest, the physician suggests that "the feverish symptoms might be abated; and, upon the whole, continual change of air, accompanied with exercise, would rather tend to cure than increase the disorder" (Clarke 1824, 9: 365-66). This turns out not to be the case. Due to his prostrating illness, Clarke is forced to remain in the boat while his companions go ashore, and he is unable to participate in pulling the boat past the many river torrents they have to traverse. For a whole week he is so ill that he lies "like a corpse, upon the bottom of one of the boats, so excessively weak as to be almost unable to move" (Clarke 1824, 9: 425). In other words, he travels as an invalid, passive and increasingly despondent, and at times entirely dependent on the assistance of his companions.

Only the primitive lack of roads, which makes travel by river in "the gentle easy conveyance of a boat" necessary, enables him to carry on as far as Enontekis (Clarke 1824, 9: 425). And there he reluctantly has to let Cripps set out alone to climb some mountains from which they can still (on 25 July) see the midnight sun: "as their ascent promised some degree of fatigue, and the journey must be performed on foot, the author, owing to illness, was compelled to relinquish all thoughts of the undertaking" (Clarke 1824, 9: 463-64). Since one goal of his northern journey had been "to witness the remarkable appearance exhibited [...] by the presence of the solstitial sun through the entire night" (Clarke 1824, 9: 153), his inclusion of a long footnote citing an account by Cripps that replaces the report that he himself ought to have written, functions as a signifier of his complete failure to live up to the heroic role of explorer.

His inability to digest the strange local diet exacerbates Clarke's health problems. He praises the water, which is "so clear and cool, that it afforded us many a refreshing draught, during the sultry hours of the day" (Clarke 1824, 9: 373), but rejects with disgust staples such as dried reindeer meat, salted fish and sour milk. One memorable passage describes – in nauseous detail – the local diet consisting "only of biscuit made of the inner bark of the birch-tree, chopped straw, and a little rye" that he observes his boatmen eating. This they wash down, he explains, with sour fermented milk "*Lapland* nectar; a revolting slime, '*corrupted*,' as *Tacitus* said of *beer*, 'into a semblance of *wine*'" (Clarke 1824, 9: 400-01). Even the fresh reindeer milk that the travellers are offered on a visit to a camp of "nomade Laplanders" is a problem for his delicate stomach. Although deliciously "thick, and sweet as cream", it is also "rather difficult of digestion, and apt to cause head-ache in persons unaccustomed to it, unless it be mixed with water" (Clarke 1824, 9: 444). While the other members of his party sometimes suffer from lack of provisions, Clarke claims that he himself had survived most of the Lapland journey on "only bread and water, and was scarcely able even to swallow this" (Clarke 1824, 9: 415).

In Acerbi's narrative the ubiquitous mosquitoes, though described as a terrible nuisance, are treated humorously and usually in passing. Clarke, however, is obsessive about the agony they inflict and the failure of all forms of covering to provide sufficient protection against them. Like the unpalatable food, the mosquitoes aggravate his bodily suffering. But although he goes so far as to make the improbable claim that their powerful probosces "will penetrate very thick leather; the gloves upon our hands not being sufficient protection from their attacks"

(Clarke 1824, 9: 389), he is reluctant to follow the advice of his local interpreters and imitate the Lapland practice of covering the face, arms, ears and neck in a mixture of cream and tar. Doing so would clearly undermine the crucial distinction between the naturally fastidious metropolitan traveller and the native population in its most primitive aspect. Only when Clarke and Cripps are no longer able to endure another sleepless night caused by the noise and stings of the mosquitoes, do they submit to being smeared with "the darksome unction", thus becoming "*literally* prepared to keep the *Laplanders* in countenance" (Clarke 1824, 9: 434). As Clare Brant points out, the issue of submerging national identity by adopting local dress or customs, as opposed to preserving native habits, is an important one in travel books of the period. When Clarke chooses the former option and finally allows himself to be tarred, he destabilizes the simple binaries (Brant 2000: 131). But as his narrative shows, by allowing himself to be changed, he paradoxically preserves the self.

A similar pattern of initial resistance to and eventual acceptance of local customs is represented by Clarke's account of his illness. At the start of his Lapland journey, when he is waiting for the physician from Torneå, he and his companions are told by the local inhabitants that they ought to learn from them "to cure all ills ourselves, without depending upon others for remedies" (Clarke 1824, 9: 363). Although he belittles this advice by calling the people who offer it "simple", his narrative proves them right. When reaching Enontekis and believing himself to be close to death, he also achieves a surprising cure in the form of the indigenous cloudberry. "The *Swedes* call it *Hiortron*; the *Laplanders* give it the name of *Latoch*; the inhabitants of *Westro-Bothnia* call it *Snotter*; and in *Norway*, its appelation is *Multebær*," he explains:

The same plant is found upon the highest mountains and in some of the *peat*-bogs of the north of *England*; on which account, perhaps, it is called *Cloud-berry* in our island: but it is not likely that its fruit ever attains the same degree of maturity and perfection in *Great Britain* as in *Lapland*, where the sun acts with such power during the summer. Its medicinal properties have certainly be overlooked, owing, perhaps, either to this circumstance, or to its rarity in *Great Britain*. (Clarke 1824, 9: 371-72)

Hence, as a naturalist he endows the story of his cure with a general and scientific as well as a personal significance.

Nothing in the Lapland section of Clarke's *Travels* is described with such evident delight as the cloudberries. On a walk in early August, for example, he finds such an abundance of them "that the whole surface of the morasses was covered by its plump and fair berries, inviting us to a delicious feast by their blooming appearance" (Clarke 1824, 9: 534). His account of how the combined gastronomic and aesthetic pleasures of this fruit may have powerful healing effects is equally poetic. In Enontekis, Clarke and Cripps stay with the local pastor Erik Grape and his family, and this is where his cure takes place:

In the evening, Mr. *Grape*'s children came into the room, bringing with them two or three gallons of the fruit of the *Cloudberry*, or *Rubus Chamæmorus*. The plant grows so abundantly near the river, that it is easy to gather bushels of the fruit. As the large berry ripens, which is big as the top of a man's thumb, its colour, at first scarlet, becomes yellow. When eaten with sugar and cream, it is cooling and delicious, and tastes like the large *American* hautboy-strawberries. Little did the author dream of the blessed effects he was to experience by tasting of the offering brought by these little children; who, proud of having their gifts accepted, would gladly run and gather daily a fresh supply; which was as often blended with cream and sugar, by the hands of their mother; until at last he perceived that his fever rapidly abated, his spirits and appetite were restored; and, when sinking under a disorder so obstinate that it seemed to be incurable, the blessings of health were restored to him, where he had reason to believe he should have found his grave. The symptoms of amendment were almost instantaneous, after eating of these berries. (Clarke 1824, 9: 470-71)

He even lets his emotions at this miraculous cure spill over in a long personal footnote concluding with two stanzas from his favourite poet Thomas Gray's "Ode on the Pleasure arising from Vicissitude":

See the wretch, that long has toss'd
On the thorny bed of pain,
At length repair his vigour lost,
And breathe, and walk again:

The meanest floweret of the vale,
The simplest note that swells the gale,
The common sun, the air, the skies,
To him are opening Paradise.

As he explains, this quotation is not coincidental: "It is only in the moments of such a recovery, and at such a distance from one's native land, that the [...] lines of *Britain*'s deathless Bard can be called to mind" (Clarke 1824, 9: 471). Writing about Clarke's youth, William Otter underlines his friend's ardent love of English poetry, particularly Gray, "every ode and every line of whose writings were familiar to him" (Otter 1825, 1: 71). In *Travels* Clarke on several occasions quotes Gray to articulate his more lyrical sentiments, but in the footnote quotation he goes beyond such incidental embellishments and uses Gray's poem as a way of expressing emotions – of homesickness as well as of exhilaration – that he clearly feels are inappropriately intense and personal in the context of a naturalist travel narrative.

In spite of the cure described in the *Travels*, Clarke privately summarized his Lapland journey in terms of unabated suffering. "I had the melancholy task of telling Cripps how to commit my poor carcass to a grave, and go home," he writes in the letter to his friend Otter that I have used as one of the epigraphs of this article. Here he also confesses to serious psychological symptoms like fainting spells and hallucinations. "All my illness arose from fatigue," he explains, "and neglect of sleep, and perhaps from the effect of climate on a constitution unarmed to encounter a frigid zone" (Otter 1825, 1: 471). His metaphorical use of "unarmed" is telling. Adventurous though he is, he has been physically and mentally unprepared for the extreme strains of a northern journey. Thus the struggle for self-preservation described in his narrative literally become a losing battle against a hostile environment.

Like Lamb's South Sea travellers (Lamb 2001), Clarke demonstrates the great personal risks of exploration, but his vulnerability does not necessarily undermine his role as an observer and natural historian. On the contrary, as John Tallmadge has pointed out in a study of Charles Darwin's plotting in *The Voyage of the Beagle*, the admittance of weakness and loss of control was read as an indication of candor that rhetorically gave added credibility to a traveller's knowledge claims (Tallmadge 1980: 340-41). Moreover, the emphasis on personal risk was an important factor in the popularity of exotic travel writing among metropolitan readers "curious about the singularities of self-preservation" as Lamb phrases it (Lamb 2001: 7). But it is only in the private letter to Otter that Clarke is able to articulate his almost inexpressible experiences. His solution in the *Travels* is the quotation from Gray's poem, which may be interpreted as an effort to translate the emotional impact of his illness into terms that are readable for his audience at home.

Acerbi's Embarrassment

Although Clarke in his personal correspondence from Sweden mentions "a game at romps with some Lapland lasses" (Otter 1825, 1: 461), his published *Travels* is without even such oblique references to sexuality. Only his sick and suffering body is present in the text. When describing the Finnish sauna – a subject of titillation in many northern travel narratives – his tone is carefully neutral:

There is not a village, nor indeed a dwelling, without a *steam-bath*; in which the inhabitants of both sexes assemble together, in a state of perfect nudity, for the purpose of bathing, at least once in every week; and oftener, if any illness occur among them. These *steam-baths* are all alike: they consist of a small hut, containing a furnace for heating stones red hot, upon which boiling water is thrown; and a kind of shelf, with a ladder conducting to it, upon which the bathers extend themselves, in a degree of temperature such as the natives of southern countries could not endure for an instant: here they have their bodies rubbed with birch boughs dipped in hot water; an office which is always performed by the females of each family, and generally by the younger females. It is to these *baths*, and to the natural cleanliness and temperate habits of the people, that the uninterrupted health they enjoy may be ascribed. (Clarke 1824, 9: 366-67)

In spite of his view that the sauna promotes the health as well as the hygiene of the local inhabitants, Clarke does not seem to have thought of it as a possible treatment for his own illness. He none the less explicitly connects it to the other civilized virtues, such as a general cleanliness and good manners, that he observes in remote regions of Lapland.

Like Clarke, Acerbi believes that the sauna has health benefits, but in his opinion it exemplifies the primitivism of the north. "Nothing could be more curious than to describe the odd and fantastic customs of the northern nations, and the gross indelicacies practiced among them on certain occasions," he claims, adding that he will confine his remarks to marrriage customs and the Finnish manner of bathing. Of the latter he writes:

Men and women use the bath promiscuously, without any concealment of dress, or being in the least influenced by any emotions of attachment. If, however, a stranger open the door, and come on the bathers by surprise, the women are not a little startled at his appearance; for, besides his person, he introduces along with him, by opening the door, a great quantity of light, which discovers at once to the view their situation, as well as forms. Without such an accident they remain, if not in total darkness, yet in great obscurity, as there is no other window besides a small hole, nor any light but what enters in from some chink in the roof of the house, or the crevices between the pieces of wood of which it is constructed. I often amused myself with surprising the bathers in this manner, and I once or twice tried to go in and join the assembly; but the heat was so excessive that I could not breathe, and in the space of a minute at most, I verily believe, must have been suffocated. (Acerbi 1802, 1: 297)

For Acerbi the communal sauna is not only primitive and bizarre, but indecent because nakedness to him equals sexuality. To a modern reader, however, the most bizarre aspect of the above passage is the narrator's prurient and unabashed voyeurism. Would he have allowed himself to behave in the manner he describes – and more pertinently, would he have admitted to such behaviour publicly – if he had not considered the bathers uncivilized? Even so, as Heidi Hansson rightly emphasizes in a discussion of the sauna as a site of cultural encounter in travel narratives from Scandinavia, Acerbi obviously finds the spectacle of the men and women naked together sexually arousing (Hansson 2002: 167).

But it is Acerbi's presence and gaze that sexualizes the bathers. Until he exposes them to daylight by opening the door of the sauna, their modesty has been protected by darkness. In the sudden light, as the illustration in his book shows, the bathers – like Adam and Eve after the fall – become conscious of their nakedness (Hansson 2002: 166-67). But to what extent does this image represent Acerbi's subjective interpretation of the scene? Clarke, in contrast, relates an almost parallel episode without equating nakedness with indecency. Arriving at a remote village one night, he and his companions think it has been deserted until their local boatsman opens the door of one of the saunas, "for all the world like a cow-house, and out rushed men, women, and children, stark-naked, with dripping locks and scorched skins, and began rolling upon the grass" (Clarke 1824, 9: 368-69). By focusing on – to outsiders – the comic and absurd behaviour of the bathers, and mentioning children as well as adults, Clarke diffuses any potential erotic associations attached to the image of a group of naked men and women. At the same time, his emphasis on the comic has a distancing effect, and he shows himself less willing than Acerbi to engage with the local inhabitants and their customs.

Unlike Clarke, Acerbi is not only an observer. In spite of his misgivings, at Kemi in northern Finland he is persuaded to join a local pastor in a sauna bath. He looks upon this, he explains, as a kind of anthropological experiment that will enable him to "become more familiar with the manners and customs of the natives" (Acerbi 1802, 1: 338). Instead his account, which I will quote in full, represents a painful initiation into the many ambiguities attending the practice of participant observation:

The stones in the small apartment of the bath were [. . .] heated, and a young girl of eighteen years of age, who had the office of attending, informed us when every thing was ready. After we had entered the bath, the girl first stripped us naked, and then began to throw water as usual upon the stones. She presented us with a bason of cold water, and birch rods, with which we were to switch ourselves. Feeling as a stranger, I was quite out of countenance at my present situation, but strove to keep up my spirits by constantly turning my eyes towards my companion, and endeavouring to imitate, as much as possible, his most exemplary indifference. The heat of the vapour rose to fifty degrees of Celsius: at first I felt a violent oppression, and had it quickly augmented, I believe, naked as I was, I should have made my escape from the bath; but forcing myself to persevere, I became gradually accustomed to it, and after some time was able to support a heat of 65 degrees. Under this heat it was an extreme pleasure to throw water upon the head, and to feel it running all over the body. The birchen rods were garnished with leaves, and by dipping them in the bason of cold water, and afterwards lashing the body, one enjoys nearly the same sensation. Having been about half an hour in the bath, my friend [. . .], as I declined being the first to submit to all the usual discipline of the place, entered upon the process without delay, in order that I might see how I ought to conduct myself in my turn. The girl gave him a little stool to sit upon, threw cold water upon his head, squeezed his hair, and with soap and water washed his whole body, and rubbed him down to the girdle. She then went to his feet, and rubbed his legs completely, particularly his ankles, and the tendon achillis. Meanwhile I was extremely attentive, and almost stupified at the whole operation: but what astonished me most was the perfect apathy with which the minister endured this long and stimulating process. When it came to be my turn to submit, I found myself in a state of extreme embarrassment – and at last was very glad to get on my clothes, and walk out of the bath. (Acerbi 1802, 1: 338-39)

What is revealed here is not only the narrator's own naked body and some of its intimate sensations of discomfort, pleasure and arousal, but the transformation that takes place when he has stepped inside the sauna and allowed himself to become a participant rather than an observer of local customs.

Whereas in the first sauna scene Acerbi causes the embarrassment of the bathers (most clearly depicted in the illustration by the figure concealing his face) by opening the door and letting in the daylight, in the second it is he himself who becomes embarrassed. In Rom Harré's words, embarrassment is "a very bodily emotion" (Harré 1990: 181), and the "extreme embarrassment" with which Acerbi concludes his account is obviously a euphemism for an involuntary erection. His erection also represents an embarrassment, in the modern sense of "constrained feeling of manner arising from bashfulness or timidity" (first used, according to the *Oxford English Dictionary*, by Edmund Burke in 1774), because it undermines the personal dignity that is preserved and protected in the first scene by clothing. But the reason Acerbi's nakedness in the sauna makes him vulnerable is of course that he is in the presence of others. As Charles Darwin writes in his pioneering study *The Expression of the Emotions in Man and Animals* (1872), about the most common physiological manifestation of embarrassment, the blush, it is caused by "self-attention". Darwin ties the blush to a consciousness of personal appearance which "through the force of association" is related to moral conduct: "It is not the simple act of reflecting on our own appearance, but the thinking what others think of us, which excites the blush," he argues (Darwin 1998: 324). This view has been followed up by recent theorists of embarrassment, who usually distinguish between shame as a private feeling and embarrassment as a form of social anxiety. Hence, for Robert Edelmann, "embarrassment has to do with 'unmasking' – with an observation that we have not acted or behaved in the way we would have wished" (Edelmann 1987: 11).

Acerbi's reference to the local pastor's "most exemplary indifference" and "perfect apathy" during the ablutions administered by the young woman may be ironical. At the same time, it is his own inability to live up to the pastor's example that causes his feelings of embarrassment. In other words, Acerbi's erection "unmasks" him as a violator of the local norms of modesty and civilized behaviour. Assuming for a moment the perspective of the Other, he is unable to maintain his usual attitude of cultural superiority. The second sauna scene, then, indicates the extent to which the struggle for self-preservation in travel narratives is connected to the issue of immersion or non-immersion in local cultures. When Acerbi concludes the scene by describing his relief at reestablishing a physical distance by getting dressed and leaving the sauna, he implicitly admits to his own unheroic susceptibility.

Torture and embarrassment are only two aspects of the discourses of vulnerability and self-preservation that inform Acerbi's and Clarke's Lapland narratives. The effect of these discourses is to enhance our sense of the North as a particular place that does not only promote heroic masculine qualities and naturalist careers, but is also a veritable battleground where the unarmed traveller is bound to be humbled if not defeated. A later Lapland traveller, Xavier Marmier, puts it memorably in his *Letters sur le Nord* (1840), in a personal confession omitted from the official report of his journey: "J'ai courbé le front sous le sentiment de mon impuissance" – in Wendy Mercer's translation: "I bowed my head in the knowledge of my impotence" (Mercer 2006: 7).

References

Acerbi, Joseph (Giuseppe) 1802: *Travels through Sweden, Finland, and Lapland, to the North Cape, in the Years 1798 and 1799.* 2 vols. London: Joseph Mawman.

Austen, Jane 2003 (1818): *Northanger Abbey.* Harmondsworth: Penguin.

Barton, H. Arnold 1998: *Northern Arcadia: Foreign Travelers in Scandinavia, 1765-1815.* Carbondale: Southern Illinois University Press.

Batten, Charles L., Jr. 1978: *Pleasure and Instruction: Form and Convention in Eighteenth-Century Travel Literature.* Berkeley: University of California Press.

Brant, Clare 2000: Climates of Gender. *Romantic Geographies: Discourses of Travel 1775-1844.* Ed. Amanda Gilroy. Manchester: Manchester University Press.

Buch, Leopold von 1810: *Reise durch Norwegen und Lappland.* Berlin: G.C. Nauck.

Buch, Leopold von 1813: *Travels through Norway and Lapland, during the Years 1806, 1807, and 1808.* Trans. John Black. London: Henry Colburn.

Clarke, E.D. 1824: *Travels in Various Countries of Europe, Asia and Africa. Part 3: Scandinavia.* Vols. 9-11. London: T. Cadell.

Darwin, Charles 1998 (1872/1889): *The Expression of the Emotions in Man and Animals.* London: HarperCollins.

Dolan, Brian 2000: *Exploring European Frontiers: British Travellers in the Age of Enlightenment.* London: Macmillan.

Edelmann, Robert J. 1987: *The Psychology of Embarrassment.* Chichester: John Wiley & Sons.

Hansson, Heidi 2002: Kulturmöte i bastun. *När språk och kulturer möts: Festskrift till Tuuli Forsgren.* Ed. Heidi Hansson, Raija Kangassalo and Daniel Lindmark. Umeå: Johan Nordlander-sällskapet: 162-75.

Harré, Rom 1990: Embarrassment: A Conceptual Analysis. *Shyness and Embarrassment: Perspectives from Social Psychology.* Ed. W. Ray Crozier. Cambridge: Cambridge University Press: 181-204.

Humboldt, Alexander von 1852: *Personal Narrative of Travels to the Equinoctial Regions of America, during the Years 1799-1804.* Trans. Thomasine Ross. Vol. 1. London: Henry G. Bohn.

Lamb, Jonathan 2001: *Preserving the Self in the South Seas, 1680-1840.* Chicago: University of Chicago Press.

Leask, Nigel 2002: *Curiosity and Aesthetics of Travel Writing, 1779-1840.* Oxford: Oxford University Press.

Mercer, Wendy 2006: Arctic Discourses: People(s) and Landscapes in the Travel Writing of Xavier Marmier. *Edda* 106, 1 (2006): 3-17.

Mellor, Anne K. 1993: *Romanticism & Gender.* New York: Routledge.

Nencioni, Giuseppe 2004: Italienare i Norr. Reseberättelser från 1400-talet til idag. Unpublished typescript.

Niemi, Einar 1997: Sami History and the Frontier Myth. *Sami Culture in a New Era: The Norwegian Sami Experience.* Ed. Harald Gaski. Karasjok: Davvi Girji: 62-85.

Otter, William 1825: *The Life and Remains of Edward Daniel Clarke.* 2 vols. London: George Cowie.

Ryall, Anka 2002: Paradoxes of Encounter in Edward Daniel Clarke's Narrative of Lapland. *Scandinavica* 41 (May): 21-36.

Said, Edward W. 1994 (1978): *Orientalism.* New York: Vintage Books.

Stadius, Peter 2004: Bilden av Norden. *Det nya Norden efter Napoleon.* Stockholm Studies in History 73. Eds. Max Engman and Åke Sandström. Stockholm: Almquist & Wiksell.

Tallmadge, John 1980: From Chronicle to Quest: The Shaping of Darwin's "Voyage of the Beagle". *Victorian Studies* 23 (Spring): 325-45.

Thomson, William 1796: *Letters from Scandinavia, on the Past and Present State of the Northern Nations of Europe.* 2 vols. London. G.G. and J. Robinson.

Tuttle, Charles R. 1885: *Our North Land: Being a Full record of the Candian Northwest and Hudson's Bay Route, Together with a Narrative of the Experiences of the Hudson's Bay Expedition of 1884.* Toronto: C. Blackwell Robinson.

Wollstonecraft, Mary 1989: *The Works of Mary Wollstonecraft.* Ed. Janet Todd and Marilyn Butler, with Emma Rees-Mogg. Vol. 6. London: Pickering.

STEPHANIE BUUS

Disappearing Tracts

The Vanishing of Christen Pram and his Travel Account of Norway 1804-1806

Although a well-known and influential figure while he lived, the feisty and out-spoken Norwegian civil servant, novelist, dramatist, poet, editor, and social critic, Christen Henriksen Pram (1756-1821), would bear witness to his own fall into personal and professional obscurity at the end of his life – an obscurity that has not lessened with time.[1] A figure generally mentioned in passing rather than in detail, Pram is probably best remembered as the shadowy, unhappy husband-figure in a love triangle featuring Pram himself, Pram's wife, and the Danish author, Jens Baggesen, whose adoring poems to his married muse (Seline) remain popular today (Nettum 2001: 15-16; Bull 1916: 427). Despite the magnitude of Pram's authorship and his significant role in the culture and politics of the late eighteenth early nineteenth century Danish conglomerate state[2] – particularly his repeated attempts to advance the position of his native Norway within this state – Pram has been the object of only a handful of literary and historical accounts since his death.

An example of Pram's authorship that remains as, or even more, obscure than its author is his unpublished, nine-volume account of his topographical-statistical travels through Norway between the years of 1804 and 1806 – an account that bears a title almost as exhaustive as its contents: *Indberetning til det Kongelige General Land-Oeconomie og Commerce-Collegium indeholdende oeconomiske Bemærkninger paa en efter Kongelig Befaling i Aaret 1804 foretagen Reise i Norge* (Report to His Majesty's Department of Land Economy and Commerce Containing Economic Remarks on Travels Conducted in Norway in the Year 1804 Commissioned

---

1   A book-length biographical study of Christen Pram by Rolf Nyboe Nettum first appeared in 2001.

2   The Danish conglomerate state consisted of the kingdoms of Denmark and Norway, the German Duchies of Schleswig and Holstein, and a few overseas colonies. The 'Dual Monarchy' of Denmark and Norway was extremely centralized with most power and nearly all institutions located in Copenhagen (Brincker 2003; Degn 1999: 224; Østergaard 1992; Thyssen 1980: 31).

by Royal Order).[3] Although one of the most comprehensive descriptions of the economic, social, and structural conditions in Norway preceding the dissolution of Norway's more than four-hundred-year union with Denmark at the end of the Napoleonic Era (the Treaty of Kiel in 1814), Pram's Norwegian travel account has yet to be published in anything approaching its entirety. Instead, Pram's momentous work continues to rest demurely in the Danish Royal Library as it has done for centuries, awaiting the attention of a Scandinavian publisher undaunted by the challenge posed by its formidable size and chaotic form.[4]

A Travel Account Without an Audience

In this chapter, I argue that Pram's Norwegian account was one of the major factors contributing to Pram's fall into obscurity at the end of his life. As it turned out, the particular type of travel account that Pram chose to write garnered him success in the short run, but made him unpopular and in many respects 'useless' to the newly-separated nation-states of Denmark and Norway in the longer run. Pram disappeared from the scene in post-1814 Denmark and never made it to the scene of post-1814 Norway because he no longer had anything to offer either of these countries ideologically. In Denmark's case, the disappearance of Pram's Norwegian travel account may not strike the reader as particularly unexpected. After all, Pram's account was no longer topical the moment that Norway ceased to be a part of the Danish multi-national state in 1814. Prior to 1814, Pram's account was extolled for its documentary zeal in providing an inventory of contemporary economic, social, and structural conditions in Norway – a remote northern part of the Danish conglomerate state that remained relatively unknown and little researched. After 1814, Pram's account became a textual reminder of Danish territorial and political losses at the beginning of the nineteenth century, functioning now as a sort of cenotaph marking a body of land that now rested elsewhere/outside the boundaries of Danish control and concern. Quite literally, then, Pram's account was *out of place* in Denmark after 1814.

In Norway's case, the travel account that Pram wrote proved to be *out of time* in the nationally charged ideological climate that characterized the country after 1814.[5] Whereas Pram's account promoted a vision of Norway framed in terms of its

---

3   This is the title of the initial set of four volumes (National Archives of Norway, vol. 1320-1323). The subsequent set of four volumes (vol. 1324-1327) has almost the same title. The final volume (vol. 1328) of Pram's account consists of an appendix with economic and statistical tables.

4   An entire reproduction of Pram's nine-volume Norwegian travel account is located in the National Archives in Oslo.

5   For a discussion of events in Norway immediately before and after the signing of the Treaty of Kiel, see Seip (1974), Mykland (1983: 198-211) and Lunden (1992).

STEPHANIE BUUS

present and most particularly its future, the nation-building project underway in Norway in the years immediately after 1814 pursued a vision of the country framed primarily in terms of its independent and unspoiled past (Christensen 1998: 2). Among other things, the value scale informing Pram's travel account was turned on its head in post-1814 accounts of Norway: what Pram had earlier viewed as poor and uncultivated was now hailed as picturesque or sublime by many leading figures in Norway after 1814, among them Henrik Wergeland (1808-1845) (Fjeldstad 1998: 165). The atavistic national project espoused by many Norwegian literati and supported to varying degrees by ruling Norwegian elites after 1814 was therefore wholly incompatible with the progressive enlightenment project driving Pram's account, a situation that would leave Pram struggling to find common ground to stand on once the Napoleonic dust had settled.

The Danish Case

In the turbulent years of the Napoleonic Era leading up to and following the definitive end of the Dual Monarchy in 1814, many Danes attempted to turn away from the troubling business of the world outside of Denmark's borders and to focus instead on the business of conquering the world within Denmark's borders, pursuing an introvert strategy of national reconsolidation that would later become a popular motto after the definitive loss of the duchies of Schleswig and Holstein in 1864 following the second Schleswig-Holstein war: "what has been lost without must be won within" ("Hvad udadtil tabes skal indadtil vindes"). In a spirit of *revolution* in its regressive sense, a 'rolling back' or a return to a point before occupied[6] – in this case, a return to the presumed Danish 'core' of the conglomerate state – pamphlets such as Frederik Stoud's *Tabet af Norge til Medborgernes Efter-tanke* (Norway's Loss for the Reflection of Citizens 1815) urged Danes to "make up for the loss of Norway by reclaiming their own undeveloped wastelands" in historically neglected parts of Denmark (Barton 1986: 378-379). In contradiction to its title, Stoud's pamphlet and others like it advocated a 'revolutionary strategy' of internal colonization in response to losses incurred in the near present – one that actively rejected reflection and mourning over recent events in favour of an energetic, forward-looking program focused on the physical reclamation of 'lost' interior spaces (Frandsen 1996; Olwig 1984).

---

6   Late L. *revolutio* (n-), from *revolvere* (v): *re-* 'back' (also expressing intensive force) + *volvere* 'roll'. See "Revolution *n*" and "Revolve *v.*" *The Concise Oxford Dictionary.* Ed. Judy Pearsall. Oxford University Press, 2001. *Oxford Reference Online.* Oxford University Press. September 2004. Available at: <http://www.oxfordreference.com/views/ENTRY.html?subview=Main&entry=t23.e47671>.

In contrast, other contemporaries of Pram, among them lesser remembered literary figures such as Christen Molbech in his wistfully-entitled travel account from 1811-1815, *Ungdomsvandringer i Mit Fødeland* (Youthful Travels in My Native Country) as well as canonical figures like Adam Oehlenschläger in his famous poem from 1803, *Guldhornene* (The Golden Horns), pursued a 'revolutionary' course that was distinctly nostalgic and narrative in its response to the events of the Napoleonic Era (Rerup in Feldbæk 1991: 326-330; Østergaard 1992). The works of these and other Danish writers mourned the loss of various Danish Golden Ages comfortingly removed from the present and decidedly tarnished age in which these writers now found themselves, even as their authors strove to reclaim these ages through the act of writing about them (Damsholt 1999; Bredsdorff 1999; Nielsen 1996). In a post-1814 Denmark keenly intent on remaking itself, in part by moving speedily forwards *beyond* 1814; in part by moving speedily backwards *before* 1814, there was thus little room for Pram's Norwegian travel account, since it focused on a time and a place now foreign to the time(s) and place(s) that occupied the ruling elites involved in the Danish national project taking shape after 1814.

Pram's travel account thus became incongruous the moment that Denmark was forced to relinquish Norway to Sweden in the 1814 Treaty of Kiel. From that point, Pram's utilitarian and fact-driven account of Norway's resources, its population, the state of its roads and factories, seaweed burning practices, and disgruntled Norwegian fishermen – all of this information became esoteric reading rather than instrumental reading for a Danish audience. Since Norway was no longer a Danish territory, there was nothing to be gained from reading Pram's travel account except the acquisition of knowledge – or a bit of readerly pleasure. As very little in Pram's account constitutes particularly pleasurable (i.e. literary) reading – its title alone clearly indicates its utilitarian intentions – one imagines that there would have been little to attract a more general Danish public to the account once its instrumental value vanished (cf. Batten 1974).

Whether or not contemporary Danish readers found Pram's Norwegian travelogue instructive or pleasurable after 1814, the events of 1814 transformed Pram's Norwegian travel account into a *document of loss* in Danish eyes. Pram's account no longer served as an inventory of the Dual Monarchy's Norwegian possessions, but had now become an inventory – a textual memorial, as it were – of Denmark's powerlessness and its numerous losses during the Napoleonic Era – loss of face, loss of territory, loss of population, loss of resources, and, it should be noted, loss of valuable Norwegian skills and expertise.[7] The fact, then, that Pram's Norwegian

---

7   Iron production was an area of Norwegian expertise that Danes desperately lacked following the separation of the two kingdoms. Denmark was forced to import Norwegian and English labour to meet this need immediately after 1814 (Christensen 1996: 362-363).

travel account remains tucked quietly away at the Danish Royal Library as it has been for nearly two centuries is not especially surprising.

The Norwegian Case

The fact that Pram's Norwegian travel account has almost no publication history in Norway is quite another matter, however, and presents us with a far greater mystery. With the exception of the 1964 publication of *Kopibøker fra Reiser i Norge 1804-1806* (Letter-books from Travels in Norway 1804-1806), a collection of letters that Pram wrote to his employer and colleagues as a running epistolary supplement to his main account, only scattered excerpts from Pram's travel account have been published in Norway before 1964, and nothing more substantial has been published since. In addition to its scant publication history, Pram's Norwegian travel account is rarely mentioned in the literature on topographical accounts in Norway during the eighteenth and early-nineteenth centuries – a situation that has likely contributed to the continued obscurity of both the account and its author.[8] Why did Pram's Norwegian travel account fail to arouse interest in Norway in 1814, particularly when Norway was the sole subject of the account and its raison d'être? Why does this still appear to be the case today?

As revealed in letters to friends between 1814 and 1817, Christian Pram certainly believed that his pragmatic account of the state of things in Norway at the beginning of the nineteenth century would find a significant and enthusiastic audience in the new Norway, and, if he so desired, provide him with sufficient patriotic capital to purchase a one-way ticket back to his native country after fifty years of residence in Denmark (see letters in Bull 1916: 433; Amundsen 1969: 435). Commissioned by the Danish King Frederik VI in 1804, Pram's Norwegian account not only possessed the legitimacy of royal decree, but was also well-received by the King, by Pram's employer, the Department of Commerce, and in Dual-Monarchy governmental circles more generally. Indeed, Pram's initial account of his travels through the central and northern parts of Norway as far north as Trondheim (1804-05) met with such approval that he was quickly re-commissioned to undertake a second journey to the south and west of Norway as far west as Stavanger (1805-06). Given the success of his Norwegian account prior to 1814 (Bull 1916: 433; Amundsen 1969: 435), Pram had no reason to believe that its contents would not meet with the approval of Norwegian authorities after 1814, many of whom had, like Pram, been civil servants under the Danish King during the Dual Monarchy or

---

8   Supphellen's study of eighteenth-century topographical-historical literature includes a bibliography that extends as late as 1825, more than twenty years after Pram's Norwegian account. Pram's account is never mentioned, however (1979: 210-11; 205-06).

remained loyal to Denmark and hoped for a new Norwegian-Danish union even after Norway's stipulated confederation with Sweden (Mykland 1983: 198-211).

Pram's Norwegian travels are, in fact, an excellent example of the cartographic project of 'discovery' begun in several parts of Europe during the mid-1700s, the aim of which was to open up and map out the resources, geography, and populations of previously unexplored or under explored places throughout the world (Pratt 1992: 29-37; Stafford 1984). Norway represented one such under-explored periphery at the dawn of the nineteenth century, a veritable *terra incognita* for the ruling elites within the Danish multi-national state (Christensen 1998). As Roald Aanrud points out, travellers to Norway during Pram's time generally relied on Christian Jochum Pontoppidan's map of southern Norway (*Det Sydlige Norge*) from 1785.[9] It wasn't until the 1840s that domestic and foreign travellers received more – as well as more accurate – topographical information on Norway in the form of additional travel guides and maps in Norwegian and English (Aanrud, forthcoming: 18; Rogan 1998: 51-55).

Pram's objective in this case was thus to act as "the King's Eyes" (La Cour 1943: 114). His task was to see *for* the King; to see *as* the King and to provide the royal administration with the information he believed they needed to know, in this case a more definitive account of the state of infrastructure and manufacturing in a relatively uncharted and remote part of the Danish realm (Supphellen 1979). From Trondheim, the northernmost point of his Norwegian journey, Pram wrote to a colleague at the Commerce Department:

His Majesty has ordered me to go out into the provinces of his realms to look around as an organ of the department whose member I have the honour of being. First, I received orders to come here, to this, the end of his kingdom, so far away from the centre. I set out to look around here, saw that everything was much better than one might have expected at 64° latitude, and found many excellent people [...] (1964: 41).

Pram's travels to Norway and the nine-volume account that resulted from them therefore possessed the authenticity and authority of royal decree as well as the authenticity and authority of an eyewitness account documenting large parts of Norway that few in Denmark (and arguably, Norway) had ever seen.[10] There was therefore every reason to believe that the "intuitive knowledge" (intuitiv Belærelse) contained in Pram's topographical-statistical account would meet with spontan-

---

9   Pontoppidan's map of northern Norway (*Det Nordlige Norge*) appeared ten years later (Aanrud forth-coming: 17-18).

10   See Justin Stagl on the connection between authenticity and power in topographical travel accounts purporting to depict places the public have never been (1995).

STEPHANIE BUUS

eous acceptance in Norway itself, a country greatly in need of topographical information for its own nation-building project after 1814 (see Letter in Bull 1916: 439).

Such topographical information also constituted Norway's primary way of presenting itself to other nations in the first decades of the nineteenth century. In effect, topographical accounts such as Pram's served as a form of early advertising, a way of informing as well as enticing not only foreign, but also domestic travellers to visit unknown Norwegian shores. Steinar Supphellen writes of the significance attached to topographical literature in late-eighteenth-century Norway:

…the country [Norway] was to be discovered and presented both for countrymen and for other nations. Norway, which had hitherto been one of the least-known countries in Europe, ought to become one of the best-known countries. There were so many remarkable things there waiting to be discovered […]. (1979: 205)

Finally, Pram's belief that his topographical-statistical account of Norway would function as his passport to Norway after its separation from Denmark was very much in tune with the general view of domestic travel itself before and during Pram's time. As Justin Stagl points out, there was a strong European tradition dating back to the Renaissance of viewing travel within one's native land as an act of love for one's country, whatever the additional goals of such travel might be (Stagl 1995: Chapter 5). Olav Christensen writes of the patriotic value ascribed to the writer of topographical accounts as well as the patriotic value that these accounts in turn 'allowed' Norwegians to ascribe to their local landscapes during the eighteenth century:

Writing topographical texts was understood as a concrete expression of 'Love for the Fatherland' and civic obedience, a theme that prefaces [to these accounts] often revolved around. But topographic literature was also a means of glorifying the nation and one's place of origin […]. (1998: 60)

The historic connection between domestic travels and love for one's country meant that Pram's allegiance to Norway after 1814 ought to have required little, if any, proof. The proof was in his travels – a connection so conventional by Pram's time that it hardly seemed possible that he might be forced to defend his right to be called a Norwegian or to view his long residence in Denmark as constituting an identity not merely separate from, but indeed, *opposed to* a Norwegian identity.[11]

---

11   For more on the ethnic-civic distinction, see for example Anthony D. Smith, *The Ethnic Origins of Nations* (1986). See also Damsholt (2000).

Similar to other Norwegians in Copenhagen, many of whom were there as civil servants of the Dual Monarchy, Pram's writings reveal a less entrenched view of national identities and loyalties – a view that often encompassed shifting combinations of civic and ethnic definitions of collective belonging (Feldbæk 1998; Nettum 2001). In the words of another of Pram's contemporaries, Johan Nordahl Brun (1745-1816), a well-known poet, dramatist, and bishop who was also Pram's colleague in Copenhagen's famed Norwegian Society (Norske Selskab): "In a natural sense, Norway is our Fatherland; in a civic sense, both Denmark and Norway are." (Brun in Supphellen 1979: 206).[12]

As Pram was a lifelong and very vocal proponent of a more independent Norway *within* the confines of a continued Danish-Norwegian union, the way in which domestic travel seemed to offer him a quick ideological passport to Norway without forcing him to relinquish all ties to his previous life must have been an enormous comfort (cf. Nettum, 2001: 91). Theoretically, at least, the equation of domestic travels with love of one's native country allowed Pram to have his cake and eat it, too: on a mission of love for Norway after 1814; on a mission of patriotic duty for King and conglomerate state before, and even after 1814, should the Danish King decide to lay claim to Norway again.

The Patriotic Traveller Without a Letter

What works in theory, however, may not always work in practice, and such was the case with Pram. As it turned out, Pram's travel account did not rescue the author from a war of identities (a war that Pram would lose) nor did it earn him a place of glory in Norway or Denmark after the dissolution of their union. Indeed, Pram found himself unable to capitalize on his account in any way – politically, socially, or financially.[13] In Pram's first and only official letter to the newly-formed Norwegian nation in the summer of 1814, he cites his Norwegian travel account as proof of his worth as a Norwegian and urges the newly-formed government there to allow him "to be counted as a Norwegian" (at gielde for Nordmand) on the strength of its existence. In addition to his more abstract demand to be counted as a Norwegian, Pram's letter also asks the receiver for more concrete gifts, including immediate residence in Norway and the provision of employment there. As part

12 Øystein Sørensen suggests that the weight placed on allegiance to the King was another way in which Norwegian-Danish 'go-betweens' publicly negotiated questions of civic versus ethnic identity (2001: 41).

13 Pram failed to garner enough subscriptions to fund the publication of his collected writings (Bull 1916: 442-443).

STEPHANIE BUUS

of his plea for citizenship, Pram emphasizes the great achievement that his Norwegian travel account represents:

I [...] have struggled all of my life, especially in my thirty-three years of civil service, to mould myself after and to work almost entirely for my Norwegian Fatherland – that the most important and finest works from my once not-obscure authorship were dedicated to my Fatherland – that I, for this reason, took advantage of the King's order of a little more than ten years ago to procure important economic-statistical local knowledge about the State [of Norway], and that I visited more parts of the country's extensive districts in two travels lasting over two years than easily any other civil servant in his mature years; and, without other helpful aids, managed to find the opportunity to obtain intuitive knowledge, a knowledge that I then received a 4-year leave-of-absence to rework, to synthesize and complete with what I unearthed in archives and libraries, and which I…turned into many volumes [...] All of this may be something a great many of you are unaware of. (Bull 1916: 439)

In a strange turn of events, however, Pram never received a response to his letter. Norway simply failed to write back – a blow that Pram appears to have taken quite personally and a topic he returned to with great bitterness in letters to friends and acquaintances. As he writes in one letter:

Since my Fatherland's immense repudiation with hurtful silence of my modestly-expressed wish to live in and to serve this country so dear to me, I have quite naturally lost [...] the courage to present myself to any Norwegian as a compatriot [...] I must, God knows why, be in general disfavour in Norway. (Bull 1916: 441)

And in another letter:

Not one word in reply! Not one little excuse! Not even a feigned shadow of hope that there might with time come a small position that I could rejoice at in my final days, useful to my Fatherland [...] (Letter to Johan Collett dated 27 July 1814. In Nettum 2001: 23).

The mystery of the unanswered letter remains unsolved to this day, and has rarely been addressed in the literature available on Pram (see, for example, Bull 1916: 438). One exception is Rolf Nyboe Nettum's more recent bibliography, in which Nettum argues that Pram was the victim of his own outspoken opposition to a Norwegian union with Sweden prior to the signing of the Treaty of Kiel – an opposition that caused him to be blacklisted in Norway-Sweden once the union between them was a fact (2001: 94). There were, however, other Norwegians in Copenhagen who openly opposed the new union alongside Pram but did not suffer the same fate after 1814.[14] In a country struggling to consolidate and grow in the wake of 1814, as Norway was, any sort of information useful to the country's project of modernization ought to have been of great interest to the ruling elites both in Norway and even in Sweden – Norway's other half in the dynastic union forcibly established with the signing of the Treaty of Kiel (Eriksen and Sørensen 2001: 93; Barton 2002).[15] Pram's extensive statistical-topographical account of Norway *should* have found an interested audience among economically liberal circles in Norway, if nowhere else.

It is important to note, however, that Norway's modernization project – a project led by a large group of energetic civil servants, students, and young intellectuals in Oslo known as 'the intelligentsia circle' – did not in fact gain momentum in Norway until the mid-1840s (ibid.). It was only then that a nationwide project aimed at building and expanding Norway's fragile, and, in many places, non-existent infrastructure sprang to life (Eriksen and Sørensen 2001: 94). Perhaps, then, Pram's Norwegian travel account was simply written too early to be of use to Norway after 1814, a Norway whose immediate national concerns apparently lay elsewhere despite at the time, a severe lack of decent roads, internal trade and communication routes, and strong manufacturing base (Rogan 1998: 25-40).

Gerhard Schøning and Christen Pram

Like Pram, this chapter is inclined to treat the mystery of the unrequited letter and Norway's silence on the matter of Pram's Norwegian citizenship in symbolic terms, the missing letter representative of a relationship gone astray between sender and receiver – in this case, between Pram and Norway. In Pram's letter to the Norwegian government asking to be "counted as a Norwegian," it is his account of Norway that he offers up as evidence of his lifelong dedication to "my Norwegian Fatherland." His right to lay claim to a Norwegian identity is then directly linked to the value that he presumes this account and its "useful economic-statistical local knowledge" will have for the new state of Norway. This evidence elicits no response, however, a fact that could be attributed to an administrative oversight or a negligent mail carrier were it not for Pram's relative fame in Dual Monarchy

---

14   Jonas Anton Hielm was a fellow 'subversive' in Copenhagen in 1814, who, like Pram, openly opposed the union between Sweden and Norway. Hielm later became a successful lawyer and politician in Norway (Nettum 2001: 89-94).

15   Unfortunately, this chapter cannot address the reception of Pram's Norwegian account in Sweden after 1814. However, preliminary research suggests that Pram's account received little attention there, either (see, for example, Bring 1954: 111; 140 and Barton 2002).

STEPHANIE BUUS

circles at the time[16] and his many fruitless attempts to ascertain the fate of his letter in correspondence with high-profile figures in Norway (see Bull 1916; Nettum 2001; Amundsen 1969). Why did Norway fail to respond?

Norway's failure to respond to Pram's letter was an indication that Pram's *form* of patriotism, as much as Pram's patriotism itself, was in question. As it turned out, Pram allied himself with an unpopular portrait of Norway in his letter, one that lacked rhetorical force with the letter's readers. Despite a pronounced need for more topographies and other accounts mapping out the country's population, resources, provinces, and overall economic industrial position, many nation-builders in post-1814 Norway were not interested in the kind of utilitarian knowledge – and by extension, utilitarian "Norway" – that Pram had to offer in his nine-volume account. While a number of scholars have argued that the development of 'Norwegian-ness' was in many respects a political phenomenon in Norway after 1814; that Norway's constitution-makers and their political agenda were strongly influenced by the same Enlightenment, cosmopolitan, and liberal-capitalistic principles driving Pram's account of Norway (Witoszek 1997: 84-7; Schnitler 1911), other scholars have argued equally convincingly that Norway's aesthetic agenda was drawn early on to decidedly more romantic and nostalgic images of Norway (Eriksen and Sørensen 2001: 82-85; Fjeldstad 1998: 164-165).

Indeed, a number of ruling Norwegian elites, whose search for national symbols and pictures intensified in the wake of the events of the Napoleonic Era, developed at an early stage a set of tastes – an aesthetic tradition, one might say – that favoured the kind of atavistic ethno-historical accounts and images of Norway formulated not by Pram, but by those before Pram, particularly the Norwegian historian Gerhard Schøning (1722-1780) in his three-volume work entitled *Norges Riiges Historie* (The History of Norway) from 1771-81 (Sørensen 1998). Evidently, Schøning's timeless, Golden-Age images of unyielding wild fells and the self-sufficient heroism of the hearty Norwegian 'noble savage' – half-naked, belly full of Norwegian nature's unrestricted bounty, asleep on a pillow of snow – proved more attractive after 1814 than Pram's reports on manufacturing capacity at John Collet's aluminium factory in Trondheim or provost Abraham Pihl's request for a new threshing-machine from the Department of Commerce (*Kopibøker* 1964: 16; 19-20).

The Norway, then, that appealed to ruling elites in Norway in the wake of 1814 was highly incompatible with the vision of Norway that Pram espoused in his travel account. It was a picturesque Norway, not a progressive Norway that

---

16   After Johannes Ewald's death, Pram was briefly considered the leading poet in the Dual Monarchy (Nettum 2001). Together with Knud Lyhne Rahbek, Pram also co-founded the esteemed Copenhagen literary and social periodical *Minerva*.

dominated textual and visual portrayals of the country after 1814. This was a rural and epic Norway of the kind expressed in Erik Paulsen's painting, *Sarpsfossen i Norge*, from 1789 (Hagland 2001: 169) – a Norway uncorrupted by the works of man, untouched by the world (particularly the Danish world), and based vaguely on notions of primitive community and a pre-capitalistic society. These were visions intentionally far removed from – perhaps a defence against – the turmoil that Norway had experienced at various points at the beginning of the nineteenth century and visions that might also be interpreted as a rejection of the Danish multi-national state itself – its civic foundations and strongly urban focus, i.e. Copenhagen (Sagmo 1998: 85). This rural-epic topos was also one already long in vogue in the rest of Europe, and it featured regularly in numerous travel accounts of the Nordic countries written by non-Nordic travellers both before Pram's time as well as after Pram's death (Larsen 2001; Sagmo 1998; Barton 1998).

Perhaps, too, the myth of a happier, primitive Norway was a defence more generally against the freer and increasingly aggressive liberal economic politics espoused by theorists such as Adam Smith in his *Wealth of Nations* (1776) and gradually adopted by most European governments in the latter 1700s, the Danish Dual Monarchy among them (Dyrvik & Mykland 1976: 116-119). While the middle civil-servant class in Copenhagen was strongly supportive of freer trade, freer competition, and minimal state interference, civil servant elites in Norway advocated these policies even as they supported, or at least did not contest, a form of land ownership that was quite in opposition to contemporary liberal economic doctrine. Dating back to the Middle Ages, the law of *odelsrett* (allodial right) strongly contradicted notions of free competition and open markets, privileging instead the right of inheritance and the notion that hereditary property "could not be sold outside the family without its common consent and could be repurchased from an outside buyer upon demand of a family member at the buyer's purchase price within twenty years" (Barton 1986: 23). Allodial right clearly solidified and defended the position and influence of Norwegian peasant freeholders, but it did so at the expense of the open market because it obstructed the circulation of property and "the raising of credit against collateral." (Ibid; Kirby 1995: 74). Although many in Denmark and Norway took issue with the 'backwardness' of allodial rights and attempted to abolish this institution in 1811 and again around 1860, allodial rights were officially incorporated into the Norwegian Constitution at Eidsvoll in 1814 and continue to exist in Norway today (Barton 1987: 347; Eriksen and Sørensen 2001: 37).

In contrast, Pram's account offered an image of Norway based primarily on its cities and towns – on places of cosmopolitan exchange, circulation, and liberal-economic enterprise. Pram thus directed his gaze and his travel itinerary towards

STEPHANIE BUUS

urban centers and urban people, primarily civil servants, and he spent his days touring their factories, discussing methods that might increase production or decrease costs, and arguing the case of these struggling Norwegian industrialists to colleagues in the Department of Commerce. Indeed, Pram's account in no way idealizes the countryside or the pleasures of travelling through it. Upon arriving in the city of Trondheim in July of 1804, Pram writes most unsentimentally: "The date on my letter to the Department shows you that I have arrived here after a most difficult journey over the mountain that has the honour of being my birthplace" (*Kopibøker* 1964: 5).

Moreover, Pram travels to Norway as a representative of the Danish King and the Dual Monarchy. What he sees in Norway – and whom he sees – have therefore little to do with allodial farmers and almost everything to do with improving the state of manufacturing in Norway along liberal economic lines as well as maintaining ties and keeping the channels of communication between Denmark and Norway open during a time of crisis for the Dano-Norwegian union. In general, Pram has little interest in or use for the Norwegian farmer and he attaches no particular symbolic national importance to this figure. Indeed, he even seems to view the Norwegian farmer as a hindrance to Norwegian national interests precisely because he believes them to be provincial, backward, and less motivated than other groups in Norwegian society:

Everything [in Moss] shows signs of increasing wealth [...] The farms here are very small, reaching up to twenty acres of cultivated fields. The farmers run the farms least well, although increased motivation among them has also become more common. But everything seems to confirm the point that none of us will acknowledge, that agriculture begins to flourish when it leaves the hands of *farmers.* (1964: 3)[17]

In short, Pram's Norwegian travel account focused on what he perceived to be civilized nature and civilized people – on the developed landscape and the industrious citizen. Rather than adopting an atavistic stance, Pram's account of Norway was about how to reach the future, and its descriptions and letters emphasize technology, civilization, and capital as the best means to this end. Pram's Norwegian travels are thus the farthest thing possible from a picturesque voyage. They are, rather, a re-enactment of the forward March of Progress. As Pram writes of Vang, a place he passes through on his northwards trek to Trondheim:

17   Pram later states that "people outside of the farmer class" (Mennesker udenfor Bondestanden) are more cultured. *Kopibøger* 1964: 26.

One not only sees everywhere signs of lively fruitfulness, everything cultivated, everything protected, and enclosed; but one sees culture's effects, wealth in the tidiest abodes and well-built houses near each other; the roads now, too, are altogether excellent where once they were quite poor (1964: 25).

Not unlike its incongruous position in Denmark after 1814, Pram's travel account became equally trapped in an aesthetic time warp in Norway after 1814 – out of step with the current needs and tastes of the ruling elites in the country: too modern to be authentic; too cosmopolitan to be Norwegian, and too pragmatic to be epic. Ironically for Pram's account, it was Schøning's images of Norway that went national, or were nationalized, after 1814 and became the veritable "bible" of the Norwegian nation-building project after the 1820s (Olsen 1984: 400). Despite the fact that Schøning's 'map' antedated Pram's more modern version of a cosmopolitan, technological, and economically liberal Norway, it was this ethnohistorical map that painters, poets, and other travellers tended to follow when they went in search of the real 'Norway'. It is Schøning's *History of Norway* that is frequently named in the large and multi-faceted body of scholarship that exists on Norwegian nationalism, and it is Schøning's topographical accounts of Norway[18] that have been re-published in their entirety not once, but twice: first by Karl Rygh in 1910-1926 and most recently by Wilhelm K. Støren in 1979-1980 (Hagland 2001: 169). In the preface to the 1910-1926 edition of Schøning's topographical account, Rygh stresses precisely its seminal role in the Norwegian national project:

It is the most important literary account to emerge in Norway in the last part of the eighteenth century [and tells of] the eager efforts born of love for the Fatherland to learn more about the country and its conditions and to disseminate this knowledge. Almost simultaneously as well as later, the account generated a series of landscape and local descriptive accounts. (quoted in Hagland 2001: 170)

Conclusion: A Traveller Without an Audience

Not unlike Christian Molbech (1783-1857), a younger Danish contemporary of Pram, who chose rather unwisely in his travel account to search for proof of a glorious Danish past within the confines of an aesthetic largely antithetical to this search (Buus 2002; Damsholt 1999), Pram, too, was unfortunate enough to adopt a style and form of travel that literally frustrated his claims to nation. Pram chose

18   *Rejse som giennem en Deel af Norge i de Aar 1773, 1774, 1775 paa Hans Majestets Kongens bekostning er giort og beskreven* (Travels Conducted through a part of Norway in the Years 1773, 1774, 1775 Commissioned by His Majesty). Published in 1887.

to model his travelogue after Voltaire (Bliksrud 1999: 9; 40) when he ought to have modelled it after Rousseau The Enlightenment-style account that then resulted – cosmopolitan and multi-national, focused on Norway's infrastructural and industrial development, receptive to manufacturers and critical of farmers – would not provide Pram with any ground to stand on when the time came to lay claim to his Norwegian-ness. What proved ironic in Molbech's case, however, proved tragic in Pram's case, since Pram's claim to nation was not only more urgent than Molbech's, but the consequences of the 'rejection' of that claim proved far more harrowing for Pram personally.

Welcomed by some and vigorously opposed by others, the end of the 434-year union between Denmark and Norway in 1814 brought with it an end to Pram's domestic civil service career, his authorship, his life in Scandinavia, and ultimately, Pram's very existence. While Norway's star began to emerge from a long period of centralized, and by some accounts, colonial control at the hands of Denmark,[19] Pram's star headed south in April 1820 to the island of St. Thomas in the Danish West Indies and expired there in November 1821 after a fatal bout with yellow fever (Nettum 2001: 25-29).

The once-robust Pram, admiringly described by Adam Oehlenschläger as 'a fiery Norwegian full of spirit and heart,' spent his final days as an anonymous and ailing customs agent in an exotic place far from both Denmark and Norway, spurned and apparently forgotten not only by the country of his birth, but also by the country in which he had resided and worked for most of his life (Nielsen 1963: 62). In an indignant and anguished letter to a friend written three years after the end of the Dano-Norwegian union, Pram wrote of his increasingly vulnerable position as an ethnic Norwegian 'left' to reside in Denmark after 1814 and the eventual necessity of migrating to more distant climes:

As I am no longer able to bear living – disowned by my real Fatherland and treated the way I have been in Denmark because I have the misfortune to be born in Norway [...] – I now intend to leave this place and go – this will seem strange to you – to the West Indies [...] The former Deputy Councillor of State; Knight of the Dannebrog; widely-known, sevenfold-crowned author and poet; member of a great number of learned societies, and President of the Scandinavian Literary Society – he will leave in his 62nd year to become a broker on the Caribbean island of St. Croix [a Danish colony in the West Indies] – Sic transit gloria mundi. (Letter in Bull 1916: 442)

19   See, for example, Bagge and Mykland 1987: 8-9.

The way in which Pram's life ended and his subsequent place, or lack thereof, in the annals of Scandinavian literature after his death suggest a complicated tale of disgrace and disappearance. This in turn makes Pram a fascinating character to study, since his double-edged disappearance and the various reasons for it are so little acknowledged and so little studied on either side of the North Sea. Perhaps Pram's is the tale of the dark side of, if not exactly nationalism, then certainly the taking of sides and the loss of common ground that taking sides necessarily entails. Unlike Ludvig Holberg (1684-1754), whom both Denmark and Norway have scrambled to claim since the two countries separated, neither country seems particularly interested in claiming Pram. There is, for example, Willy Dahl's bewildering definition of Pram, whom he describes as "a Danish author it has been customary to include in Norwegian literary histories [...] He was Danish, but his writings are also part of Norwegian tradition" (2001: 214-219). As Dahl's definition of Pram would seem to indicate (a definition that manages to be muddled and categorical at the same time), it may well be that Pram's consistent attempts to play the *go-between*; to merge sides, or at least to keep them together as long as he could, ultimately left him with no side at all to stand on at the end of his life.

Though his transfer to the West Indies in 1817 was ultimately self-imposed, the move clearly represented an act of forced displacement in Pram's eyes – one born not of inclination, but of political, social and economic necessity.[20] What was codified, then, in the 1814 Treaty of Kiel was not only the permanent separation of Denmark and Norway but, in effect, the disenfranchisement of Pram as well. Like the letter that Pram waited for and never received from Norway, Pram, too, would eventually go missing. An examination of the reception of Pram's Norwegian travel account in the two countries for which it was written offers us one means of returning to the scene of this disappearance and re-tracing some of the steps that led to Pram's demise.

---

20   Pram's post as Deputy Advisor in the Department of Commerce disappeared, and he was given early retirement at one-third his earlier salary (Nettum 2001). See Maurseth (1983: 110) and Gøbel (2000) on the consolidation and abolition of many administrative departments and civil service posts at this time.

STEPHANIE BUUS

References

Aanrud, Roald (N.d.) Statens kartverk, Historie-prosjektet. Norwegian Mapping Authority.

Amundsen, Leiv 1969: Et brev Fra Christen Pram til Johan Collett. *Edda* LXIX.

Bagge, Sverre and Knut Mykland 1987: *Norge i dansketiden: 1380-1814*. Oslo: Cappelen.

Barton, Arnold H. 1986: *Scandinavia in the Revolutionary Era, 1760-1815*. Minneapolis: University of Minnesota Press.

Barton, Arnold H. 1998: *Northern Arcadia: Foreign Travelers in Scandinavia, 1765-1815*. Carbondale, Ill.: Southern Illinois University Press.

Barton, Arnold H. 2002: *Sweden and Visions of Norway: Politics and Culture, 1814-1905*. Illinois: Southern Illinois University Press.

Batten, Charles 1974: *Pleasurable Instruction: Form and Convention in eightteenth-Century Travel Literature*. Berkeley: University of California Press.

Bliksrud, Liv 1999: *Den smilende makten. Norske Selskab i København og Johan Herman Wessel*. Oslo: Aschehoug, 1999.

Bring, Samuel 1954: *Itineraria Svecana: bibliografisk förteckning över resor i Sverige fram till 1950*. Stockholm: Almqvist & Wiksell, 1954. Bredsdorff, Thomas 1999: Oehlenschläger's Aesthetics. Allegory and Symbolism in 'The Golden Horns' - and a Note on twentieth Century Eulogy of the Allegory. *Edda* IC: 211-21.

Brincker, Benedikte 2003: A 'Small Great National State': An Analysis of the Cultural and Political Factors that shaped Danish Nationalism 1760-1870. *Journal of Historical Sociology*, Vol. 16, No. 4: 407-431.

Buus, Stephanie 2002: Travel, Translation, and Self in Scandinavian Travel Accounts of the Napoleonic Era. Ph.D. diss., University of California Berkeley.

Christensen, Dan Ch. 1996: *Det Moderne Projekt. Teknik & Kultur i Danmark-Norge 1750-(1814)-1850*. Copenhagen: Gyldendal.

Christensen, Olav 1998: En nasjonal identitet tar form. Sørensen, Øystein ed.: *Jakten på det norske: perspektiver på utviklingen av en norsk nasjonal identitet på 1800-tallet*. Oslo: Ad Notam Gyldendal AS.

Dahl, Willy 1965: *Stil og struktur. Utviklingslinjer i norsk prosa gjennom 150 år*, 2nd ed. Oslo: Universitetsforlaget.

Damsholt, Tine 1999: En national turist i det patriotiske landskab. *Fortid og Nutid. Tidsskrift for kulturhistorie og lokalhistorie*, 1: 3-26.

Damsholt, Tine 2000: *Fædrelandskærlighed og borgerdyd. Patriotisk diskurs og militære reformer i Danmark i det sene 1700-tal*. Copenhagen: Museum Tusculanums Forlag.

Dyrvik, Ståle and Mykland, Knut 1976: *Norge Under Eneveldet 1720-1800*, 6, II. Bergen: Universitetsforlaget.

Feldbæk, Ole 1998: *Danmark-Norge 1380-1814. 4. Nærhed og adskillelse: 1720-1814*. Esben Albrectsen, Øystein Rian, Ståle Dyrvik, and Ole Feldbæk eds. Oslo: Universitetsforlaget.

Fjeldstad, Anton 1998: Fedreland og nasjon. Johnsen, Egil Børre and Eriksen, Trond Berg eds.: *Norsk litteraturhistorie. Sakprosa fra 1750-1995*. I. Oslo: Universitetsforlaget.

Frandsen, Steen Bo 1996: *Opdagelsen af Jylland. Den regionale dimension i danmarkshistorien 1814-64*. Århus: Århus Universitetsforlag.

Gøbel, Erik 2000: *De styrede rigerne: embedsmændene i den dansk-norske civile centraladministration 1660-1814*. Odense: Odense Universitetsforlag.

Hagland Jan Ragnar, 1998: Nordisk fortid og 1700-talets filologiske prosjekt. Johnsen, Egil Børre & Trond Berg Eriksen eds.: *Norsk litteraturhistorie. Sakprosa fra 1750-1995*. I. Oslo: Universitetsforlaget.

Kirby, David 1995: *The Baltic World 1772-1993: Europe's Northern Periphery in an Age of Change*. Harlow: Longman Publishing.

La Cour, Vilhelm 1943: *Mellem Brødre. Danske-Norske Problemer i det 18. Aarhundredes Helstat.* Birkerød: C.A. Reitzels Forlag.

Larsen, Stian Bones 2001: Gerhard Schøning, Gothicism, and the Re-evaluation of Northern Landscapes. *Acta Borealia* 18, 2: 61-84.

Lunden, Kåre 1992: *Norske grålysing. Norsk nasjonalisme 1770-1814 på allmenn bakgrunn.* Norway: Det Norske Samlaget.

Maurseth, Per 1983: Forvaltningen i Danmark-Norge før atskillelsen. Supphellen, Steinar and Kjelland, Arnfinn eds.: *Studier i norsk historie 1537-ca. 1800: Tvillingriket 1660-ca. 1800.* Oslo: Universitetsforlag.

Mykland, Knut 1983: Christian Frederiks støtter – Stormannsmøtet – Partidelingen – Embetsstandens grunnlov.

Supphellen, Steinar ed.: *Norske Historikere i Utvlag IX. Studier i norsk historie omkring 1814. Ein nasjon stig fram.* Oslo: Universitetsforlaget.

Nettum, Rolf Nyboe 2001: *Christen Pram. Norges første romanforfatter.* Oslo: Aschehoug.

Nielsen, Erik A. 1996: Runen. *Som Runer paa Blad.* Copenhagen: Akademisk forlag: 53-67.

Nielsen, Torben 1963: Prams Rejser i Norge 1804-06. *Fund og Forskning i Det Kongelige Biblioteks Samlinger* X: pp 60-98.

Olsen, Albert 1984: Norsk nationalisme. *Studier i norsk historie 1538-ca. 1800.*: Imsen, Steiner and Steinar Supphellen. Eds. Oslo: Universitetsforlaget.

Olwig, Kenneth 1984: *Nature's Ideological Landscape: A Literary and Geographic Perspective on its Development and Preservation on Denmark's Jutland Heath.* London: Allen & Unwin.

Pram, Christen 1964: *Kopibøker fra Reiser i Norge 1804-1806.* Oslo: Norske Kunst- og Kulturhistoriske Museer.

Pram, Christen 1804-1806: *Indberetning til de kongelige Land- Oeconomie- og Commerce Colzkninger paa en efter kongelig allerhøieste Befaling i Aaret 1805 fortsat Reise i Norge.* Unpublished manuscript. 9 vols. Copenhagen.

Pratt, Mary Louise 1992: *Imperial Eyes: Travel Writing and Transculturation.* London & NY: Routledge.

Rerup, Lorenz 1991: Fra litterær til politisk nationalisme: Udvikling og udbredelse fra 1808 til 1845. Feldbæk, Ole ed.: *Dansk Identitetshistorie: Et yndigt land 1789-1848,* 2. Copenhagen: C.A. Reitzels Forlag.

Rogan, Bjarne 1998: *Mellom tradisjon og modernisering. Kapitler av 1800-tallets samferdselshistorie.* Oslo: Novus Forlag.

Sagmo, Ivar 1998: Norge – et forbilde eller et utviklingsland? Sørensen, Øystein ed.: *Jakten på det norske: perspektiver på utviklingen av en norsk nasjonal identitet på 1800-tallet.* Oslo: Ad notam Gyldendal.

Schnitler, Carl 1911: *Slegten fra 1814: Studier over norsk embedsmandskultur i klassicismens tidsalder 1814-1840.* Kulturformene: Christiania.

Schøning, Gerhard 1771, 1773, 1781: *Norges Riiges Historie.* I-3, Sorøe.

Seip, Jens Arup 1974: *Utsikt over Norges historie. Tidsrommet 1814-ca. 1860.* I. Oslo: Gyldendal.

Stafford, Barbara Marie 1984: *Voyage into substance: Art, Science, Nature and the Illustrated Travel Account, 1760-1840.* Cambridge, Massachusetts: MIT Press.

Stagl, Justin 1995: *A History of Curiosity. The Theory of Travel 1550-1800.* Switzerland: Harwood Academic Publishers.

Supphellen, Steinar 1979: Den historisk-topografiske litteraturen i Noreg i siste halvparten av 1700-talet, regionalisme eller nasjonalisme? *Heimen* XVIII: pp. 198-211.

Sørensen, Øystein 2001: *Norsk Idéhistorie. Kampen om Norges sjel,* 3. Eriksen, Trond Berg and Øystein Sørensen eds.: *Norsk Idéhistorie.* Oslo: Aschehoug.

Witoszek, Nina 1997: Fugitives from Utopia: The Scandinavian Enlightenment Reconsidered. Sørensen, Øystein and Bo Stråth eds.: *The Cultural Construction of Norden.* Oslo: Scandinavian University Press.

STEPHANIE BUUS

Østergaard, Uffe 1992: Peasants and Danes: The Danish National Identity and Political Culture. *Comparative Studies in Society and History*, 34, 1.

Østergaard, Uffe 2002: The State of Denmark – Territory and Nation. *Comparare. European History Review* 2: 200-220.

Original Quotes

Hans Majestæt [har] befalet mig, at forføye mig ud i hans Rigers Provindser, for, som det Collegii Organ, hvis Medlem jeg har den Ære at være, at see mig om. Først fik jeg Ordre at gaa hid eller til denne fra Centret saa fierne Ende af hans Stater. Jeg gav mig til at see mig om her, saae alting meget bedre end man skulde vente det under 64° Brede, fandt mange fortreffelige Mennesker […]. (*Kopibøker* 1964, 41)

… landet skulle oppdagast og presenterast både for landsmenn og andre nasjonar. Noreg som hittil hade vore av dei minst kjende land i Europa, burde bli av dei mest kjende. Så mange merkverdige ting var der å oppdaga […]. Supphellen (1979, 205)

Å skrive topografiske tekster ble forstått som konkret uttrykk for 'Kierlighed til Fædrenelandet' og statsborgerlig underordning, et tema forordene gjerne sirkler omkring. Men topografisk litteratur var også et middel til å prise nasjonen og sitt hjemsted […]. (Christensen 1998, 60)

I en naturlig forstand er Norge vort Fædreneland; i en borgerlig er baade Danmark og Norge det. (Supphellen 1979, 206)

Gjennom forestillingen om nordmennenes spesielle kongetroskap var enevoldsregimet i København både ønskelig og nødvendig. Norge og nordmennene skulle finne sin plass innenfor dobbeltmonarkiet. Gjerne en mer fremtredende plass. Men nordmennene hadde en dobbelt binding. På den ene side et statsborgerlig, fornuftsmessig fellesskap med danskene og de andre etniske gruppene i monarkiet. På den annen side en direkte troskap til enevoldsmonarken som gikk utover statsborgerlige og fornuftsmessige forbindelser […] Den særnorske kongetroskapen, slik den ble forstått hos Johan Nordahl Brun og andre norske patrioter, utgjorde en ideologisk barriere

mot en norsk politisk nasjonalisme. (Sørensen in Eriksen and Sørensen 2001, 41)

At jeg […] har stræbt mit hele Liv igiennem, især paa min treogtrediveaarige Embedsbane, at danne mig for, og at virke for aldeles hovedsageligen mit norske Fædreland – at af mit engang ej obscure Forfatterliv dets vigtigste og modneste Frembringelser, var mit Fædreland indviede – at jeg saaledes benyttede det, mig for nu lidt mere end ti Aar siden af Kongen givne Bud, at søge at indhente nyttig oeconom-statistisk local Kundskab om Staten, saa jeg ved meere end to Aars Omrejser besøgte en større Deel af Landets vidtløftige Egne end lettelig nogen anden Embedsmand i de modne Aar, og ej ganske blottet for dertil hørende fundamentale Kundskaber, nogensinde fik min Lejlighed til at skaffe sig intuitiv Belærelse, en Belærelse, som jeg fik derpaa 4 Aars Otium til at diregere, at sammenholde og fuldstændiggiøre, med det jeg her opstøvede i Archiver og Biblioteker, og som jeg […] bragte til Resultater i mange Volumina […] Alt dette kan vel en heel Mængde blandt Eder være uvidende om. (Bull 1916, 439)

Siden mit Fædrelands Vældige forstødte med saarende Taushed mit ydmygeligt yttrede Ønske at leve og virke i og for dette mig saa kiære Land, har jeg heel naturligen tabt […] Modet til at fremstille mig for nogen Normand som Landsmand […] jeg, Gud veed af hvad Aarsag, maa staae meget ilde anskreven i Almindelighed i Norge. (Bull 1916, 441)

Ikke eet Ord til Svar! Ikke en lille Undskyldning! Ikke engang en fingeret Skygge af Haab at der maaske blev med Tiden en Smule Post, hvor jeg kunde fryde mig ved under Anvendelsen af mine sidste Dage, til Nytte for mit Fædreland […]. Letter to Johan Collett dated 27 July 1814 in Nettum. (2001, 23)

At jeg er kommen hid, efter en saare besværlig Rejse over det Field, som har den Ære at være mit Fødested, viser dig mit Brev til Collegium af Dags Dato. (*Kopibøker* 1964, 5)

Alting viser stigende Velstand [...] Bønder-gaardene ere her meget smaae, høyt til 20 Tønder Agerland. Bønderne ere de, som mindst vel drive Landhuusholdningen, dog begynder den bedre Drivt blandt dem ogsaa at blive almindeligere. Men alting synes at bekræfte den hos os ej erkiendte Sætning, at Landvæsenet kommer først i Flor, efterhaanden som det kommer ud af *Bøndernes* Hænder. (*Kopibøker* 1964: 3)

Man seer ej alene overalt Tegn til livlig Frugtbarhed, og god Cultur, alting dyrket, alting indfredet og hegnet, men man seer Culturens Virkning, Velstand, i idel pyntelige Boliger og velbygte Huuse nær hinanden; ogsaa ere nu Vejene, som hidtil vare temmelig slette, ofte heel elendige, nu aldeles fortreffelige. (*Kopibøker* 1964: 25)

Det er det betydeligste litterære vidnesbyrd om de ivrige, af varm fædrelandskjærlighed baarne bestræbelser for at lære landet og dets forhold bedre at kjende og udbrede kjendskabet til det videre, som træder frem i Norge i sidste halvdel af det 18de aarh., og som omtrent samtidig og senere ogsaa har affødt en række af landskabs- og bygdebeskrivelser. (Hagland 2001, 170)

Da jeg nu ikke længer kan holde ud at leve, forstødt af mit egentlige Fædreland, og saaledes behandlet i Danmark, fordi jeg har den Ulykke at være født der [...] så lægger jeg nu an paa at komme herfra, for at gaae – hvad der vil synes Dem pudseerligt – til Vestindien [...] Den forrige Deputerede Etatsraade, Ridder af Dannebrog – vidtbekiendt syvfold kronede Skribent og Digter – Medlem af en heel Deel lærde Corporationer, det scandin. Lit. Selskabs Præsident – gaar, i sin Alders 62de Aar som Mægler til den caraibiske Øe Ste Croix – Sic transit gloria mundi. (letter in Bull 1916, 442)

en dansk novellist som det har vært vanlig å ta med i norsk litteraturhistorie [...] Han var dansk, men hans diktning er en del også av norsk tradisjon. (Dahl 1965, 33)

STEPHANIE BUUS

KAREN LANGGÅRD

John Ross and Fr. Blackley
European discourses about Inuit and Danes
in Greenland 1700-1850

After several other Inuit cultures in Greenland, the Inuit forefathers of the Green-landers had emigrated from Alaska into Greenland by the end of the twelfth cen-tury A.D.[1] The Norsemen had settled there some 200 years earlier, had adopted Christianity soon afterwards, and had submitted to the Norwegian king in the eleventh century, but disappeared during the fifteenth century.

In 1700 the Inuit Greenlanders did not really consider Greenland to be part of Scandinavia! But from a Scandinavian viewpoint, Greenland – even without contact – was under the sovereignty of Denmark-Norway because of the Norse subjection to the Norwegian king. Some Norse Christians were imagined still to live in Østerbygden (the Eastern of their two settlements in Greenland), and Øs-terbygden was thought to be in East Greenland, but inaccessible because of drift ice.

In 1721 the priest Hans Egede started the Danish mission and the colonization of Greenland. In 1733 the Moravian Brethren (= the Herrnhuts) came, too. A cul-tural meeting resulted between Nordic Europeans (Danes and Norwegians) and Southern Europeans (the German Moravians and various other Europeans who were whaling or on voyages of discovery), and of course the Inuit.

This paper delineates the views of non-Nordic Europeans about the Inuit and the Nordic Europeans in Greenland from 1700-1850. The main focus is on the re-ports from two trips made in the 1820s, written by John Ross and Fr. Blackley. Both of them have a double context: the European negotiation of ethnicity in its dis-courses on 'savages'/native others (especially the Inuit in Greenland and Canada) and the European negotiation of nationality in its discourses on other Europeans. The questions are to what degree the Greenlander's conversion to Christianity in-fluenced European views of the Inuit, and how non-Nordic Europeans looked on Nordic Europeans in Greenland.

---

1   For this dating – 200 years later than formerly presumed – see Gulløv (ed.) 2004.

Concepts from Postcolonial Studies and Cultural Studies will be used in the analysis of the texts and their use of the discourses on Inuit. Ethnic identity is thus seen as negotiable.

Greenland before Hans Egede

The Vikings did not doubt their own superiority when they first encountered the Inuit in Vinland. They called them 'Skraellings' (i.e. weaklings). With regard to Greenland, we have a narrative on how Vesterbygden (the Western of the two settlements) was found abandoned and at the mercy of the Skraellings (Bárdarson mid-fourteenth century, in Jónsson 1930). The European contact to Greenland ceased. The sailing route sank into oblivion in the fifteenth century and Eric the Red's Greenland became the Old/Lost Greenland to Europeans. The (new) Greenland was Spitzbergen (see e.g. Martens 1675), where whaling took place until it moved west in the eigthteenth century and became Straat Davis Trade (see e.g. Zorgdrager 1723(1720).

Up until colonisation by the Danes, sources based on older texts or rumours focus on the fate of the Norse population. However, if they do mention the Inuit, they see them as the exterminators of Vesterbygden (e.g. Arngrim 1688; Torfæus 1706); hairy trolls (e.g. Blefken 1606); pygmies, in full accordance with Aristotle's climatology, or even pirates – sinking ships from their kayaks by *boring holes from under the water* (e.g. Olaus Magnus 1555:68ff and Grønlands Historiske Mindesmærker I-III 1979(1838-1845), espec. II: 464ff).

Old Greenland was rediscovered by John Davis in 1585-87 and expeditions meant new data on the Inuit. Davis describes the Greenland Inuit as idolators of the sun, co-operative and easily inducible to politeness, but extremely thievish (Davis 1930(1589)).

In the seventeenth century the Danish kings again showed interest in Old Greenland and took the lead in expeditions (e.g. Lindenow 1605 and Cunningham 1605, David Dannel 1654). They even took part in the quest of the North West Passage (e.g. Jens Munch 1619), and on the request of the monarch such expeditions brought home specimens of 'savages'. This became the theme in poetic works written by Jens Bielke 1608, C.C. Lyschander 1608, and Adam Olearius 1656. Lundgreen-Nielsen (1989 and undated), and later Harbsmeier (2001) describe how a pattern recurs in these poems: the savages behaved as if untameable, but were kept down with an iron hand and appeared totally tamed and subjugated to the king and his guests (see also Bobé 1927:5ff). Isaac de Peyrère (1647), who gathered information in Denmark about Danish sources, made data accessible to Europeans through his writings.

Because of thefts by the Inuit and abductions by the Europeans, even trading encounters between them grew violent in many cases. The aim of an otherwise rather positive and detailed description of the Inuit – written by Lourens Feykes Haan and based on his own experiences – was clearly to warn European travellers: page after page he describes how cruel and dangerous the Inuit can be towards the Europeans, but neglects to mention the European abductions (Haan, 1914(1720)).[2]

Hans Egede and sons. The Moravian Brethren and their historian Crantz

The decisive turning point in the description of Greenland's population came with Hans Egede (1686-1758) and his sons. They settled down as a family and were not scared off by the climate. Having the Norrlandene north of the Polar Circle as a standard of comparison, they started learning Greenlandic, and although this was difficult for Egede, he acknowledged the paramount importance of language. Furthermore, by proving themselves different from the European travellers and whalers, the Egede family won to a certain degree the confidence of the Greenlanders over the years, especially when an epidemic of smallpox struck the population.

Egede's attitude to the pagan Inuit was rather pragmatic: he showed much flexibility as long as it did not compromise his Christian faith. However, driven by the impatience of those financing the Mission and his own zealous wishes, he sometimes felt compelled in his verbal fights with the Greenlandic shamans to threaten to kill them – he would add that the Greenlanders already knew him well enough not to take the threat seriously. Sometimes he referred to the power of the Danish King not only as a threat, but also as a protection against other Europeans (e.g. Egede 1925:151 ff). Although his zeal made him complain about the indifference of the adults, and underline that the Inuit would have to obtain more knowledge about this world before they could understand Christianity, he also emphasized that the children learned whatever was taught as easily as European children.[3] Furthermore, he compared their "superstitions" with those known from Antiquity or from the Jews. Egede's writings show him discussing not with trolls but with human beings, and responding to their arguments. In his descriptions the Inuit appeared as individuals to the European readers.

Strack (1994) claims that Egede operated within more discourses: first and foremost within the religious-assimilative discourse, without any room for religious ideas outside those of European Christianity. Lack of Christian religious

---

2   For this section, see Gad 1967.

3   See e.g. concluding pages of *Perlustration* (Egede 1925).

concepts was seen as lack of reason. The morality of the Greenlandic way of life was reduced to an innate virtue given by Nature. However, insight into the Greenlandic culture drew Egede and his sons to describe the Inuit culture on its own premises using the descriptive-scientific discourse, and therefore, his descriptions were very heterogeneous. Pragmatic flexibility without religious compromising would be a more adequate characterization of Egede.

Ever since Antiquity two discourses on the barbarians/the savage others have spread throughout Europe: the savage as an animal versus the noble savage – as well as two discourses on the development of the world: decay versus progress. The savage other has been one of the significant others to the Europeans. During the Renaissance the holistic perspective on man split into a religious sphere and a secular sphere, and the secular sphere would then be described without direct reference to Christianity, but within a Christian frame. Most people would still consider man as originating from Adam and Eve. It was discussed what happened to the savages after the creation of man, since they must have lost their original knowledge of God. It was considered how to convert them. The more knowledge that was gathered by Europeans about the savages, the more complex the picture of their culture became – and the more difficult it became to fit them into the stereotypes of the overall models (Høiris 2000). Egede's reports were written within this Christian period and before the Danish enfolding of the Enlightenment, i.e. under religious constraints (see Bredsdorff 2003) which however would be in accordance with Egede's missionary project. Hans Egede looked, as even Haan did, for signs of a former acquaintance with God. As was the habit of the Jesuits among American Indians (Høiris 2001:20), he had to decide which of the Greenlandic customs should be abandoned for the sake of salvation, and which should not be abandoned. After having considered seriously whether the performances of the Inuit shamans should be seen as devilry, Egede chose first and foremost to undermine the shamans by showing the Greenlanders that they were fakes and should be condemned.

To the Europeans, the work done by the Egedes together with the Moravian Brethren meant the conversion of some savage heathens, and so they became less mysterious and less dangerous. Egede's message to the Danish authorities and to his other European readers was that the Inuit culture had to be changed basically by conversion to Christianity, and that this was possible.

The Moravian Brethren had their own missionary policies, but in many ways they were in line with Egede's. In the mid-1760s David Crantz wrote a history of Greenland, first and foremost to describe the missionary achievements of the Moravians. Apart from what he witnessed during his one-year stay in Nuuk, he built on Egede's writings and on letters and reports sent by the Moravians to Neu Herrnhut since 1733.

Both Egede's and Crantz' reports showed how Greenlanders had critical attitudes and asked critical questions. The Moravians would report this as stupid and wicked, while Egede – and even more so his son, Poul Egede,[4] (1939(1788)) – would be less condemning. Deconstructing the texts of the Egedes and the Moravians, Greenlanders are seen to exert a high degree of agency in the cultural transformation taking place through their cultural meeting with the missionaries. Both Egede and Crantz showed the readers how individual Greenlanders responded in individual ways to their fate and to the Europeans and Christianity. The Inuit were lifted away from myth and anonymity, and considered individual human beings.

Crantz's work was published in 1765, after Hans Egede's descriptions of Greenland had been published in German, English, Dutch and French.[5] Both Crantz and the translations of Egede into European languages disseminated the picture of the Inuit as human beings who with slow progress, but beyond doubt, could be converted and who already possessed some morality and some human intellect and reason concerning their own mutual relations. The reputation of the Greenlanders could change from dangerous savages to converted natives with some degree of civilisation, living in model colonies established by the Danes.

Crantz, the European, stressed the ground-breaking contribution made by Egede before the arrival of the Moravians, and the theological and intellectual weight of Egede versus the Moravian Brethren, who were not scholars. This was indeed a great tribute and mark of respect to a man from the northernmost part of Scandinavia, regardless of the tensions which must have existed between the two missions.[6]

After Hans Egede

With access to Egede's and Crantz descriptions of Greenlanders, and of their meetings with Danes and Germans in Greenland, what were the views of non-Nordic Europeans about Greenlanders and about Nordic people living in Greenland? Accounts of knowledge compiled about Greenland/the polar areas/West Nordic countries,[7] and travel reports from the same areas,[8] are influenced by the tone set by Egede about the Greenlanders, and keenly distinguish between pagan Inuit

---

4   Thanks to a greater language competence, but also thanks to the fact that he could write more freely because the editing took place when the cultural climate in Denmark had changed and the Enlightenment had begun.

5   For a list see Bobé's introduction to Egede 1925.

6   For new details, see Bredsdorff 2004.

7   E.g. Anderson 1746; Kergeulen 1771, Barrow 1818; Lesley, Jameson and Murray 1835; Nicoll 1840.

8   E.g. Giesecke 1910(1813); O'Reilly 1818; Manby 1822; Ross 1819 and 1835; Blackley 1939.

and Greenlanders under the impact of Christianity. They are all positive towards Egede and even glorifying biographies were written about him, such as, *Hans Egede und seine Gattin unter den heidnischen Grönländern. Ein schönes Lebensbild für Jung und Alt* (Hans Egede and his wife among the heathen Greenlanders. A lovely model for Young and Old people) 1852.

However, this does not mean that information on Egede and his work reached far and wide. In some descriptions a cultural lag is seen. Further, the focus can differ from Egede's: the important thing for Egede and for the other missionaries was conversion. Egede mentioned, for example, the stench in Inuit dwellings, but added that when one eventually grew accustomed to it, it was not so unbearable (Egede 1925:369). Others (e.g. Half Hour 1883:141f) would, by contrast, make many more comments on stench and the like.

An analysis below of two travel reports written by Sir John Ross and by the Rev. Fr. Blackley – the latter in Minstrel form – will demonstrate in more detail how the varying discourses were used and mixed according to personality and goals.

John Ross' encounters with Inuit and Danes in Greenland 1829

In the eighteenth century the quest for Straat Davis and the North West Passage started. In the first half of the nineteenth century both whaling and exploring accelerated in the Arctic region. Most of the expeditions were carried out by the British Navy, and most of these ran into serious problems. They were not supposed to use indigenous knowledge and those who did had more participants than the native groups and the land could sustain. Even when somebody experienced how useful collaboration with Indians and Inuit could be and how much one could learn from them about survival strategies, the Navy did not use that knowledge (Feeney 1997). Nor did it use all the know-how of the whalers (among these especially Scoresby) (Fleming 1998). John Barrow ruled with cynicism as Second Secretary of the British Admiralty 1816-1845. Failure was failure, no matter how conditions had been (Fleming 1998).[9]

John Ross (1777-1856) was in command of two expeditions searching for the North West Passage in 1818 and from 1829 to 1833, and a third one searching for Franklin from 1850 to 1851. Sent by the Navy in 1818 he met the Polar Eskimos and then went on to Canada, but without success there. It was a very cold period, and Ross was very cautious. He was heavily criticized afterwards and was never em-

---

9   According to Fleming 1998:11 Barrow was called the father of Arctic exploration, but should rather be called the father of global exploration.

ployed by Barrow again. Barrow had even invested prestige in him by publishing his expectations of him and the first expedition (Barrow 1818).

On his second expedition in 1828, a mutiny forced Ross to sail off with only one ship and half the crew – an advantage in collaborating with the Inuit. This time supported by a private businessman he could travel further into the Arctic than before. Furthermore, he and his men were experienced with arctic conditions. His nephew, Commander James C. Ross (1800-1862) had even been with Parry near the area to which they were now heading.

The climate was more favourable, the ship better constructed, and John Ross eager to do better than last time. They forced their way into the Canadian straits, beyond the point reached by then from the East. Areas were mapped and named. The British colours were planted on many spots. They survived four winters in Arctic Canada, not least by establishing good relationships with local groups of Inuit.

Pratt (1992) describes how the expedition reports evolved during the eighteenth century from the adventure genre into the scientific one, justifying the expeditions by professing a pure scientific goal. The report written by Ross (1935) is a mixture containing a narrative part and a systematic part. He describes the narrative part as "my narrative, which is carried on in the shape of a journal, was written by myself daily." (xii). It was of course edited later; Ross often sums up an incident or an evaluation in the perspective of the whole expedition.

Ross was expected to bring back scientific results by collecting specimens and by gathering data about the weather, the geological occurrences and the magnetic North pole, but clearly the first priority was to facilitate British commercial interests. His expeditions made him doubt any commercial outcome. According to him, the British Empire ought to carry the explorations through to a successful mapping of the Arctic, as "a matter of just boast to Britain"(xviii).

Ross's attitudes towards Greenland

On 23 July 1829, Ross anchored near the coast of West Greenland, just north of the Polar Circle. He was positively surprised by the landscape and its picturesque mountains.[10] On his first voyage in 1818, snow had obscured everything. The near by island even reminded them (61): "of the far fairer lands which we had quitted but a month before". Although aware of some dogs on the island, they were taken by surprise at the sight of a Danish flag, accompanied by kayaks:

10   Very different from most of the landscape he would find in Canada (a burden for a European during a period with a passion for the picturesque mountain landscape as found in Switzerland and later in Norway).

They were alongside almost as soon as they were seen; and we were pleased to find that there were two Europeans in the crowd, which at first seemed to consist of Esquimaux alone; being dressed in the usual clothing of the natives. (62)

Ross's stereotyping of the Europeans' clothing overwrote the message of the Danish flag. He had to revise his wrong ideas, especially when told that these two Danes represented the Danish State, one in charge of the district, the other as a clergyman. His vocabulary changes: the man from the Trading Company is described as a person of very prepossessing manners and appearance, and is placed in the military rank hierarchy, while the clergyman, Kjer,[11] is "with the manners and language of a well educated and intelligent man" (63). The presentation switches to a much more formal language code. When Ross bought some supplies from a shipwrecked whaler that was left under the Danish governor's charge, the negotiations are also reported in a rather formal language.

However, Ross was still unprepared for the settlement's ability to provide hospitality, and was taken by surprise when they landed under a salute:

… an honour which I did not expect, but which we returned afterwards, of course, as soon as an opportunity occurred. (66)

Paying tribute to the Danes by using the word "mansion", Ross continues his narratives:

We were received by Mrs Kijer, who was in waiting to conduct us to their hospitable mansion. … Fortunately, knowing the Danish myself, I was enabled to converse with this lady also, as her knowledge did not, like her husband's, extend to the English language. We were treated with what we might here consider an elegant repast of venison and other things, and served by Esquimaux females in their native costumes, but far surpassing in cleanliness those with whom we had been in communication on former occasions, and moreover decorated with a profusion of beads, while their hair was bound with pink handkerchiefs.

After dinner we inspected the settlement … (66)

Ross further notices that the Inuit actually helped them with the ship (70), and that he even experienced the honesty of the Inuit (72). His conclusion:

11   1802-65, missionary in Sisimiut 1823-1831

… I do but justice to the natural character of this race, almost every where within our experience, to say that they are among the most worthy of all the rude tribes yet known to our voyagers, in whatever part of the world. (73).

During this cultural meeting in Sisimiut, Ross thus experiences several feelings and responses. He is on the alert, until he realizes that the crowd includes two Europeans. Finally, he can even relax while natives are present, thanks to the civilization process being carried out by the Danes. However, while he does pay homage to the work being done by the Danes in Greenland, he never at any point abandons the feeling of being superior by being British.

Ross's attitudes in relation to Arctic Canada

While Ross's systematic description from the Canadian Arctic is quite sober, the narrative is much harsher than the Greenlandic. It reveals more clearly the author's personal pattern of reaction, depending on the theme – but even more on the degree of pressure felt – and thereby throws light on the dynamics of the Greenlandic meeting. The following key themes illustrate first some of his positive attitudes, and then some of the negative ones:

Food and clothing: Ross's text was open-minded and pragmatic on the very sensitive subjects of food and clothing, both being clearly part of the ethnic-national self-respect of Europeans fearing 'to go native' – the food maybe even more than the clothing (Oct. 1829):

… This [i.e. to be well-fed], doubtless, explains in a great measure, the resisting powers of the natives of these frozen climates: their consumption of food, it is familiar, being enormous and often incredible. (200).

… that in every expedition or voyage to a polar region, at least if a winter residence is contemplated, the quantity of food should be increased, be that as inconvenient as it may. It would be very desirable indeed if the men could acquire the taste for Greenland food; since all experience has shown that the large use of oil and fat meats is the true secret of life in these frozen countries, and that the natives cannot subsist without it; … (201)

[and many expedition men would have been saved] if they had been aware of these facts, and had conformed, as is so generally prudent, to the usages and the experience of the natives. (201)

Ross even tried to prove to the crew that if the fat is removed, the flesh of sea birds and seals is tasty (38-39,134-135), but he did not convince them (615).

Contact with the Inuit: January 1830, Ross and his men got into contact with the Inuit around Boothia and Netsilik (241). Much later they understood that the Inuit had been watching them for some time. Although the Europeans were the 'displaced persons' in strange surroundings, they adapted to some degree to the conditions – at least in comparison to those from the British Navy expeditions.

Ross described the Inuit as well dressed (243). Later on he bought some clothes from them:

If our meeting with the Esquimaux had been, in many ways, interesting as well as amusing to us, so was it an acquaintance which could be rendered serviceable. They had already furnished us with some dresses, much more useful to the men than those which we had brought from England, and we had reason to expect more.

It was probable also that they might supply us with fresh meat; thus enabling us to economise our own stores.

The information which they had given us was of even higher importance: while we now also hoped, that by means of their dogs and sledges, we should be able to examine a great deal of the coast, so as to decide on our future motions by sea, long before we should be released. ….. (278).

Ross was very impressed by the Inuit's ability to map the area (263). When he tested them about areas already mapped by the British, he got valuable knowledge from them several times – as had Parry. Certainly, he acknowledged their hunting competence and benefited from it.

Control and ethnocentrism: Impressed or not, Ross made every effort always to be seen as the person in control of situations in order to ensure the safety of his expedition, but also to maintain a feeling of superiority, although he often had to admit that the Inuit were much better in certain situations. However, it was important for him to ensure that they, 'the Others', were impressed and he would often attain this end through something not reckoned as anything special by the British themselves. For example, Ross impressed the Inuit when his carpenter made a wooden leg for one of them:

… and we felt, of course, carpenter and all, the full triumph of superior civilization; as the people themselves evidently admitted that we were a more cunning race than they, though we could not equally harpoon seals at an ice hole, nor eat walrus flesh stewed in train oil. (271f)

Ross fully acknowledged ethnocentrism among the Inuit, without however reflecting much on his own:

KAREN LANGGÅRD

... that custom alone, were vanity of no account, causes the savage to estimate his own clothing, or the want of any, at a much higher rate than all which even a Stultz could produce, to value and cling to his own modes of life, and his own food, repulsive as it may be to ourselves, far beyond all that can be offered in exchange. ... (272).

Although he understood the need for "Greenlandic food", his prejudices show up first and foremost about the Inuit's interest in eating and their capacity for it. His prejudices in this regard also become more abundant when problems arise for the expedition or for Ross himself. To express how atrocious it is to him, in April and July 1830 he uses expressions like these:

... feeding, much like swine, ... (320)

... since, while we found that one salmon, and half of another (boiled), was more than enough for all of us English (5), these voracious animals (12) had devoured two each. At this rate of feeding, it is not wonderful that their whole time is occupied in procuring food: each man had eaten fourteen pounds of this raw salmon, and it was probably but a luncheon after all, or a superfluous meal for the sake of our society. .... would doubtless outrival a glutton and a boa constrictor together. .... The Esquimaux is an animal of prey ... like the vulture and the tiger. . (446-48).

In comparison, Parry ate Inuit food while visiting Inuit dwellings, and saw their enormous consumption as an improvident and unhealthy habit, but without the derogatory vocabulary used by Ross (1824:290 and 293; 1824:412-13).

Dislocation: When forced to winter over for the second time, Ross described the dislocation (Dec.1830):

The whole life is here curtailed ... a sound philosopher would come to the conclusion that it is the Esquimaux alone who here know the true secret of happiness and the rational art of living; ... The Esquimaux eats but to sleep, and sleeps but to eat again as soon as he can ... The adaptation is perfect, his happiness is absolute. Had we been better educated, we should have done the same; but we were here out of our element, as much in the philosophy of life as in the geography of it. (489).

After having been considered dead for two years, when they finally reach their fellow Brits again in 1833, Ross begins to see themselves once more with the imperial gaze, and the Irish beggar replaces the Inuit as the significant Other:

... no beggar that wanders in Ireland could have outdone us ... dressed in the rags of wild beasts instead of the tatters of civilization ... (721).

Ross under pressure

In Arctic Canada the pressure on Ross became extreme in the harsh surroundings combined with his growing awareness of the limitations set by his age. In Volume I (the more narrative part of his report) his tirades towards the Inuit became full of contempt – one could even say full of savage rage, especially concerning their eating habits.

He admitted the kindness of the Inuit and their good workmanship. But the more he came under pressure, the more he needed to show his contempt for their eating habits and to show how incompetently they responded to European technical skills and European culture, and how profound their lack of fine arts or anything on a par with European philosophy was. The captain starts as a captain, but ends up as a human being fighting for survival and for control. The development and the special features of Ross's response to situations become very clear when compared with the ways Parry and Lyon describe things in the same area of the Canadian Arctic (Lyon, 1825; Parry 1968(1821) and 1969(1824)).

We witness parallels to the dichotomy of Orientalism in Ross's travel report, intersected with humanism whenever he, for a while, is open minded and reflecting on cultural diversity. But he suppresses his humanism whenever he wants to honour his country and his own culture – and even more whenever he is under pressure.

No matter how much Ross has to admit that the Inuit are those who are best adapted and with full agency in the Arctic, and the fact that he and his men have been dependent on their services, the European hierarchy and the British imperial hierarchy are nevertheless upheld and not to be shaken (as is Ross's upper-class discourse towards his crew also). His attitudes must be seen as part of a cultural context, where the view of savages is a topic with a long history in European thinking (see above), but this doesn't explain his indignant tone.

The more systematic Volume II of Ross's report refers to Volume I for detailed descriptions, whenever such are already included there. However when describing eating habits in Volume II, he is quite sober in his vocabulary and ascribes it more to "the necessity of doing something" i.e. being an energetic and active people (20). This is in full accordance with the picture he draws of the Inuit he met; a picture, which in many ways is an empathic and positive one. Further, he makes the Canadian Inuit become individual human beings: Volume II contains a series of illustrations depicting Inuit individuals, with biographies added.

316   KAREN LANGGÅRD

Ross seems to have tried to manipulate the description of his own role to a very high degree, and the narrative is edited.[12] However, the narrative (Volume I) of his second report still shows us a man desperately fighting not to totally lose his influence and agency and his authority. It shows us a man who needs to underline time and again that he is taking care of his crew in a very competent manner. The more stress, the more fierce verbal attacks he makes in his report on the real others, the Inuit.

Blackley: The Greenland Minstrel

The Greenland Minstrel, a poem in Six Cantos with an Introductory Narrative. Illustrated from Drawings taken on the spot during a voyage to Greenland in the year 1826 was, according to the title page, published by Rev. Frederick R. Blackley, curate of Rotherham in 1839. I found no further data on him. The voyage is said to have taken place in 1826, three years before Ross' visit to Sisimiut.[13] Even if he never was in Greenland, his poem still contains attitudes towards the Others.

In his introductory narrative Blackley describes how he set out from Edinburgh on a journey to the North on board the ship "U- of H- commanded by Captain J – ", visited Greenland, saw the inhabitants and in the midnight sun saw parts of North America. However, the ship hit an iceberg and called at Sisimiut, where Blackley became familiar with missionary Kjer and spent one of the most interesting periods of his life. He quotes a long passage from John Ross's report on Sisimiut (xv ff). Kjer's life full of hardships impressed Blackley deeply. He praises the work done by Kjer and the whole Danish Mission and especially "the great Egede". After mentioning the dangers that he had been through (as a real traveller should), he describes the Inuit and their patterns of reactions, apparently in order to establish as a fact already here that the Inuit are not "devoid of" good characteristics like affection, devotion and gratefulness (especially after having received guidance from Christian missionaries). The Inuit neither lack predisposition to civilization when tutored, nor are they devoid of reason and initiative: "Christianity is doing great things for them" (xxv). For each of these characteristics he adds examples to substantiate his statements. "Greenlanders possess courage, and that is often tested when on hunting, and they are not devoid of compassion and energy: the Greenlanders of Sisimiut often rescue the shipwrecked" – and:

12   He was severely attacked in writings, especially after the second expedition, for not having taken care of his men and for not attributing to his next in command, his nephew commander James C. Ross the honour that he deserved (Huish 1985; Dennett 1839). He would pay tribute to others but only as long as this would contribute to his own role as leader. It would stop as soon as he felt his superior status to be threatened. However, it is not the focus here to discuss this further.

13   Langgård 2006 contains more quotes from Blackley.

Where the natives have received instruction they have made considerable progress in civilization; their houses are better built … books are valued and preserved with great care. (xxv).

Thus he is positive towards the Greenlanders and Greenland. But when he describes significant parts of the Arctic nature, he ends up with the magnificent English nature:

They soon reached their happy home, and felt more and more attached to England, the highly-favoured land of their nativity. (xxxi).

He urges the British to make a greater effort in their missionary work in the Arctic, in North-America, and in Greenland. To strengthen his case he includes a quote from Bishop Heber's *From Greenland's icy mountains* (xxxii)[14].

A small postscript tells that he has later on been to Continental Europe, staying for two years in Switzerland. He draws parallels between Greenland and Switzerland regarding the landscape, but also regarding the close attachment of the mountain dwellers to their birthplace.

His introductory prose narrative thus shows that his basic goal is to stimulate the British to start missions in the Arctic area. He depicts the Inuit in a very positive way in general, and especially those who have been exposed to the mission, without mentioning anything negative. He is effusively positive about the work done by the Danish Mission.

Cantos I-V

In the cantos, the positive attitude continues but, in several ways, more clearly within the British imperial discourse. Reading the cantos we find the concept of *terra nullius*: In Canto I, Greenland is a *terra nullius*, except for some vagrant dwarfish savages – or later in connection with the Norse population, the Skreelings (Canto I):

Mine be the task to sing of lands of snow,
Of icy grandeur spread, where'er you go
Where dwarfish tribes in state untutor'd stray,
And Greenland wonders tempt the ventr'ous lay; (3).

---

14   For the hymn written by Heber (1783-1826), Anglican Bishop of Calcutta, see s.v. Heber Greenland Icy on Google, e.g. www. theotherpages.org/poems.

Whether by hunger, cold, or Skreelings slain
Their settlements in ruins now remain! (6)

After the Norse period, Greenland is "this lost island" and it is deserted, "where once a hundred towns have flourished well". There is no direct mention of the Inuit's presence in this Norse perspective, but hints to the explorations during the times when nobody could find the way to Greenland. The British are mentioned with praise for their efforts: "The matchless sons of fair Britannia's shore!" (12).

Nature is seen as anxiety-provoking. The scenery of ghastly nature (e.g. Canto I, p 4: "These strike the traveller's mind with solemn dread, …") is a recurrent theme of the cantos. Nature is harsh in Canto II, but Gothic with sublime scenery, too (not least because of its mountains). It's even "perfect" as part of the Creation. The Greenlanders are remerging in the perspective. The Greenlanders love their birthplace, their country (like those in Switzerland) and have no interest in all the riches of the world (Canto II, p 24), i.e. the poem adhedes to the idea of the noble savages. They are seen both as human beings who actually love their country and as barbarians because of their choice of a country not comparable to Greece and Rome. Yet, when Blackley personifies the moon, it is seen as a counterpart to Phoebus – out of poetic convention. Blackley sort of oscillates (e.g. Canto II):

The Greenland regions no such sweets convey
But scenes peculiar and sublime display;
And rocks, and hills, and seas, and vallies show,
God's works, all perfect in that world of snow!
Man too finds here, in northern lands a home,
And loves, unknown, in barb'rous clans to roam,
Although the summer scarce may tinge the plain
With verdant hues, ere winter comes again
How diff'rent this from genial lands,
…. (16).

Blackley depicts the tough life of the Greenlander: The Greenlander himself makes his tools "with greatest care" etc, as he possesses great know-how on the environments, but he is surrounded by "one endless night" (47). The cold of the area binds everything "cementing nature in one complex whole / of isles, seas, glaciers, round the northern pole!" Sometimes the seal will come soon enough, but often it won't and the Greenlander is overcome by hunger (48). The poem describes how some British reach a settlement and find all dead (Canto IV).

The theme on nature and the British is twofold. First Blackley dwells on the beauties of his own country and on his feelings when away from it, before he turns to the wilds of Greenland, which fill the traveller with *dire dismay* (Canto II). Second, since Britain wants to show leadership at sea through its exemplary conduct in relation to moral virtues, Blackley – in order to enhance admiration for Britain – draws attention to the danger associated with sailing – especially in the Arctic regions. He exemplifies this through a tearful description of a shipwreck (not a symbolic one, but a real one to show the real danger) (Canto III).

The subject of Greenlanders' encountering other ethnicities is covered in Canto V. This is a narrative on the Greenlander as a traveller, Indians as bestial enemies of the sweet-tempered Inuit, and the European abductions of Inuit in former times – all condensed in the fate of one Greenlander.

Canto VI - and the overall idea of the minstrel

Cantos I-V thus introduce the readers to a lot of themes and attitudes about Greenland and Greenlanders. The view of the Inuit starts with dwarfs and Skraellings, goes on to the pagan Greenlander in the ghostly nature, and ends up with the travelling Greenlander with a sad fate. Canto VI, the final ballad, expresses Blackley's message: more Christian missionary work in the Arctic regions. The narrative consists of many details that are only loosely knitted together. For dramatic effect, it starts with yet another heartbreaking shipwreck to show the danger. Blackley then turns to their own less dramatic shipwreck, which is used to show the influence of the Christian mission: They were rescued by a Christian Greenlander who risked his life (Canto VI:106).

Throughout the book, background information is added with references to Egede, Crantz, Anderson, etc. Although praised already in the introduction, Sisimiut and missionary Kjer get a long note in Canto VI. It mentions his extraordinary work with building a congregation of 600 souls who live a civilized life. The ballad itself switches between praising this small, happy and peaceful enclave, Hans Egede and the King of Denmark (107), and then preaching the fight against paganism: "against Pagan darkness, ignorance and crime" (109). The mission has brought the dwarfish natives from dying without mercy to be safely sheltered by Christianity.[15]

---

15 Pagans can be removed from the status of being part of nature by the mission. However, Blackley does not at any point describe the mission as saving the pagans from "shipwreck", which would be an obvious metaphor in the setting, where paganism and the dreadful nature are intertwined in long passages.

The future aim is to establish many such places. Innumerable natives, and among them the Inuit, are still in the dark – indeed even part of the evil – without any sense of moral crime in the damaging climate: a dying man having a rock for a pillow and foreseeing the fate of his wife and his children without any merciful comfort in the belief in Paradise; the aging parents left behind to die; and finally, the Inuit mothers killing their babies. The author admonishes his readers to evangelize, in order to fight paganism and reach the stage when all finally can join and sing the praise of Jehovah (117-118).

The discourses thus live side by side in Blackley's work, of course basically borne by the sharp distinction: either Christian plus approaching civilization, or pagan and dangerous, vicious and evil. However, I find a discrepancy between his introductory narrative which has a moderate and positive view of the Inuit, and the poem itself which gets its poetic drive first and foremost by placing Inuit as part of the Arctic nature and thereby describing them as a people who causes horror and deadly fear in the European.[16] The more of this, the greater is the praise of the Northern European for bringing the mission and the civilization, and creating peaceful enclaves inhabited by natives who are almost transmuted from dwarfish barbarian savages into brave, helpful and pious human beings who live under the ringing bell of church. While the introduction implicitly turns away from the old discourse on Skraellings, the poem itself includes exactly that discourse in order to throw into strong relief the merits of the mission and to admonish further the fight against paganism.

Blackley's text shows, according to my reading of it, how old general discourses about the savages exist in the same author's work side by side with newer data on savages from a particular geographical area, although the newer data produce quite another discourse on the Others.

From trolls, via pagans, to human individual beings

In a project that deals with European views of the Scandinavian countries from 1700-1850, the inclusion of Greenland indeed adds an extra perspective to the viewpoints of the non-Nordic Europeans with regard to their fellow Europeans living in the North. The savages/natives /and those of another ethnicity, help to prove that without a third "savage", unknown and strange culture, the Europeans are in fact much more similar than might otherwise be apparent. Furthermore, the sources show that the "savages" are considered more or less wild, depending on

---

16   The description of the nature may well be inspired by Ross (1835) on Arctic Canada, even more since Blackley did not winter in the Arctic.

how much they have been influenced by the mission. Egede and Crantz described the Inuit of Greenland as individual human beings, and not as a horde of trolls or the like. The explorers of Arctic Canada did the same a hundred years later while staying among Inuit there for longer periods, as did Parry and Ross.

Both Ross's and Blackley's texts are typical examples of British self-image: they show how the British saw themselves as unambiguously superior to other Europeans and to all other Others for that matter.

On the other hand, both texts pay respect to the evangelization/colonisation of Greenland in a similar manner to other sources I have seen, but they do so from two different angles.

Blackley's text shows us the relation between the Europeans and the British self-image, but also how this discourse is competing with the discourse of the Christian brotherhood and community feeling and its fight for the souls on the borders of paganism. The real Other for Blackley is the pagan Other.

For Ross the focus is on civilized life. Religion seems to have more to do with the upholding of discipline and civilized ways on the expedition. The mission is not his goal. The real Other for him is the uncivilized non-British Other. Civilization is on Blackley's agenda, too. The mission is seen to have given the 600 souls the possibility of living a civilized life and making progress. On a deeper, more general level the important thing to both of them (and to all Europeans) is the ethnocentric European awareness of their common culture seen as civilisation, contrasting the savage way of life, i.e. the fear of the Others, hiding behind contempt for the uncivilized life. One might say that Blackley only has an auxiliary approach, but certainly a very dominating one, i.e. the focus on the goal of evangelization.

In general, Hans Egede's and Crantz' descriptions of the Inuit had an impact on the overall accounts of different types, whenever they include Greenland. For example, Nicoll describes the pagan Inuit more or less by the old discourse, and then stresses the change towards civilization brought about by the mission. The focus of such works varies according to the author's interest in religion, but the main points are fixed: the mission brings the Inuit within the reach of civilization and this holds true even for other worldwide works (e.g. Malte-Brun, 1834).

The European exploration of the North is the story of how the predicate of being the evil and dangerous savage moves gradually further away the more information is gathered on those who are nearer. The border to the unknown moves, and so do the stereotypes.[17]

---

17   Internally in Greenland this process was repeated in the nineteenth century: East Greenlanders were seen as dangerous, indeed even cannibalistic Others (Langgård 1998/99).

References

Anderson, John 1748: *Efterretninger om Island, Grønland og Straat Davis: til Videnskabernes og Handlens sande Nytte.* Copenhagen: Gabriel Christian Rothe.

Arngrimi, 1782 (1688): *Arngrim Jonssøn: Grønlandia, eller Historie om Grønland … .* Copenhagen

Barrow, John 1818: *A chronological history of voyages into the Arctic Regions.*

Blackley, Frederick R 1839: *The Greenland Minstrel, a poem in Six Cantos with an Introductory Narrative.* London: Simpkin and Marshall.

Blefken, Dithmar 1652 (1615): *Korte en klare beschryvingh von Yslandt en Groenlandt.* Amsterdam: Nicolaus van Ravensteyn.

Bobé, Louis 1926/27: Grønlændere i Danmark. *Det grønlandske Selskabs Aarsskrift 1926/27*:5-28. Copenhagen: G.E.C. Gad.

Bredsdorff, Thomas 2003: *Den broged.e oplysning.* Copenhagen: Gyldendal.

Bredsdorff, Thomas 2004: A Moravian Brother in Greenland. Bredsdorff, Thomas & Anne-Marie Mai, eds: *Enlightenend networking. Import and Export of Enlightenment in eightteenth century Denmark.* Copenhagen: Museum Tusculanum.

Bårdssön, Ivar 1930: *Det gamle Grønlands beskrivelse af Ívar Bárdarson (Ivar Bårdssön) udgiven efter håndskrifterne af Finnur Jónsson.* Copenhagen. Levin & Munksgaards Forlag.

Crantz, David 1765: *Historie von Grönland.* Leipzig: Barby: Heinrich Detlef Ebers: in Commission bey Weidmanns Erben und Reich.

Davis, John 1930 (1589): *Tre rejser til Grønland i Aarene 1585-87.* Copenhagen: Gad.

Dennett, John Frederick 1839: *The voyages and travels of captains Ross, Parry, Franklin, and Mr. Belzoni.* London: William Wright.

Egede, Hans 1925: *Relationer fra Grønland 1721-36 og Det gamle Grønlands ny Perlustration 1741.* Copenhagen: C.A. Reitzel. Boghandel.

Egede, Poul and Niels Egede 1939: *Continuation af Hans Egedes Relationer fra Grønland samt.* Copenhagen: C.A. Reitzel. Boghandel.

Feeney, Robert E 1997: *Polar Journeys. The Role of Food and Nutrition in Early Exploration.* Washington and Fairbanks: University of Alaska Press.

Flemming, Fergus 1998: *Barrow's Boys.* New York: Atlantic Monthly Press.

Gad, Finn 1967: *Grønlands Historie Vol. I.* Copenhagen: Nyt Nordisk Forlag.

Giesecke, Karl Ludwig 1910: *Mineralogisches Reisejournal über Grönland 1806-13.* Copenhagen: C.A. Reitzel Boghandel.

Grønlandske Historiske Mindesmærker – udgivne af Det kongelige Nordiske Oldskrift-Selskab. I-III. 1838 og 1845: Copenhagen: Oldskrift-Selskabet, udg. af Carl Chr. Rafn, Finn Magnusen o.fl.

Haan, Lourens Feykes 1914 (1720): *Beskrivelse af Straat Davids tilligemed sammes indvåneres sæder, skikke og vaner.* ed Louis Bobé. Grønlandske Selskabs Aarskrift: 63-88. Copenhagen: Det Hoffenbergske Etabl.

Half Hour 1883: *The Half Hour Library of Travel Nature and Science For Young Readers. Half Hours in the Far North.* London: Wm. Isbister Limited.

Harbsmeier, Michael Hg., 2001: *Stimmen aus dem äussersten Norden. Wie die Grönländer Europa für sich entdeckten.* Stuttgart: Jan Thorbecke Verlag.

Huish, Robert 1835: *The Last Voyage of Capt. Sir John Ross.* London: John Saunders.

Høiris, Ole 2001: Teologi, Antropologi og Arkæologi. Om de fremmede som vor fortid og oprindelse. Aarhus Universitet: Arbejdspapirer. Center for Kulturforskning.

Høiris, Ole 2000: Forfald og Fremskridt. Analytiske hovedfigurer i den antropologiske erkendelseshistorie. Aarhus Universitet: Arbejdspapirer. Center for Kulturforskning

Langgård, Karen 1998/99: Vestgrønlænderes syn på østgrønlændere gennem tiden. *Grønlandsk Kultur- og Samfundsforskning 98/99*: 175-200. Nuuk: Ilisimatusarfik og Forlaget Atuagkat.

Langgård, Karen 2006: *En minstrel fra 1839 om Grønland år 1826. Wiener Studien zur Skandinavisk Band 15.*

Leslie, John, Robert Jameson and Hugh Murray 1830/35: *Narrative of discovery and adventure in the Polar Seas and regions.* Edinburgh.

Lundgreen-Nielsen, Flemming 1989: *C.C-Lyschanders Digtning. I-II, ved Flemming Lundgreen-Nielsen og Erik Petersen.* Copenhagen: C.A. Reitzel.

Lundgreen-Nielsen, Flemming undated: *Forfatterportræt af Claus Christoffersen Lyschander.* Arkiv for Dansk Litteratur. www.ald.dk

Lyon, G. F. George Francis 1971 (1825): *A brief narrative of an unsuccessful attempt to reach Repulse Bay, 1824.* Toronto: Coles.

Malte-Brun , M. 1834: *System of Universal Geography.* Vol. II, Boston: Samuel Walker

Manby, George William 1822: *Journal of a Voyage to Greenland, in the year 1821.* London: G and W.B. Whittaker.

Martens, Federico 1675: *Spitzbergische oder Groenländische Reise-beschreibund. 1671.* Hamburg: in Verlegung Hohann Naumans und Georg Wolffs.

Munk Jens 1980: *The Journal of Jens Munk 1619-1620.* (Ed.) W.A. Kenyon. Toronto.

Nicoll, James 1840: *A historical and descriptive account of Iceland, Greenland and the Faroe Islands.* Edinburgh.

Olaus Magnus 1555: *Historia de gentibus.* Rom: Pont. Max.

O'Reilley, Bernard 1818: *Greenland, the adjacent seas and the North-West Passage 1817.* London: Baldwin, Cradock and Joy.

Parry, William Edward 1969 0(1824): *Journal of a second voyage for the discovery of a north-west passage 1821-22-23.* New York: Greenwood.

Parry, William Edward 1968 (1821): *Journal of a voyage for the discovery of a north-west passage 1819-20.* New York: Greenwood.

Peyrère, Isaac de 1647: *Relation du Groenland.* Paris.

Pratt, Mary Louise 1992: *Imperial Eyes. Travel Writing and Transculturaltion.* London and New York: Routledge.

Ross, John 1835: *Narrative of a second voyage in search of a North-West Passage. I-II.* London: Longman.

Strack, Thomas 1994: *Exotische Erfahrung und Intersubjektivität.* Paderborn: Igel Verlag Wissenschaft.

Torfæus, Thormod 1706: *Groenlandia antiqva.* Hafniæ. Kerguelen, Trémarec de 1771: *Relation d'un voyage dans la mer du Nord … 1767 et 1768.* Paris.

Zorgdrager, Cornelis Gisbert 1723 (1720): *Alte und neue Grönländische Fischerei und Wallfisch-fang.* Leipzig: Peter Conrad Monath.

KAREN LANGGÅRD

KAREN KLITGAARD POVLSEN

Persistent Patterns
The Genre of Travel Writing in the Eighteenth Century

"In Western Europe there has undoubtedly been a movement away from allegorical narratives towards impressionistic narratives", writes Tzvetan Todorov in respect to the generic development of travelogues (Todorov (1996 (1991)): 292). As examples of this development, he refers to two travelogues by Chateaubriand, an allegorical one from America in the 1790s and an impressionistic one from the Orient (1811):

The former submits the traveller's observations to a preconceived design that they are used to illustrate; the latter neglects the world and concentrates on the self, recounting the successive impressions of that self. (293)

This broad perspective no doubt contains some truth, but Todorov's use of the works of Chateaubriand could imply that this development takes place around 1800 in conjunction with the romantic breakthrough, and that this could have something to do with the subject matter of the travelogues. In the following, I shall call into question the linear view of this development and show that the allegorical and subjective travelogues intersect each other and that the allegorical, less subjective travelogue continues to exist even today – for instance, in the works of Claudio Magris or to a lesser degree in the two German travelogues of Wolfgang Büscher. Magris and Büscher write learned and sentimental travelogues, travelling in places as well as in time and historical layers of history and art which they find described in past literature. They do not however travel in and with their selves in the tradition of the Bildungsroman which today is a stereotypical format of the genre.

I shall roughly limit myself to the eighteenth century, approaching it from a generic perspective. The geography is northern: England, Germany, Sweden and Denmark, and one of my points is that generically it does not matter whether the travelogues are about northbound or southbound journeys. Generic patterns prevail with no sense of place, and the generic track is a beaten one and when it changes – as it does in the second half of the eighteenth century – the reason lies somewhere outside the question of place or actual topography.[1]

Travelling by the book

The first characteristic of travel writing described by Todorov is its position between science and autobiography, the second is its specific position in time and space or place – or, to borrow Bakhtin's word – its chronotope (Bakhtin 1981, 1986). It is a genre reflecting deviances and infringements as well as progress. At its base is a tension between the traveller/writer and the topography, and for Todorov colonialism is always in play, securing the balance between personal experience and the visited place, a point that was supported from a postcolonial viewpoint by Mary Louise Pratt (1992). The visitor is a stranger, but convinced of his or her own superiority as a person or as a scientist. The genre as such thus balances between personal experiences and objective registrations. Again, in the wide perspective this may seem convincing. But how does it look applied to the eighteenth century – to non-fiction travelogues that are not scientific?

In his reading of the formal criteria of eighteenth-century English travelogues, Charles L. Batten (1978) stressed Joseph Addison's *Remarks on Several Parts of Italy* (1705) as reflecting a generic pattern of prevailing importance for most of the century, which Batten described as "a new era in which non-fiction travel literature achieved an unparalleled popularity" (Batten 1978: 1). Batten claims that the 1770s was a turning point, as exemplified by Smollet's *Expedition of Humphry Clinker* (1771) (Ibid.: 19-20), but implicitly he acknowledges that Smollett's work was influenced by Laurence Sterne's *A Sentimental Journey* (1768). According to Batten, the generic change in travelogues was mainly caused by the theories of the picturesque, which created a new way of depicting the landscape that was reflected by William Gilpin's books in the 1780s and 1790s. But Edmund Burke's theories of the sublime had already popularised a new pathetic mode of depicting of mountains, seas and so forth (Klitgaard Povlsen 2001: 11-13), and in 1712, in several issues of *The Spectator* (1711-12), Joseph Addison proposed distinguishing between the beautiful, simple and nice on the one hand and, on the other, the sublime, chaotic and turbulent so contradictory to the good taste of the neo-classicists (Ibid.: 13). So Batten's historical outline of the genric of the travelogue might not be satisfactory.

The German tradition of travelogues is described by Peter J. Brenner (1989, 1990), Wolfgang Griep (1986, 1991) and others (Maurer 1999).[2] Like Batten, they

---

1   See also Charles L. Batten 1978: part one.
2   Klitgaard Povlsen 2002: 415ff.

KAREN KLITGAARD POVLSEN

emphasize the latter half of the eighteenth century as the culmination of the popularity of the genre, which continues to develop into a more personal, subjective and sentimental genre around the year 1800. The pattern is the same as in England: most travellers were men and most of them travelled southwards on their "Grand Tours"; after 1750, however, many more men and few women travelled northwards – and wrote about their experiences. The focus in the German studies on travelogues is still on Johann Wolfgang von Goethe and his *Italienische Reise* (*Italian Journey*) from 1785-86, which was partly published in periodicals in the following years, but finally published as a book in 1816. Goethe was and is perceived as representing a subjective and romantic turning point in German travel literature.

In *Deutsche Reisende in der Spätaufklärung unterwegs in Skandinavien* (2000), Regina Hartmann analyses 35 travel accounts and 12 travel guides from Denmark, Sweden, Norway and the Sámi regions. She has also found 32 reviews of travel accounts in German periodicals, which she interprets as a symptom of the public acceptance of the images represented. She rightfully stresses that the travel literature of the eighteenth century has to be understood and read as literature today. Her theoretical focus is on the construction of images and on the different stereotypes, or "hetero-stereotypes", included in the same text. This seems profoundly relevant as she looks for incoherencies in the texts analysed. Hartmann is on the outlook for anterior texts (pre-texts) and the intertextuality of travel accounts, but since she structures her work in relation to the geography of Scandinavia and splits up most books into three or more thematically oriented readings, she offers no generic or formal analysis. One of her insights is nevertheless important within the framework of the present article. Especially in the chapter on Norway, Hartmann describes the stereotypical representation of Nordic Switzerland as a utopia of the strong, free and healthy mountain dweller throughout the century. At the same time, contemporary nature is depicted as cruel and icy, as it is destroyed by hard wood cutting, mining industry and so forth. The Swiss poet Albrecht von Haller had however already introduced this dichotomy in his famous poem on *The Alps* from 1729. The well-educated German travellers knew Haller's work, of course, and through the translations of his and their own later works, this matrix was exported to other languages as well. Elements of new sublime or even picturesque descriptions of landscapes (the Swiss author Salomon Gessner called them "idyllic") – descriptions very similar to what Batten in England dated from Gilpin onwards as the great turning point of the century – are found earlier in German – and other – literature. Hartmann's work shows how important it is to look for generic patterns in different languages and cultures. In the eighteenth century, most writers were able to read languages other than their own because they belonged to the well-educated middle classes or to the aristocracy, so many anterior texts existed as a reservoir for the travel account – one of them being travel itself (Todorov 1996(1991)).

Patterns and pre-texts

In an introduction to the English translation of Jean Viviès's study on English travel literature, Alain Bony sketches the overall pattern of English travel accounts in the eighteenth century: "From A(ddison) to W(ordsworth) by way of S(terne)" (Viviès 2002: 3). The German poet Johann Wolfgang von Goethe was nevertheless very important to German-speaking travel authors, several of whom will be introduced further below, so at this point we shall turn to Goethe's Italian travel account rather than to Wordsworth's. Bony emphasizes Joseph Addison's *Remarks on Several Parts of Italy* as a book "that marked an epoch as soon as it was published in 1705" (Ibid.). Addison is the source of the travel literature genre of the eighteenth century – as Batten also claims. Like many writers in the eighteenth century Addison produces many citations of earlier travel accounts, including Richard Lassel's *Voyage to Italy* (1670), at the time the most complete guid e to Italy available. As Jean Viviès shows, the travel writers of the eighteenth century travel as naturally through the world of books as through the topographies of the world. The travel accounts also echoed each other, establishing a kind of meta-library (Ibid.: 5); this is a point also made by Hartmann (2000), and several of the chapters in this book confirm this tendency.

Addison's voyage went south, but we recognize the pattern of his travelogue in much travel literature from the North (cp. Pär Eliasson's chapter on learned German writers in Sweden in this volume). Addison's travel account was not a guide to solving the practical problems of the journey; it was a guide to the best classical authors that one could and should read when travelling through specific places. In a letter from 2nd October 1840, his friend Horace Walpole wrote that Addison travelled: "…through the poets and not through Italy for all his ideas are borrowed from the descriptions and not from reality" (Ingamells 1997: 21). This approach was announced in the preface and was first seen in Addison's travel account, written at a time when searching for facts and experiences was important to most travel writers. In the chapter on mythology, we have seen how Robert Molesworth's travel account from Denmark (1693) stressed the fact that Molesworth had seen and experienced what he wrote about. We have also seen, however, that he borrowed stereotypes of the North and South (Greenland and Italy) that he himself had not experienced. In this manner, Molesworth's account resembles most travel accounts of the eighteenth century, which try to convince the readers that they are eye-witness accounts, but nearly always borrow elements from earlier

KAREN KLITGAARD POVLSEN

travelogues – in other words, from the represented experiences that others might have had or that may just have been stereotypes for a long time.

Addison did try to convince his readers that his actual journey was the empirical basis for his travelogue, his pre-text. He nevertheless constructed a plot based on another combination of time and space, a chronotope in which time became the important factor always present in space. As Chloe Chard stresses:

> [...] despite Addison's own eagerness to establish his commitment to observation as well as to scholarship: he has, he says, read passages from classical authors "as it were upon the spot", comparing them with 'the Natural face of the Country'. (Chard 1999: 87)

Chard shows how Laurence Sterne and Henry Fielding criticise Addison for his scholarliness, and how it became a stereotype in travelogues describing the English Grand-Tour to insist on marking a distance to Addison (Ibid.: 88). Still, in this genre, the eyewitness traveller continued to "suddenly" or "spontaneously" recall relevant classical quotes and works from different time eras.

What made Addison's pattern so attractive was that it allowed him and others to stress universality by doubling the times of the place. The important topographies were described by the author as an eyewitness, and this eyewitness, like a detective, traced the past of the place through literature or art, thus creating two or more imagined time zones in the same place: present and past merged in the specific topography, the author became a cultural correspondent between ancient descriptions and modern sites, and the place became a space for imagined cultural meetings (Klitgaard Povlsen 2004). This plot structure was suitable for both northbound and southbound travel accounts because the effect also was a sentimental one: an emotion/affect invited the reader to join with his or her own experiences and emotions.

Such plots gave way to endless digressions, discussions with other authors on art works and name-dropping *ad infinitum*. It created a text consisting of fragments, and in reality this technique announced Sterne and his sentimentality:

> Even the principle of citation contributes to this effect: The *Remarks* can be read in part as an anthology of Latin descriptive poetry, with a series of literary fragments interrupting the textual space much in the way ancient ruins would have dotted the Italian landscape. (Bony's preface to Viviés 2002: 7)

This sentimental doubling of times in one space was an allegorical technique. Underlying the first time was another time connected to the same place or sign. This created a distance in the text, a reflexive relation which made room for the sentimental affect produced in the imagination of the reader – as it probably had been produced in the mind of the writer. The text became a palimpsest of layers of anterior texts. The problem became one of convincing the reader that an actual contemporary eyewitness had experienced a here and now in the vast and sometimes seemingly endless time span he produced in his text.

Sentimental irony and reflexive subjectivism

Sterne's *A Sentimental Journey* (1768) became an extremely popular bestseller among readers in many European countries. In spite of its ironic mode and fictional character, most readers could easily imagine the figure Yorick moving slowly and "near-sightedly" from place to place, stumbling from accident to accident. The book, which is now read as a novel, was read as a travel account during the eighteenth century (Adams 1983: 198) and created a travel writing trend throughout Europe. Sterne also created a palimpsest of his own. His book was explicitly written according to the eighteenth-century tradition of the travelogue – but in a satirical tone. Apart from the satire, Sterne was unique in placing Yorick himself, rather than the journey or places, at the centre of the account.

In Denmark, the author Jens Baggesen adopted Sterne's narrative method, but placed himself as the first-person traveller/writer in his *Labyrinten* 1-2 (1792-93, *The Labyrinth*). Sterne's Yorick was a fictional character, Baggesen's travel literature was explicitly autobiographical but the subjective effect was even stronger in his book. In both Sterne's and Baggesen's accounts, the plot revolves around the protagonist and his journey through and to himself, so these travelogues both represent, but not in quite similar ways, the impressionistic turn referred to by Todorov at the beginning of this article.

Even more impressionist is Goethe's travel diary on his travels in Italy in 1786-87, *Italienische Reise* (1816, *Flight to Italy* 1999), which was partly published in periodicals starting in 1789. Goethe's style was already well known in Germany before 1800. His personal diary entries and selection of letters offered a multi-facetted portrait of the writer as a private person writing for himself and in relation to other people (in the letters). The travel account does therefore not consist of one genre, but of at least two, and this duplicity emphasized the impressionism and subjectivity we have seen in the works of Sterne and Baggesen. Like Baggesen's protagonist, Goethe found himself in Naples and decided, at the peak of his travels, what he was going to do with his life. Travelling back home to oneself has been the general pattern for modern travel accounts ever since, as has accentuated and self-reflexive subjectivity. Goethe also made use of anterior or pre-texts such as the travel accounts of Italy by his friend and, in part, fellow traveller Karl Philipp von Moritz (1792), with whom he discussed the art of travel writing (1993 (1816): 391), as well as the art of writing mythology into descriptions of contemporary topographies and arts.

So, while Goethe also tried to write other eras and times into his work, he was not as explicit as Addison. Like most visitors to Rome and Naples, Goethe saw many works of art and met many artists, and it is often through his descriptions of people and art rather than topographies and places that he implicitly refers to preceding texts. He does not explain the works of art to the reader, but rather describes them with a "feeling eye", showing the effect of what he sees on his feelings, and the emotions produced in him and by him by looking at landscapes or works of art. On the surface, it may seem that the erudition of Addison's travel account has disappeared, but, in fact, it has been transformed and written implicitly into the text. In order to be able to see Goethe's palimpsest, it is necessary to know his references, to be very well educated and to have a fine sense of imagination. Addison is easier to read; his explicit references educated the reader to follow him and to imagine the same time-spaces that he himself did. Sterne is situated in between, with his mocking satire revealing another form of distance. The well-educated and imaginative reader from around 1800 tended to find Addison boring – he was always criticised – but Sterne seemed funny and Goethe an enjoyable challenge. The same might be true for Wordsworth's travel accounts. The question now is how the minor writers travelling northward related to these patterns that they no doubt knew to some extent. Did other patterns occur?

Travelling as a woman – in a landscape of previous texts

Chloe Chard (1999) and Brian Dolan (2001) have emphasized that not only men and male writers travelled during the eighteenth century; women travelled too, and many of them did so in order to become writers in their own right.

One of the less well-known writers today is Friederike Brun, born Münter, who lived in Copenhagen most of her life (1765-1835), but who also travelled extensively and published many travel diaries or travel letters on her travels (Klitgaard Povlsen 2001b). Most of Friederike Brun's travels went to Germany, Switzerland, France and Italy, but she also published two minor texts on her northbound travels – one to Kullen in Sweden and the other through Sweden and Stockholm to St. Petersburg. The journey to Kullen took place in 1786, the same year Goethe visited Rome.

Friederike Brun wrote in German, raised as she was in the German circle in Copenhagen, where her father was a popular vicar who preached at the royal court and was a well-known author of religious texts and psalms. Having received an excellent education, Friederike Brun spoke and read many languages, and she began writing at an early age, publishing her first travel diary and a collection of poems when she was only sixteen. She married a wealthy tradesman and she continued her travels, often joining him on his European journeys with or without their four children. The small piece on her northern journey to Kullen in Sweden was originally published in the periodical *Deutsches Magazin* in 1791, but was later reprinted a number of times, indicating its popularity among readers.

This popularity might have to do with the fact that Kullen was (and is) a rather popular place to visit. It is the only cliff, or small mountain, visible from Denmark north of Copenhagen. Considering how popular mountains and seas were in the latter half of the eighteenth century, it is not surprising that the cliff appealed to sentimental journeys and descriptions or even to idyllic or picturesque ones. At least, this is what the opening lines of her account touch upon. Friederike Brun begins in *medias res* by stating the date and time of year – at six in the morning on 26th June 1786 "we left" (verliessen wir 1799: 179)[3] the coast of Zealand. The indefinite "we" slowly reveals itself as the wife, husband, child and the wife's parents, who are on a family excursion. The small Øresund is grey and calm, but to the left lies the "limitless North Sea" (unbegräntzte Nordmeer; ibid.) with bigger waves, and to the right the bluish Kullen is visible. The writer makes us see the small boat ("our Nutshell"; ibid.). This is a picturesque image painted with words in the classical tradition of *ut pictura poesis*, and has a touch of the sublime. The composition is classical: to the left the sea, to the right the mountain, and in the middle is the tiny protagonist in her tiny boat between two big creations of nature.

The family arrives in Helsingborg, a small town not to the liking of the writer but with friendly inhabitants. The first-person narrator climbs a hill on top of which stands a gothic tower. From here, she describes the panoramic view across the Øresund towards Copenhagen and Zealand, which appears verdant and lush in the distance while the Swedish surroundings are dull. The tour continues in a carriage up and around the mountain. Again, the composition consists of panoramic descriptions focused on the right and the left – one sight after another. On the one hand, we see idyllic images of peasants working in their fields and girls and women harvesting cabbage in their gardens filled with flowers, roses and lilacs. On the other hand, we see grey cliffs and big stones in chaotic heaps. The same views give the impression that the Kullen is near – or very far away. When the family is near the mountain it is "horribly beautiful" ("furchtbarer Schöne"; ibid.: 183); when they are farther away, they see idyllic fields with rolling hills and fields with oat and barley, "sweet shades" ("lieblichen Schattierungen"; ibid.: 184), soon to be

3   The translations of Friederike Brun's texts are by the author of this article.

332   KAREN KLITGAARD POVLSEN

replaced by rough cliffs with "hanging ruins and shuddering clefts" ("hangenden Ruinen und schaurigen Klüften"; ibid. 184-85). The first-person narrator reflects upon the very different views, establishing a wonderful unity as an image of the creative genius behind this scenery.

With the above description in mind, it becomes evident even to a twentieth-century reader that this account is to be read in the long tradition of 'The Great Book of Nature' revealing the presence of God behind the scenery. Its composition with alternating idylls and sublime horrors is known from Albrecht von Haller's *Die Alpen* (1729) and numerous texts of the eighteenth century that repeat this pattern with descriptions of the Alps and other mountain landscapes. For his part, Haller refers back to Dante and the Purgatory section of the *Divine Comedy* from the thirteenth century – an important text in the tradition of travel accounts – and I could go on revealing other former texts (Salomon Gessner's idylls are self-evident examples). Yet, it should now be clear that this is an example of a piece of popular travel literature using generic patterns referring to other texts and concepts. One of these is the soul of nature revealing itself to the admiring eye and manifest in many personifications or animations in the text, as quoted above; another is the implicit reference to the creator behind this, and a third is the implicit parallels between this small northern mountain and the impressive Alps, as well as between the friendly, happy, beautiful Nordic peasants and the Swiss peasants, though the former live in smaller circumstances. In this period, Norway was generally presented as the Switzerland of the North, but this text presented Sweden as another Nordic Switzerland. Of course, this idea had utopian political dimensions, in that the account claimed that the Swedish peasants could be as free and healthy as the Swiss if only they owned their own fields in the same way as they apparently owned their own gardens.

Denmark or Zealand appears in faraway glimpses as a cultivated lush garden, in contrast to the dual character of Sweden's natural environment, which alternates between the picturesque and the sublime but is also nearer God. The family proceeds to the top of the cliff, which is the culmination of the text. It is fearful (sublime) to stand at the top looking down at the sea, but it is also soothing because from a distance the sea looks like a tranquil mirror with murmering waves – a place to reflect. The first-person is struck by her own reflection:

Quick as lightning my thoughts flowed through my mind, not of the living – of the dead – living there! Andreas, the tender youth, smiling towards heaven all his life! My fragile infant, who greeted the world and crying left it again! O all my beloved ones who have gone before me and who now enjoy the light of a softer sun. (Ibid.: 188)

At the top of the cliff, the first-person narrator meets her own reflection, her memories of the dead situating her in the text with affective emphasis. She meets her dear departed ones just before the sun sets, not in the sea, but in the convergence of the Baltic and North Seas. So the 'Book of Nature' shows the first-person narrator how to reconcile life and death, East and North. Everything unites in the end. When the sun finally disappears into the two seas, a big breath is audible, the wind rises, and the waves sound louder. Again, these are tokens of the creative genius behind it all.

The descent from the mountain begins and continues as dusk settles, the colours disappear, darkness prevails. Everything seems gothic and filled with horror; the world seems limitless, disappearing into the dark vastness. The writer looks for friends' names that she knows have been inscribed in the cliff, but all except one have disappeared into nature's *Vanitas*. Descending even further, she sees the name of a woman, "Emilia". The name was carved into the stone by the woman's husband, Ernst von Schimmelmann, before she died at a young age, and in Copenhagen in the 1780s this was the essence of sentimental love. With this reference, the text thus expresses a hope for eternal love. It also expresses something else. The name Ernst von Schimmelmann does not appear in the text; Emilia is the only name that appears. However, people in Copenhagen would have known who Emilia was because her husband had erected a stone in her name at his mansion north of Copenhagen. From an eye in the stone an eternal waterfall flowed into a small basin at its base: Emilia's quell. A footnote in the travel account tells the reader that it was the husband that had engraved their names on the cliff. This explicit information shows that Friederike Brun's ambition was to be read outside of Denmark and that she wanted this travelogue to be read as a literary work.

The descent from the mountain resumes and the small group discovers a cave at the bottom of the cliff. The writer imagines this to be the seat of Poseidon, the Greek god of the sea. The text is not ironic about this: Having reconciled life and death, sea and land, North and East, the mythologies of North and South needed to be reconciled. Thus having done this, the text ends not back where it started but with a parallel to its beginning. The party returns to the flat gardens of Denmark: "So a more limited happiness is our real destiny, I thought" (Ibid.: 197).

This elegiac idyll with its sublime, intense spots and a clear composition containing a beginning and an end with a climax in between where beginning and end are reconciled is typical of Friederike Brun's early travel literature. It is evident that her ambition is to write literature. It is also evident that the text comes alive when she herself 'enters' the account as a mourning mother on top of Kullen. It is obvious that on the one hand the composition of the text appeals to the imagination of the reader, but, on the other, also to a certain amount of knowledge of classical and modern literature and art – knowledge that is not as self-evident to a modern reader as it was to the eighteenth-century reader.

Friederike Brun seemed to travel with a book in her hand – or at least, like Addison, with a number of books in her mind. Her references are not as explicit as his were, but her text is also a text spotted with ruins like a landscape outside Rome – or like a Nordic landscape inscribed with runes. Here the literate 'runes' are the names of her friends and dear ones, but they offer the reader the possibility of imagining her feelings. The names are of course explicit references to living or departed persons. In this respect it seems curious that no one in the small group has his or her name mentioned by the writer. The first-person narrator is the writer's 'eye', it is looking on behalf of someone else – be it the reader or the creative genius. The style is extremely scenic, with one composition following after another. The climax occurs exactly at the top of Kullen exactly in the middle of the text. The text is composed like a painting by the German painter Casper David Friedrich.

Like Addison, Friederike Brun was well read, but her ambition was to give her readers the experience of travelling in a painting or a panorama. Her style is not the least ironic; instead, the text is pathetic, especially in connection with the sublime landscapes. Parts of the texts that I have emphasized less in this reading are quite different in nature from those described above. Some of the idylls are rather long due to Friederike Brun's thorough descriptions of the Swedish peasants – their clothes, teeth, hair and manners. In some of her other texts this is even more evident, giving them an anthropological flavour, and at times they contain very detailed descriptions of agriculture, fertilizers, kitchens, oils and so forth. Her thirst for empirical information is evident and as a result her style is not in the least like the subjective style of Goethe's travel diary from the same year.

The subjectivity of Friederike Brun's travel account is discrete – well into the text. At the top of Kullen, she at last reveals herself through her departed child and her friends – after which she descends into mythical darkness and returns to ordinary life in the plain gardens of Denmark.

Travelling as a man with good taste

Friederike Brun's travel writing was situated between the patterns of Addison and Goethe but in the tradition of Albrecht Haller and Dante. As a writer, she was an intermediary between (at least) two cultures and languages and she was perceived as 'neither-nor' during the nineteenth century with its emphasis on national languages and literature.

She was often visited by Germans travelling to Denmark. One of these was Friedrich Wilhelm Basilius von Ramdohr, who met her in 1792. He published a book on this journey to Denmark the same year: *Studien zur Kenntniss der schönen Natur, der schönen Künste, der Sitten und der Staatsverfassung aus einer Reise nach Dänemark* (Studies on the knowledge of beautiful nature, the fine arts, manners and the constitution of the state from a journey to Denmark). One year later, Friederike Brun published her piece on Kullen. Rather than going into detail on this work, I shall discuss it in relation to the idea that Friederike Brun was a new version of the generic pattern going back to Addison. The literary travelogues subsequent to the model offered by Friederike Brun still followed the persistent patterns, but many travellers wrote diaries as a personal project to keep track of time and place, persons met, and so on. Ramdohr's travel account could also be regarded as a kind of time manager – or as proof of having been there.

Ramdohr was a traveller of the kind described by Pär Eliason in his chapter on German travellers in Sweden. He was learned, well educated, and quite sure of his own and of his culture's superiority to Danish culture. He had already been to Italy on his Grand Tour, but since he had family in Denmark, he travelled north. He stayed in Denmark for four months and used his relatives as informants to tell him about Danish culture. So, in essence, Ramdohr was a travelling ethnographer looking at the native Others and their surroundings and keeping an exact record of his impressions. He was a traveller in the colonial tradition (Todorov and Pratt), placing himself at a more advanced level of civilisation. His book is an empirical list of everything he has seen, but in his list of the views, art works, buildings and landscapes, he compares Nordic phenomena with what he knew from home or from Italy. He measured everything according to the classical norms. It made him blind towards his experiences in this northern country and his travel book seems from another era or even outdated in relation to the work of Friederike Brun. In reality, Ramdohr wrote somewhat along the lines of Addison, and only in comparison with Ramdohr does it become evident that Friederike Brun wrote travelogues of quite another kind.

Ramdohr described his travels through Lüneburg, Hamburg and Copenhagen. Everywhere he found several if not many Rembrandts, Rubens and Ruysdals, and he tried to convince his readers of his expert gaze and thus of his cultural superiority in deciding quickly and concisely whether a particular piece or painting might be an original or a copy. His southern-trained eyesight also measured the landscapes. If Friederike Brun travelled and wrote about her travels to mirror herself in God's book of nature and to reflect upon her life and memories through this mirror, Ramdohr travelled and wrote to prove that he knew the standard of beauty and good taste. Already at the beginning of the travelogue, which starts outside of Hamburg, he states his method of comparison explicitly:

KAREN KLITGAARD POVLSEN

These surroundings reminded me intensely of the shores of Brenta between Padua and Venice. However the absence of an attractive style of the garden houses and the unprepossessing costumes of the local people here prevented the complete illusion to believe to stay near the place where my imagination is mostly heightened and also mostly satisfied. (Ramdohr 1792: 3)

Describing sociability in the northern cities of Hamburg and Copenhagen, Ramdorh decided that he liked the hospitality of Naples best, while distancing himself from the formal French tone. He even wrote a short essay on good social behaviour and included it in the travelogue. The dichotomy seemed clear: South was good and North was bad.

But his descriptions seem less dichotomous when he is actually in Copenhagen. For example, when he describes how the sun descended into the sea, he draws a parallel between this experience and one he had of seeing the sun rise from the sea outside of Genua (Ibid.: 81). Northern nature thus seems equivalent and comparable to southern nature and the literatures and arts of Denmark and Norway would be so much better if only they concentrated on depicting Nordic nature in relation to the classical standards. According to this acceptance of a picturesque Nordic landscape, the climax of Ramdohr's travelogue then occurs in nature – not in culture. Once again he sees the sun descend into the sea, but this time he can also see the Swedish coastline of Skåne on the horizon:

In brief! If mountains enwreathed the horizon, then you might consider the location of Copenhagen to be among the most beautiful in the world. (Ibid.: 204)

At Marienlyst he saw his mountain – behind the Øresund was Kullen – and even Ramdohr had to admit that he was in one of the finest places in Europe (Ibid.: 226-227), inspiring him to continue for several pages with a short treaty on the picturesque and sublime beauty of nature. Ramdohr and Friederike Brun thus 'meet' in their views on Kullen. But Ramdohr did not write to create a chronotope of times crossing one another in a particular place. His work was contemporary, even practical. The short treaty on the picturesque is, for instance, followed by another short treaty on how to create beautiful gardens (Ibid.: 253-54ff.) and pleasant and cultivated sociability (Ibid.: 308ff). Ramdorh therefore ends up in accordance with Mary Wollstonecraft's *Letters Written During a short Residence in Sweden, Norway and Denmark* (1796; see the introduction to this book), stating that the democratic assemblies found in England are the true utopias of a new 'Geselligkeit' – or sociability.

Clearly, Ramdohr wrote with books and theories in mind. His aim was however not to establish vast historical horizons in the places he visited, providing them with imaginative force and affect. His travelogue is 'flat' and contemporary and his vision was to establish one true standard instead of discussing varying historical standards. Ramdohr was certainly a man of good taste; unfortunately, this did not enable him to establish either an allegorical or an impressionistic travelogue genre. A truly impressionistic travelogue of the time was the Swiss preacher Johan Kasper Lavater's *Reise nach Kopenhagen im Sommer 1793* (Journey to Copenhagen in the summer of 1793).[4] Lavater was subjective and private, travelling with his daughter to visit the Danish or Nordic 'circle of light' in Holstein and in Copenhagen, a group of aristocrats experimenting with early spiritualism. He had hoped to see John the Baptist in a spiritual gathering arranged by the northern freemasons, but he did not succeed in having this vision. However, he did manage to meet many important Danish civil servants in and around the court. He describes the people he met as individual persons, and throughout the diary entries he expresses concern for the well being of his young daughter. The first volume was regarded as utterly boring and much too long, so the second and following volumes were never published. Today (2007), it seems quite easy to read and very personal and modern. Lavater had given up any literary ambitions relating him to the generic pattern from Addison onwards. Simple stories like his – much more personal and direct than Goethe's travelogue account – transgressed the eighteenth-century horizons and reached into the twentieth century where travelogues like Lavater's can be found everywhere – in bookshops, in magazines and in weblogs.

Friederike Brun represents a typical eighteenth-century travel writer, writing according to the generic model dating back to Addison, Haller, Dante and so on. She represents the tradition of travel writing as a literary genre and was read as a literary author – at least up until around 1810. After that, the persistent patterns from the travel writing of the eighteenth century became marginalised – maybe even more for Friederike Brun because she was a female writer and an intermediary between at least two languages and cultures: German and Danish.

---

4   A Danish version was published by Louis Bobé in 1898: *Johan Caspar Lavaters Rejse til Danmark i Sommeren 1793*. Copenhagen: Lehmann & Stages Forlag.

KAREN KLITGAARD POVLSEN

References

Adams, Percy G. 1983: *Travel Literature and the Evolution of the Novel.* Lexington: University Press of Kentucky.

Bakhtin, Mikhail 1981: Forms of Time and Chronotope in the Novel. *The Dialogic Imagination.* Austin: University of Texas: 84-258.

Bakhtin, Mikhail 1986: The Bildungsroman and Its Significance in the History of Realism. *Speech Genres and Other Essays.* Austin: University of Texas: 10-59.

Barton, Arnold 1998: *Northern Arcadia. Foreign Travelers in Svandinavia, 1765-1815.* Carbondale: Southern Illinois University Press.

Brun Friederike 1799 (1791): Reise nach den Kullen in Schonen 1786. *Prosaische Schriften II.* Zürich: Orell Füssli: 179-200.

Batten, Charles L. Jr. 1978: *Pleasurable Instruction. Form and Convention in eightteenth Century Travel Literature.* Berkeley: University of California Press.

Brenner, Peter J. 1989: *Der Reisebericht.* Frankfurt am Main: Suhrkamp.

Brenner, Peter J. 1990: *Der Reisebericht in der deutschen Literatur.* Tübingen: Max Niemeyer Verlag.

Chard, Chloe 1999: *Pleasure and Guilt on the Grand Tour.* Manchester: Manchester University Press.

Dolan, Brian 2001: *Ladies of the Grand Tour.* London: HarperCollins Publishers.

Griep, Wolfgang und Hans-Wolf Jäger 1986: *Reisen im 18. Jahrhundert.* Heidelberg: Carl Winter Universitätsverlag.

Griep, Wolfgang 1991: *Sehen und Beschreiben.* Eutin: Eutiner Forschungen.

Hartmann, Regina 2000: *Deutsche Reisende in der Spätaufklärung unterwegs in Skandinavien.* Frankfurt am Main: Peter Lang.

Ingamells, John 1997: *A Dictionary of British and Irish Travellers in Italy 1701-1888.* New Haven: Yale University Press.

Klitgaard Povlsen Karen, 2001a: Det sublime øjeblik. Eds.: Elin Andersen and Karen Klitgaard Povlsen: *Tableau – Det sublime øjeblik.* Aarhus: Klim: 7-24.

Klitgaard Povlsen Karen, 2001b: Standsningens attitude i krop og tekst. Ibid.: 93-116.

Klitgaard Povlsen Karen, 2002: Rejselitteratur i 1700tallet. Forskningsoversigt over den tyske og engelske litteratur efter 1990. *HTF-Historisk Tidskrift för Finland* 3: 2002: 415-428.

Klitgaard Povlsen 2004: Stedets blik: Kulturmøde som naturmøde. *Kontur* 8: 50-58.

Maurer, Michael 1999 ed.: *Neue Impulse der Reiseforschung.* Berlin: Akademie Verlag.

Pratt, Mary Louise 1992: *Imperial Eyes.* London and New York: Routledge.

Stagl, Justin 1995: *A History of Curiosity. The Theory of Travel 1550-1800.* Sidney: Harwood Publishers.

Todorov, Tzvetan 1996 (1991): The Journey and Its Narratives. Eds.: Chloe Chard and Helen Langdon: *Transports: Travel, Pleasure, and Imaginative Geography, 1600-1830.* New Haven: Yale University Press: 287-296.

Viviès, Jean 2002: *English Travel Narratives in the Eighteenth Century. Exploring Genres.* Burlington: Ashgate.

Original Quotes

Friederike Brun:

Schnell wie ein Blitz durchströmten mich Gedanken, nicht an Lebende – an Todte – die d o r t
leben! An Andreas den sanften Jüngling, der sein
ganzes Leben hindurch dem Himmel entgegen
lächelte! An meinen zarten Säugling, der weinend
die Erde begrüsste, weinend sie wieder verliess!
Ach an Euch alle ihr vorangegangenen Geliebten,
denen eine mildere Sonne leuchtet! (1799: 188)

So ist denn eingeschränkteres Glück unser ei-
gentliches Los, dacht' ich. (Ibid.: 197)

Ramdohr:

Diese gegenden erinnerten mich lebhaft an die
ufer der Brenta zwischen Padua und Venedig.
Aber der mangel schöner bauart an den garten-
häusern und die unvortheilhafte tracht des hiesi-
gen landmanns hinderte die völlige illusion, mich
in der nähe des orts zu glauben, wo meine einbildungskraft mit am stärksten gehoben, und mit
am vollkommensten befriedigt ist. (1792: 3)

Kurz! Wenn berge den horizont bekräntzten, so
könnte man die lage von Kopenhagen zu den
schönsten in der welt rechnen. (1792: 204)

PÄR ELIASSON

The order of Stockholm: The "State" of the Swedish Capital Around the Year 1800

The German travellers of the period 1795-1820 which I discuss in this paper were all men of literature. Their itineraries reflect their special interests as they spent a lot of time in the few existing learned milieux of Sweden, i.e. in the capital city of Stockholm, and in the university town of Uppsala. These writers can be described as enlightened encyclopedic travellers trying to explain the 'state' of the social and political life of Sweden. Here, they will be related to the German tradition of encyclopedic travel and I will focus on their descriptions of Stockholm as both a natural and a cultural milieu.

The majority of foreign travel books published about Sweden at that time were written in German, so my choice of German travel writers reflects both the travel and publishing patterns of the era (Bring 1954). The many personal relationships that existed between Swedish and German learned men also contributed to the German interest for Sweden. Until 1815 Sweden had a university in Greifswald, in Swedish Pomerania, and Swedes also visited German universities such as Göttingen. At both these universities journals were published that reported on Swedish matters and often literary and scientific news travelled via Germany to Sweden.

The political dimension of Enlightenment travel

Charles L. Batten has described the famous English travel writer Joseph Addison as the "model writer if not a totally typical traveller" of the eighteenth century (Batten 1978: 9). Batten argues that Addisons's style, his choice of topics, and his ambition to tell something new about the already familiar places he described, set an example for others to follow. (Batten 1978: 14-15). His style of writing was later critized for being merely descriptive and lacking any individual touches by the author. But Addison had an enlightened political agenda as well. During his journey to Italy in 1705 he seemed to notice a strong connection between despotism and Catholicism in some parts of Italy, especially in the Papal States, which led to economic backwardness. (Müllenbrock 1982: 116).

During the latter part of the eighteenth century a new kind of travel literature emerged in Germany that is described as 'statistical and topographical' or 'staatskundlichen' in German. These books contained up-to-date data on the constitutions and institutions of nations and cities, on trade and economy, city planning and architecture, and they also described the mentality, customs and beliefs of the inhabitants. The authors of these 'statistical' travel reports saw themselves as being without any bias as they only objectively described what they had seen with their own eyes during their journeys. (Bödeker 1986: 281).

The most extreme representative of this kind of enlightenment 'statistical' travel is Friedrich Nicolai (1735-1811), a publisher and journalist from Berlin who published a very extensive travel report in 12 volumes on his journey in Germany and Switzerland. (Nicolai 1783-96, Möller 1977: 108-109). The purpose of Nicolai's journey was to describe the state of learning, industry, religion and morals in the German states that he had visited in 1781. Sure enough Nicolai saw himself as a social scientist, a teller of true tales who stood above party politics. But Nicolai also had an enlightened political agenda as he noted any deficiencies he found and even recommended possible remedies (Martens 1979: 45-67, Möller 1977: 108-110). The information given in his travel description could be used to improve the state of the German lands. Nicolai's book should then be read as a kind of applied social science handbook (Martens 1983:100, Stewart 1978: 252-262).

Nicolai's description of the Habsburg capital Vienna may be read as enlightenment model topography of a city, indicating what was important to include in such a text. He begins by describing the plan of the city and the architecture of its official buildings. He discusses the 'Policey-Wesens', a broad category that both included the police department and the cleaning of the streets. Institutions such as hospitals, prisons, postal services, universities, academies, libraries, natural history collections, museums, and bookstores are described. Nicolai finaly discussed the public life on the streets and he ended his topography with a long paragraph on the morals and behaviour of the inhabitants of Vienna (Martens 1979: 48-49, Möller 1977: 128-131).

Nicolai's paragraphs on the 'Policey-Wesen' in Vienna are full of superlatives. The streets were clean and all official buildings and institutions were kept in very good order. Despite the large nummer of coaches on the streets there were no traffic problems in Vienna as order prevailed everywhere on the streets. The word 'order' ('Ordnung') thus had very positive connotations for the enlightened traveller Nicolai (Martens 1979: 49).This word 'order' is also used by foreign travellers when they describe the state of Stockholm in the first decade of the nineteenth century.

Friedrich Nicolai is a remarkable example of the kind of ambitious enlightened encyclopedic German traveller that existed at the end of the eighteenth cen-

PÄR ELIASSON

tury. I believe that his meticulous descriptions of the state of – especially the larger – German cities and the political conclusions he drew from his many observations of city life could have been used as a model for other German travel writers in the era.

Intertextuality: Establishing a position in the text as a teller of true tales

Enlightenment travellers tried to establish a position in their texts as trustworthy tellers of up-to-date facts. They especially wanted to make sure that the reader understood that they, the writers, knew more than earlier travellers had known. Nicolai was critical of the antiquarian travellers of the eighteenth century that did not discuss the contemporary social realities. This does not mean that Nicolai was not interested in history, as historical investigations could help the social scientist understand how a certain society had developed until its present state (Bödeker 1986: 288-89).

Thus a knowledge of history was also crucial when writing an up-to-date description of Sweden. Present conditions had to be compared to what had been told by other travellers to Sweden, as this was the easiest way for a traveller to get some knowledge of recent history. This method explains why especially the travel genre can be described as intertextual, travel books always refer to other travel books. References to earlier works are not seldom used in a polemic against those predecessors who got things wrong and now had to be corrected (Hartmann 2000: 10-12).

A splendid example of this kind of intertextuality is the many explicit and implicit references made to the Italian traveller Joseph Acerbi by foreign travel writers in the early nineteenth century. The Italian Giuseppe (Joseph) Acerbi, who travelled in Sweden in 1798-99, was critized for being a liar and he was perhaps also a dangerous Jacobin. (On Acerbi see Anka Ryall in this volume). When Acerbi's travelogue was published in 1802, Swedes were enraged by his many negative comments on the 'state' of Sweden. Acerbi even described the Swedish king, Gustav IV Adolf, as a despotic reactionary. The Swedish authorities were so troubled by Acerbi's book that it was forbidden. The Swedish poet Carl Gustaf Leopold was commissioned to comment on Acerbi's book and this comment was later translated into German by the Greifswald scholar and expert on Sweden, Friedrich Rühs.

Rühs also wrote critical comments in the German translation of Acerbi's book. (Acerbi 1802/1803, Willers, 1945: 104-110, Önnerfors 2003, 416-418).[1]

The German traveller Johann Gottfried Seume gives us another good example of intertextuality when he writes in his travel report that he had not written it for the reader that already knew everything about Scandinavia, but neither was it for the reader that knew nothing at all. Seume thus informs his readers that his travel book should be read as only one minor contribution to the entire corpus of books on the region. (Seume 1806: Vorrede, IV). Seume also refers to the enlightenment tradition of Nicolai which recommended that the traveller should first try to describe the 'state' of things and then suggest remedies for the social ills found. Seume admits that he had given some harsh judgements on Scandinavia, but all his judgements were based on his own experiences of the realities of the region at the time of his journey (Seume 1806: Vorrede, IV). Seume, when later editing his book, tries to convince his readers that he has been true to what he had seen himself during the journey. He states: "I have not anticipated anything but I have scrupulously described everything as it was at the time and what I thought about it then" (Seume 1806: Vorrede, VII). Seume's descriptions ought then to be read as "snapshots" of Sweden from the summer of 1805, which reflected the ideas he had at that time.

In 1806 the Leipzig Professor Johann Georg Eck published *Reisen in Schweden* (Leipzig, 1806), a book that was especially appreciated in Sweden as an antidote to Acerbi (Eck 1806, Willers 1945: 100, Önnerfors 2003: 418). Eck declares in his preface that he has only told his readers the correct information as acquired from the leading Swedish experts. He wanted to give his readers as many new facts as possible, thus he had tried to avoid writing about what was already known, but sometimes he had to correct the information given by other travellers (Eck 1806: Vorrede, 2-3). Eck's statement is typical for the travel genre that always stressed the ideal of 'novelty', as it is described by the German historian of travel Regina Hartmann. Hartmann points out that critique of earlier writers forced the travel writers to refer to older texts in various ways. This is another good example of the intertextuality of the travel genre (Hartmann, 2000: 13-14).

The many intertextual connections between these travel books puts the texts in an established literary genre, the encyclopedic 'statistical' travel book of the enlightenment. They also indicated to the contemporary readers that these texts

---

1   Joseph Acerbi, *Travels through Sweden, Finland and Lapland to the North Cape, in the years 1798 and 1799* (London, 1802), the German translation, done by Philipp Christopher Wyland, was edited and "corrected" by Friedrich Rühs, as *Reise durch Schweden und Finnland bis an die äussersten Gränzen von Lappland in den Jahren 1798 und 1799* (Berlin, 1803). Uno Willers, *Ernst Moritz Arndt och hans svenska förbindelser: Studier i svensk-pommersk historiografi och svensk oponionsbildning* (Stockholm, 1945), 104-110, see also Andreas Önnerfors, *Svenska Pommern: Kulturmöten och identifikation 1720-1815* (Lund, 2003), 416-418.

PÄR ELIASSON

should be interpreted and read as belonging to an entire corpus of travel books on Sweden.

Urban criteria of enlightenment

What criteria could be used by German enlightened encyclopedic travellers to measure the "state" of Sweden around the year 1800? From which circumstances could a traveller passing through a nation and its capital determine the quality of literature, science or the performing arts, or, for that matter, the morals of its inhabitants and the possibility of social and economical improvements in the future?

The German literary historian Friedrich Wolfzettel argues that French preromantic or enlightenment travellers saw themselves as members of a European cosmopolitic and universialistic enlightenment culture of equals. When these travellers visited other countries they always lived in the social milieux they were comfortable in. Wolfzettel points out that these travellers did not really understand or appreciate anything that was foreign or unknown as they, in a sense, never left home (Wolfzettel 1986: 17).

The literary historian H. Arnold Barton also believes that the Age of Enlightenment was cosmopolitan in its outlook. Civilization was then regarded to be one and indivisible, and having some essential attributes that were judged by the standards of Europe's cultural capitals, above all Paris and London. These attributes were: cities, literature and the arts, science, scholarship and learning, royal courts, government and its functions, and the manners and mores of polite society. Barton writes that, together, they created a nations's 'public visage', and by scrutinizing this 'public face' foreign travellers could determine a nation's level of civility (Barton 1998: 23). These are also the areas of life that interested statistical enlightenment travellers such as Nicolai. But in Sweden cities were few and far between, thus the capital Stockholm became *the* place to describe for these enlightenment travellers. It was only in larger cities – especially the capitals, that foreign travellers could find the known attributes of civilization (Barton 1998: 29).

The cityscape of Stockholm: Nature and culture mixed

Enlightenment travellers were focused on what could be seen and described, i.e. the outer appearance of civilization that could be observed for instance in the street life. Nicolai had found many such visible attributes in his description of Vienna that could be labelled 'order'. Did Stockholm, the Swedish capital, meet these expectations of regularity and order? What did these German travellers think of the setting or cityscape of Stockholm?

In the early nineteenth century three categories or aesthetic labels were used by travellers for describing landscapes: the sublime, the picturesque and the beautiful. The sublime landscape was wild and dramatic and associated with awesome natural phenomena, the beautiful landscape was man-made and controlled by man, while the picturesque landscape was a mix between these two extremes. (Fjågesund & Symes 2003: 280-287).

It was important for the travellers of the era to find a good vantage point from which the overall shape of a landscape or cityscape could be analyzed using these aesthetic labels. This awareness of the importance of viewing from exactly the right spot is reflected in the description of Stockholm given by the German traveller Carl Gottlob Küttner in 1798 (Küttner II 1801). He spent three days walking around the city as he wanted to see it from many different angles, and then he wrote a short topography of Stockholm. This chapter gives the reader the feeling that he accompanies Küttner on a stroll through the city, as good views and suitable perspectives are indicated by the author. (Küttner II 1801: 227-229).

What impression did Küttner get of Stockholm? After complaining about the dirty look of the suburbs he states: "However I also found here some pretty views and some picturesque parts, because Stockholm just has that special aspect: it combines the picturesque and romantic with the pomp and beauty of a capital" (Küttner II 1801: 233). He found it difficult to describe Stockholm in the contemporary aesthetic terminology as, for him, it was a city of extremes. The central parts of the capital were very beautiful with the Royal palace, the stone palaces from the seventeenth century and the large regular squares, but most buildings in the capital were peasant houses built of wood. Sweden's capital could best be described as a peculiar mix of elegant houses and simple peasant dwellings. Küttner uses the German word 'mahlerisch', which means picturesque, to describe the over-all view of the city itself. (Küttner II 1801: 236-7).

Küttner even states that in the suburbs of Stockholm he sometimes believed he was in the Alps as he saw nothing but simple wooden buildings scattered among wild, naked and romantic cliffs. The proximity of the capital was sometimes not even felt in the suburbs, but:

When you climb such a cliff, from different spots you get the most romantic and, at the same time, the most splendid views of a beautiful seat of government; succinctly, in one glance you can observe palaces, churches, towers, islands, lakes, harbours filled with ships, beautiful culture, naked cliffs and the wildness of the Alps, all mixed together. These are the things that perhaps make Stockholm one of a kind. Never before have I from the same vantage point, within the limits of a city, seen anything so beautiful, splendid and grandiose, and never anything so simple, wild, and Alps like (Küttner 1801 II: 237).

346

The German traveller August Wilhelm von Nordenfels mentions that Stockholm was called 'The Venice of the North' (Nordenfels 1830: 173). However, Nordenfels argues that this designation was not correct at all as the panorama of Stockholm could not be compared to the classical panoramas of the southern cities of Constantinople, Naples or Genoa. The impression these cities gave was that of an amphitheatre rising above a single large bay, easiest to describe in the picturesque manner according to Nordenfels. When Nordenfels standing on the hill of Mosebacke looked out over Stockholm, he was impressed by the incredible diversity of the panoramic view: "Not quite in any other place on earth do art and nature appear in their full pure grandeur, so sharply divided and not mixed, but standing side by side. Where the Stockholm palaces end, the wild romantic cliffs immediately appear covered with their primeval and awesome pinewoods" (Nordenfels 1830: 173- 174). To Nordenfels this was not really a picturesque sight; rather, this beautiful cityscape and the perhaps dangerous, sublime landscape seemed to co-exist side by side.

Johann Gottfried Seume writes that Stockholm is called the paradise of the North (Das Paradis des Nordens). This designation is suitable if one refers to the beautiful location of the capital. Seume also thinks that it is the peculiar mix of urbanity and rural landscape that makes the panorama of Stockholm unique. (Seume 1806: 187-188). Seume directs his readers to the descriptions of Stockholm written by Acerbi and Küttner, and – like Nordenfels – Seume tells his readers that they should stand on the hill of Mosebacke if they wished to see the best possible panoramic view of Stockholm (Seume 1806: 188). This is another good example of intertextuality. Mosebacke Hill now becomes established as the vantage point from which to view the cityscape of Stockholm. In most European cities these 'fixed' points emerged. According to these German travellers the city of Stockholm was situated in a wild and romantic landscape of tree-covered cliffs, from which water could be seen everywhere. And, even if many of its buildings were simple, the capital had its share of impressive palaces and nicely decorated squares and streets. In the then contemporary aesthetic terminology the mixed views of the cityscape of Stockholm given by these travellers could perhaps best be labelled picturesque, but it seems like no aesthetic label was really suitable.

Model descriptions of the sights of Stockholm

It is obvious that the descriptions of the learned and artistic milieux of Stockholm in the German travelogues that I have read are very similar in content. In 1801 Küttner wrote that, at the time, only one description existed of Stockholm written in Swedish. And, as a stranger could not cope without a guidebook, Küttner decided to write a short topography of Stockholm to be included in his travelogue (Küttner II 1801: 227-229). In this text Küttner listed the important buildings and institutions of the capital (Küttner II 1801, 229-241), and as he anticipated, his list was read and used by other travellers. Seume wrote that as he was no good himself at writing descriptions, he instead recommended Küttner's and Acerbi's descriptions of Stockholm to his readers (Seume 1806, 188).

The German vicar of Stockholm, Dr. Lüdeke, wrote an inventory of the sights of the capital, which he normally gave to foreign travellers. According to the German traveller Johann Georg Eck, however, Lüdeke's list was too long and also recommended sights that could hardly be called sights at all. For that reason Eck then presented his own list of the sights of Stockholm, which contains 51 items (Eck 1806:145-149). Eck was not satisfied with Küttner's topography either, as Eck believed that even if Küttner's work was based on Lüdeke's inventory, Küttner had made unnecessary and incorrect additions to the original. Eck writes in a footnote that he was compelled to make this remark about Küttner's topography because many at that time considered Küttner's book to be one of the classic works on Sweden (Eck 1806: 146). Eck's criticism of the inventories of Lüdeke and Küttner is another very good example of the complex intertextuality that Hartmann discusses. (Hartmann 2000: 122-123).

There were other guidebooks for foreign travellers interested in the sights of Stockholm. Carl Fredrik Fredenhielm, the director of the Royal Museum, wrote in 1796 an unpublished guidebook on the collections. According to the Swedish art historian Anne-Marie Leander Touati, this description did not reflect the actual disposition of the collections; rather, it was hierarchically disposed beginning with the least important items and ending with the most important items, the statues of Apollon and Endymion (Leander Touati 1993: 48-49).

In 1794 Fredenhielm had also published *Ex Museo Regis Sveciae*, a short illustrated catalogue of some parts of the collection. The catalogue was reviewed in the influential German journal *Göttingische Anzeigen von gelehrten Sachen* in the same year, and Leander Touati convincingly argues that the German reviewer must have had access also to the unpublished guidebook (Leander Touati 1993: 50-51). It is thus possible that this unpublished guidebook was known to German travellers as well.

The sights of Stockholm: Buildings, institutions and people described

I shall try to analyse the views held by these German travellers on the state of the scientific and artistic life in Sweden, as could be understood from their descriptions of the learned and intellectual milieux of Stockholm. These descriptions are short and quite matter-of-fact, and are really only inventory lists of what could be observed in Stockholm, together with a few comments. These lists may well be compared to the specimen lists made by contemporary natural-historians when they travelled in foreign lands, but they did reflect the 'present state' or the existing prerequisites for learning and artistry in Sweden. It was actually up to the readers then to draw their own conclusions.

Museums and collections

We will begin by following our travellers to the royal art collections kept in the Royal Palace: While the Gallery of Paintings would not be of any significance in Italy, in the far distant and poor country of Sweden it was all that could be expected, stated Küttner. And, although some good paintings were to be found there, the collection could not really be called a 'royal collection'! (Küttner II 1801: 242). The Dutch traveller Johan Meerman visited Stockholm in 1797-98, and his travelogue was published in Dutch in 1804. It was translated into German by Freidrich Rühs in 1811. Meerman agreed with Küttner that the Gallery of Paintings had some excellent works of art but most paintings were second-rate. (Meerman I, 1804/1811: 315-316). It is obvious that this gallery did not meet these travellers expectations with regard to a national or royal art collection.

More impressive was the large Royal Collection of Drawings and Engravings, all made by famous painters, among these were about 40,000 portraits. Not all of these items were first-rate and the collection was not kept in the best order argued Meerman. (Meerman I, 1804/1811: 316). Eck also visited these two royal art collections and he believed that the collection of drawings was perhaps the best and most complete collection in Europe. (Eck 1806: 203-204). At least, then, the collection of drawings was up to the expected standard of a national collection.

The Royal Museum or the Collection of antique Greek and Roman statues and other art objects, established by the late king Gustavus III, was much more impressive than any of the other royal art collections, writes Küttner. Its rooms in the Royal palace were nicely decorated and the objects had been arranged with great taste. The most impressive item was the Roman statue of the Sleeping Endymion (Küttner II, 1801: 242). Both Meerman and Eck agree with Küttner's opinions on the the Royal Museum and they also praise the Endymion (Meerman I, 1804/1811: 315-317, Eck 1806: 199-202).

It is quite possible that Küttner's, Meerman's and Eck's descriptions of the Royal Museum follow Fredenhielm's guidebook mentioned above, at least they list the items in the same order as he does. Meerman and Eck both met Fredenhielm in person and the Swedish curator gave Eck some engravings of the statues of the collection, this may refer to Fredenhielm's *Ex Museo Regis Sveciae*. (Meerman I, 1804/1811: 314, Eck 1806: 199-202).

The artists and painters of Sweden: Sergel and the others

The art collections of Stockholm did not really seem to impress these cultivated and enlightened travellers. What about the Swedish painters of the era? Küttner lists the Swedish painters and artists that were active at the time of his visit in 1798 and he informs the reader that he has met all the artists he had heard about. He states that Stockholm has a greater number of artists than one could expect in such a city (Küttner II, 1801: 280). Meerman and Eck also presents short biographical lists of the Swedish painters, but they are not impressed by them. (Küttner II, 1801: 280-282, Meerman I, 1804/1811: 312-314, Eck 1806: 183-185).

The only Swedish artist that the travellers held in the highest regard was the famous sculptor Johann Tobias Sergel. He was the only Swedish artist that Küttner was really impressed by, and Sergel's statue of Gustavus III was splendid even if it perhaps lacked some of the dignity of the Roman statues that served as its model (Küttner II, 1801: 281-284). This statue of Gustavus III was praised by Seume as being a good blend of the modern and antique styles, because it actually reflected the Antique spirit (Seume 1806: 189). Eck also visited Sergel and he was impressed by Sergel's statues of Amor and Psyche. He had never seen anything that came even close to them: when he gazed at them, it was as though the marble was alive! Eck insisted that Sergel was even better than the Italian Canova in the use of marble (Eck 1806: 163-164). According to Meerman, Sergel was one of the best sculptors in Sweden, but Meerman believed that because Sweden was such a backward country in the arts, Sergel was not given either the recognition or resources that he needed (Meerman I, 1804/1811: 311-312).

Sweden thus had at least one artist who could be compared with the foreign masters: the sculptor Sergel, whose classical training in Italy, and mastership of the prevailing classical style in sculpture supported this foreign recognition. However, as Meerman indicated, conditions for artists were not good in Sweden, and not even Sergel got the recognition there that he deserved. Therefore, with the sole exception of Sergel, it is obvious that these foreign travellers were anything but impressed by the Swedish artists.

The Academies of Sweden

Meerman argues that the late King Gustavus III was influenced by French models when he established the academies of Stockholm. The Royal Swedish Academy of

Sciences (Kungliga Vetenskaps-akademien) had 93 Swedish fellows in 1805, many of these from the nobility, and it had 64 foreign fellows. The Academy had its own elegant building in the city and its *Proceedings* were famous and well-regarded abroad. It had a natural history collection, a collection of physical instruments and a library containing both Swedish dissertations and foreign books of science. Meerman was given a tour of the building by the secretary of the Academy (Meerman I, 1804/1811: 303-304).

Eck was shown the natural history collection of the Academy of Sciences by the curator Dr Conrad Quensel. The Academy itself was, according to Eck, highly regarded for its many excellent contributions to all the sciences and many prominent foreign scientists were fellows of the Academy. Interestingly, his list of 49 Swedish fellows of the Academy presents their professional titles as well as their scientific interests and writings. Eck states that many of these fellows were prominent men of science who had spread the light of science both in Sweden and abroad (Eck 1806: 207-215).

However, the most popular and esteemed academy in Stockholm was, according to Meerman, the literary Swedish Academy (Svenska Akademien). Some of its fellows were from the nobility, who also considered it a great honour to become an elected fellow of this Academy. Its public meetings, held at the Exchange, were usually visited by many citizens of the capital (Meerman I, 1804/1811: 305-306). Eck also considered the Swedish Academy as the most prominent academy in Sweden. It was modelled after the Academie Française and had 18 fellows, all Swedes. Its proceedings gave recommendations on the correct use of the Swedish language, and it also contained poetry and biographies of prominent Swedes. According to Eck, the Italian traveller Acerbi had written a terrible caricature of the Academy. And as Acerbi's description was full of lies, Eck felt he had to give a true picture of the fellows of the Swedish Academy by producing a detailed biographical list describing their many merits (Eck 1806: 219-29).

The Royal Academy of Sciences and its fellows seemed to meet the high expectations of the foreign travellers. The Academy was at the time well-known abroad, as ever since the middle of the eighteenth century Sweden had had a very good reputation for its many contributions to the world of science. Around the year 1800, however, the literary Swedish Academy was perhaps more esteemed in Sweden which could indicate that the conditions for doing scientific work had deteriorated.

According to the Swedish historian of science, Karin Johannisson, the status of science went down in Sweden at the end of the eighteenth century, as science lost some of its economic and practical function and also lost most of its social function as it simply went out of fashion. One of her sources is Acerbi, who gives a negative picture of the state of Swedish science and learning around 1800. (Johannisson 1979/1980: 109-110, 153-54). But the learned German travellers referred to above do not necessarily confirm Johannisson's analysis of the state of Swedish science at the turn of the century 1800.

The 'public visage' as displayed in the street life of Stockholm

But there were also matters to observe in the streets for these observant, enlightened, encyclopedic travellers. Eck remarked on the dress habits of the higher strata of society who, without exception, followed the French style. The Swedes were also fond of orders and medals, and these were valued more than even money. The nobility was held in very high regard in Sweden and men of science as well as merchants all wanted to become enobled. This, Elk believed, was bad for the Swedish economy as the progressive values of the bourgeois would then be looked down on (Eck 1806: 231-232). The same conclusion had been drawn by Friedrich Nicolai when he described the worst prejudice of the citizens of Vienna as the 'prejudice of birth' ('Vorurtheil der Geburt'). Nicolai did not criticize the nobility as such, but was very critical of the interest of Viennese society in becoming enobled ('Nobilitierungssehnsücht') (Martens: 1983: 111-112).

The question of the order of Sweden

According to the foreign travellers referred to in this paper, most Swedish institutions, collections, scholars, scientists and artists of the early nineteenth century could not match the standards of similiar establishments and people in other countries. The sole exception to this rule was the excellent Swedish men of science at the Royal Academy of Sciences. Originality in the world of art was seldom to be seen, even if the sculptor Sergel was among the best in his field. The royal art collections were rather small and did not contain many valuable items. However, the Royal Museum with its antique sculptures was very good.

But at least institutions like the academies seemed to be well organized. Could this Swedish tendency towards order and organization perhaps be observed in other places in the capital? Even in the streets?

Eck argued that the architecture of Stockholm was of the highest standard and quality. All official buildings and most of the private houses were symmetrical and built in good taste, despite the fact that there existed no architectural handbooks in Sweden. Everytime Eck wandered in the city he was impressed by the tidiness and social stability he believed he could observe and he was convinced that the local police contributed to this prevailing order (Eck 1806: 153). The archictecture and the clean streets of the city seemed to bear witness to the social order of Sweden, if one is to believe one of the reflections Eck made from his observations of street life in Stockholm. The capital was the site of the court, of all governmental institutions, of scientific and learned academies and of commerce. All these institutions seemed to have a positive influence on the public spirit of Stockholm believed Eck, even if the old French influence of the eighteenth century could become problematical again (Eck 1806:153-154). The last comment is typical for German travellers who disliked any foreign influences – and especially anything French.This description of Stockholm is reminiscent of a similiar picture Friedrich Nicolai gave of Vienna as a place of order in 1781.

Seume concluded his description of Sweden with another interesting characterization of the nation: "Sweden is perhaps the most humane and friendly country in the North. Despite all the poverty, that one cannot disregard or hide, there prevails everywhere an order and an appearance of well-being" (Seume 1806: 217). Even if poverty existed in Sweden, everything seemed to be kept in very good order; obviously the entire country was being supervised by a benevolent and enlightened regime. Especially the countryside of Sweden looked prosperous, and Seume writes that he had not seen any village in Sweden in which he would not have lived, if he had ever wished to do so (Seume 1806: 217). Regina Hartmann convincingly argues that Seume's enthusiasm for this patriarchal Swedish rural order must be understood as a contrast to the feudal disorders of the serfs of Livland in Russia. Hartmann argues that Seume's Russian experience pre-condition his views on Sweden. Thus Russian disorder is set against Swedish order (Hartmann 2000: 181-185).

Order is then used as a word of praise by both Eck and Seume, but with rather different connotations. Eck talks about the visible rational order of the capital, perhaps an effect of the benevolent influence of the urban cosmopolitan civilization, while Seume praises the rational patriarchal order of the Swedish countryside. Hartmann gives further examples of this enthusiasm for order, as other German travellers compare the industry, efficiency and technical knowledge of the Swedish farming community and rural industry with the indolence and ignorance of German farmers (Hartmann 2000: 161).

The different 'orders' of Sweden that foreigners such as Eck or Seume seemed to find, also had a function in their texts. As enlightenment travellers they wanted to fully understand the society in which they travelled. The many disparate descriptions that their travelogues are filled with could better be understood if the author imposed a kind of rational order from above. If you believed that Sweden was a rational society, where the authorities were in control of both the city and the countryside, any anomaly could be explained away and reforms could be imposed.

Perhaps the time had come at the beginning of the nineteenth century to establish a new kind of order in Sweden? The word did have political implications during the era of the Napoleonic wars. And in 1809 a new political order was established in Sweden when the despotic king was toppled and a new, more democratic, constitution was accepted by the Diet.

References

Acerbi, Joseph 1802: *Travels through Sweden, Finland and Lapland to the North Cape, in the years 1798 and 1799* London: J. Mawman.

Acerbi, Joseph 1803: *Reise durch Schweden und Finnland bis an die äussersten Gränzen von Lappland in den Jahren 1798 und 1799*. Ed., Friedrich Rühs. Berlin:Vossische Buchhandlung.

Barton, H. Arnold 1998: *Foreign Travelers in Scandinavia, 1765-1815*. Carbondale & Edwardsville: Southern Illinois University Press.

Batten, Charles. L. Jr. 1978: *Pleasurable Instruction: Form and Convention in Eighteenth-Century Travel Literature*. Berkeley, Los Angeles & London: University of California Press.

Bring, Samuel E. 1954: *Itineraria Svecana: Bibliografisk förteckning över resor i Sverige fram till 1950*. Stockholm: Almqvist & Wiksell.

Bödeker, Hans Erich 1986: Reisebeschreibungen im historischen Diskurs der Aufklärung. *Aufklärung und Geschichte: Studien zur deutschen Geschichtswissenschaft im 18. Jahrhundert*. Eds., Hans Erich Bödeker, Georg G. Iggers, Jonathan B. Knudsen, & Peter H. Reill. Göttingen:Vandenhoeck & Ruprecht.

Eck, Johann Georg 1806: *Reisen in Schweden* . Leipzig: C.H. Reclam.

Fjågesund, Peter & Symes Ruth A. 2003: *The Northern Utopia: British Perceptions of Norway in the Nineteenth Century*. Amsterdam & New York: Editions Rodopi.

Hartmann, Regina 2000: *Deutsche Reisende in der Spätaufklärung unterwegs in Skandinavien: Die Verständigung über der "Norden" im Konstruktionsprozeß ihrer Berichte*. Frankfurt am Main: Peter Lang.

Johannisson, Karin 1979/1980: Naturvetenskap på reträtt: En diskussion om naturvetenskapens status under svenskt 1700-tal. *Lychnos* 1979-80.

Küttner, Carl Gottlob 1801: *Reise durch Deutschland, Dänemark, Schweden, Norwegen und einen Theil von Italien, in den Jahren 1797, 1798, 1799*, I-II. Leipzig: Georg Joachim Göschen.

Martens, Wolfgang 1979: Zum Bild Österreichs in Friedrich Nicolais 'Beschreibung einer Reise durch Deutschland und die Schweiz, im Jahre 1781'. *Anzeiger der Österreichischen Akademie der Wissenschaften: Philosophisch-Historische Klass*e 116:2 (1979).

Martens, Wolfgang 1983: Ein Bürger auf Reisen. *Friedrich Nicolai 1733-1811: Essays zum 250. Geburtstag*. Ed., Bernhard Fabian. Berlin: Nicolaische Verlagsbuchhandlung.

Meerman, Johan 1811 (1804): *Reise durch den Norden und Nordosten von Europa in den Jahren 1797 bis 1800*, I-II, translated by Friedrich Rühs. Wien: B. Ph. Bauer.

Heinz-Joachim Müllenbrock 1982: Die politischen Implikationen der 'Grand Tour': Aspekte eines spezifisch englischen Beitrags zur europäischen Reiseliteratur der Aufklärung. *Arcadia* 17.

Möller, Horst 1977: Landeskunde und Zeitkritik im 18. Jahrhundert: Die Bedeutung der Reisebeschreibung Friedrich Nicolais als regional- und sozialgeschichtliche Quelle. *Hessisches Jahrbuch für Landeskunde* 27.

Nicolai, Friedrich 1783-1796: *Beschreibung einer Reise durch Deutschland und die Schweiz, im Jahre 1781: Nebst Bemerkungen über Gelehrsamkeit, Industri, Religion und Sitten.* Berlin & Stettin.

Nordenfels, August Wilhelm von 1830: *Denkwürdigkeiten und Reisen des vestorbenen herzoglich Braunschweigischen Obristen von Nordenfels, Commandanten der Stadt Wolfenbüttel, Ritter des Guelphen-Ordens u.s.w. Nach dessen hinterlassenen Tagebüchern bearbeitet und herausgeben von C. Niedmann.* Braunschweig & Leipzig: Im Verlags-Comtoir.

Seume, Johann Gottfried 1806): *Mein Sommer 1805* . s.l.

Stewart, William E. 1978: *Die Reisebeschreibung und ihre Theorie im Deutschland des 18. Jahrhunderts.* Bonn: Bouvier Verlag, Martin Grundmann.

Touati, Anne-Marie Leander 1993: Den första museivägledningen: Carl Fredrik Fredenhielms text med inledning och kommentarer. *Kongl. Museum: Rum för ideal och bildning.* Ed., Solfrid Söderlind, Årsbok för Statens Konstmuseer 39. Stockholm: Streiffert Förlag AB.

Willers, Uno 1945: *Ernst Moritz Arndt och hans svenska förbindelser: Studier i svenskpommersk historiografi och svensk oponionsbildning* . Stockholm: Hugo Gebers Förlag.

Wolfzettel, Friedrich 1986: *Ce désir de vagabonde cosmopolite:Wege und Entwicklung des französischen Reiseberichts im 19. Jahrhundert.* Tübingen: Max Niemeyer Verlag.

Önnerfors, Andreas 2003: *Svenska Pommern: Kulturmöten och identifikation 1720-1815* . Lund: Avdelningen för Idé och lärdomshistoria.

Original Quotes

Ich habe nicht vorgegriffen, sondern gewissenhaft alles gegeben, wie es damals war, und wie ich darüber dachte. (Seume 1806: Vorrede VII)

Indessen fand ich auch hier einige hübsche Aussichten und einige mahlerische Partien; denn Stockholm hat nun einmal das Besondere, dass es das Mahlerische und Romantische mit dem Pomp und Schönheiten einer Haupstadt vereiniget. (Küttner II 1801: 233)

Ersteigt man hier und da einen solchen Felsen, so bekommt man beydes die romantischten und zugleich die prächtigsten Aussichten auf eine schöne Residenzstadt; kurz, man übersieht mit einem Blicke Palläste, Kirchen, Thürme, Inseln, Seen, mit Schiffen angefüllte Häfen, schöne Cultur, nackte Felsen und Wildheit der Alpen, alles durch einander. - Diess sind die Dinge, welche machen, dass Stockholm viellicht einzig in seiner Art ist. Nie habe ich etwas so Schönes, Prächtiges, Erhabenes, nie etwas so Armes, Wildes und Alpenartiges aus dem nähmlichen Geschichtspunkte gesehen, innerhalb der Umzäunung einer Stadt gesehen. (Küttner II 1801, 237)

Nicht leicht auf irgend einem andern Plätzchen der Erde treten Kunst und Natur in ihrer vollen reinen Grösse so scharf gesondert und unvermischt neben einander. Denn wo die Päläste Stockholms aufhören, da beginnen sogleich die wildromantischen Felsenhöhen mit ihren uralten schaurigen Fichtenwaldungen bedeckt. (Nordenfels 1830: 174)

Schweden ist wohl im Norden das humanste und freundlichste Land. Bey aller Armuth, die nicht zu läugnen und nicht zu verbergen ist, herrscht doch überall eine Ordnung und ein Anschein von Wollhabenheit. (Seume 1806, 217)

SYLWIA SCHAB

The Undiscovered North

Polish Travel Narratives of the Seventeenth and Eighteenth Centuries

Contacts between countries and their mutual image are to a large degree shaped under the influence of pragmatic factors.[1] Among the most crucial are the political and economic relations between particular countries. The form of these contacts is also influenced by factors which one might generally label 'mutual attractiveness' in terms of landscape, culture, or the educational opportunities. In the history of Poland the seventeenth and eighteenth centuries were a tumultuous period, filled with both internal conflict and wars with neighbouring countries – incl. rivalry with Sweden to dominate the Baltic region; a period which saw the beginning of the process of the 'destruction' and 'archaisation' of Poland (Gerner 2002: 67-71), eventually leading to the country's complete loss of statehood. Thus, the Polish traveller of the period found his way to Scandinavia at a very special moment in the history of his state; quite often he was a soldier, refugee, castaway or an investigator looking for Polish books and documents stolen in wartime. It was a rather unusual starting point and it seems inevitable that an unconventional perspective would consequently be adopted in their perception of the lands they visited; the more so, that due to the scarcity of direct travellers' accounts[2] the view of Nordic countries in Poland had not yet been fully shaped.

This article will attempt to answer the question of what elements in the life and organisation of the countries visited aroused these Poles' interest, and in what way the authors of the travel narratives built an image of 'the other'. The various levels of the intercultural translation process, as well as its implications for the construction and transmission of the picture of the *Norden* and its inhabitants in Poland will also be analysed. My key point is that Scandinavian countries were interpreted according to the current political situation in the traveller's own homeland – his attitude to the motherland being one of the most important factors determining

---

1   I would like to thank Waldemar Lýs and Keith Stewart for proof reading of this article.
2   Despite Polish visitors to Scandinavia, few early travellers' accounts have survived. One of the first was Daniel Vetter's book *Islandia abo krótkie opisanie wyspy Islandii* published in 1638. Indirect information about Scandinavia was most often contained in historical accounts.

his perception. The most striking example in support of this statement being a reversal in the image of Sweden – once interpreted as an incarnation of the devil and the main enemy, but later on depicted as a bastion of modernity, social justice and peace. The most surprising thing about those first travel narratives is the fact that the characteristics ascribed to Northern countries in them are still prevalent in the modern Polish picture of Scandinavia. Many of them have survived as stereotypes concerning Scandinavian customs or national characteristics. In this sense they have become "cultural cosmologies" or "'stubborn' narratives" (Witoszek 1997: 74), which have created specific channels for understanding this part of Europe.

Another question reflected upon is the small number of reports by travellers from this part of Europe and the reasons for this scarcity. The key factor in finding the answer to these question is the historical context, including the wars and their consequences for the Polish state and its culture, as well as the mental historical space showing a lack of any deep-rooted mythical constructs connected with the European North, such as the Gothic tradition. During the period discussed here, the Polish gentry developed its own myth emphasizing its independence, supremacy and special position among other noblemen in Europe. Although Poland used to be placed among the Nordic countries,[3] Poles had in general been heading for the European South and wanted to be regarded as belonging to the culturally highly developed South rather than to the barbarian North.

This analysis is primarily based on three source texts: *Pamiętniki* by Jan Chryzostom Pasek (who stayed in Denmark during 1658-59), letters by Jan Chrzciciel Albertrandy (who journeyed through Denmark and Sweden during 1789-90), and memoirs of Julian Ursyn Niemcewicz (who journeyed through Finland and Sweden in 1796), which contain the broadest reflections based on travels in Scandinavia during the aforementioned period.

Nobleman investigating Danish customs

Written in the 1690s and published in Poznań in 1836, *Pamiętniki* (Memoirs) by Jan Chryzostom Pasek (1636-1701) occupies a special place in the Polish literary canon. This diary of a minor nobleman from the Mazowsze region, who had received only an elementary education at a Jesuit college, played a major role in shaping the self-image of seventeenth century Poland.[4] Researchers agree that *Pamiętniki*

---

3   See Hendriette Kliemann-Geisinger's contribution in this volume.

4   This image was popularized by *Potop* (The Deluge), a novel by the Nobel laureate Henryk Sienkiewicz, where the Swedish invasion in Poland in 1655 forms the historical background for the plot. Written in a heroic-patriotic vein 'to cheer people's hearts', this novel became one of the most popular and influential Polish literary works of the nineteenth century. The popularity of *Pamiętniki* by Pasek is further proved by the number of its editions – the book has been published over 50 times since 1836.

should not be treated as a historical document.[5] However, what rivets the attention are the literary qualities, the stylistic and linguistic vividness, as well as the humour of this "most outstanding diary of the Baroque" (Hernas 1989: 259). J.Ch. Pasek arrived in Denmark with a Polish military expedition commanded by Stefan Czarniecki (1658-59). It was the period of the Danish-Swedish war (1657-1660), as well as the Swedish 'deluge' of Poland (1655-1660)[6], Poland being Denmark's ally in the conflict against Sweden. The diarist presents the reasons for which the two countries became allies in the fight against their mutual enemy, emphasizing the role of the eternal conflict between these Scandinavian neighbours, but also brings up the somewhat demagogical argument that "his nation [the Danes] had been *ab antiquo* favourably inclined towards the Polish nation, as old documents show" (Swiecicka 1978: 77-78).[7] Pasek devotes several pages of his diaries to the description of his stay in Denmark: he recreates the battle episodes of Czarniecki's expedition and his soldiers' relations with the locals; outlines the characteristics of the country's inhabitants – in particular the ladies and their customs and attitude to religion[8]; but he also describes the natural world – mainly marine animals. Pasek is an accidental traveller, essentially unprepared to dwell on and analyse a different culture; thus, he mainly sees what is different, odd, what "both awakens primitive curiosity, and captures one's imagination" (Rosznecki 1896: 167). The style of *Pamiętniki*, which is a collection of anecdotes associated with the person of the narrator, is described as 'a nobleman's tale',[9] and its narration is full of fancifulness and exaggeration in presenting people and events. The narrator of *Pamiętniki* writes out his observations into roles, assuming (sometimes only ostensibly) different points of view, which, on the level of the writer's strategy, reveals itself in 'giving the floor' to persons with whom he made contact during his visit to Denmark. This device is subordinated to the strategy of the traveller, "'a stranger' who wants to get to know and mentally comprehend an unknown reality" (Chemperek 2001:69). Pasek assumes several roles – a soldier, an observer of local customs, a

---

5   This judgement is based on the diaries having been written down thirty years after the events to which they refer, as well as the inclination of the author – a well-known raconteur – to embroider numerous details and events.

6   A reference to Czarniecki's expedition also found its way into the Polish national anthem: "Like Czarniecki to Poznań, after the Swedish invasion, We will come back across the sea to save our motherland".

7   All quoted reference from Pasek's *Pamiętniki* come from the translation by M.A.J. Swiecicka, 1978.

8   Other accounts describing Czarniecki's expedition have also survived. These include one by Jakub Łoś, who contents himself with a description of the military aspects to the complete exclusion of the country and its inhabitants. He only remembers that the Danes admired the Poles' courage and military prowess (Łoś 2000: 88).

9   A genre of epic prose in Polish literature centred upon the life of the gentry. It is characterized by the lack of a compositional framework combined with a loose treatment of particular motifs, repetitions, and an anti-intellectual character.

naturalist, or a romantic lead – and differentiates the style of his narrative to suit the needs of the given area of observation he is currently covering. Describing an unknown reality Pasek employs the 'per analogiam' principle, and when this proves impossible, he resorts to a description revealing fantastic and fairy-tale-like elements.

A prominent place in his account is occupied by references to the appearance and behaviour of the inhabitants of Denmark, in particular these of the Danish women, who surprised Pasek not only with their good looks, but also with their temperament:

The Danish people are good-looking; the women are pretty but somewhat too fair. They dress nicely but in cities as well as in villages they wear wooden clogs. (…) In showing affection, the Danish women are not as restrained as the Polish women are, for even though they show some unusual shyness at first, they fall madly and passionately in love at the first meeting after exchanging merely a few words and they do not know how to conceal this amorousness. They are all too eager then to give up father and mother and a rich dowry, and are ready to follow their beloved even to the ends of the earth .(Swiecicka 1978:84)

Moreover, Pasek could give a very, in his eyes, reliable example of the aforementioned behaviour – in the form of a letter which he was supposed to have received from a Danish noblewoman, who fell passionately in love with him. The young lady – Eleonora af Croes Dyvarne – expressed her feelings for "a splendid hero of a famous nation" (Swiecicka 1978:133) and a desire for "the presence of your Honor in the house of my father" (ibid:135). However, this episode is rather an act of self-creation by the author.[10]

A diarist who was raised under bashfulness-commanding Catholic morality, finds the habit of completely undressing before going to bed – even in the presence of visitors – a very meaningful customary trait. However, the inquisitive traveller finds a practical explanation for such behaviour: constructing the narrative, he gives the floor to Danish women, who bring up arguments of a theological and hygienic nature:

When we told them that this was shameful and that in our country even a wife did not do this in front of her husband, they used to tell us that in their land no shame was attached

---

10   Also in other travel narratives, Danish women seem to occupy a special place on the attractiveness scale. Other Scandinavian women are described as rather pretty (with the most outstanding exception being Lappish women who are so ugly that they do not look like human beings at all), but lacking gracefulness, which is "much easier to achieve having a smaller body and living in a warmer climate" (Tripplin 1844: 71), and temperament: "a dead fish has more temperament than a Norwegian peasant woman and at least as much sense of humor" (ibid: 231).

to this because one should not be ashamed of one's limbs, which were created by God. As for their sleeping in the nude, they said: "The chemise and other articles of clothing which are of service to us and cover us during the day, deserved a rest and should be allowed to have one at least at night. Besides, of what use are they to us and why should we take fleas and bugs to bed with us and allow them to bite us, thus interfering with our sweet dreams?" (Swiecicka 1978: 85-86)

Pasek's observations on the temperament and behaviour of Danish women as very distant from what he knew from his own parochial world, can be traced back to at least two different circumstances. The first one is connected with the religious context – a Polish Catholic (and in this sense a representative of the South European cultural circle) meets a Danish Protestant, who is not bound by any restrictive moral dictates rooted in the religious milieu. The second one concerns the social context – a Polish nobleman meets a Danish peasant. I would see the latter one as more explanatory. The bias pervading the description of the country, its inhabitants and the prevailing relationships stems from a feeling of superiority by a Polish peer, who finds himself ennobled by the ancient origin of his kind – an attitude consistent with the then widespread myth of the so-called Sarmatians.[11] It has to be stressed that it is this superiority of the Pole-nobleman over the Dane-peasant which thus reveals a class, rather than a national characteristic. One of the central elements of such an attitude was the conviction that the Polish nation enjoyed unique divine protection. Its origin goes back to this very period of the Polish-Swedish wars, and is directly related to repulsing the Swedish siege of the Jasna Góra Heavenly Mother Sanctuary in Częstochowa in 1655. The myth of divine protection found its sanction in declaring the Blessed Virgin Mary Queen of Poland (Gerner 2002: 66). In Pasek's *Pamiętniki* God became an ally of the Polish cause, and in conflicts between Poles and their enemies always takes the side of the former. Denmark is perceived as a country on a lower level of development, one that can neither pride itself on the nobility of its origin nor its customs, as well as being a country of heretics (although the religious aspect is interpreted according to the prevailing alliances). Swedes, the enemy, are heretics who cannot count on God's mercy. When, during an assault launched on the stronghold of Kolding where a castle tower and its Swedish defenders were blown up, the diarist presents his cause in the form of St. Peter's direct address to "sinners":

11   The notion of *Sarmatism* gained popularity with the Polish nobility in the sixteenth and seventeenth centuries. It referred to the myth of its ancient origin from the Iranian warrior tribe of Sarmatians, which subordinated the Slavonic tribes inhabiting the lands later referred to as "Polish". The key elements of the Sarmatian attitude were national-class megalomania, religious conservatism, as well as the belief that the Polish Commonwealth of the "Golden Age of (the Nobleman's) Freedom" was the most perfect form of the state (Bockenheim 2003: 6-7).

The wretches wanted to flee from the Poles to Heaven, but they were not admitted there. St. Peter closed the gate immediately and said: "Ah, scoundrels! You maintain that the grace of the Saints is useless, that their intercession with God is meaningless and unnecessary. (…) Even there God saved those who should have been saved. (…) Also now you have directed heavy fire at the Poles and yet you did not kill many of them – why? Because they are guarded by the angels and you by the black devils – now you see what their service is like!" (Swiecicka 1978: 99)

The description of the religiousness of the ally, the Danes, who were Lutherans just like the Swedes (!), is imbued with a different atmosphere: one full of tale and anecdote. Being 'homo religiosus', Pasek praises the beauty of churches, once Catholic, yet better preserved and offering "more beautiful" services "than those of our Polish Calvinists" (Swiecicka 1978: 87). He takes part in services celebrated by Protestant clergy, who respect the Catholic guests and are cautious not to say anything 'contra fidem' [against the faith]. In Pasek's narrative the pastor goes as far as to assume a line of mild defence of his creed, explaining: "We believe in what you believe, and you call us dissenters in vain" (Swiecicka 1978: 87). The description of the service is augmented with anecdotes about the conversion of Lutherans into 'the genuine faith', i.e. Catholicism; it also recounts the positive attitude and merry atmosphere in the church – laughter which brings the Lutherans and Catholics together and plays a cathartic function that helps avoid scandal.[12]

The war trail of Stefan Czarniecki's army led through a number of Danish towns in Jutland and Fyn. Pasek does not, however, pay much attention to their appearance, contenting himself by describing two of them, Århus and Ribe, as "pretty". Perhaps the judgment reflects the author's (who came from Mazowsze, a poor district of Poland) restricted point of reference. What he is interested in though is the country's fauna, mainly the marine life: in a semi-fantastic manner he lists and describes several species of fish, e.g.

Plenty of various kinds of fish was available there, of the talking and the groaning kind except for carp, which was scarce. (…) They have a horrible fish there, resembling the demon painted on church walls, with flames coming out of its mouth. (Swiecicka 1978:110-111)[13]

---

12 Apprentices to Polish officers steal prayer books, which, on the one hand is a breach of the *sacrum*, on the other, evidence that in Poland – a country with a rather low level of literacy – the book was considered a symbol of high intellectual and material status (Chemperek 2001).

13 Writing about fish, Pasek mentioned Greenland – probably confusing it with Zealand (!) – which "has so much fish that if people did not keep fishing there would be no *fretum navigabile* [navigable straits]" (Swiecicka 1978: 127).

The last description concerns the ray, which was popular in Scandinavia at the time. As the diarist's knowledge of nature is insufficient to recognize particular species, sober information is supplanted by entirely fanciful descriptions bringing to mind a visit to the 'Wunderkammer', the popular curiosity attraction of the era.

In his account, which serves – he admits – the purpose of a presentation of his own life, being a specific form of self-creation rather than a presentation of "those provinces and their natural resources", Pasek confuses numerous details; e.g. local names, the position of towns in relation to one another and the political status of particular territories; so he calls the county of Holstein a German province and confuses the inhabitants of Fyn with Finns (Polish: Fiończycy – Fińczycy). However, what seems more important for the analysis of the cultural aspect, is what elements Pasek consciously embellishes or plainly omits. According to his account, one might think that the relations between the allied forces and the inhabitants of the areas in which they were stationed were adequate, to say the least. We learn from historical sources, however, that cases of robbery, rape and exploitation of the local population were not infrequent (Ślaski 1977: 166).[14] In numerous places Pasek's report demonstrates the narrow horizons regarding his knowledge of the world, including a lack of references to countries other than his own, and his perplexity over the question of social relations in Denmark – so he accords the living standards of bourgeoisie and affluent peasants with an inflated social status (Chemperek 2001:70), mildly conservative religious views, and a certain kind of megalomania which has its origin in his proud membership of a social class of ancient descent, the beneficiaries of 'the Golden Freedom'. In spite of this, Pasek creates a positive image of the Danes, and juxtaposes it with a negative assessment of the Swedes – the very embodiment of evil. These negative stereotypes have survived in proverbs and sayings which originated in the 'post-Deluge' period, such as 'as evil as a Swede', 'as filthy as a Swede', 'Swedes have brought trouble to Poland' (Bystroń 1933:181), and 'to do something the Swedish way', i.e. insincerely (Krzyżanowski 1972:419).

---

14   Stanisław Rosznecki recalls folk tales relating to the stay of Polish troops in Denmark. They mainly talk about the cruelty of the Polish allies, their strange ways of behaviour and the supernatural skills of the Poles (e.g. an excellent sense of smell, which helped them nose out money and valuables), or soldiers' places of burial (the so-called *polakhullet*) (Rosznecki 1896: 183-203). Pasek related an anecdote about his own special skill as an 'interpreter' – he was sent as a delegate in order to get a contribution from the Danish peasants. He pretended not to know any foreign language and kept answering "Geld" to all questions until he got the money (Swiecicka 1978: 106-107).

After the wars with Sweden, despite attempts to introduce internal reform and modernise the Polish state, a slow process of political and economic disintegration of the Polish Commonwealth of Two Nations – Polish-Lithuanian – began. The weakened country became both an object and the arena for the political games played by its ever mightier neighbours: Prussia, Russia and Austria. This led to subsequent partitions of Poland (1772, 1793, 1795), in whose wake the Polish state vanished from the map of Europe for 123 years. Dynastic relations with and the political interests of the countries of the Scandinavian North lost significance following the ousting of the kings of the Swedish Vasa family from power in Poland (1668).

In a cultural sense, Poland was oriented towards such countries as Italy, France, Germany, England and the Netherlands – going there to study; seeking creative, artistic inspiration; and going on pilgrimages. The above tendencies are evidenced in data concerning Polish students at Scandinavian universities: the student register at Copenhagen University for the years 1720-1796 contains only one Polish name, and the registers from Uppsala and Lund – none (Ślaski 1977: 239). Historians also attribute a negative role to the Reformation movement in the development of mutual relations, although in the second part of the eighteenth century this factor seems to have lost its importance.

It is also for these reasons that eighteenth century Polish travel reports from the Nordic countries are scarce. Among the most interesting ones are two rhymed pieces by Jerzy Karol Skop (1754);[15] Tobiasz Grotkowski's *Podróż morska dwu studiujących Polaków*[16] of 1760; as well as letters written during 1789-90 by the royal envoy, Jan Chrzciciel Albertrandy; plus the memoirs (1796) of Julian Ursyn Niemcewicz: fragments of *Pamiętniki czasów moich* and *Podróż Juliana Ursyna Niemcewicza z Petersburga do Szwecyi w drodze do Ameryki roku 1798*. Tobiasz Grotkowski (d.1822) wrote his piece in 1760 when he was principal of a secondary school in Słuck. He recollects his return journey after a three-year period of study at Leiden University (1755-58). He arrived on the shores of Norway by accident – his ship foundered off the coast by the town of Grimstad. The circumstances did not engender a joyous impression upon the traveller: his only memories are related to scarce food supplies (except for fish and seafood). The author was able to fully experience the unrefined qualities of the food and drink as he spent approximately

15 In the Latin collection of poems the author included short characterizations of Denmark, Norway and Sweden, underlining Sweden's wealth in natural deposits, the harsh climate of Norway, as well as describing the Danes as the least strict of all Northern nations (Ślaski 1977: 261).

16 Full title: *Podróż morska dwu studiujących Polaków, gdy się z Amsterdamu do Gdańska okrętem pławili powracając z Akademiej Lejdeńskiej do granic ojczystych, opisana krótka przez Tobiasza Grotkowskiego, konrektora gimnazjum słuckiego w Słucku miesiąca lipca roku 1760.*

364

ten weeks in Norway, of which "none was merry". The piece, of which only five stanzas were devoted to his stay in this Northern country, also contains a jocular description of the Norwegian landscape disguised in the form of a riddle:

(…) in a land people in the land do dwell,
Though no land in their land they hold. (Kotarski 1973: 169)[17]

Scholar searching for stolen books

A much more abundant material for analysis is contained in the letters by the Polish scholar Jan Chrzciciel Albertrandy (1731-1808), a member of a legate mission to Sweden,[18] written to Pius Kiciński, head of the King's Chancellery. In the years 1789-90 Albertrandy was sent by King Stanisław August to Denmark and Sweden to verify books and Polish documents as well as other materials concerning Polish-Scandinavian relations, which were kept at local libraries – most of them stolen by the Swedes during 'the Deluge'. Albertrandy not only reports on his library queries and the search carried out in private collections, but also gives interesting descriptions of the countries and their social relations, as well as the mentality of their inhabitants. Unlike the previously quoted J. Ch. Pasek, Albertrandy was a well educated and erudite man who knew several European countries and languages. His letters were not very personal, mainly employing a report-like style, particularly in the parts concerning the progress of the mission he was entrusted with. They are not, however, completely devoid of literary elements, and contain numerous practical remarks relating to the manner of travelling, accommodation, and the appearance of the places visited; so when describing Scandinavian churches Albertrandy emphasizes their abundance, notices the copper-covered roofs (Wójcicki 1856:160), and draws comparisons to Polish churches – comparing the Roskilde cathedral to the one in Gniezno, the first capital of Poland, as well as recalling a place also renowned in Poland, the monastery in Vadstena, which owed its status to the St. Bridget's cult. Albertrandy, a canon and Jesuit, finds observations concerning the religious sphere and the ecclesiastical state interesting. As a scholar he recognizes the high material status of the Swedish clergy, and at the same time underlines their fairness (Wójcicki 1856:163). Finally, he praises the level of religiousness in Swedish society, making comparisons to other Protestant countries:

17   All quoted references from the narratives, other than *Pamiętniki*, were translated by Waldemar Łyś.
18   The so-called Stockholm Mission was related to the 1789-1795 legation of Jerzy Michał Potocki, whose goal was to win Gustav III to the Polish cause (Anusik 1993).

The folk here are quiet, docile, even more pious in their religion than other Luther's countries. Not a day without a service in one or more churches, and these services with zeal they frequent. (Wójcicki 1856: 165)

His narration does not show any signs of disapproval of Protestants; religious differences seem to take second place.

Albertrandy does not devote much attention to the beauty and qualities of the Scandinavian landscape and climate. He writes about their 'tardiness', which not only brings about later harvests, but is also to be blamed for the character of the inhabitants of the Northern lands. Using such argumentation he outlines the theoretical framework of the so called 'climate theory', which seem to be very fitting in understanding the inhabitants from this part of Europe:[19]

With order, safety and ordering of the custom, one should expect that the citizens [of Denmark - S.S.] are happy. Things, however, turn out different; the climate is rough and so unstable, that the citizens are envious of the Swedes, and they consider them far happier than themselves. The air is foul, the waters unwholesome, and thence comes the catholic melancholy, which over all extends its rule, and against which people of even the merriest nations cannot defend themselves, when a few years in Copenhagen they dwell. This melancholy conducts even the commoners' minds. (Wójcicki 1856: 156)

A similar observation concerns the Swedes themselves; their mentality, however, was drawn by the Polish scholar in somewhat brighter hues: "The character of the nation is a certain chilliness and melancholy, but peaceful, not desperate, like in Denmark." (Wójcicki 1856: 165)

It is worth stressing that the mental picture of Sweden has not only been reversed since Pasek's time, but that Sweden, little by little, has become more interesting and amicable than Denmark in Polish eyes.

Furthermore, the author of the letters emphasizes the honesty of the Swedes (he points to the feeling of security, common public order, and scarcity of theft), and their hospitality. His attention is also drawn to their egalitarianism and social solidarity as exemplified by the lack of any material gap between different members of the society, a phenomenon so typical of social relations in the Polish Commonwealth:

---

19   See also the other contributions in this volume.

This folk's character is basically good, but in the province better still than in the capital. (…) Thus, it seems, an equality of fortunes is commonplace, a lot of passion taming, and excessive luxuries which can bring enviousness, are scarce. (Wójcicki 1856: 165)

The picture drawn by the author of the letters is not, however, explicitly positive. Albertrandy diagnoses "two major flaws" in the Swedes. The first is the universal and daily consumption of liquor, also by women and children (sic!), to which the exceptionally great number of taverns greatly contributes. He does, however, do justice to Swedish gourmets of alcoholic beverages with hidden criticism of the Polish habit in the matter:

(…) however, be it a habit, be it a head constitution, or ability to hide excess, scarcely a drunk is to be seen, while our more inferior in rank Poles more often put on this show for Swedes than Swedes for Poles. (Wójcicki 1856: 166)

Another "major fault" is loose morals – the former Jesuit condemns "excessive ease" and straightforwardness, with which the populace "adores" the pretty Swedish women, accosting them in the street with winking, gestures or unrefined words.

This "poor country" commands attention for the good organization of its social life and services, including the high quality of the roads, and the efficient operation of the post; which "in Poland runs, in Brandenburg walks, in Denmark rushes, in Sweden shoots and less than in Poland costs" (Wójcicki 1856: 159); as well as the quality of handicraft services offered at reasonable prices. Swedish towns are made of wood, but well-built; the houses are "within convenient and neat". In a letter of October 1789 Albertrandy lends his epistolary talents to a meticulous description of a "beautiful town", Copenhagen, and its most impressive buildings: Christiansborg, Amalienborg, the Marble Church and Kastellet, which he compares to buildings he saw in Italy and Germany. Copenhagen is presented as European, although somewhat provincial as a metropolis, e.g. the author observes the beautiful marble on the stairs of the Christiansborg, but also expresses an opinion that it has been used tastelessly.

This traveller's attention is also attracted by the reorganization process of the Danish countryside, which began with Struensee's reforms and consisted among other things in driving farmsteads out of the hearts of villages into their outskirts, and enclosing all grounds and pastures (Wójcicki 1856: 153). These do not find acceptance in the eyes of this scholar both for purely practical reasons (the necessity to wait for the opening of passage-blocking barriers), and for wider, social reasons, as it contributes to a disintegration of rural communities. Furthermore, as a scholar he does not express a particularly favourable opinion about the state of education in the country, including the low level of their knowledge of Latin, although he stresses common knowledge of French both among the clergy and laymen.

The image of Denmark and Sweden in the letters of this Polish canon seems relatively balanced. The countries described are somewhat sleepy European provinces, where life follows its own rhythm, and whose inhabitants are free from the plague of unfairness. In these geographical latitudes one would seek in vain for surprising distinctness or elements to impress a newcomer from continental Europe; he is, however, in danger of falling into a peculiar stupor and melancholy. Constructed this way, the utopia is thus marked with cracks whose character removes it from the image of a carefree idyll. Though the importance of those imperfections for the whole image should not be overestimated.

Soldier missing his homeland

Only six years later the Scandinavian North was visited by Julian Ursyn Niemcewicz (1758-1841), a patriot actively fighting – with pen and sword – for the independence of his motherland, and who, as aide-de-camp to Prince Czartoryski, made several trips in Europe in his youth. In 1796, being released from Pietropavlovsk hold, he accompanied Tadeusz Kościuszko, the great hero of the Polish fight for independence, who – en route to America – travelled through Finland and Sweden. The experience of several months of isolation, as well as the political situation in the motherland (after the third partition in 1795 when Poland ceased to exist as an independent state) which exerted a profound influence upon his perception and interpretation of the world.

In his account, written in the form of a literary diary, he devotes a lot of attention to a description of the Finnish winter landscape, which – inaccessible and dangerous – intensifies the feeling of alienation. Ice and snow become dangerous Northern elements which cover with a thick blanket the lush forests full of wild animals, including the reindeer, which Niemcewicz sees for the first time, and become the source of numerous problems related not simply to travel itself, but also to getting food supplies: "Not only drink, water, but meat, poultry, and fish so frozen that everything had to be cut up with an axe." (Niemcewicz 1957: 202). The author also emphasizes the problems of finding food in the Swedish capital; he writes: "(…) where did they send us to get parsley and horseradish? – to a chemist's." (Niemcewicz 1858: 13). Some meals and particular dishes seem to arouse a special interest in this traveller, who recalls "very wholesome and singularly tasty" (Niemcewicz 1858: 9) Finnish beer, 'knicka-broë' bread as well as the method of its storage, the pickling of vegetables, and the frequent consumption of fish, but also seal-meat dishes which he found repulsive.

SYLWIA SCHAB

Like Albertrandy's, his reflections on the climate and the difficult living conditions are combined with conclusions concerning the character of the nation inhabiting the land. In the following statement they are based on a contrast between a passionate love of the motherland and the image of the deadly ice-crust covering the Finnish land:

Besides, there is silence everywhere, and icy deadness. The traveller traversing the land, having to experience the local winter lasting six or seven months, must deplore the fate of its inhabitants; yet if he were to investigate them, he would soon realize that they think Finland the most beautiful and pleasant land in the world. Man's inherent love of the motherland is nature's greatest benefit (…) (Niemcewicz 1858: 7)

A similar statement comes from one of the Swedish officers that the author met in Eckerö on Åland. To answer Niemcewicz's regret-ridden question on how one could live "in a country this desolate with a climate this harsh" (Niemcewicz 1858:18), the soldier replies with an extensive and pompous monologue, in which he praises the abundance and fertility of the land, the merits of the climate which cannot be found anywhere else like white nights and northern lights, as well as the courage, toil and dignity of its inhabitants. This declaration – contained in the narration in the form of a direct address, a statement by a proud member of Swedish society – is intended to add credibility to his words, but also constitutes a deliberate stylistic device. Its closing keystone is an extensive metaphorical phrase describing the path of life: "along the tract of life we pick our own flowers, and die, like others, having learned the earthly happiness" (Niemcewicz 1858: 19), which emphasizes not only the feeling of dignity and independence, but also points to the universal character of the human experience.

For this Pole, a fighter for national independence, observations of patriotic feeling, as well as those bringing to mind his own motherland, seem to be of crucial importance. It is in this context that we should see his reflections upon the wretched fate of the Polish nation made during a visit to Stockholm and Drottningsholm. Having seen portraits of the Swedish ruler from the time of the Great Northern War, Niemcewicz wrote about him: "Charles XII, who so needlessly awakened the barbarous Peter I" (Niemcewicz 1957: 205), thus indicating a change in the attitude to the Swedes as an embodiment of the devil incarnate. The negative role played by the Swedes in the disintegration of the Polish state fades into the background and becomes hidden behind the veil of time; so increasingly there are more and more examples of a favourable disposition and a willingness to help by the once hostile neighbours from across the Baltic Sea. For example Polish soldiers who fled the country after the fall of the Kościuszko insurrection (1794) enjoyed a very warm reception:

These decent people cannot overpraise the humanity and fairness they found with the Swedish folk. Whenever they said they were Poles, they instantly found aid and support. What a kind-hearted people! (Niemcewicz 1858: 21)

Also, Swedish hospitality and sociability produce a favourable opinion in a stranger (Niemcewicz 1858:12), though he labels some of the hosts' habits, like the custom of serving soup at the end of the meal, or serving wine with sugar, as straying from the European norm. This unexpected local exoticism cannot, however, change his overall positive attitude to the hosts: "This supper, offered with such honest and sincere hospitality, more pleased my taste than the grandest and most excellent feasts." (Niemcewicz 1858: 10).

This traveller's notice is also drawn to the situation of the Swedish peasant, a free man – as opposed to his Polish equivalent who is bound to the land – who exerts an influence upon the legal system, as well as receiving "an adequate up-bringing and schooling" (Niemcewicz 1957: 203). In Niemcewicz's eyes, another sign of social equality – greater than he is familiar with at home – are the relations between the baron of Wrede, the governor of the province, and a neighbouring leaseholder:

He greeted the baron the English way, which is by shaking his hand. This greeting let me better understand the rule and customs of this nation, than all treatises and books. Indeed, having seen any old leaseholder living in such familiarity with one of the first lords of the kingdom, (…) I said to myself that the folk, perhaps, must have their say in the rule of the land, and in their leaders only see elder brothers. (Niemcewicz 1957: 14-15)

This traveller brings further evidence of the good organization of the social and economic life of the countries he visited – he emphasizes the good condition of the Swedish roads and peasant farmyards, thriving commerce in port towns such as Gothenburg, and an efficient courier-postal system. What Niemcewicz's account does not contain, however, are extensive descriptions of the architecture and municipal attractions. The author himself explains this "negligence in the chronicler's duty" with reference to the political situation in Poland:

I shall not say much about Stockholm and about our visit there. In times happier I would try to please my innate curiosity by watching everything that is worth the while, yet to one who has lost his motherland everything becomes immaterial. (Niemcewicz 1858: 26)

SYLWIA SCHAB

In his diary Niemcewicz devotes considerable attention to questions that up to his time had been absent from Polish travel narratives – to Laplanders, their language and customs. A brief contact with the Lapps, who were their hosts at one of the stopovers, sparked his interest in this mysterious, nomadic people.[20] He observes that the people, who used a language unlike any other, "the Northernmost dialect in Europe" (Niemcewicz 1858: 17), is poor, non-expansive, and very attached to its territory. The Laplander is aware of political reality – the division of Lapland between Russia, Sweden and Denmark – but the situation does not exert a meaningful influence upon the daily life of the inhabitants of the region: "They pay very little, live independently, wage frequent wars between themselves, assault one another to their governments' ignorance." (Niemcewicz 1858: 19)

In the latter part of his diary he relates conversations with neighbours of the Laplanders, some Swedish officers who described to him the Lapps' character, manner and appearance:

They are of short height, mighty unsightly, their women being particularly appalling. Hospitality is one of their chief virtues; they like foreigners and treat them to the best milk, cheese and meat of reindeer. (Niemcewicz 1858: 19)

The mental isolation of Laplanders and their position – not only in a geographical sense – on the outer edges of European civilization, have been highlighted by the statement that "as a matter of fact they are only by name Christians" (Niemcewicz 1858:19). This mysterious tribe of nomads and shamans appears to be one of the last refuges of paganism in Europe.

This Polish patriot, who yearns for an independent motherland, emphasizes the Laplanders' attachment to their land and lifestyle. In his narrative he relates in a short story about sending a few Lappish families to Chantilly where they were to become attractions in the prince's garden. Despite good living conditions, the beauty of the place and ease of existence, all the time they would sigh for their rocks, snow and ice (Niemcewicz 1858: 19), and eventually had to be sent back up north because otherwise they would have paid with their lives for the aristocrat's whim. The historical and personal context of the author's experience enables us to see this stylistic device as one of the many measures intended to promote the ideal of love for the motherland and the inalienability of man's right to attain it. In the countries of the North Niemcewicz seeks and finds what he cannot experience in his own motherland: he pictures the Nordic countries as a utopia of freedom, equality and harmony. He does not deny the North the quality of exoticism, but it

20   See also Anke Ryall's contribution on this topic.

is more of a "familiar" type, one that does not evoke the feeling of cultural exclusion. The North is in this Pole's eyes an open and friendly land.

Nearby exoticism

Accounts by Polish travellers of their visits to Scandinavia in the seventeenth and eighteenth centuries are sporadic and incidental; they do not result from deliberate choice preceded by appropriate preparations, but see the light of day as if "by chance". One of the reasons for that is the fact that the 'Scandinavian axis' was never a dominant one in Polish culture and politics. Polish students went to Italy, Germany, France and the Netherlands; artists searched for inspiration in Italy and Greece; pilgrims visited the Pope and the Holy Land; and exoticism was found in Turkey or China. In the same vein, contacts with its two mighty neighbours – Russia and Germany – were of crucial importance for strategic reasons. Moreover, this lack of interest seems to be reciprocated on the Northern side of the Baltic Sea – there are no substantial Scandinavian travel narratives from Poland in the said period either.

The elements of a foreign reality, to which these Polish travellers predominantly draw attention, are the landscape and climate of the countries visited; as well as the inhabitants, their appearance, customs (in particular those related to eating), manner, and mentality. In these travellers' eyes the above mentioned two worlds remain mutually interrelated, following the popular understanding of the notion of human behaviour being climatically determined. Other vital areas of observation include questions of religion: these being related both to church infrastructure and the cultivation of one's faith. This, in turn, is directly related to the question of the religious differences between Poland and Scandinavia. The Polish traveller feels more important as a follower of 'the true faith' among the Scandinavian dissenters, who 'got lost' on the way to salvation. Such an attitude can be found especially in Pasek's memoirs and seems in any case to be associated with his Sarmatian outlook. Although other travellers do not seem to attach much importance to this particular aspect, one can say that what they observe are indications of the practical implementation of the Scandinavian world of meaning, with its ideal of unconditional personal freedom and an individual ethos, which was also formed by religion (including pre-Christian ones) (Witoszek 1997: 76-78).

Observers of the Enlightenment era are also interested in social problems: the ratio between poverty and affluence, the position and role of the peasant in society, or the state of education. The 'translation' of a different culture into the categories of one's own involves the employment of three interrelated strategies: the negation of observed phenomena or their interpretation on a fantastic plane;

SYLWIA SCHAB

the assumption of a detached attitude and a critical perception of the "foreign" reality; as well as the application of the 'per analogiam' principle, which lets one 'annex' some of its elements and shift them to one's own outlook. Foreign cultures become a discursive referential framework for the travellers' cultural self-understanding. This analysis also revealed vital factors determining the perception of the Northern countries by Polish travellers; including not only the authors' own life experience, the scope of their knowledge of the world, and membership of a different cultural circle, but – perhaps, most importantly – the circumstances that determined Poland's political situation at a given historical moment. Due to the scarcity of direct reports from Scandinavia it is difficult to determine the role of the quoted travel reports in shaping the image of the North in Poland; one can, however, assume the establishment of certain channels of interpretation, which appear surprisingly current from a contemporary point of view. On the one hand, the 'Norden' becomes a stronghold of modernity and progress in terms of civilization and society; on the other, the discussed accounts evoke popular associations of Scandinavia with a 'centre' of moral looseness or depression. The Polish traveller of the era was rather inclined to choose the south European destinations for his – and very rarely her – trips, however, if he finds his way to the North, he is most likely to visit Sweden. The image of Sweden has undergone many changes: from enemy, dissenter in faith, traitor – through being a poor and peaceful land – to an ally.[21] Norway is almost absent from travel narratives before the era of Romanticism; Lapland is used as an image of European 'Barbaricum' and the 'Ultima Thule' of the period.

Furthermore, it has to be stressed that the discussed pieces were published only in the nineteenth century, in the wake of Polish Romantics' increased interest in the 'Northern Arcadia'. It is also at that time that the first translations of the literary works of that region are published (e.g. parts of *Edda* translated by Joachim Lelewel, 1807). This interest produced a great number of reports on travel in the countries of the North, and the process of "discovering" the North for the Polish reader gained momentum.

---

21   Though the reversal of that image was not complete – according to Aleksandra Niewiara there were still traces of a suspicious attitude towards the Swedes among the Polish people in the nineteenth century (Niewiara 2000: 172-176).

References

Anusik, Zbigniew 1993: *Misja polska w Sztokholmie w latach 1789-1795*. Łódź: Wydawnictwo Uniwersytetu Łódzkiego.

Bockenheim, Krystyna 2003: *Dworek, kontusz, karabela*. Wrocław: Wydawnictwo Dolnośląskie.

Chemperek, Dariusz 2001: Pasek w Danii – literackie i kulturoznawcze jakości *Pamiętników*. *Studia Filologiczne*. Sandomierz.

Gerner, Kristian 2002. The Swedish and Polish-Lithuanian Empires and the formation of the Baltic Region. W. Maciejewski ed.: *The Baltic Sea Region. Cultures, Politics, Societies*. Uppsala: The Baltic University Press.

Hernas, Czesław 1989: *Literatura baroku*. Warszawa: Państwowe Wydawnictwo Naukowe.

Kotarski, Edmund (introduction and commentary) 1973. *Trzy podróże. J. Kochanowki "Pamiątka Janowi na Tęczynie", A. Zbylitkowski "Droga do Szwecyjej", T. Grotkowski "Podróż morska"*. Gdańsk: Wydawnictwo Morskie.

Łoś, Jakub 2000: *Pamiętnik towarzysza chorągwi pancernej*, (edited by R. Śreniawa-Szczypiorski). Warszawa.

Niemcewicz, Julian Ursyn 1858. *Podróż Juliana Ursyna Niemcewicza z Petersburga do Szwecyi w drodze do Ameryki roku 1796*. Poznań.

Niemcewicz, Julian Ursyn 1957: *Pamiętniki czasów moich*. Państwowy Instytut Wydawniczy (edited and introduced by J. Dihm).

Niewiara, Aleksandra 2000: *Wyobrażenia o narodach w pamiętnikach i dziennikach z XVI-XIX wieku*. Katowice: Wydawnictwo Uniwersytetu Śląskiego.

Pasek, Jan Chryzostom 1952: *Pamiętniki*. Biblioteka Narodowa (introduction by W. Czaplński).

Rosznecki, Stanisław 1896: *Polakkerne i Danmark 1659. Efter Jan Paseks erindringer*. København: Gyldendalske Boghandels Forlag.

Swiecicka, M.A.J. (translation and introduction) 1978: *The Memoirs of Jan Chryzostom z Gosławic Pasek*. New York.

Ślaski, Kazimierz 1977: *Tysiąclecie polsko-skandynawskich stosunków kulturalnych*. Gdańsk: Instytut Bałtycki.

Tripplin, Teodor Teutold 1844: *Wspomnienia z podróży po Danii, Norwegii, Anglii, Portugalii, Hiszpanii i państwie marokańskim*. (part 1: Dania i Norwegia). Poznań.

Witoszek, Nina 1997: Fugitives from Utopia: The Scandinavian Enlightenment Reconcidered. *The Cultural Construction of Norden*, eds.: Ø. Sørensen and B. Stråth. Oslo: Scandinavian University Press.

Wójcicki, K. W. ed. 1856: Listy Jana Albertrandego do Pijusa Kicińskiego od r. 1789-90. *Archiwum domowe do dziejów i literatury krajowej*, Warszawa.

Original Quotes

(…) lubo ten naród jest ab antiquo przychylny narodowi polskiemu, jako dawne świadczą pisma (…) (Pasek 1952:11)

Lud też tam nadobny; białogłowy gładkie i zbyt białe, stroją się pięknie, ale w drewnianych trzewikach chodzą wieskie i miescke.(…) W afektach zaś nie tak są powściągliwe jako Polki, bo lubo zrazu jakąś nadzwyczajną pokazują wstydliwość, ale zaś za jednym posiedzeniem i przymówieniem kilku słów zbytecznie i zapamiętale zakochają [się] i pokryć tego ani umieją: ojca i matki, posagu bogatego gotowiusieńka odstąpić i jechać za tym w kim się zakocha, choćby na kraj świata. (Pasek 1952:19)

Kiedyśmy im mówili, że to tak szpetnie, u nas tego i żona przy mężu nie uczyni, powiedały, że "tu u nas nie masz żadnej sromoty i nie rzecz jest wstydzić się za swoje własne członki, które Pan

SYLWIA SCHAB

Bóg stworzył". Na to zaś nagie sypianie powiedają, że "ma dosyć za swe koszula i inszy ubiór, co mi służy przez dzień i okrywa mię; powinna też przynajmniej w nocy mieć swoją ochronę, a do tego co mi po tym robaki, pchły brać z sobą na nocleg do łóżka i dać się im kąsać, mając od nich w smacznym spaniu przeszkodę!" (Pasek 1952:20-21)

Chcieli nieborzęta przed Polakami uciec do nieba, aleć ich tam nie puszczono; zaraz św. Piotr przywarł fortki, mówiąc: "A, zdrajcy! Wszak wy powiedacie, że świętych łaska na nic się nie przygodzi, instancyja ich do Pana Boga nieważna i niepotrzebna. (…) a przecię i tam pań Bóg obronił od śmierci, kogo miał obronić (…) I teraz strzelaliście gęsto, a niewieleście nabili Polaków – czemuż? Bo ich aniołowie strzegą, a was czarni, atoż macie ich usługę". (Pasek 1952:33-34)

(…), my w to wierzymy, co i wy, daremnie nas nazywacie odszczepieńcami" (Pasek 1952:21)

From Sacred Scenery to Nuclear Nightmare:
Rjukan and Its Myths

By capitalising the four rather prosaic compass points and adding to them the definite article – the East, the West, the North and the South – we are suddenly dealing with phenomena which in most people's minds trigger a wide register of associations to fact as well as fiction, reality as well as myth. The present book offers a wide and fascinating insight into the world of the North as it was perceived more than two centuries ago, primarily but not exclusively by foreign travellers and commentators. This final chapter is not an attempt to provide a concluding summary of a highly complex picture. Instead, it will very deliberately and by way of a case study from a small but rather extraordinary Norwegian town, go far beyond the historical period covered by the book itself and look at how eighteenth- and early nineteenth-century perceptions even today continue to influence our interpretation of the place and the events connected with it, despite a radically different historical context. Hopefully, it may also serve as a reminder that a genuine understanding of the present can only be acquired through a thorough understanding of the complex palimpsest of the past. But first and foremost, this is a study of myths: how they operate and how they survive and how they sometimes dress the facts in a garb that requires interpretation and analysis in order to be fully understood.

Rjukan is situated in a remote and mountainous region in the interior of Telemark in southern Norway. During the Second World War this place witnessed a series of spectacular commando raids and sabotage operations that have since acquired almost mythical proportions and attracted the attention of tourists, adventurers, military historians and Hollywood scriptwriters alike. The result has been a steady stream of articles, books, films and TV programmes. Only in 2003 the British survival expert Ray Mears produced a three-part TV series for BBC and a book, both of them entitled *The Real Heroes of Telemark*. For most visitors to Rjukan, this is what makes the place famous and serves as a focus for the visit. But Rjukan also has a very different story to tell: the dramatic events of the War were played out against an historical backdrop going back almost two centuries, to the almost obsessive preoccupation with untouched natural scenery, and to the very first discovery, by both Norwegians and foreign travellers, of Norway as a tourist destination. It is necessary, in other words, to go back in time in order to find the roots and the different layers of the myth.

During the whole period of the Grand Tour and even during the early period of what may be termed modern tourism in Britain and on the Continent, the interior of Norway was essentially an uncharted and undescribed wilderness, at least from the point of view of the small number of foreign travellers venturing on a journey to these northern shores. The great majority of commercial travellers would not go very far beyond the coastline, and the eighteenth-century travellers of any category would hardly have much of an appetite for what was to be seen in the country's inaccessible interior. The discovery of Rjukan, therefore, coincides with a radically new landscape aesthetics.

In 1810, rumours reached Christiania (now Oslo) and the Danish vice-governor, Prince Friedrich of Hesse, that a huge waterfall had been discovered somewhere in the upper regions of Telemark. The Prince immediately wrote a letter to Professor of Geology, Jens Esmark, who was reported to have seen and measured the fall. The letter is interesting, because it contains passages suggestive of a new aesthetic outlook. In it, Prince Friedrich claims that such an observation would be of interest to "any admirer of Nature's grandeur", and he regrets that although the waterfall was briefly mentioned in a local account a few decades earlier, one has, "until now, not at all found this phenomenon worthy of attention".[1] Professor Esmark's response to the vice-governor is not known, but in 1812, he published his report and made the information about the waterfall available, claiming among other things that it was the highest waterfall in the world, and from the 1820s onwards, Rjukan started to attract a steadily increasing number of visitors. Thus, whereas a few years earlier the waterfall had been in effect both unknown and uninteresting simply because there was no aesthetic 'market' for it, travellers now thronged to Rjukan to see it and, on their return, to publish enthusiastic accounts which elevated it to religious heights.

To the typical traveller of the eighteenth century, Rjukan would indeed have had very little to offer. Except for a handful of farms, it was essentially an empty landscape.[2] Furthermore, it was situated almost literally in the middle of nowhere, nearly as far from the coast as it is possible to get and in an area so mountainous and inaccessible that the early descriptions of the arduous journey there (from the early decades of the nineteenth century) are strikingly reminiscent of Joseph Con-

---

1   Quoted in *The Yearbook of the Norwegian Tourist Association 1881*, 114-15. Translated from the Norwegian by P.F.

2   The adjective 'empty' is of course in itself suggestive of an aesthetic outlook which presupposes a degree of human presence for the landscape to have a 'content'.

rad's descriptions of Marlow's strenuous journey into the heart of darkness. The roads were either non-existent or, as a Danish traveller from 1830 puts it, "at times hardly visible" (Rørbye 1930: 85). But with the aesthetic eyes of the early nineteenth century, this area suddenly became interesting. And to complete the picture, Rjukan was partly surrounded by the Hardangervidda, the largest and least hospitable mountain plateau in northern Europe. Also, as the Hardangervidda plays a significant role in the later drama at Rjukan, it seems relevant to include some observations of it, all of them from around the middle of the nineteenth century. The German writer Theodor Mügge,[3] describing Møsvatn, the largest lake at the Hardangervidda, seems as late as 1844 to revert to the eighteenth-century terminology of the sublime, adopting phrases reminiscent of Edmund Burke on the terrifying and awesome aspects of the bleak landscape:

Møsvatn lies at the utmost edge of that world which man could occupy, close to the region he must for ever leave to the wild beasts, because no effort can wring out of this dreary soil any more nourishing grass. Still, even at the other side of these miserable shores, nature now and then, in the middle of this rocky desert, has placed some hidden spark of life, and with Aaron's rod touched these terrible cliffs so that they divided, withdrew, and gave room for a small valley, a hut, a pasture, a tiny field which, with inexpressible effort, was cleared and sown, but which often vanished under snow and ice before its harvest could be reaped. (Mügge 1844: 388)[4]

The British travellers John Willis Clark and Joseph W. Dunning, who in 1857 appear as "Two Unknown Quantities", similarly offer a chilling description of their encounter with the area in question:

For six hours we traversed a vast and wild expanse of hideous barrenness. If there be upon earth a spot disregarded by its Creator, where conscience-stricken spirits roam, seeking in their unrest to escape themselves, surely on the Hardanger fjeld must be that spot! Oh, the monotony of that dreary ride! a monotony that crept into one's very vitals, stopped the flow of conversation, and thus increased seven-fold its own dismal horrors. It was not that calm and peaceful solitude in which man delights to commune with himself, and which calls forth oft-times the highest aspirations of his soul. It was a solitude where everything bore the blank aspect of desolation: even the humpy hills that rose above the plateau looked like the deformed excrescences of a neglected body, and possessed no beauty of form: the

---

3   Journalist, travel writer, novelist and short-story writer (1806-61) from Berlin. His collected works in 33 vols. were published 1862-67.
4   Translated from the German by P.F.

scattered rocks and withered herbage told only of ruin and despair. (Clark and Dunning 1857: 134-5)

These descriptions echo an ancient perception of mountains and highland wastes as products of the Fall, and as warts, blisters and physical monstrosities on the otherwise flat and even surface of the world.[5] Thomas Forester, however, who visited Rjukan in 1848, takes a radically more sentimental view of the Hardangervidda. Approaching the "high altitudes", he says:

In such situations, the great purity of the air, the unbounded solitude, and the grandeur of the scale of the objects presented, concur in affecting the mind with feelings of serenity, of freedom, and of awe. One seems to be lifted above the turbid atmosphere in which the cares and turmoils of the world unceasingly estuate; to be emancipated from the thraldom of passion and all gross and sordid influences; at the same time that the spirit is bowed, in the presence of the majesty of Nature, under a profound sense of one's own insignificance. (Forester 1850: 136)

Thus, for traditional travellers seeking manifestations of such human achievements as cathedrals, libraries and picture galleries, the Hardangervidda and the rest of the Rjukan area had indeed very little to offer. To the breed of travellers, however, who had really taken on board the powerful gospel of nature worship and sensibility, it had everything. As a matter of fact, it is interesting to note how writers of the same generation adopt rather different aesthetic perspectives. In some cases even one and the same account displays a variety of different responses. This is particularly conspicuous in the description of the waterfall – the Rjukanfossen – itself.

In a letter dated "Bergen, July 31ˢᵗ, 1830", Charles Boileau Elliott starts his description in the tradition of the eighteenth-century sublime:

I do not remember to have seen a sight so calculated to inspire terror. The Moen [Måne-elven] rushes through a rock blackened by time, and falls from a height of four hundred and fifty feet perpendicularly into a caldron of the same dark material. The foam, or *riuken*, rises so high as to conceal from the distant spectator the depth of the fall, which we could duly appreciate only when lying on the ground and looking over the edge of the precipice at its highest point. Whether real or fancied, the earth seemed to tremble under the concussion of the continuous torrent.

---

5   For a more comprehensive discussion of this phenomenon, see Nicolson 1959 and Fjågesund and Symes 2003: 302-20.

PETER FJÅGESUND

FIG. 23:

Nineteenth-century Rjukan, represented first of all by the spectacular waterfall, acquired a world-wide reputation as a place of sublime, untouched scenery and "nature red in tooth and claw". Illustration from Alfred Smith: Sketches in Norway and Sweden (1847).

He then quickly moves into a different register, namely that of pantheistic nature worship, coupled with a Christian sentimentalism echoing the Covenant and the dawn of human history:

At this moment the sun burst from behind a cloud, and, shining upon the falling water and the playful spray, cast obliquely on the dark background a perfect double rainbow approaching nearly to a circle. The effect was exceedingly striking. Placed in the only point where the circumference was incomplete, we saw ourselves clothed with the rainbow. Unprepared as we were for so extraordinary a position, it was too sublime; and we almost shuddered at the glory of the vesture with which we were surrounded: while in the beauty and grandeur of this masterpiece of His hand, we recognized the power of Him who "weigheth the mountains in scales," and "covereth Himself with light as with a garment". (Elliott 1832: 111-12)

Mügge, likewise, who was quoted above on the "terrible mountains" around the Møsvatn lake, exemplifies a Romantic sensibility which transforms the scene in front of him from a mammoth cauldron of black rock into a natural cathedral with the waterfall itself as the shimmering and altar-like focal point:

For hours and days one could sit here, and stare over and over again into this roar and splendour; because waterfalls and ocean waves have got the power to rock man's soul into dreams and, with their surging rhythm of coming and going, to awaken imagination and yearning. … Such phenomena make the sensitive human good. To view Nature in her highest majesty is so wonderful, so pure and profoundly touching, that it makes one forget much of what would otherwise reduce the impression of her greatness. (Mügge 1844: 349)[6]

Robert Bremner, who witnessed the waterfall in 1836, offers a long and detailed account in a similar vein, concluding along the lines of Wordsworth's "emotion recollected in tranquillity", that "[t]he beauties of such a scene … cannot be analysed at the moment when the mind is agitated by their effect", and:

The thoughts which occupied our minds while beholding this majestic exhibition, were among the most elevated – may we add, among the most edifying we have ever experienced. Who, with such a spectacle before him, would not have been driven to ask, Whose hand upholds these lasting bulwarks? Whose bounty feeds these everflowing springs? the heart must indeed be cold that does not here rise to a great Contriver (Bremner 1840, 2: 154-5).

6   Translated from the German by P.F.

Mention should also be made here of the Maristien, a narrow and dangerous path along the steep and slippery rock face above the waterfall. All visitors to the waterfall were told the tragic story of Mari, the daughter of a wealthy farmer, who fell in love with a peasant boy and who went mad after her lover fell down into the waterfall as he came along the path to meet her. Thus, to complete the picture, the natural drama of the fall was supplemented by a sentimental and romantic love story, adding a human touch to a scene otherwise monopolised by an empty, inhuman landscape.

In addition to the waterfall, however, Rjukan could also boast another natural attraction, namely the Gausta, the highest mountain in southern Norway, towering nearly 5,000 feet above the narrow floor of the Rjukan valley and about half as much above the surrounding mountain plateau. Again, attempting to describe the awesome spectacle, the travellers struggle to find words,[7] falling back on such poetic devices as personification and religious imagery. One writer is struck by the Gausta's "massive dignity" (Goodman 1896: 59). Another claims that "the moment when, for the first time at such close range, I had the courage to set my eyes on the King of southern Norway's mountain giants, will remain unforgettable for as long as I live" (Lobedanz 1875: 145)[8]; whilst a third, drawing a picture of a man-like gargantuan creature, mentions how the mountain's "whole swollen bulk stood alone amid a wilderness of dark moors and table-lands", before comparing it to "a cathedral of the Titans" (Paterson 1886: 285).

Rjukan, then, with the 10,000 km² expanse of the Hardangervidda next-door: "the most magnificent waterfall in Europe" (Bremner 1840: 111) – "so terrible, so mysterious, so oblivion-like, as well as, eternity-like!" (Popplewell 1859: 67); the Gausta, looking "like a colossal wedge of fire against the violet sky" (Taylor 1858: 349); and the "grandly desolate" valley (Goodman 1896: 59), like an abyss between dark, spruce-clad mountain sides – all this made even the Alps look civilised. And out of these dramatic and diverse elements, the nineteenth century forged a powerful and long-lived myth of a place which in effect contained the whole varied register of the period's nature worship: a combination of John Martin-like[9] apocalyptic canvases of breath-taking, terrifying landscapes, on the one hand, and sen-

---

7   This is what Chloe Chard calls "hyperboles of indescribability", whose effect is "that of affirming their own status as eye-witness, who have encountered the objects of commentary in person, and undergone an experience beyond the imaginative grasp of those who know these objects only through the mediation of literature and art. It is the eye-witness alone, such hyperboles suggest, who is capable of experiencing the sense of uniqueness that supplies the precondition for wonder" (Chard 1999: 85).

8   Translated from the Danish by P.F.

9   As a matter of fact, it has been convincingly argued that the dramatic landscapes of the famous Romantic painter John Martin (1789-1854) were partly inspired, via his colleague Francis Danby (1793-1861), by Norwegian mountain scenes (Adams 1973: 56).

FIG. 24:
The Rjukan valley in the years after industrialisation, with Mount Gausta in the background. The main factories were built in the lower part of the valley (photo), whereas the heavy water was produced next to the power station further up the far steeper and less accessible part of the valley. ©Norwegian Industrial Workers Museum

timental, Eden-like scenes, on the other. Common to both, however, is a view of nature in which man turns into a small and insignificant speck of dust in relation to the overpowering surroundings. In short, Rjukan turned into a myth, produced perhaps mainly through the numerous travelogues, but other literary genres also contributed. Mügge, for instance, did not just write a travel account from the area; he also wrote a short-story – partly based on the Maristien legend – from Rjukan in the 1840s, about a German businessman whose daughter falls in love with the son of a local farmer. The story, interestingly, implies a rather unequivocal condemnation of the German bourgeois materialism of the period, whilst the farmer, who is a direct descendant of a Viking king, epitomises all the admirable and Rousseauesque qualities of the Norwegians. The French writer Jules Verne visited Rjukan in 1862 and wrote a whole novel, *Un Billet de Loterie* (*The Lottery Ticket: A Tale of Tellemarken*, 1886), which is set at Rjukan, and which was published in several editions and translations. Furthermore, poems were written in various languages to celebrate both the waterfall and the Gausta. Even the British Poet Laureate, Lord

PETER FJÅGESUND

Tennyson, visited Rjukan during a brief stay in Norway in 1858, and although he did not produce a poem from the scene, he reported in a letter to his wife from 2 August that "I have seen the Ruikan [sic] Foss. Magnificent power of water; weird blue light behind the fall" (Tennyson 1981-90, 2: 205).[10]

However, although foreign travellers and writers contributed strongly to making Rjukan famous, the Norwegians themselves were also quick to realise the potential of using the area as an image of their country's natural, if not political, grandeur. In the nationalistic aftermath of the Constitution of 1814 and independence from Denmark, Norwegian artists and intellectuals, mildly intoxicated by British and Continental Romanticism, thronged to Rjukan and celebrated its sublimity in a profusion of paintings, prints, poems, songs and stories. Even the local farmers, as in Mügge's story, were neatly woven into this overall picture of dramatic and breathtaking scenery in whose protective bosom people eked out a simple but harmonious living.[11] One of the early Norwegian travellers was the physicist and astronomer Christopher Hansteen (1784-1873), who is not only regarded as the 'father of Norwegian science', but who also played a central role in the nation-building project of the years following 1814. In the summer of 1821, he visited Rjukan together with two officers and the painter Johannes Flintoe. Later Hansteen devoted a whole chapter in his account of the trip to descriptions of the natural beauty and to scientific observations of the area.[12] Thus, in the course of the nineteenth century, Rjukan was almost perceived as a miniature version of the nation's grandeur, and with the growth of modern tourism from the 1850s onwards, including improved communications and accommodation, it provided a breath of activity and optimism which gave promise of a brighter future.[13]

Still, the myth of Rjukan as a spectacularly condensed version of the Norwegian nature experience was only the first of three myths which, in the course of the nineteenth and twentieth centuries, were to be spun around the place. Just as the

10   That the reports about the Rjukan waterfall spread far and wide is underlined by Tennyson's Pre-Raphaelite friend, the sculptor Thomas Woolner, who in a letter soon after Tennyson's return from Norway writes to Lady Trevelyan: "The Tennysons were in town a few days ago; he had been in Norway, and for the short time he was there the country pleased him very much; one waterfall 900 feet high particularly struck him". (Tennyson 1981-90, 2: 205)

11   The best example is the giant farmer Eystein Hansson at the farm Ingolfsland, who is mentioned with great admiration by numerous travellers, and who is also very clearly the model for the farmer in Mügge's story.

12   Hansteen's travel account was published in 1859 under the title *Bemærkninger og Iakttagelser paa en Reise fra Christiania til Bergen og tilbage i Sommeren 1821* (Notes and Observations on a Journey from Christiania to Bergen and back in the Summer of 1821), having previously been published in both German (1854) and French (1857) translations.

13   When The Norwegian Tourist Association, which was very much part of the nationalist movement, was founded in 1868, Rjukan was on the agenda: at the very first board meeting, the association decided to buy Krokan, a small farm with a view of the waterfall, to be used as a place of accommodation for the tourists. (Dahl 1983, 1: 9)

first myth focused primarily on the waterfall, so did the second. But before moving on to the second myth: with the benefit of hindsight it is interesting to note how the travel writers of the second half of the nineteenth century, though still within the grasp of the first myth, increasingly see the fall with a kind of double vision, namely with that of the modern engineer and that of the Romantic nature lover. Hansteen's detailed measurements of the waterfall and the Gausta, combined with enthusiastic descriptions of the natural scenery are perhaps the first indication of this shift of emphasis.[14] In 1850, Thomas Forester, similarly mixing expectations of the final days with the terminology of industry and steam engines, observes

…the hoarse breathings of the mysterious spirit which, with unwearied energy, has worked since time was in that marvellous laboratory, and, with ceaseless throbs, will yet discharge those mingled volumes of steam and water, until that final catastrophe, when some yet mightier power of nature shall dissolve even the solid framework of those granite cliffs. (Forester 1850: 99-100)

Thirteen years later, the German travellers Th. Demuth and M. von Schick exclaim, as they realise the enormous natural resources of the river: "And this wonderful water power remains unexploited in the valley; no factory, no industrial enterprise, not even a simple mill forces this power to be of service to it" (Demuth and von Schick 1863: 46).[15] However, no dramatic changes took place before the turn of the century. Even as late as 1896, the British traveller E. J. Goodman, perhaps somewhat naively, comments on the modern road that is being built and how this will open the place to "visitors by thousands". Neither does he seem to suspect anything when mentioning, in passing, that the waterfall has recently been purchased by "herr Kielland-Torkildsen, the head of the Kreditbank of Skien" and "Herr Borchgravink [sic], an engineer" (Goodman 1896: 69).

But the end of the waterfall did not have to wait for Forester's "final catastrophe". By 1911 it was gone, and the water was led through a huge tunnel deep inside the mountain, down through enormous water pipes, and into the ten turbines of the Vemork power station, the largest hydroelectric power station in the world. The industrialisation of Rjukan and the exploitation of the enormous resources of the Mån river were an achievement of modern engineering almost as remarkable as the waterfall itself. In the course of little more than a decade, Rjukan was transformed – through the injection of enormous sums of money – from a sleepy back-

14   Mary Louise Pratt's discussion of the eighteenth-century obsession with "classificatory systems" such as that of Carl von Linnaeus, together with the general mapping of the world, comes to mind here (Pratt 1992: 30-31). It also gives interesting perspectives on myth number two below.

15   Translated from the German by P.F.

water with a handful of traditional farms, into a town of 10,000 people, virtually all of whose livelihoods depended on a futuristic and almost science fiction-like technology. It is hardly an exaggeration to claim that the scale of the development at Rjukan – in modern terms it could perhaps most usefully be compared to that of the oil installations in the North Sea – was of major national significance for a country which had only a few years earlier gained independence from Sweden.[16] Thus, whereas in the course of the nineteenth century Rjukan acquired a myth primarily connected with an untouched and largely unproductive nature in a rural and primitive environment, the twentieth-century myth was radically different: it was a myth connected with a kind of urban, industrial progress profoundly dependent on a strictly scientific harnessing and control of the natural forces. The only common characteristic between the two was that both played a role and were effectively utilised in the country's nation-building process, despite the fact that the development of Rjukan was more dependent on foreign (i.e. Swedish, German and French) than on Norwegian capital.

In the course of this metamorphosis from being a place of timelessly beautiful scenery into becoming an exhibition window of state-of-the-art technology, Rjukan also exemplifies in a graphic way a significant feature of Romantic nature worship, namely the sense of potential or actual loss. The celebration of untouched nature so typical of the early nineteenth century, especially in Britain, clearly cannot be separated from the rapidly growing industrialisation and urbanisation which together devoured more and more of the natural scenery.[17] Even in the interior of Norway, therefore, the nineteenth-century travellers who came from countries where industrialisation had already transformed the landscape must have had a sense of foreboding: that the march of progress would eventually extend even to these areas so remote and apparently beyond the reach of contamination. And a visitor to Rjukan in 1910 would, as already suggested, have found all his fears confirmed. The result is a profound sense of loss coupled with nostalgia, both of which are fundamental to the third and final stage in the myth-building process, which rises out of the dramatic events of the Second World War.

The factories at Rjukan were indeed closely connected with the march of progress. With a rapidly growing world population and a steadily increasing need

---

16 By 1911, the investments had amounted to ca. NOK 100,000,000, which at the time was the equivalent of the Norwegian state budget (http://www.hydro.com/en/about/history/1900_1917/1906.html, accessed 29 November 2004).

17 In the Lake District, for instance, which in many ways could be called the Telemark of Britain, Wordsworth himself had spoken out against the plans to extend the railway to Grasmere, thus threatening to bring modernity and contamination to the area. This kind of protest, which in modern jargon is called nimbyism (not-in-my-back-yard), is still frequently used and is clearly a legacy from the Romantic period.

for better food supplies, artificial fertilisers were an important clue to feeding the hungry millions around the world, and the more than 100 megawatt power station made it possible to manufacture huge quantities of this product at a very low price. By a fatal coincidence, however, the isolation of hydrogen from water, which was an essential part of the process, gave a by-product called deuterium oxide, more generally known as heavy water. It was this apparently innocent water molecule, in which the hydrogen atom has an extra neutron, that was destined to draw Rjukan to the attention not only of foreign travellers, but also of foreign armies.

Aware of the special properties of heavy water, the Norwegian company Norsk Hydro started a separate production of it as early as 1934 (though without having an obvious market for it), and by the time of the German occupation of Norway in April 1940, both German and Allied scientists were aware of its crucial significance for the potential production of a nuclear bomb. Consequently, the Germans, having immediately taken a series of precautions to fortify the factory, made every possible effort to intensify the production. Thus, although the Norwegians had already started the production before the War, in the myth-building process the belligerent use of the heavy water is almost exclusively associated with the Germans.

This is not the place to recapitulate in detail the dramatic events that took place at Rjukan during the Second World War, but a brief summary will be necessary as a background to the myths that were created and to the reasons why, more than half a century later, they have acquired what appears to be a self-perpetuating appeal.

By the early months of 1942, the Allies concluded that the German heavy water production had to be stopped.[18] After lengthy discussions, the SOE (Special Operations Executive) – "Britain's highly secret army specialising in 'irregular' warfare" (Mears 2003, 10) – was entrusted with the task. The SOE immediately started recruiting a number of young Norwegian commandos, most of them with an intimate knowledge of the area. However, having been dropped down over the snow-covered Hardangervidda on 18 October and survived under gruelling conditions, they were only intended as an advance party for the main attack a month later. On 19 November 1942, two bombers, each with a glider on tow, took off from Scotland. The gliders contained altogether thirty-four Royal Engineers who were to land on the Hardangervidda, find their way to Rjukan, blow up the factory, and then split up in pairs and escape to Sweden. The operation – called 'Freshman' – was a complete disaster from beginning to end: the planes were unable to find

---

18   The following highly condensed version of events at Rjukan during the Second World War is primarily based on the detailed accounts in Mears 2003, Dahl 1983-2000 and Njølstad et al. 1995. Reference to sources has only been added in connection with specific information and direct quotes.

PETER FJÅGESUND

the landing place and decided to return. Having frozen, the tow rope on one of the gliders snapped over the Norwegian coast, and the plane crashed, killing most of the commandos, while the bomber returned to base. The other bomber and glider also crashed on the coast. In both cases those who had not been killed in the crashes were summarily shot by the Germans.

Then three months later, during one of the hardest Norwegian winters in living memory, a small group of Norwegian commandos conducted one of the most spectacular raids of the entire war. Spending the winter at the Hardangervidda under extreme conditions and scraping through on rapidly dwindling rations and the odd reindeer (including the nutritious moss in the reindeers' stomachs), they stayed in touch with the SOE in London, receiving new and urgent plans for an attack on the plant. On 17 February 1943, a British plane dropped six men who were to join up with the others, and on 28 February, after another pitched battle with the elements, the group of nine approached the valley. They climbed down the nearly vertical mountainside, which was covered in ice and snow, and decided that the apparently only access to the plant – the guarded suspension bridge – was impossible to traverse without raising the alarm. Instead, they went all the way down to the bottom of the deep gorge, where they just managed to ford the river, and climbed up on the other side. Having quietly cut their way through two gates, they moved past the barracks of the German guards and took up positions before the demolition group entered the building in two pairs. Inside the production hall in the basement a Norwegian night watchman was kept in check while the explosives were secured. With only thirty seconds to go, the fuses were lit, and they rushed out of the building, taking cover and awaiting the reaction of the Germans. Steering clear of the flashlight of a German guard by a couple of inches, they managed to escape and were already crossing the river when the sirens went off. Lorries with reinforcements were rapidly coming up the valley from Rjukan, but thanks to the total confusion of the Germans as to the whereabouts of the saboteurs, the latter were already well on their way up the mountainside and heading for the Hardangervidda.

The so-called Gunnerside operation was unique in the history of the Second World War, in particular because no shot was fired and no life was lost. Sadly, that may not be said about the remaining two operations at Rjukan. The Germans succeeded in rebuilding the plant and resuming the production of heavy water sooner than expected by the Allies, and on 16 November 1943 the Vemork plant was subjected to a massive bombardment from 162 American Flying Fortresses. However, whereas the needlepoint operation of the Norwegian commandos had been bloodless and efficient, only eighteen of the nearly one thousand bombs actually hit the plant, claiming, in addition to German losses, twenty-two civilian lives and destroying no more than sixty litres of heavy water. The production unit itself was practically undamaged.

Still, although the bombing was largely a fiasco, soon after the Germans decided to move the production of heavy water to Germany, a decision which opened up for the fourth and final act in the drama of the War at Rjukan. The stocks of heavy water in the plant were once again considerable, and according to local intelligence sources, the Germans planned to transport the entire supplies on Sunday 20 February 1944. A number of options were considered, but it was eventually decided at top level to try and blow up the ferry that was to carry the heavy water down the Tinnsjøen lake before it was to be put on the train to Germany. Despite massive German security measures during the transport from the plant and down to the ferry, an hour after midnight on 20 February, four Norwegian saboteurs, one of whom had also taken part in the Gunnerside operation, managed to get on board the ferry. Here they placed close to ten kilos of explosives in the engine room, set to go off, by the help of ordinary alarm clocks, at 10.45 the following morning. Then they slipped unseen from the ferry and the port. According to schedule, the ferry, which also carried civilians, left the port at about 9 a.m. with more than 10,000 litres of heavy water on board. At 10.45 the explosion ripped up the bow, and within minutes the ferry sank in the middle of the lake at a depth of 400 metres. A number of people were saved, but fourteen Norwegian civilians and four German soldiers died.

During the War and after, the breathtaking events at Rjukan were broadcast around the world. As a result, Rjukan has been transformed into a multi-layered myth, whose timeless appeal can be compared to that of such fictional counterparts as the siege of Troy and the love story of Romeo and Juliet. But that is not all. In the Norwegian context, Rjukan has also been turned into a national icon that thousands of Norwegians visit every year as a silent celebration of events which confirmed, at a critical moment in the nation's history, that the Norwegians still possessed the mettle of their Viking ancestors. Just as Eidsvoll, the seat of the Constitutional Assembly in 1814, became a national shrine epitomising Norwegian independence, so has Rjukan played a similar role in the post-War years. It has simply acquired a prominent place in the collective memory of the nation.

Some questions remain to be answered, however. What exactly are the constituent parts of this powerful story? Why are scriptwriters from Hollywood intrigued by it? Why have two internationally acclaimed films been made at Rjukan, and why does it continue, as with the BBC series from 2003, to fascinate generations of people who themselves were born long after the War? In short, why is it 'such stuff as dreams are made of'? And finally, what is the connection between the events of the Second World War and the two-hundred-year long history of Rjukan outlined above?

These questions are perhaps best answered by approaching the story of the saboteurs – which, it should be remembered, is very clearly the story of the conquering side – as if it were a work of fiction, i.e. a text requiring a literary interpretation. With such a perspective, a new and slightly different recapitulation of the story itself might go something like this: The main characters of this tale, a handful of young men in their early twenties, most of them from the local area and with a perfectly ordinary background, receive basic training abroad and are then dropped behind enemy lines, into their own country. Here they seek the solitude, the desolation and the protection of the Hardangervidda, the playground of their childhood. In this wilderness, they live for months from hand to mouth under extreme conditions, but survive by humbly accepting whatever the barren landscape has to offer. Like the stereotyped life of the Norwegian farmer described in the old travelogues, they exist at the mercy of and in harmony with a strict but unblemished Mother Nature. A simplicity of life that would make Rousseau himself blush with admiration is the very recipe for survival. Even the primitive mountain cabins in which they seek shelter from the raging snowstorms and their enemies are twentieth-century echoes of the innumerable huts which in Romantic fiction and poetry serve as a persistent image not only of the genuine rural life, as opposed to the squalor of urban living, but also of such human virtues as friendship, loyalty, solidarity, endurance and independence. In this first phase of the story, in other words, the young and as yet unproven heroes live the lives of their nineteenth-century ancestors: they go back, at a time of crisis, to the foundation of their forefathers, thereby confirming myth number one described above: a life in perfect harmony with a nature which is essentially untouched, or at least undamaged, by human activity. The very different accounts of the Hardangervidda by various nineteenth-century travellers here almost imperceptibly melt into one: it is a place of inhospitality and terrifying sublimity, and at the same time a place that provides beauty, sustenance and protection.[19]

Then, in the tradition of such timeless heroes as the Biblical David, in his battle against Goliath, of Robin Hood, or of others who against all odds challenge a powerful enemy, this tiny band of warriors make a swift and daring visit to 'the Valley of the Shadow of Death'. This move from the Hardangervidda into the Rjukan valley is almost like a descent from a prelapsarian world into a Dantean underworld, the heavily industrialised valley representing a giant laboratory

---

19   Claus Helberg, who will be discussed in more detail below, expressed it very clearly in an article written many years later: "Hardangervidda was never occupied" (Helberg 1978: 72).

where a dangerous intruder is using modern science to develop a lethal weapon, a threat not just to the Norwegians but to all of humanity. Despite the fact that the Norwegians themselves were responsible for the industrialisation of Rjukan, in the context of the War, it is transformed from a natural utopia, via a utopia of modernity and progress, into a scientific dystopia.

This symbolic reading could be taken even further: the heavy water could be interpreted as an evil travesty of the life-giving waters which once flowed freely on their way to the sea and provided travellers with the profoundly edifying and religious experience of the untamed waterfall. The whole industrialisation of Rjukan, with the water forcefully channelled into subterranean tunnels and colossal metal pipes, is suddenly placed in the service of death and destruction rather than life and progress, which had been the original intention. Thus, the black and giant abyss of the vanished waterfall becomes a symbol of the rape committed against Mother Nature herself. The panorama unfolding in front of the approaching saboteurs on the night of the attack, therefore, was one of Miltonic and Tolkienesque proportions, with the factory like a Pandemonium or an Isengard seething with demonic activity and destructive energy: the fall had turned into a Fall.

Then, having performed one of the most spectacular raids in military history, sending the stocks of heavy water literally down the drains, the saboteurs retreat and seek shelter, not in the throng of a city, but once again in the protective lap of the great Mother, whose symbolic significance now takes on an additional quality. Ray Mears quotes the leader of the operation, Joachim Rønneberg, about his feelings when a few hours after the attack, they took a rest high up in the mountains, with a view of the valley where the Germans were continuing their frantic search:

It was a beautiful morning as we watched the sun rise. The sky was lit up in a lovely red colour as we sat there in silence eating chocolate and raisins and looking across the valley at the Gausta mountain peak. A bird was singing in a tree telling us that spring was on its way. We were all very, very happy. Although we said nothing as we sat there I think we all felt great pride. But we also spared a thought for our British friends who had died in the gliders disaster. They were unlucky, but someone was definitely protecting us that night.

The Germans were down in the valley below, but we were not that worried about them just now. From now on our struggle was with Norwegian nature. But we didn't fear the struggle because we had already learnt from experience that sometimes you just have to give in and accept that nature is our master. If we paid our respect we knew we would be all right. (Mears 2003: 166-7)

At this hour, and in the myth-making process that followed it, new energy is injected into the image of the mountainous wastes as a trope for Norway herself, for whose freedom they had just shown themselves willing to sacrifice their own lives. Motherland and Mother Nature become one and the same, and for the saboteur this mother figure is there to be saved and protected.[20] This symbolic significance of the Hardangervidda in combination with potential sacrifice is underlined even further in a famous incident from soon after the Gunnerside operation.

Immediately after the destruction of the heavy water plant, a massive campaign was launched in order to capture the saboteurs. So far during the War, the Germans seemed not to have realised the importance of the desolate areas around Rjukan. Now, with three thousand soldiers and a number of planes, they went systematically to work. During the following months, ski patrols were ordered into the wilderness and a number of huts were bombed or blown up (Dahl 1983-2000, 2: 290). About a month after the Gunnerside operation, one of the saboteurs, Claus Helberg, returned to the area and was visiting one of the group's hide-outs in order to recover weapons, when he was spotted by a ski patrol of three Germans. Having opened fire but failing to stop him, the Germans gave pursuit. Helberg, who was a first-class skier, out-distanced two of them after an hour, but going down-hill, the third was slowly getting closer. Eventually, according to his own account, Helberg decided to face the enemy. Armed with a Colt .32 he stopped and turned round. The German similarly stopped and raised his Luger. Helberg fired one shot, which missed. Standing in the snow as a living target, he then allowed the German to empty his magazine, knowing that whoever ran out of ammunition had lost. When the Luger finally clicked and the German turned to flee, Helberg skied closer, fired one shot, saw him slumping over his ski poles, and fled.

This duel in the snow is yet another contribution to the construction of the multifarious Rjukan myth. It could have been taken from the popular fiction of virtually any century, and for a Hollywood film-maker it is immediately recognizable as a set piece from the genre of the western movie. Furthermore, from the black and white perspective of the mythological story outlined above, there is a profound symbol of justice in the fact that the intruder into the inner sanctuary

20 The elements of war, rape and motherland (in Latin, the feminine *patria*) provide a rich supply of literary, and frequently Freudian, symbolism. In connection with the German occupation of Norway on 9 April 1940, there is one crucial event that lends itself with particular ease to such a reading. Under cover of darkness, the German surprise attack was spearheaded by the large battleship *Blücher*, which sailed across the Skagerak and – with lights turned off – into the narrow tract of the Oslofjord towards the capital. On board were not just a large number of troops (about 2,400), but also numerous officers and civil servants, who were to fill key positions in the new Norwegian government. At Drøbak, the most narrow point of the fjord, the ship was hit by two Norwegian torpedos and sunk. Thus, as a look at the map of the Oslofjord will make clear, this attempted rape or hostile phallic penetration of the motherland was prevented at the last and crucial minute, allowing among others the royal family to escape.

of the saboteurs – the Norway of Norways – spills his blood in the white snow. Similarly, in the image of the young Helberg standing as if frozen, with the bullets whistling about him but never hurting him, there is a powerful sense of the great Mother's invisible but protective hand, shielding him from danger and eventually smiting the intruder with just wrath.[21]

It is a strange coincidence – which acquires a profound significance – that all the four operations that took place at Rjukan during the Second World War contributed, in different ways, towards the construction of *one* tale of archetypal proportions. As with all such tales, its simple and fundamental theme is that of good and evil, here represented on the one hand by nature and nation and the protection of these, and on the other by an aggressively Faustian or Promethean scientific and technological search whose success would have been seen as a global disaster.[22] It should be remembered, however, that it was not only the German heavy water project that failed miserably; it was also the attempts by the Allies to destroy it by means of their apparently superior technology. Thus, from a nationalistic Norwegian point of view, the events at Rjukan may be said to have confirmed two well-established Norwegian characteristics: a faith in a simple life in close contact with the natural landscape, and a profound scepticism towards outside interference. The former is perhaps not surprising in a large country in which a small and scattered population through generations has had to adjust to difficult natural conditions; it is undoubtedly also a characteristic further emphasised by the nationalist movement of the nineteenth and early twentieth centuries. The latter is clearly connected with the fact that the country was forced into political unions with Denmark and later Sweden from the Middle Ages until 1905, thus enjoying only forty years of genuine independence before yet again being brought under the yoke of a foreign power. As a result of this, the two negative referendums on EU membership, in 1972 and 1994, simply confirm that the historical memory is a political power to be reckoned with, even in an age that may appear to look more to the future than to the past.

Admittedly, the above reading of the Rjukan myths may be regarded as an excessive over-interpretation, and it is hardly likely that the average French or Japanese – or even Norwegian – visitor to the museum at Vemork today will consciously arrive at such a conclusion. Also, a German visitor will very understand-

21   As a further indication of Helberg's heroic stature in Norway, it should be mentioned that during the 1980s and 90s he served as a sole guide for Queen Sonja of Norway and Queen Margrethe of Denmark on their ski and hiking trips in the Norwegian mountains. Queen Sonja also attended his funeral in March 2003.

22   Again, the fact that the industrial development of Rjukan was initiated by the Norwegians themselves, and that it was also an important contribution to the country's march into the modern world does not change the mythical significance of the events during the War.

ably approach the story from a radically different perspective. On the other hand, the power of myth to construct – subconsciously – stereotyped stories that influence our perceptions should not be underestimated. Against this background it is important to try and understand not just emotionally but also intellectually how these stereotyped perceptions affect us in our attitudes towards the 'Other'. It is to be hoped, for instance, that more than half a century after the War a discussion like the above of the Rjukan myths may contribute to a better understanding of how these national stereotypes may be faced and, when necessary, deconstructed. Finally, it may make us more alert to the paradoxical way in which nationalist myths sometimes come into being, namely through an intense dialogue with, precisely, the 'Other'. After all, from the early nineteenth-century travel accounts until the events of the Second World War, the 'Others' have represented an indispensable part of the Rjukan story. [23]

---

23   I am grateful to Ruth A. Symes, John Gilham and Stephanie Buus for critical comments and useful suggestions.

References

Adams, Eric 1973: *Francis Danby: Varieties of Poetic Landscape*. New Haven: Yale University Press.

Bremner, Robert 1840: *Excursions in Denmark, Norway and Sweden; Including Notices of the State of Public Opinion in Those Countries and Anecdotes of Their Courts*. I-II. London: Henry Colburn.

Brun, Jomar 1985: *Brennpunkt Vemork 1940-1945*. Oslo: Universitetsforlaget.

Chard, Chloe 1999: *Pleasure and Guilt on the Grand Tour: Travel Writing and Imaginative Geography 1600-1830*. Manchester: Manchester University Press.

Clark, John Willis and Joseph W. Dunning 1857: *A Long Vacation Ramble in Norway and Sweden, by X and Y (Two Unknown Quantities)*. Cambridge: Macmillan & Co.

Dahl, Helge 1983-2000: *Rjukan*. I-III.. Rjukan: Tinn kommune.

Demuth, Th. & Schick, M. v. 1863: *Skandinavische Fahrten. Tagebuchblätter als Manuskript für Freunde gedruckt*. Leipzig: Otto Wigand.

Elliott, Charles Boileau 1832: *Letters from the North of Europe, or a Journal of Travels in Holland, Denmark, Norway, Sweden, Finland, Russia, Prussia, and Saxony*. London: Henry Colburn and Richard Bentley.

Fjågesund, Peter 2001: *Til Telemark! Utlendingers reiser på 1800-tallet*. Oslo: Landbruksforlaget.

Fjågesund, Peter and Ruth A. Symes 2003: *The Northern Utopia: British Perceptions of Norway in the Nineteenth Century*. Amsterdam/New York: Rodopi.

Forester, Robert 1850: *Norway in 1848 and 1849: Containing Rambles among the Fjelds and Fjords of the Central and Western Districts; and Including Remarks on Its Political, Military, Ecclesiastical, and Social Organisation, with Extracts from the Journals of Lieut. M. S. Biddulph, Royal Artillery*. London: Longman, Brown, Green, and Longmans.

Goodman, E. J. 1896: *New Ground in Norway: Ringerike – Telemarken – Sætersdalen*. With Fifty-Six Illustrations, from Original Photographs by Paul Lange, Late President of *the Liverpool Amateur Photographic Association*. London: George Newnes.

Hansteen, Christopher 1969: *Til fots til Bergen, anno 1821*. 1859: Oslo: H. Aschehoug & Co.

Helberg, Claus 1978: Hardangervidda under krigen, Leif Larsen, ed., *Fjell og Vidde* (Den norske turistforening, årbok): 61-80.

Lobedanz, Edmund 1875: *Rejseskizzer og Noveller*. Kjøbenhavn: Rudolph Klein.

Mears, Ray 2003: *The Real Heroes of Telemark*. London: Hodder & Stoughton.

Mügge, Theodor 1844: *Skizzen aus dem Norden*. Erster Band. Hannover: C.F. Kius.

Nicolson, Marjorie Hope 1959: *Mountain Gloom and Mountain Glory: The Development of the Aesthetics of the Infinite*. New York: Cornell University Press.

Njølstad, Olav, Ole Kristian Grimnes, Joachim Rønneberg, Bertrand Goldschmidt, eds. 1995: *The Race for Norwegian Heavy Water, 1940-1945*. IFS Info 4/1995. Oslo: Norwegian Institute for Defence Studies. Østgaard, H.

R. 1881: *Norske Turistforenings årbok 1881, Den*. 1881. Kristiania: Alb. Cammermeyer.

Paterson, M. 1886: *Mountaineering below the Snow-Line, or The Solitary Pedestrian in Snowdonia and Elsewhere*. With Etchings by Mackaness. London.

Popplewell, John Benjamin and Sarah 1859: *Norway in 1858, Lindesnæs to the Midnight Sun: and Nordkap to Christiania*. Printed for Private Circulation by Wm. Byles, Observer Office, Bradford.

Pratt, Mary Louise 1992: *Imperial Eyes, Travel Writing and Transculturation*. London: Routledge.

Rørbye, Martinus 1930: *Maleren Martinus Rørbyes Rejsedagbok 1830*. Ed., Georg Nygaard. København: Kunstforeningen i København.

Taylor, Bayard 1858: *Northern Travel: Summer and Winter Pictures of Sweden, Lapland, and Norway*. London: Sampson Low, Son and Co.

Tennyson, Alfred Lord 1981-90: *The Letters of Alfred Lord Tennyson*. III vols. Eds., Cecil Y. Lang and Edgar F. Shannon. Oxford: Clarendon Press.

Original Quotes

Der Miøsvand liegt an der äussersten Grenze der Welt, welcher der Mensch sich bemächtigen konnte, dicht an der Region, die er den wilden Thieren auf ewig überlassen muss, weil kein Fleiss mehr diesem traurigen Boden einen nährenden Halm entlockt. Doch selbst über diese trostlosen Ufer hinaus hat von Zeit zu Zeit die Natur, mitten in der Steinwüste, irgend ein verborgenes Lebensfünkchen niedergelegt, mit dem Aaronsstabe an diese schrecklichen Felsen geschlagen, dass sie sich spalteten zurückwichen, und Raum gaben für ein kleines Thal, für eine Hütte, für einen Weidenplatz, für ein winziges Feld, das, mit unsäglichem Fleiss gereinigt und bestellt, meist in Schnee und Eis versinkt, ehe seine Früchte reifen konnten.

Stunden- und Tagelang könnte man hier sitzen, und wieder und immer wieder in dies Gebraus und Leuchten schauen; denn Wasserfälle und Meereswellen haben die Macht erhalten, die Seele des Menschen in Träume zu wiegen, und, mit ihrem Rhythmus von rauschendem Gehen und Kommen, Fantasie und Sehnsucht aufzuwecken. … Solche Werke machen den fühlenden Menschen gut. Es ist so herrlich, so edel und tief rührend, die Natur in ihrer höchsten Majestät zu schauen, dass man darüber Vieles vergisst, was sonst wohl den Eindruck ihrer Grösse abstumpft.

Det Øjeblik, da jeg første Gang paa saa nært Hold
turde fæste mit Blikk paa Kongen blant de sydlige
Norges Bjergkjæmper, vil blive mig uforglem-
melig, saalenge jeg lever.

Und diese herrliche Wasserkraft liegt in dem
Thale unbenutzt da; keine Fabrik, kein industri-
elles Unternehmen, ja nicht einmal eine simple
Mühle zwingt diese Kraft ihr dienstbar zu werden.

Contributors

Jesper Hede is Postdoc in Comparative Literature at University of Aarhus. He has a Master's degree in Italian and Medieval Studies and a PhD in European Studies. He has published articles on medieval literature, and his book *Reading Dante: The Pursuit of Meaning* is forthcoming. He is currently writing a book on *The Ontology of Rhetoric in History* financed by The Carlsberg Foundation.

Bernd Henningsen; MA, University of Munich 1972; PhD 1974, ("Die Politik des Einzelnen. Zur Genese der skandinavischen Ziviltheologie"); 1984 Habilitation ("Der Wohlfahrtsstaat Schweden"); 1985 Theodor-Eschenburg-Prize; Guestprofessor at the Universities of Minnesota/Minneapolis, Zürich, Hamburg, Trier, Erlangen-Nürnberg, Free University of Berlin, Södertörn, Örebro, Copenhagen; Several prizes, 1992-2002 Professor in Scandinavan Studies at Humbolt University; 2002-05 Professor in Greifswald and 2002-2003 Director of the *Alfried-Krupp-Wissenschaftskollegs Greifswald*; 2003- Professor at the Nordeuropa-Institut, Humboldt University. Has published widely in Scandinavian Studies, Cultural Studies and Political Studies.

Sumarliði R. Ísleifsson, MA in history, University of Iceland 1986. Historian and editor in The Reykjavík Academy. Author of books, articles and documentary films, mainly on travellers in Iceland, and icelandic images. I.e. on Jules Verne's book, *A Journey to the Centre of the Earth*, the illustrator Riou and Iceland (article 1995); *Ísland framandi land* (book 1996, Images of Iceland through the ages); Suðurganga Nikulásar, a documentary on pilgrimages from Iceland in the Middle ages (Icelandic TV 1999); "Fyrirmyndasamfélagið Ísland". Ritið (article 2002, The ideal society Iceland).

Marianne Raakilde Jespersen, PhD, MA in Comparative Literature and Gender Studies. PhD-dissertation, "Papirkroppe" (Paper bodies) (2003), on representations of the body in literature from the 1790s to the 1920s. Related publications: "En skøn sjæls krop. Goethe og tableauet i teksten" (The Body of a Beautiful Soul.

Goethe and the textual tableau) in Elin Andersen & Karen Klitgaard Povlsen (eds.): *Tableau. Det sublime øjeblik* (Tableau. The Sublime Moment, 2001) and "Den symbolske syge" (The Symbolic Illness) in Rune Gade & Marianne Raakilde Jespersen (eds.): *Krop og æstetik. Tekster om krop og køn i moderniteten* (Body and Aesthetics. Texts on body and gender in modernity, 2000).

Hendriette Kliemann-Geisinger, 2001 graduated (MA) in Scandinavian Studies and History; 2001-2004 research assistant in Scandinavian Studies and History at Blekinges Tekniska Högskola, Humboldt-Universität and Aarhus Universitet; 2004 gained doctorate (Dr. phil.), 2005-2006 research fellow at Humboldt-Universität; since March 2006 research assistant for Scandinavian Studies at Humboldt-Universität zu Berlin. Publications: "Nordens koordinater. Vetenskapliga konstruktioner av en europeisk region 1770-1850" (2005), "Norden från ett europeiskt perspektiv. Begreppshistoriska betraktelser 1770-1850" (2005). Dissertation: *Koordinaten des Nordens. Wissenschaftliche Konstruktionen einer europäischen Region 1770-1850* (2004).

Karen Klitgaard Povlsen, Associate Professor, PhD and MA in comparative literature, Gender- and Media Studies at the University of Aarhus, Department of Information and Media Studies. Has published widely in magazines, mediated youth-cultures, gender, body and eighteenth century genres, genders and cultural studies. Books on magazines (*EyeCatcher: Women's Magazines 1986, Organizing the Everyday Life 1995*), popular fiction (*Beverly Hills 90210 – Soaps, Irony and Youth Culture*, 1999), anthologies on eighteenth century culture (*Tableau – The Sublime Moment*, co-editor Elin Andersen, 2001, *Art Criticism and Cultural War*, co-editor Anne Scott Sørensen, 2005), contributor to *Nordic Salon-Culture* (ed. Anne Scott Sørensen 1998) and *Eighteenth Century Literary Culture* (ed. Ole Birklund et al. 1999).

Karen Langgård, MA, Associate Professor at the Department of Greenlandic Language, Literature and Media, Ilisimatusarfik University of Greenland, Nuuk Greenland. Research and teaching of Greenlandic literature (including hymns, old newspapers, and the newest song lyrics on CDs), Greenlandic syntax, and sociolinguistic matters in Greenland.

Bjarne Rogan, MA in 1975, Dr. phil. (PhD) in 1986. 1975-81 Civil servant; 1982-86 Researcher; 1986-92 Senior lecturer; Since 1993 Professor of ethnology, later of cultural history, University of Oslo. 1998-2001 Director of Centre de Coopération

Franco-Norvégien en Sciences Sociales et Humaines, Paris. 2003- Dean of Faculty of Humanities, University of Oslo.

Anka Ryall is Associate Professor of English at the University of Tromsø, Norway. She has published widely in the fields of travel literature and gender studies. Her latest book is *Odyssevs i skjørt. Kvinners erobring av reiselitteraturen* (Odysseus in Skirts: Women's Appropriation of Travel Literature, 2004). She is also co-author (with Jorunn Veiteberg) of *En kvinnelig oppdagelsesreisende i det unge Norge: Catharine Hermine Kølle* (A Female Explorer of Nineteenth-Century Norway: Catharine Hermine Kølle, 1991) and co-editor (with Catherine Sandbach-Dahlström) of *Mary Wollstonecraft's Journey to Scandinavia: Essays* (2003).

Karin Sanders, Associate Professor at Department of Scandinavian, University of California-Berkeley. Author of *Konturer. Skulptur og dødsbilleder i guldalderlitteraturen*, 1997. Contributing author of *Nordisk kvindelitteraturehistorie* and *Læsninger i dansk litteratur*. Has published articles on word-image relations, archaeological imagination and the visual arts, gender and literature. She is presently working on a book-length study of the use of archaeological human remains in literature and visual arts.

Sylwia Schab, MA in Danish. PhD dissertation on Nordic cooperation within culture and literature. Since 2003 researcher and teacher at the Department of Scandinavian Studies in Pozna, Poland. Has published several articles on the Danish culture and society. Her current field of interest is Polish and Scandinavian travel literature.

Peter Stadius has a PhD in history from the University of Helsinki. In his dissertation *Resan till norr. Spanska Nordenbilder kring sekelskiftet 1900* (2005) he examined the image of the North in Spanish travel descriptions, focusing on the period around 1900. He has published a number of articles on travel literature and on the mental mapping of Europe regarding north and south.

Antje Wischmann: Associate Professor of Scandinavian cultur and literary studies, Nordeuropa-Institut, Humboldt-Universität Berlin (2006-2008), senior researcher at Södertörn högskola, Stockholm (1998-2006); is author of *Verdichtete Stadtwahrnehmung. Untersuchungen zum literarischen und urbanistischen Diskurs in Skandinavien 1955-95* (On the perception of cities: An analysis of Scandinavian literary and urbanist discourse 1955-95, 2003); *Ästheten und Décadents* (Aesthetes and decadents, 1991).

Place index

Name index

Acerbi, Guiseppe   17, 21, 29, 30, 35, 46, 266,
    267, 268, 269, 270, 271, 272, 274, 277, 278,
    279, 280, 281, 282, 343, 344, 347, 348, 351
Adam of Bremen   113, 114, 126, 144, 148, 160,
    165, 166, 169, 230, 231, 239, 241, 279, 288,
    296, 299, 306, 308
Adams, Eric   31, 46, 330, 339, 383, 395
Addison, Joseph   22, 326, 328, 329, 331, 335,
    336, 338, 341
Adelung, Johann Christoph   20, 195, 196, 197,
    198, 199, 200, 201, 202, 203, 204, 206, 213,
    214, 215, 216
Albert the Great   302
Albertrandy, Jan Chrzciciel   23, 358, 364, 365,
    366, 367, 369
Alfonso III, king of Asturias   58
Ampère, Jean-Jacques   43
Anderson, Johann   114, 117, 126, 309, 320, 323
Andrés, Juan   28, 37, 38, 41, 42, 43, 44, 45, 46
Aristotle   38, 39, 112, 306
Arndt, Ernst Moritz   80, 84, 99, 344
Arrebo, Anders   159
Attila, king of the Huns   50, 52
Austen, Jane   266, 282

Bacon, Francis   35, 42
Baggesen, Jens   21, 285, 330
Banks, Joseph   117, 118, 119, 120, 122, 123, 126
Bartholin, Thomas   38
Becanus, Johannes Goropius   60
Berch, Christer   227, 228, 240

Blackley, Frederick R.   10, 22, 305, 309, 310,
    317, 319, 320, 321, 322, 323
Blom, Gustav Peter   253, 257, 259, 260, 263,
    264
Bodin, Jean   65
Bonstetten, Karl Viktor von   13, 14, 15, 22, 24,
    82, 85, 146, 147
Boorde, Andrew   114, 115, 119, 126
Bording, Anders   159
Bouterwek   37, 39
Bremner, Robert   382, 383, 395
Brooke, Arthur Capell de   246, 259, 262, 263
Brun, Friederike, geb. Münter   22, 144, 146,
    147, 331, 332, 334, 335, 336, 337, 338, 339,
    340, 395
Brun, Johan Nordahl   292, 303
Buch, Leopold von   257, 258, 261, 263, 266,
    282
Bucher, August Leopold   77, 78, 81, 85
Buhle, Johann Gottlieb Gerhard   79, 85
Bure, Johan   152
Burke, Edmund   62, 66, 138, 158, 172, 187, 188,
    189, 190, 280, 326, 379

Campbell, John   42
Cannabich, Johann Günther Friedrich   78,
    85
Canova, Antonio   164, 350
Carducci, Giosué   43
Catherine the Great   71
Charles II (Carlos II), king of Spain   66

Charles V (Carlos I), emperor 50, 59

Charles IX, king of Sweden 53

Charles XII 71, 369

Clark, John Willis 379, 380, 395

Clarke, Edward Daniel 21, 257, 258, 260, 263, 265, 266, 268, 269, 270, 271, 272, 273, 274, 275, 276, 277, 278, 279, 281, 282

Cook, James 28, 119

Coxe, William 14, 121, 126

Crantz, David 22, 307, 308, 309, 320, 322, 323

Cripps, John Marten 265, 269, 270, 272, 273, 274, 275, 276, 277

Dahl, Helge 385, 388, 393, 395

Dahl, Willy 300, 301, 304

Dalin, Olof von 135, 226, 227

Dampier, William 31, 46

Danby, Francis 383, 395

Darwin, Charles 277, 280, 282, 283

Defoe, Daniel 31, 32

Demuth, Th. 386, 395

Descartes, René 35, 39, 40, 42

Don Pelayo 58

Dunning, Joseph 379, 380, 395

Eck, Johann Georg 344, 348, 349, 350, 351, 352, 353

Egede, Hans 21, 22, 305, 306, 307, 308, 309, 310, 317, 320, 322, 323

Elliott, Charles Boileau 380, 382, 395

Esmark, Jens 378

Ewald, Johannes 143, 144, 146, 159, 295

Ferdinand II, emperor 53

Ferdinand III, emperor 53

Flintoe, Johannes 249, 254, 385

Fontenelle, Bernard le Bovier de 40, 231

Forester, Thomas 255, 256, 263, 380, 386, 395

Forsström, Johan Erik 229, 239, 240

Forster, Georg 28, 46

Forster, Johann Reinhold 83, 85

Fredenhielm, Carl Frederik 348, 349, 350

Frederik V. King of Denmark 85, 89, 129, 158, 168, 236, 247, 261, 287, 289

Freund, H. E. 160

Friedrich of Hesse, Princee 378

Fulda, friedrich Carl 200

Galeazzo Gualdo Priorato 53, 66

Garnaas, Jørgen 130

Gatterer, Johann Christoph 77, 78, 85

Geer, Charles de 20, 221, 222, 223, 224, 229, 230, 231, 234, 235, 236, 237, 238, 239

Geijer, Erik Gustaf 81, 85, 95, 154

Gerstenberg, Heinrich Wilhelm von 9, 19, 129, 137, 139, 140, 141, 142, 143, 144, 145, 146, 148, 149

Gibbon, Edward 172, 180

Gilham, John 395

Ginguené, Pierre-Louis 43

Goethe, Johann Wolfgang von 22, 30, 37, 90, 91, 94, 95, 103, 107, 108, 327, 328, 330, 331, 335, 338, 400

Goodman, G. E. 383, 386, 396

Gottsched, Johann Christoph 199

Gracián, Baltasar 65, 66

Grape, Erik 276

Gray, Thomas 13, 138, 148, 276, 277

Grimm, Jacob 20, 165, 205, 206, 207, 208, 209, 210, 211, 212, 213, 214

Grimm, Wilhelm 20, 199, 205, 206

Grotkowski, Tobiasz 364, 374

Grund, Johann Gottfried 126, 129, 130, 169, 226

Grundtvig, Nikolai Frederik Severin 18, 81, 85, 89, 93, 99, 100, 144, 147, 160, 161, 170

Gustavus Adolphus, king of Sweden 9, 49, 50, 53, 56, 57, 58, 63, 64, 66

Gustav III 228, 238, 365

Gustav IV Adolf 343

Guthrie, William 120, 121, 126